Inequality, Inclusiv and Fiscal Policy in _____

Developing Asia's sustained rapid growth has improved general living standards and lifted hundreds of millions of Asians out of poverty within a generation. Yet the region now finds itself confronting rising inequality. Countries where inequality has worsened over the past two decades collectively account for over 80% of Asia's population. As a result, governments across the region have begun to accord a higher priority to promoting more inclusive growth. The international experience, especially the experience of the advanced economies, suggests that fiscal policy can make a potent contribution to reducing inequality. This book systematically explores the relationship between both sides of fiscal policy—public spending as well as taxes and other fiscal revenues—and inequality in Asia at great depths. On the basis of the analysis, the book sets forth a number of concrete options for rendering fiscal policy a more effective tool for more inclusive growth that benefits all Asians.

Inequality, Inclusive Growth, and Fiscal Policy in Asia is written in response to an issue of growing demand in most Asian countries, and it comes at a time when Asian governments are also beginning to use fiscal policy to bridge the glaring disparities between the rich and the poor of the region. As such, the book will be a highly valuable reference for researchers, policy makers, and students as well.

Donghyun Park is currently Principal Economist at the Economic Research and Regional Cooperation Department of the Asian Development Bank (ADB), which he joined in April 2007. Prior to joining ADB, he was a tenured Associate Professor of Economics at Nanyang Technological University in Singapore. He has a PhD in economics from UCLA; his main fields of research are international finance, international trade, and fiscal policy. He has been published extensively in academic journals and books.

Sang-Hyop Lee is Professor of Economics and Director of the Center for Korean Studies at the University of Hawai'i at Mānoa. He is also an Adjunct Senior Fellow at the East-West Center and the Asian Team Leader of the Global National Transfer Accounts Network. His studies focus on population and labor and social welfare issues with particular emphasis on Asian economies. He earned his BA and MA in economics from Seoul National University and a PhD in economics from Michigan State University, USA.

Minsoo Lee is a Senior Economist in the Macroeconomics Research Division of the Economic Research and Regional Cooperation Department at the Asian Development Bank (ADB). Prior to joining ADB, he was an Associate Dean and a tenured full professor at Peking University's HSBC Business School in the People's Republic of China. His main research fields are international finance, international trade, applied econometrics, and energy economics.

Routledge-GRIPS Development Forum Studies
Edited by Kenichi Ohno and Izumi Ohno
National Graduate Institute for Policy Studies, Japan

Inequality, Inclusive Growth, and Fiscal Policy in Asia

Edited by Donghyun Park, Sang-Hyop Lee, and Minsoo Lee

CO-PUBLICATION OF THE ASIAN DEVELOPMENT BANK AND ROUTLEDGE

LONDON AND NEW YORK

First published 2015 by Routledge

2 Park Square, Milton Park, Abingdon, Oxfordshire OX14 4RN
711 Third Avenue, New York, NY 10017

Routledge is an imprint of the Taylor & Francis Group, an informa business

First issued in paperback 2018

British Library Cataloguing in Publication Data
A catalogue record for this book is available from the British Library

Library of Congress Cataloging-in-Publication Data
Inequality, inclusive growth, and fiscal policy in Asia / edited by
    Donghyun Park, Sang Hyop Lee, Minsoo Lee.
      pages cm. — (Routledge-GRIPS development forum studies)
    1. Fiscal policy—Asia. 2. Equality—Asia. 3. Economic development—
Asia. I. Park, Donghyun. II. Lee, Sang-Hyop. III. Lee, Minsoo.
    HJ1301.I54 2015
    339.5'2095—dc23
    2014044560

The views expressed in this publication are those of the authors and do
not necessarily reflect the views and policies of the Asian Development
Bank (ADB) or its Board of Governors or the governments they represent.

ADB does not guarantee the accuracy of the data included in this
publication and accepts no responsibility for any consequence of their use.

By making any designation of or reference to a particular territory or
geographic area, or by using the term "country" in this document, ADB
does not intend to make any judgments as to the legal or other status of
any territory or area.

ADB encourages printing or copying information exclusively for personal
and noncommercial use with proper acknowledgment of ADB. Users are
restricted from reselling, redistributing, or creating derivative works for
commercial purposes without the express, written consent of ADB.

Note: In this publication, "$" refers to US dollars.

6 ADB Avenue, Mandaluyong City
1550 Metro Manila, Philippines
Tel +63 2 632 4444
Fax +63 2 636 2444
www.adb.org

For orders, please contact:
Department of External Relations
Fax +63 2 636 2648
adbpub@adb.org

ISBN 13: 978-1-138-85035-4 (hbk)
ISBN 13: 978-1-138-31699-7 (pbk)

Typeset in Galliard
by Apex CoVantage, LLC

Contents

vi *Contents*

Figures

Tables

Contributors

Arnelyn Abdon is a consultant with the World Bank Office in Manila under the Mindanao Trust Fund and with the Department of Social Welfare and Development on the impact evaluation of the *Pantawid Pamilyang Pilipino,* the Philippines' conditional cash transfer program. Prior to this assignment, she was an Economics Officer in the then Economics and Research Department of the Asian Development Bank.

Arindam Das Gupta is currently Senior Professor at the Goa Institute of Management (GIM) in Goa, India which he joined in June 2010. Prior to joining GIM, he worked at several organizations including the National University of Singapore and the World Bank in Washington, DC. He has a PhD in economics from Cornell University. His main fields of consulting and research are public finance and governance. He has published extensively in academic journals and books.

Gemma Estrada is a Senior Economics Officer in the Macroeconomics Research Division of the Economic Research and Regional Cooperation Department at the Asian Development Bank (ADB). Her recent research has been on structural change, old-age security, and fiscal policy. She is also involved with the *Asian Development Outlook,* an annual flagship publication of ADB.

Almas Heshmati is currently Professor of Economics at Sogang University, Republic of Korea and has held similar positions at Korea University, Seoul National University, and the University of Kurdistan Hawler. He was a research fellow at the WIDER United Nations University from 2001 to 2004. From 1998 to 2001, he was Associate Professor of Economics at the Stockholm School of Economics. He has a PhD from the University of Gothenburg. His research interests include energy and environment, globalization, development economics, performance analysis, and technological change.

Seok-Kyun Hur is currently Associate Professor of Finance at the College of Business and Economics of Chung-Ang University in Seoul, Republic of Korea. Before joining the university in March 2011, he was a fellow at the Korea Development Institute working on the issues of household debt and public pensions in the Republic of Korea. He has a PhD in economics from the University of Chicago. His main fields of research are macro finance, money and banking, and fiscal policy.

Jungsuk Kim is currently a researcher at the Institute of International and Areas Studies of Sogang University and teaches economics at Kyoung-Hee University both in the Republic of Korea. She worked in the airline industry for more than 20 years before earning her PhD in international trade from Sogang University. Her main fields of research are international trade, econometrics, microeconomics, and fiscal policy.

Minsoo Lee is a Senior Economist in the Macroeconomics Research Division of the Economic Research and Regional Cooperation Department at the Asian Development Bank (ADB). Prior to joining ADB, he was an Associate Dean and a tenured full professor at Peking University's HSBC Business School in the People's Republic of China. His main research fields are international finance, international trade, applied econometrics, and energy economics.

Sang-Hyop Lee is Professor of Economics and Director of the Center for Korean Studies at the University of Hawai'i at Mānoa. He is also an Adjunct Senior Fellow at the East-West Center and the Asian Team Leader of the Global National Transfer Accounts Network. His studies focus on population and labor and social welfare issues with particular emphasis on Asian economies. He earned his BA and MA in economics from Seoul National University and a PhD in economics from Michigan State University.

Andrew Mason is a Professor of Economics at the University of Hawai'i at Mānoa, a Senior Fellow at the East-West Center in Honolulu, Hawai'i, and a member of the Center on the Economics and Demography of Aging (CEDA) at the University of California, Berkeley. He co-directs the National Transfer Accounts (www.ntaccounts.org) network. His current research is on the economic life cycle, intergenerational issues, and the effects of population change on development, economic growth, and public and private transfer systems. His PhD in economics is from the University of Michigan.

Donghyun Park is currently Principal Economist at the Economic Research and Regional Cooperation Department of the Asian Development Bank (ADB), which he joined in April 2007. Prior to joining ADB, he was a tenured Associate Professor of Economics at Nanyang Technological University in Singapore. He has a PhD in economics from UCLA; his main fields of research are international finance, international trade, and fiscal policy. He has been published extensively in academic journals and books.

Rathin Roy has been Director of the National Institute of Public Finance and Policy in New Delhi since May 2013 and is also an appointed member of the Seventh Central Pay Commission of the Government of India. He has worked as an Economic Diplomat and Policy Advisor with the United Nations Development Programme focusing on emerging economies and has also taught at the universities of Manchester and London. He holds a PhD in Economics from the University of Cambridge.

Ke Shen is currently Assistant Professor at the Demographic Research Institute of Fudan University in the People's Republic of China which she joined in September 2011. Her PhD in economics is from Peking University. Her major research fields include health economics, population aging, and population polices. She has published papers in academic journals, including the *Demographic Research* and *Social Science and Medicine*.

Preface

Widening income gaps in developing Asia strengthen the case for government response. The region's past economic growth boosted living standards and lifted millions out of poverty, but now widening inequality is undermining this success. During the 1990s and 2000s, more than 80% of the region's population lived in countries with worsening Gini coefficients, a common measure of inequality. The same market forces that have enhanced growth – globalization, technological progress, and market reform – now exacerbate inequality.

Fiscal policy that fosters equality of opportunity can help tackle the region's rising inequality. International experience shows that public spending can reduce income inequality. For example, government spending on education and health care increases the access of the poor to these vital services and thus their opportunities for success. Policy makers in developing Asia have, however, generally used fiscal policy more to support growth than to affect income distribution. Authorities in advanced economies, by contrast, have extensively used fiscal tools to improve social equity.

The region has benefited from a legacy of fiscal prudence. Sound fiscal positions have served the region well in the past, promoting macroeconomic stability and ensuring the ability to respond in times of economic crisis. Pragmatic fiscal policy has given many regional economies the scope today to direct more public resources toward enhanced inclusion. In the future that scope may narrow, though, as long-term demographic and environmental trends encroach on fiscal space and the spending flexibility it provides.

The dilemma facing developing Asia is how to use fiscal policy to promote inclusion while maintaining fiscal sustainability. Making growth more inclusive is likely to require some expansion of public spending, but expanding public expenditure without adequate revenue mobilization can be unsustainable. Governments thus need to calibrate spending programs to better meet the needs of the poor as they strengthen their revenue bases through improved mobilization.

To address how developing Asia might better deploy fiscal policy to tackle growing inequality, the special theme chapter of the *Asian Development Outlook* (*ADO*) *2014* published in April 2014 was "Fiscal Policy for Inclusive Growth." The *ADO* is the Asian Development Bank's flagship report published twice a year: the main report usually in April and the update usually in October. This collective volume brings together the research papers that provided the background materials for *ADO 2014* and consists of the following chapters.

Chapter 1 by Gemma Estrada, Sang-Hyop Lee, and Donghyun Park provides an overview of the relationship between fiscal policy and inequality in developing Asia. They note that up to now the region's fiscal policy has revolved around promoting economic growth. As a result, the region trails other parts of the world in equity-promoting public expenditures.

Chapter 2 by Rathin Roy provides an overview of fiscal policy, fiscal space, and inclusive growth in developing Asia and reviews the past behavior of fiscal policy in the region. He finds that by and large the data support the conventional wisdom of a fiscally prudent region where governments live within their means. As a result, the region finds itself with more fiscal space than elsewhere.

In Chapter 3, Arnelyn Abdon, Gemma Estrada, Minsoo Lee, and Donghyun Park empirically analyze the relationship between fiscal policy and economic growth in developing Asia and find that the composition of taxes and government spending can have a significant effect on economic growth. Property taxes have a more benign impact on growth than direct taxes, and spending more on education has a sizable positive impact on growth.

Chapter 4 by Seok-Kyun Hur empirically examines the effect of government spending on growth and inequality via a panel vector autoregression analysis. He finds that compared with the advanced economies, spending on public health and public education appeared to alleviate income inequality significantly more in Asian Development Bank developing members. This implies that fiscal expenditure policies may contribute more to inclusive growth in developing economies than in advanced ones.

Chapter 5 by Ke Shen and Sang-Hyop Lee utilizes National Transfer Accounts (NTA) Project data and an analytical framework to analyze the incidence of public transfers by age group, gender, income level, and urban versus rural residence in the People's Republic of China in 2009. Their analysis looked at public spending on education, health care, and pensions. Spending on education was more or less equal at the primary and secondary levels, and spending on health care equally targeted the young and middle-aged, but there were sharp disparities in pensions by income level and residence.

In Chapter 6, Arindam Das-Gupta develops a framework to assess the growth and distribution effects of tax revenues and other fiscal resources. He then uses the framework to assess the fiscal resource bases of Asian economies. His analysis suggests that in order to expand their low fiscal resource bases, Asian economies need to strengthen fiscal revenue mobilization across a wide range of revenue sources.

In Chapter 7, Sang-Hyop Lee and Andrew Mason examine the critical issue of the fiscal sustainability of Asia's current tax and spending regimes using NTA data along with demographic and income growth projections. Their main finding is that population aging will impose sizable fiscal demands on Asian governments in the future, especially for health care and social protection.

Sang-Hyop Lee and Donghyun Park review the Latin American experience with fiscal policy in Chapter 8 and draw lessons for Asia. Of particular interest is Latin America's generally successful experience with conditional cash transfer programs. Overall, the evidence suggests that these programs can be an effective tool for inclusive growth in Asia as well.

In Chapter 9, Almas Heshmati, Jungsuk Kim, and Donghyun Park review the experience of advanced economies that have a long history of inclusive fiscal policy and find that fiscal policy can definitely be a potent tool to fight inequality in Asia. Any optimism in this regard must, however, be tempered by the differing circumstances of advanced versus developing economies.

Chapter 10 by Donghyun Park summarizes and sets forth the key facts and findings that emerged from the analyses in the nine preceding chapters. Those facts and findings give rise to a number of policy recommendations that will help developing Asia better harness fiscal policy to promote equity. The summary is followed by a few final observations.

We are confident that this volume, based as it is on the collective hard and high-quality work of knowledgeable experts, will contribute to a better informed public debate about the role of fiscal policy in tackling developing Asia's growing inequality. Asian governments will have to take the lead in fostering more inclusive growth in the region; equity-promoting spending and taxation will be a key part of that effort.

Donghyun Park, Sang-Hyop Lee,
and Minsoo Lee

Abbreviations

ADB	Asian Development Bank
ADO	*Asian Development Outlook*
ASEAN	Association of Southeast Asian Nations
BRIC	Brazil, Russian Federation, India, People's Republic of China
CCT	conditional cash transfer
CFPS	China Family Panel Study
EME	emerging mega economies
EU	European Union
FY	fiscal year
GDP	gross domestic product
GNP	gross national product
HIE	high-income economies
ICT	information and communication technology
IFC	International Finance Corporation
IMF	International Monetary Fund
IRF	impulse response function
Lao PDR	Lao People's Democratic Republic
LIE	low-income economies
LPT	land and property tax
MCF	marginal cost of funds
MDGs	Millennium Development Goals
MIE	middle-income economies
NTA	National Transfer Accounts
OECD	Organisation for Economic Co-operation and Development
OLS	ordinary least squares
PPP	purchasing power parity
PRC	People's Republic of China
PVAR	panel vector autoregression
SSC	small economies with special characteristics
SVAR	structural vector autoregression
SWIID	Standardized World Income Inequality Database
UCT	unconditional cash transfers

UK	United Kingdom
US	United States
USDA	United States Department of Agriculture
VAR	vector autoregression
VAT	value-added tax
WDI	World Development Indicators
WHO	World Health Organization
WTO	World Trade Organization

Notes: The Asian Development Bank recognizes China by the name People's Republic of China. The book has been edited to conform to this usage.

1 An overview

*Gemma Estrada, Sang-Hyop Lee,
and Donghyun Park*

A. Introduction

Achieving more inclusive growth is one of the most significant long-term strategic challenges facing developing Asia. Sustained rapid growth during the past few decades has sharply lifted general living standards across Asia and has enabled hundreds of millions of Asians to lead more dignified, humane lives. Asia's record of economic growth and poverty reduction in recent years has been remarkable by any measure. According to the *Asian Development Outlook (ADO) 2012* of the Asian Development Bank (ADB), Asia's annual gross domestic product (GDP) growth rate averaged 7.0% in purchasing power parity terms between 1990 and 2010. Rapid growth helped reduce poverty – the proportion of Asians living on or below the $1.25-a-day poverty line – from 52% in 1990 to 21% in 2010.

Notwithstanding such marked progress on poverty reduction, Asia still has a long way to go in achieving fully inclusive growth that benefits the entire population. In particular, the region has seen inequality worsen in recent years, largely in response to the same forces that have caused greater inequality elsewhere. These forces include globalization, technological progress, and market-oriented reform. According to *ADO 2012*, from the early 1990s to the late 2000s, the Gini coefficient, a widely used measure of inequality in per capita expenditure or income, rose in 11 out of 25 Asian economies with comparable data. The 11 include the People's Republic of China (PRC), India, and Indonesia and account for around 82% of Asia's population. If inequality had remained constant, the same level of growth would have lifted an additional 240 million people or 6.5% of their total populations out of poverty.

Asia's widening income gaps strengthen the case for a government response. Governments can, in principle, play a more activist role in bringing about a fairer society that provides opportunities for all and distributes the fruits of growth more widely. Fiscal policy is one of the most suitable policy instruments for direct government intervention to tackle inequality and poverty. In fact, there is now a great deal of interest in leveraging fiscal policy for promoting inclusive growth in Asia; however, in contrast to the advanced economies that have long histories of using fiscal policy for redistribution as detailed in Heshmati, Kim, and Park

(Chapter 9), Asia has only limited experience in this area. To some extent, this is due to the huge gap in income levels between the two groups and hence the difference in the relative importance of growth versus redistribution. When it comes to using fiscal policy for inclusive goals, Asia also visibly trails Latin America, which is comparable in income level.

Further strengthening the case for leveraging fiscal policy for inclusive growth in Asia, public transfers from governments to children and the elderly tend to lag private transfers from families (Lee and Mason 2012). During the economic life cycle, individuals consume more than they produce when they are young and old and do the opposite when they are of working age. A combination of public and private transfers finances the gap between consumption and production in childhood and old age. The relative role of private versus public transfers in financing the consumption–income deficit for children and the elderly differs markedly across Asia, Europe, and Latin America (Figure 1.1). For children, public transfers play a bigger role in Europe than in Asia and Latin America where private transfers are more important, that is, the family bears a higher share of the cost of raising children in Asia and Latin America. The percentage of total material needs of children covered by the family stands at 70% in Taipei,China; 82% in the Philippines; and 83% in

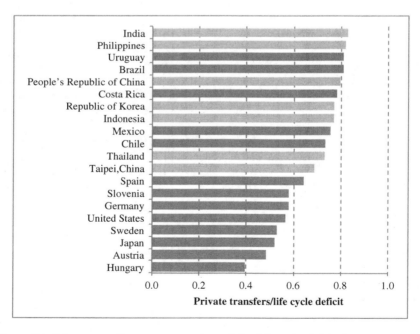

Figure 1.1 Private transfers as a proportion of the life cycle deficit for ages 0–19 in selected Asian and non-Asian economies

Source: Lee and Mason 2012.

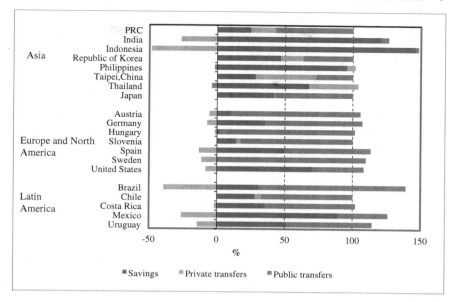

Figure 1.2 Support system for people aged 65 and older in selected Asian and non-Asian economies

Note: Negative values represent net outflows; that is, the elderly provide more support to their families than they receive. If values in one support system are negative, values in another support system can be greater than 100%. Years of data are as follows: Austria (2000); Brazil (1996); Chile (1997); PRC = People's Republic of China (2002); Costa Rica (2004); India (2004); Indonesia (2005); Republic of Korea (2000); Germany (2003); Hungary (2005); Japan (2004); Mexico (2004); Philippines (1999); Spain (2000); Slovenia (2004); Sweden (2003); Taipei,China (1998); Thailand (2004); Uruguay (2006); and United States (2003).

Source: ADB 2011, page 57.

India. For the elderly, public transfers are noticeably smaller in Asia than in Europe or Latin America, implying the smaller role of the government in supporting the elderly (Figure 1.2).

If Asia is to use fiscal policy more actively for inclusive growth, it must do so without compromising two key strategic priorities: economic growth and fiscal sustainability. For all its success, Asia still desperately needs sustained, rapid growth to raise income levels, which remain far below those of advanced economies. In addition, the region remains home to close to two-thirds of the world's poor, and further progress on the poverty front requires sustained growth. Therefore, burdensome taxation that unduly blunts the incentives of firms and workers to engage in productive activities will ultimately hinder inclusive growth. A long tradition of fiscal prudence has given Asia macroeconomic stability as well as adequate fiscal space – a highly valuable resource for fending off severe, negative shocks like the global financial crisis and for addressing medium-term fiscal demands like population aging. Expanding the role of fiscal policy in fighting poverty and inequality should not come at the expense of fiscal sustainability.

Historically, Asian countries used fiscal policy to facilitate economic growth by providing basic infrastructure while safeguarding macroeconomic stability. A tradition of fiscal prudence combined with public investments in growth-promoting physical and human capital played an instrumental role in Asia's past success. While some public spending such as that on public education contributes to higher growth and lower inequality, Asian governments were concerned first and foremost with growth. This priority was perfectly understandable in light of Asia's low income levels in the past; however, more recently, new fiscal demands have emerged. Counter-cyclical fiscal stimulus made possible by adequate fiscal space proved invaluable in fending off recession during the global crisis of 2008–2009 (ADB 2010). Going forward, a key fiscal challenge is that of leveraging fiscal policy for more inclusive growth.

B. Public spending for inclusive growth

Government expenditures in developing Asia are small by international standards. They are substantially less when compared with those in advanced countries or even in Latin America, a region comparable with developing Asia in terms of income and level of development (Figure 1.3). To some extent, this reflects the region's strong adherence to fiscal prudence, which means that the norm among Asian governments has been to avoid spending greatly beyond their fiscal resources. Roy explores trends among individual Asian economies in Chapter 2.

The role of fiscal policy in the region has been to foster economic growth, whereas other parts of the world have more broadly pursued growth-promoting equity. Thus, developing Asia has lagged the Organisation for Economic

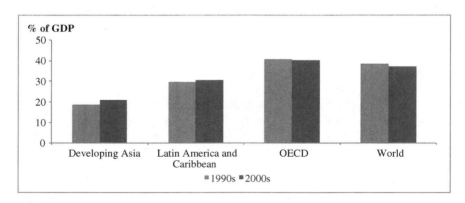

Figure 1.3 Ratio of government expenditures to gross domestic product

OECD = Organisation for Economic Co-operation and Development.

Sources: ADB estimates based on data from International Monetary Fund's World Economic Outlook database October 2013.

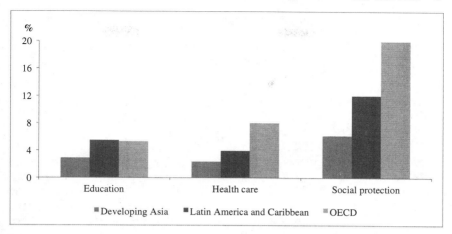

Figure 1.4 Share of education, health care, and social protection in gross domestic product, 2010

OECD = Organisation for Economic Co-operation and Development.

Source: ADB estimates based on data from World Development Indicators (accessed 27 February 2014).

Co-operation and Development (OECD) and Latin America in three equity-promoting fiscal expenditures: education, health care, and social protection. Public spending on education averages 5.3% of GDP in the advanced economies and 5.5% in Latin America, but only 2.9% in Asia (Figure 1.4). The gap is more pronounced for public spending on health care, which stands at only 2.4% of GDP in developing Asia compared with 8.1% in advanced economies and 3.9% in Latin America. On social protection, developing Asia spends about 6.2% of GDP, only half of Latin America's 12.0% and less than a third of the 20.0% in advanced economies. Clearly, Asian governments need to do more to foster inclusive growth by steering fiscal policy toward promoting greater equity.

While fiscal policy can reduce inequality from either the spending or the revenue side, evidence suggests that the impact from public spending is significantly greater (Bastagli, Coady, and Gupta 2012; Claus, Martinez-Vasquez, and Vulovic 2014). According to Bastagli, Coady, and Gupta (2012), expenditures, especially transfers without means tests, contributed more to income redistribution than did taxes. Significantly, Claus, Martinez-Vasquez, and Vulovic (2014) confirmed that the two main lessons from the broader literature for developing Asia are that fiscal expenditures, not taxation, offer the most effective means of reducing inequality and that the public spending best able to reduce inequality is on education and health care. Their analysis of data from 150 economies from 1970 to 2009 shows that despite tax systems tending to be progressive, government expenditures were more effective at redistributing income. Government expenditures on education and health care have been found to reduce income inequality in Asia and the rest of the world as Table 1.1 shows.

Table 1.1 Estimated marginal impact of government spending on income inequality (percentage points)

Spending type	Asia	Rest of the world
Social protection	0.490	–0.276
Education	–0.486	–0.034
Health	–0.241	–0.330
Housing	2.162	–0.614

Note: Minus sign indicates improved equality.
Source: Claus, Martinez-Vasquez, and Vulovic 2014.

How public spending is utilized and distributed across populations will have deep implications for inclusive growth. In particular, prioritizing programs that benefit the poor such as education and health care can help foster inclusiveness. Certain types of spending tend to be more equity-promoting than others. Another crucial issue is the need for better targeting to ensure that benefits from public spending intended to promote equity are captured largely by the poor.

1. Pro-poor public spending

Increasing access to education and health care is important for enhancing human capital, the main asset of the poor. With little or no government support, only those with sufficient incomes can pay for schooling costs or avail of health-care services. Governments therefore have a critical role in expanding opportunities for the poor and in enabling them to live more productive, decent lives through spending on education and health care. Public spending on physical infrastructure can also significantly benefit the poor. Better infrastructure improves access to markets, reduces transaction costs, and stimulates economic activity. Direct transfers are another type of spending that has significant potential to promote equity; however, direct transfers require well-designed targeting mechanisms to largely benefit the poor.

a. Public spending on education

Public spending on education can help narrow the gap in access to schooling between the poor and the non-poor. In several developing Asian economies, differences in access to schooling between the poor and non-poor are quite evident, especially in South Asia (Porta et al. 2011). Figures 1.5 and 1.6 demonstrate the wide gaps in access to primary and secondary schooling between the poorest and richest groups. For example, in Pakistan in 2006, over half of the children of primary school age among the poorest families were out of school compared to just 7% among the richest families. In India in 2005, 35% were out of school in the poorest-income group compared to 7% in the richest-income group. Similarly, there were wide gaps in secondary schooling between the two groups. Indeed, this points to the need for government support to expand coverage among the poor.

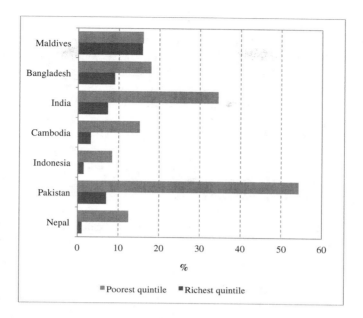

Figure 1.5 Percentage of children not in elementary school

Note: Data for Bangladesh and Cambodia refer to 2010; India, 2005; Indonesia, 2010; Maldives, 2009; Nepal, 2011; and Pakistan, 2006. Countries are ranked by the discrepancy in percentage between the poorest and richest quintiles, with Maldives having the narrowest gap.

Source: Estimated by Porta et al. 2011 using demographic and health surveys.

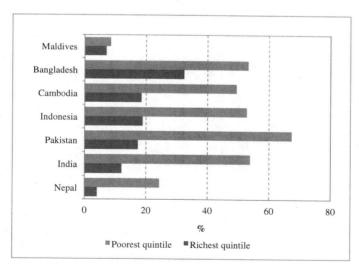

Figure 1.6 Percentage of children not in secondary school

Note: Data for Bangladesh and Cambodia refer to 2010; India, 2005; Indonesia, 2010; Maldives, 2009; Nepal, 2011; and Pakistan, 2006. Countries are ranked by the discrepancy in percentage between the poorest and richest quintiles, with Maldives having the narrowest gap.

Source: Estimated by Porta et al. 2011 using demographic and health surveys.

While increasing public financing for education may help raise access by the poor to education, there are demand-side factors that may limit it. These include perceptions of parents on the benefits of schooling, household income, and private costs to households of sending children to school. As children grow older, they are potentially more productive in the household or as child labor, and hence the opportunity cost of attending school increases. This is a main reason for falling enrollments in higher grades, particularly among the poor. Both the monetary and opportunity costs of sending children to school are higher relative to household income in poor households, which accounts for much of the difference in the enrollment rates between the poor and non-poor. Thus, it is also important to consider complementary government policies that raise returns on schooling to help improve the access of the poor to education (Roberts 2003).

Rising government investment in education has been a region-wide trend across developing Asia (Figure 1.7). This mirrors the general trend among

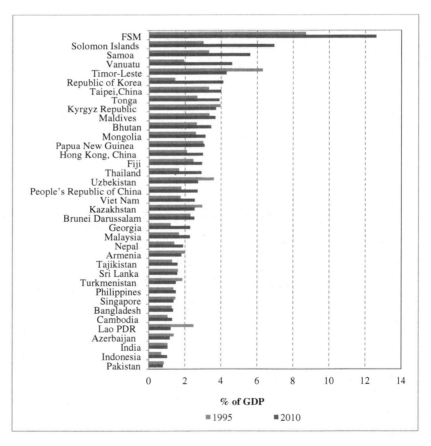

Figure 1.7 Government spending on health care

FSM = Federated States of Micronesia, Lao PDR = Lao People's Democratic Republic.

Source: Chapter 7 this volume.

developing countries to embark on huge education reforms to expand the supply of education, achieve equity in access, and significantly improve the quality of education (Tiongson 2005). While rising public spending for education bodes well for improving access to schooling, the type of intervention matters. If public spending for education is to indeed help in reducing inequality and poverty, then the poor should benefit more from it than other income groups.

Benefit incidence analysis has been used to examine whether public expenditure programs have been pro-poor or not. Studies of this type often report the average odds and marginal odds ratios of participation. The average odds for a particular quintile or income group can be defined as the ratio of that quintile's participation rate to the overall participation rate. The marginal odds of participation can be considered as the change in that quintile's participation rate associated with a change in the overall participation rate.

Studies applying benefit incidence analysis show that public spending for primary education tends to be pro-poor, particularly when the marginal odds ratio of participation is considered. Using survey data for rural India in fiscal year 1993–1994, Lanjouw and Ravallion (1999) found that since average enrollment rates tend to be lowest for the poorest quintile, then the average odds of enrollment indicate that subsidies to primary schooling would tend to favor the non-poor; however, the marginal odds of participation indicate that expanding primary schooling would be pro-poor. When considering the average odds of participation, the share of the total subsidy going to the poorest quintile is only 14%, but the results from the marginal odds of participation imply that the poorest quintile will obtain about a 22% increase in the total subsidy going to primary education. This suggests that marginal gains from expanding primary schooling in rural India appear to benefit the poor and hence contribute to lower inequality.

Benefit incidence also shows that public spending for primary schooling is more pro-poor than that for secondary schooling. For example, Lanjouw et al. (2002) found that for Indonesia, public spending on primary education tended to be pro-poor. While gross enrollment rates among the poorest quintiles were not substantially higher than the average, the large number of children in these quintiles led to a higher per capita transfer share in the bottom two quintiles compared with other three. With regard to secondary schooling, the beneficiaries tended to be the upper-income quintiles; however, after introducing economies of scale in consumption, public spending for primary education became less pro-poor, while spending for secondary schooling became more regressive. Estimates from the marginal incidence of program spending showed that primary education spending was pro-poor, but the evidence was weaker for secondary schooling. The poor would thus benefit a great deal from expanding public spending for primary education in the same way that they would be seriously hurt from reducing it.

Warr, Menon, and Rasphone (2013) found similar results for the Lao People's Democratic Republic (Lao PDR). In the case of primary education, the average odds indicated that richer households enjoyed a larger share of the total benefits than poorer households, but the marginal odds indicated the poor benefited more. For lower secondary school participation, the odds of participation showed a much higher participation rate for richer households similar to primary schooling. In contrast to primary schooling, however, the marginal odds for secondary schooling did not show the lowest-income groups benefiting more; instead, it was the middle-income quintile that was expected to gain more from expanding secondary schooling.

b. Public spending on health care

Studies have shown that the poor are significantly less healthy than the rich and that they are more likely than the rich to avail of public health-care facilities (Gupta, Verhoeven, and Tiongson 2001; World Bank 2004). This pattern is particularly evident in developing Asia. In Cambodia, Indonesia, Nepal, and the Philippines, the infant mortality rates of the poorest 20% of the population are more than twice those for infants in the wealthiest 20% (Figure 1.8). Lack of access to health services also tends to fall disproportionately on the poor in the region. While more than 60% of those in the highest-income groups in the Lao

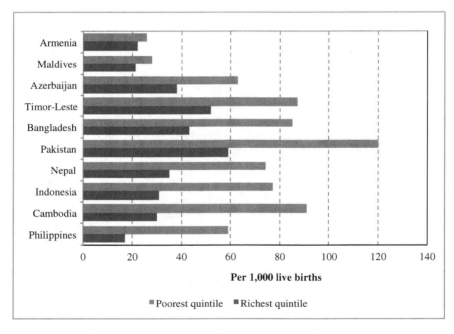

Figure 1.8 Under-5 mortality rate per 1,000 live births

Note: Countries are ranked by the discrepancy between the poorest and richest quintiles with Armenia enjoying the narrowest gap.

Source: World Health Organization 2013.

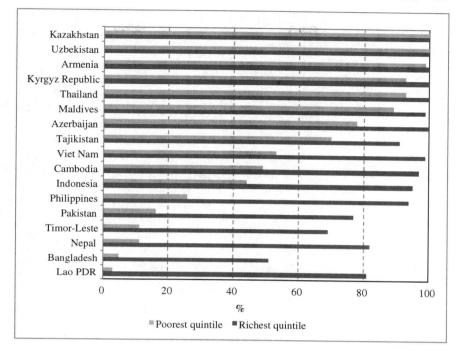

Figure 1.9 Births attended by skilled health personnel

Lao PDR = Lao People's Democratic Republic.

Note: Countries are ranked by the discrepancy between the poorest and richest quintiles, with Kazakhstan and Uzbekistan enjoying the narrowest gap.

Source: World Health Organization 2013.

PDR, Nepal, Pakistan, and Timor-Leste have births attended by skilled health personnel, the corresponding shares of those in the lowest quintile are just under 20% (Figure 1.9).

Health deficiencies can make the poor more vulnerable, generating a vicious cycle of poor health and poor incomes. Spending for critical illness can push poor households into deeper poverty or move the non-poor, especially those living at the margins, into poverty. For example, in 1998, health expenses were estimated to have pushed about 3 million people in Viet Nam into poverty. Seldom are the poor enrolled in voluntary insurance schemes or compulsory public programs that provide protection against health expenditure shocks (World Bank 2004). As Bidani and Ravallion (1997) have highlighted, public spending on health care tends to matter more to the poor. Improved health can enable them to be more productive in school and later in their working lives.

Empirical evidence shows that public spending can substantially improve the health outcomes of the poor and can narrow the gap in health outcomes between the poor and the non-poor. Examining the impact on the poor with respect to the non-poor, Gupta, Verhoeven, and Tiongson (2001) found that public spending on health had a greater impact on the poor as a 1% increase reduced their child mortality by twice as many deaths compared with the non-poor. The relationship between public health spending and the health status of the poor also tends to be stronger in low-income countries; the impact is more apparent when measured in absolute terms considering the higher levels of child mortality. Indeed, if implemented well, increased public spending for health can be quite beneficial for the poor.

Benefit incidence analysis has been widely used to determine how the benefits of public health spending are distributed across populations. There are studies such as those by Chakraborty, Singh, and Jacob (2013) for India and Kruse, Pradhan, and Sparrow (2012) for Indonesia that examine the distribution of benefits from public health spending by income groups in general or from health-care financing reforms. Examining both inpatient and outpatient health services, Chakraborty, Singh, and Jacob (2013) found that India's public health expenditure tends to be inequitable. The poorest quintile captured around 9% of the total net public expenditure in the health sector, while the richest group got around 40%. On the other hand, for Indonesia, Kruse, Pradhan, and Sparrow (2012) found that the health system tends to be pro-poor as increased local public health spending led to net transfers from the richest to the poorest quarter of the population as it increased both public health-care utilization by the poor and average health benefits. Given initial utilization shares, however, the bulk of the benefits were still captured by the middle-income groups; thus, it was recommended that increased public health spending be complemented by more directly targeted demand-side interventions for the poor such as price subsidies or social health insurance.

Other studies such as those by Lanjouw et al. (2002) and Warr, Menon, and Rasphone (2013) compared the distribution of benefits among the types of public health-care interventions. The study by Lanjouw et al. (2002) examined the distribution of benefits between primary health care and hospital services using survey data in Indonesia. In terms of utilization, primary health care was found to be fairly evenly distributed; however, utilization of public hospitals tended to be pro-rich since the richest quintile was three times more likely to visit a public hospital than the poorest quintile. Estimates from benefit incidence analysis indicated that public spending on health care was indeed pro-poor, while benefits from public hospitals were less frequently captured by the poor. In public health hospitals, per capita transfers going to the richest quintile were about four times greater than those received by the poorest quintile. Even after allowing for economies of scale, public spending for primary health care remained pro-poor, while public transfers for hospital care remained regressive. Marginal benefit incidence analysis indicated that changes in government spending on primary health care would benefit the poor substantially. Warr, Menon, and Rasphone (2013) found similar results for the Lao PDR. Primary health care tended to benefit the lower-income quintiles more but not public hospitals as benefits from using either outpatient or inpatient public hospitals were captured largely by higher-income households.

Applying benefit incidence for the PRC, in Chapter 5 Shen and Lee found that in 2009, benefits from publicly funded health care tended to be fairly equally distributed across income groups until age 60. For those aged 60 and older, public health spending per capita was highly skewed in favor of the top quartile. This inequity at old age reflects the lack of health insurance among the poor as well as low incomes since the use of health care tends to rise with income. The distance from health centers of many of the elderly poor also partly explains their limited access. This suggests that in the absence of programs that carefully target the poor, or in this case the elderly poor, inequality may increase.

c. Public spending on physical infrastructure

Developing countries tend to allocate limited fiscal resources to develop the infrastructure that supports economic activities and growth. This is apparent in spending on public gross fixed capital formation, which can be viewed as a rough proxy for physical infrastructure: communications, electricity, sanitation, transportation, and water. Since 2000, the average ratio of public gross fixed capital formation to GDP in Asia was 7.7%, which was much higher than the 4.3% average for OECD members (see Chapter 4). Thus, while the region is lagging in terms of public spending for education and health care, it tends to perform better in terms of spending for physical infrastructure.

There are several reasons for the positive growth effect of good infrastructure. A good road network or reliable electricity supply raises productivity across industries and firms and hence the economy as a whole. In addition, Winters (2014) points out that there are large potential gains from infrastructure-dependent trade, both within the economy and across borders. The empirical literature broadly supports the view that infrastructure investment boosts growth, especially in developing countries with low infrastructure stocks (e.g., Arslanalp et al. 2010; Easterly and Rebelo 1993). On the other hand, the relationship between infrastructure and inequality is conceptually more ambiguous. Using data from 1960 to 2005 for over 100 economies, Calderon and Serven (2010) found that both the quantity and quality of roads, telephones, and electricity had a significant beneficial effect on both growth and inequality. For inequality, an important additional finding was a significant relationship between inequality and the access of the poor to infrastructure.

In Chapter 4, Hur explores the link between public spending and inequality by constructing a model that accounts for the links between fiscal spending, income inequality, and economic growth. The analysis does not find a significant link between public gross capital formation and changes in the Gini coefficient, but it does find a strong growth impact. As shown by Kraay (2006), growth is the single key determinant in overcoming poverty.

Winters (2014) provides some possible explanations for the failure to find a positive, direct effect from physical infrastructure on inequality. In particular, he points out that infrastructure can exacerbate inequality in part because of its unfair allocation, but also because the better-off are better positioned to take advantage of the economic opportunities it creates. Similarly, Estache and Fay (2007) showed that access to infrastructure was highly skewed against the poorest. This reflects lack of physical access as well as limited affordability. Therefore, maximizing the inclusive impact of infrastructure requires extending access to the poor and making it affordable for them.

d. Government direct transfers

Developing Asia provides fewer direct transfers compared with other parts of the world (Figure 1.10). According to Bastagli, Coady, and Gupta (2012), direct transfer programs are difficult to establish in Asia because of the presence of large informal economies. Expenditure on social assistance programs for the poor was low and poorly targeted. Heavy spending on regressive general price subsidies such as fuel subsidies restricts the space for equity-promoting social transfers. Access to social insurance programs such as pensions is often limited to high-income workers in the urban formal sector and public sector. In many developing countries, in-kind public spending on key services such as education is regressive in the aggregate, although it may be progressive for individual components such as primary education (Davoodi, Tiongson, and Asawnuchit 2010; Lustig et al. 2011).

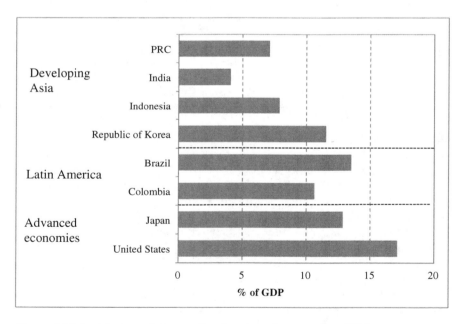

Figure 1.10 Social protection spending in selected economies, 2010

Note: Data for the People's Republic of China (PRC) are from 2004.

Source: ADB estimates based on data from the World Development Indicators (accessed 3 February 2014).

In recent years, conditional cash transfers (CCTs) have emerged as a promising option for magnifying the equity impact of public spending in developing countries, especially in Latin America. In essence, such programs provide monetary transfers to low-income households in exchange for their investing in the education and health of family members. In developing Asia, there are CCT programs in Bangladesh, Cambodia, India, Indonesia, Nepal, and the Philippines. Through the *Pantawid Pamilya* CCT program in the Philippines, for example, poor households with children receive education and health grants in exchange for education and health investments.

In Chapter 8, Lee and Park find limited and mixed evidence on the effectiveness of CCT programs in Asia. For example, the program has been found to be more successful in Cambodia than in Bangladesh because of the better targeting scheme in Cambodia. As the chapter highlights, there is no guarantee that programs that work well in Latin America will also work well in Asia. On one hand, many developing Asian governments lack the complex administrative structure to monitor large-scale programs. On the other, local communities are more organized in the region compared with Latin America, suggesting that the programs could fare better in Asia.

Further strengthening the impact of public spending on inequality will require careful targeting. As discussed in the next section, the case for improved targeting is crucial in light of the experience in implementing government subsidies.

2. Need for better targeting: the case of energy subsidies

In general, government subsidies aim to provide consumers, especially low-income groups, access to essential goods at more affordable and stable prices. Despite these sound intentions, rather than promoting equity, a large part of the subsidies have been found to benefit the better-off, as is the case with energy price subsidies.

Studies have shown that energy subsidies primarily benefit upper-income groups. There is a tendency for fuel consumption to rise substantially with income, so general subsidies will largely benefit non-poor households (Hope and Singh 1995). In low- and middle-income economies, on average, the richest 20% of households capture six times more in total fuel product subsidies than the poorest 20%. The distributional effects of subsidies vary markedly by product with gasoline being the most regressive (i.e., subsidy benefits increase as income rises) and kerosene the most progressive (International Monetary Fund [IMF] 2013a). In Indonesia, more than 90% of fuel subsidies benefit half of the richest households. In India, the richest 10% of households receive seven times more in benefits than the poorest 10% (Agustina et al. 2008; Anand et al. 2013).

Energy subsidies entail significant fiscal costs. In 2008, subsidies on coal, refined petroleum products, natural gas, and electricity consumption were equivalent to about 3%–8% of GDP in India, Indonesia, Malaysia, Pakistan, Thailand, and Viet Nam (Burniaux and Chateau 2011). Subsidies have remained substantial despite past efforts to implement energy price reforms.

In theory, removing subsidies is expected to generate economic gains arising from an increase in consumer welfare and from a more efficient reallocation of resources. Burniaux and Chateau (2011) analyzed the impacts of gradually removing oil subsidies globally from 2013 to 2020 based on data from 37 economies that comprise about 95% of global subsidized fossil fuel consumption. The unilateral removal of fossil fuel subsidies would result in welfare gains to most economies or regions ranging from 0.3% to more than 4% in 2050 relative to the baseline of 2008. In a multilateral removal of subsidies, India would benefit from welfare increases by 3% and the PRC by more than 0.5% relative to the baseline, but other countries such as oil-exporters would no longer obtain welfare gains as efficiency gains from improved resource allocation would be more than offset by the terms-of-trade losses associated with a sharp cut in world energy prices and demand.

In recent years, escalating international energy prices have put more pressure on governments to phase out energy subsidies. In India, domestic retail prices of petrol were liberalized in 2010, but diesel retail prices continue to be regulated by the government. Subsidies for kerosene and liquefied petroleum gas have often been much greater than for petrol and gasoline. Anand et al. (2013) found that eliminating subsidies in the country would have a substantial negative impact on real incomes of households ranging from about 4% for the lowest-income groups to 5% for higher-income groups, but since lower-income groups receive a very small share of total fuel subsidies, it should be possible to generate net fiscal savings from subsidizing them. Since the cost of fully compensating the poorest 40% of households was less than 0.2% of GDP, and the gross fiscal savings from a subsidy reform would be 1.9% of GDP, net fiscal gains from a targeted subsidy scheme would equal 1.7% of GDP. This suggests that huge fiscal gains can be reaped from implementing a well-targeted social safety net mechanism.

In Indonesia, estimates by Agustina et al. (2008) indicated that reducing the amount of fuel subsidies in the country by 25% could generate savings of about 0.2% of GDP and lessen the fiscal sector's vulnerability to movements in international energy prices. There was a risk, however, that removing subsidies without any compensation would lead to greater poverty, as fuel spending accounted for about 5% of total spending of the poorest households (Mourougane 2010). In general, the high direct and indirect welfare losses from the removal of subsidies imply that it will be politically challenging to implement such reforms (Table 1.2); hence, it may be important to introduce compensating measures to support the income of the poorest households once subsidies are removed.

Governments have been wary of removing subsidies maintaining that it may unduly harm poor households, yet phasing out subsidies could generate savings that could otherwise be used to provide direct transfers to the poor. Making public spending more inclusive requires well-targeted schemes rather than general subsidies. CCTs implemented in Latin American countries are a good example of a government spending program that is well-targeted and has significant equity impacts.

Overall, public spending can promote more inclusive growth by focusing on programs like primary education and basic health care that benefit the poor. Removing costly general subsidies while at the same time putting in place well-targeted schemes

Table 1.2 Direct and indirect welfare losses from fuel price increases (% of household consumption)

Region/County	Direct impact	Indirect impact
Africa	2.0	3.8
South and Central America	1.4	2.4
South and Southeast Asia	3.9	2.1
Bangladesh	1.7	1.5
Sri Lanka	2.7	2.6
Cambodia	2.2	NA
India	3.6	NA
Indonesia	8.8	NA
Middle East and Central Asia	5.8	4.2
All regions	2.8	3.3

NA = data not available.

Note: Examples of direct impact are higher prices for fuels used for cooking or lighting. Indirect impact occurs as prices for other goods and services rise because of higher production costs associated with more costly fuel.

Source: del Granado, Coady, and Gillingham 2010.

can also render public spending more inclusive. In addition to managing public spending well, governments also need to ensure that fiscal resources are sufficient to fund equity-promoting spending. Achieving fiscal sustainability to meet both current and future challenges can have far-reaching implications for inclusive growth.

C. Fiscal resources to foster inclusive growth

The previous section discussed how public spending can promote more inclusive growth in developing Asia. Given the considerable amount of public spending required to significantly narrow inequality and reduce poverty, the region needs sufficient fiscal space as more public spending in the absence of sufficient fiscal space may jeopardize fiscal sustainability and macroeconomic stability, which would adversely affect both economic growth and inclusive growth.

1. Enlarging fiscal space

Trends since 2000 indicate that developing Asia in general has maintained a prudent fiscal stance despite more aggressive public spending in the post-global financial crisis era. Since the crisis, spending has been ramped up in line with the massive fiscal stimulus implemented to counter declining external demand. Increased spending since the crisis has led to somewhat weakened fiscal positions; countries with sizable fiscal deficits such as India and Pakistan have witnessed deteriorating fiscal positions. In contrast, others such as Kazakhstan, the

18   *Gemma Estrada, Sang-Hyop Lee, et al.*

Republic of Korea, Singapore, and Turkmenistan have continued to post surpluses, but for many economies in the region, average fiscal balances have yet to reach their pre-crisis levels. While there is an obvious need for fiscal consolidation in many economies in developing Asia, overall the region has maintained a healthier fiscal position compared with other parts of the world (Figure 1.11).

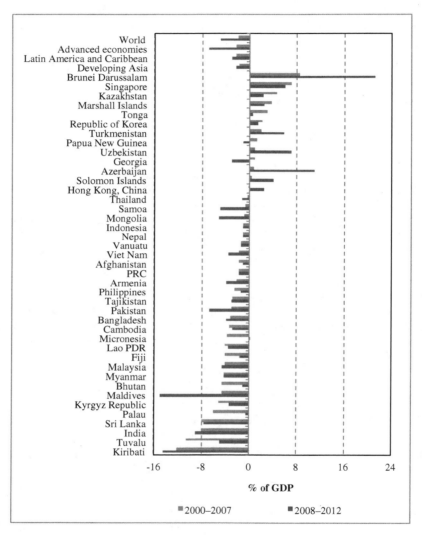

Figure 1.11 Average fiscal balance of selected economies (% of gross domestic product)

GDP = gross domestic product, Lao PDR = Lao People's Democratic Republic, PRC = People's Republic of China.

Sources: International Monetary Fund's World Economic Outlook database October 2013 and ADB estimates.

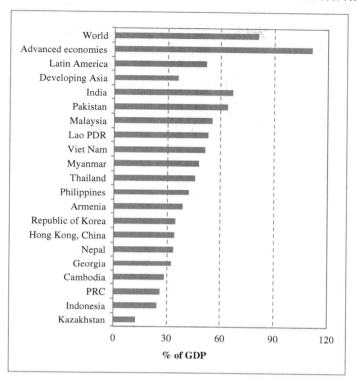

Figure 1.12 Gross government debt in selected economies, 2012 (% of gross domestic product)

GDP = gross domestic product, Lao PDR = Lao People's Democratic Republic, PRC = People's Republic of China.

Sources: International Monetary Fund's Fiscal Monitor database October 2013 and ADB estimates.

Prudent fiscal behavior has enabled developing Asia to maintain lower government debt compared with that of other regions (Ferrarini, Jha, and Ramayandi 2012). Gross government debt ratios across several Asian economies are comparable to the average for Latin America and are much lower than those of advanced economies (Figure 1.12). For developing Asia as a whole, the gross government debt ratio is lower by more than 10 percentage points compared with that of Latin America, and relative to the debt ratio of advanced countries, that of developing Asia is only about a third. Low debt ratios and favorable fiscal balances suggest that the region's overall fiscal stance is within sustainable levels, but there is a great deal of diversity among individual economies. The PRC, Indonesia, and Kazakhstan have the lowest debt ratios at less than 30%, while India, Pakistan, and Malaysia have debt ratios of 50% to 70%. For the latter, there is a need to closely monitor debt levels to ensure that they do not reach alarmingly high levels.

While the region appears to currently have sufficient fiscal space to finance equity-promoting programs, that does not guarantee the future availability of fiscal space as major structural changes may create additional fiscal demands that will affect it. The single biggest medium- to long-term structural challenge confronting the region is population aging. While there is considerable demographic diversity across subregions and economies, the region as a whole is in the midst of a shift toward markedly older populations. In Chapter 7, Lee and Mason explain how expected changes in demographic structures will affect public spending especially on education, health care, and social protection. Governments need to boost their revenues if they are to adequately meet the demands from these structural changes.

2. Raising fiscal revenues

Developing Asia needs to raise more revenues to finance public spending. A comparison of the trends for the 1990s and 2000s indicates that the region has trailed other parts of the world in tax revenues as they are less than half those of the OECD, as is graphically illustrated in Chapter 3. The gap between developing Asia and the OECD may be explained in part by the tendency for tax revenues to rise with per capita income, but developing Asia also lags Latin America – a region with comparable income and development – in both tax and non-tax revenues (see Chapter 6). From 2005 to 2011, Asia's tax revenues as a percent of GDP were only about three-fourths those of Latin America and barely half of the latter's non-tax revenues. Overall, the trends suggest that there is considerable scope for boosting developing Asian revenues.

Taxes are the primary sources of fiscal revenues. As Das-Gupta explains in Chapter 6, a large part of the region's revenues are accounted for by current revenues that in turn are dominated by taxes. Among the different types, taxes on goods and services and taxes on income are the two main sources. Across subregions, there are differences on which type of tax plays a more dominant role (Figure 1.13). The share of goods and services taxes is more pronounced

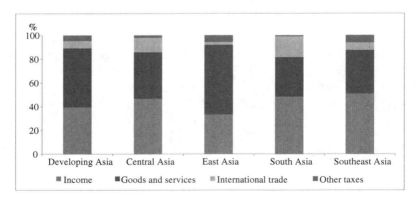

Figure 1.13 Contribution of major tax groups to total tax revenue, 2005–2011 (% of total share)

Source: ADB estimates based on data from WDI (accessed 27 February 2014).

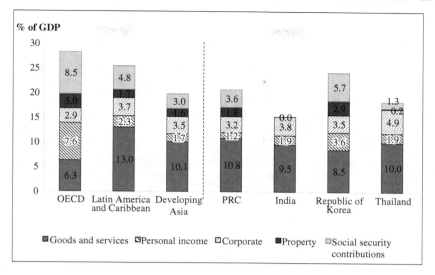

Figure 1.14 Tax composition in developing Asia, Latin America and the Caribbean, and the Organisation for Economic Co-operation and Development

GDP = gross domestic product, OECD = Organisation for Economic Co-operation and Development, PRC = People's Republic of China.

Notes:

Developing Asia includes Afghanistan; Armenia; the PRC; Hong Kong, China; India; the Republic of Korea; Mongolia; and Thailand.

Latin America and the Caribbean comprises Barbados, Brazil, Colombia, Costa Rica, Dominican Republic, El Salvador, Guatemala, Honduras, Jamaica, Paraguay, Peru, Trinidad and Tobago, and Uruguay.

The OECD consists of Australia, Belgium, Canada, France, Greece, Iceland, Israel, Japan, Luxembourg, Norway, Poland, Portugal, Slovenia, Spain, Switzerland, and the United States.

Source: ADB estimates based on International Monetary Fund's Revenue Data.

in East Asia, but in Central Asia, South Asia, and Southeast Asia, income taxes account for a larger share.

Figure 1.14 shows a comparison of the GDP share of corporate income tax, personal income tax, goods and services tax, and social security contributions among OECD members, Latin America, and developing Asia. The regional averages are weighted by the GDPs of member economies. The sum of tax composition is lower in developing Asia compared with the other two regions. The shares in GDP of income tax and property tax in developing Asia are less than those in OECD and Latin America. Goods and services taxes have a greater share in developing Asia compared with the OECD, but compared with Latin America, the share in developing Asia is less. The evidence confirms that indirect taxes are more important than income taxes in developing economies but that the opposite holds true in advanced economies. Developing Asia also collects less in social security contributions relative to GDP indicating its social security systems are less developed than those of the OECD and Latin America.

Data on tax composition for the PRC, India, the Republic of Korea, and Thailand indicate some common features and differences. A distinct feature among the four economies is the dominant role of goods and services taxes. Corporate income tax also accounts for a substantial share in all four with Thailand having the largest share, while personal income tax and property tax are more significant in the Republic of Korea compared with the other three. Among the large Asian economies in Figure 1.14, only the share of social security contributions in the Republic of Korea is comparable with that of advanced economies, although PRC is not too far behind. This signifies that the two East Asian countries have more advanced social security systems.

While taxes in general tend to deter growth, there are certain types of tax that are considered less detrimental than others. In Chapter 3, Abdon et al. simulate the impact on growth of altering the tax composition and find that reducing the reliance on income tax while raising the use of consumption and other taxes can raise GDP growth over the long run. Another finding is that raising property taxes while reducing income tax can be more beneficial to growth. Property taxes are likely to be borne more by the rich since they are expected to own more property holdings than the poor. This implies that raising the property tax can be a sound option in terms of both boosting revenues and promoting equity.

The huge role of taxes in the region's fiscal revenues suggests that stronger revenue mobilization will require reforms in tax systems. Different types of tax have varying effects on growth and income inequality. In addition to revenue and economic growth impacts, tax reforms must therefore consider the expected consequences for income distribution. Beyond tax revenue measures, there is a need for governments in the region to explore other options that will enable them to raise much-needed resources to enlarge their fiscal space and promote inclusive growth.

D. Concluding observations

The region has achieved rapid economic growth driven by globalization, technological progress, and market-oriented reforms, but that growth has occurred alongside a deterioration in income distribution. Rising inequality strengthens the case for Asian governments to do more to ensure a more equitable distribution of the benefits of growth and for fiscal policy to play a more fundamental role in fostering inclusive growth.

Evidence indicates that public spending on education, health care, and direct transfers can reduce inequality. In fact, some public spending can promote both growth and equity. The region has trailed other parts of the world in using fiscal policy as a tool to improve income distribution; however, expanding public expenditure without boosting fiscal resources can jeopardize fiscal sustainability.

The key challenge is how to use fiscal policy to make growth more inclusive while maintaining fiscal sustainability. Developing Asia has traditionally maintained fiscal prudence, which has helped the region achieve macroeconomic stability and enabled it to respond well in times of economic crisis, but future structural challenges such as the rapid demographic transition can significantly narrow the region's fiscal space.

Asian economies need to thoroughly examine their range of options. Evidence shows that government expenditure rather than taxation has a substantial effect on inequality. Economies need to consider that the composition of public expenditures, including their design and implementation, matters greatly. Furthermore, economies face limited resource bases; thus, strengthening fiscal mobilization and exploring more sources of revenues will be crucial.

Bibliography

Agustina, C.D.R.D., J.A. del Granado, T. Bulman, W. Fengler, and M. Ikhsan. 2008. Black Hole or Black Gold? The Impact of Oil and Gas Prices on Indonesia's Public Finances. *Policy Research Working Paper.* No. 4718. Washington, DC: World Bank.

Anand, R., D. Coady, A. Mohommad, V. Thakoor, and J.P. Walsh. 2013. The Fiscal and Welfare Impacts of Reforming Fuel Subsidies in India. *IMF Working Paper.* No. WP/13/128. Washington, DC: International Monetary Fund.

Arslanalp, S., F. Bornhorst, S. Gupta, and E. Sze. 2010. Public Capital and Growth. *IMF Working Paper Series.* No. WP/10/175. Washington, DC: International Monetary Fund.

Asian Development Bank (ADB). 2010. *Asian Development Outlook 2010: Macroeconomic Management beyond the Crisis.* Manila: ADB.

———. 2011. *Asian Development Outlook 2011 Update: Preparing for Demographic Transition.* Manila: ADB.

———. 2012. *Asian Development Outlook 2012 Update: Confronting Rising Inequality in Asia.* Manila: ADB.

Bastagli, F., D. Coady, and S. Gupta. 2012. Income Inequality and Fiscal Policy. *IMF Staff Discussion Note.* No. SDN/12/08. Washington, DC: International Monetary Fund.

Bidani, B. and M. Ravallion. 1997. Decomposing Social Indicators Using Distributional Data. *Journal of Econometrics.* 77 (1). pp. 125–139.

Burniaux, J.-M. and J. Chateau. 2011. Mitigation Potential of Removing Fossil Fuel Subsidies: A General Equilibrium Assessment. *OECD Economics Department Working Papers.* No. 853. Paris: Organisation for Economic Co-operation and Development.

Calderon, C. and L. Serven. 2010. Infrastructure and Economic Development in Sub-Saharan Africa. *Journal of African Economies.* 19 (Supplement 1). pp. i13–i87.

Chakraborty, L., Y. Singh, and J.F. Jacob. 2013. Analyzing Public Expenditure Benefit Incidence in Health Care: Evidence from India. *Levy Economics Institute Working Paper.* No. 748. New York: Bard College.

Claus, I., J. Martinez-Vasquez, and V. Vulovic. 2014. Government Fiscal Policies and Redistribution in Asian Countries. In R. Kanbur, C. Rhee, and J. Zhuang, eds. *Inequality in Asia and the Pacific: Trends, Drivers, and Policy Implications.* London and New York: Routledge and Manila: ADB.

Davoodi, H. R., E. Tiongson, and S. S. Asawnuchit. 2010. Benefit Incidence of Public Education and Health Spending Worldwide: Evidence from a New Database. *Poverty & Public Policy.* 2 (2). pp. 5–52.

del Granado, J. A., D. Coady, and R. Gillingham. 2010. The Unequal Benefits of Fuel Subsidies: A Review of Evidence for Developing Countries. *IMF Working Paper.* No. WP/10/202. Washington, DC: International Monetary Fund.

Easterly, W. and S. Rebelo. 1993. Fiscal Policy and Economic Growth: An Empirical Investigation. *NBER Working Paper.* No. 4499. Cambridge, MA: National Bureau of Economic Research.

Estache, A. and M. Fay. 2007. Current Debates on Infrastructure Policy. *Policy Research Working Paper.* No. 4410. Washington, DC: World Bank.

Ferrarini, B., R. Jha, and A. Ramayandi, eds. 2012. *Public Debt Sustainability in Developing Asia.* London and New York: Routledge and Manila: ADB.

Gupta, S., M. Verhoeven, and E. Tiongson. 2001. Public Spending on Health Care and the Poor. *IMF Working Paper.* No. WP/01/127. Washington, DC: International Monetary Fund.

Hope, E. and B. Singh. 1995. Energy Price Increases in Developing Countries: Case Studies of Colombia, Ghana, Indonesia, Malaysia, Turkey, and Zimbabwe. *Policy Research Working Paper.* No. 1442. Washington, DC: World Bank.

International Monetary Fund (IMF). 2013a. *Energy Subsidy Reform: Lessons and Implications.* Washington, DC: International Monetary Fund.

————. 2013b. Fiscal Monitor Database October 2013. http://www.imf.org/external/pubs/ft/fm/2013/02/fmindex.htm (accessed 22 November 2013).

————. 2013c. World Economic Outlook Data Forum. http://forums.imf.org/forumdisplay.php?3-World-Economic-Outlook-(WEO)-Data-Forum (accessed 27 February 2014)

Kraay, D. 2006. When Is Growth Pro-Poor? Cross-Country Evidence. *Journal of Development Economics.* 80 (1). pp. 198–227.

Kruse, I., M. Pradhan, and R. Sparrow. 2012. Marginal Benefit Incidence of Public Health Spending: Evidence from Indonesian Sub-national Data. *Journal of Health Economics.* 31 (1). pp. 147–157.

Lanjouw, P., M. Pradhan, F. Saadah, H. Sayed, and R. Sparrow. 2002. Poverty, Education, and Health in Indonesia: Who Benefits from Public Spending? In Morrisson, C., ed. *Education and Health Expenditures, and Development: The Cases of Indonesia and Peru.* Paris: OECD Development Centre.

Lanjouw, P. and M. Ravallion. 1999. Benefit Incidence, Public Spending Reforms, and the Timing of Program Capture. *The World Bank Economic Review.* 13 (2). pp. 257–273.

Lee, S.-H. and A. Mason. 2012. The Economic Lifecycle and Support Systems in Asia. In Park, D., S.-H. Lee, and A. Mason, eds. *Aging, Economic Growth, and Old-age Security in Asia.* Cheltenham, UK and Northampton, MA: Edward Elgar Publishing.

Lustig, N., S. Higgins, M. Jaramillo, W. Jimenez, G. G. Molina, V. Paz Arauco, C. Pereira, C. Pessino, J. Scott, and E. Yañez. 2011. Fiscal Policy and Income Distribution in Latin America: Challenging the Conventional Wisdom. *Tulane Economics Working Paper.* No. 1124. New Orleans: Tulane University.

Mourougane, A. 2010. Phasing Out Energy Subsidies in Indonesia. *OECD Economics Department Working Paper.* No. 808. Paris: Organisation for Economic Co-operation and Development.

Porta, E., G. Arcia, K. Macdonald, S. Radyakin, and M. Lokshin. 2011. *Assessing Sector Performance and Inequality in Education: Streamlined Analysis with ADePT Software*. Washington, DC: World Bank.

Roberts, J. 2003. Poverty Reduction Outcomes in Education and Health: Public Expenditure and Aid. *CAPE–ODI Working Paper*. No. 210. London: Centre for Aid and Public Expenditure, Overseas Development Institute.

Tiongson, E. 2005. Education Policy Reforms. In Coudouel, A. and S. Paternostro, eds. *Analyzing the Distributional Impact of Reforms: A Practitioner's Guide to Trade, Monetary and Exchange Rate Policy, Utility Provision, Agricultural Markets, Land Policy, and Education*. Washington, DC: World Bank.

Warr, P., J. Menon, and S. Rasphone. 2013. How Expansion of Public Services Affects the Poor: Benefit Incidence Analysis for the Lao People's Democratic Republic. *ADB Economics Working Paper*. No. 349. Manila: ADB.

Winters, L. A. 2014. Globalization, Infrastructure, and Inclusive Growth. ADBI Working Paper Series No. 464. Tokyo: Asian Development Bank Institute.

World Bank. 2004. *Services Provision for the Poor*. Washington, DC: World Bank.

———. 2014. World Development Indicators (WDI) online database. http:// databank.worldbank.org/data/views/variableSelection/selectvariables.aspx?source= world-development-indicators (accessed 3 February and 27 February 2014).

World Health Organization. 2013. *World Health Statistics*. Geneva: WHO.

2 Room at the top

An overview of fiscal space, fiscal policy, and inclusive growth in developing Asia

Rathin Roy

A. Introduction and some analytical considerations

The sustainability of policies to create fiscal space is a function of what the fiscal space is used for. The balance of emphasis placed on the stabilization, allocation, and distribution and growth functions of fiscal policy would differ according to the time frame of the analytical framework and the context of the political economy.[1] Finding sustainable fiscal space for inclusive growth therefore involves asking what the purpose of public spending is, the time frame for its implementation, and the context within which it is implemented.

An important question to consider, therefore, in assessing whether fiscal space exists for inclusive growth is to examine the extent to which fiscal policies are generally prudent and whether or not there is room to increase fiscal space. In this context, it is worth repeating that one of the requirements for inclusive growth is that growth must be steady and stable. Inclusion as an objective of fiscal policy is expected to complement, not compromise, the growth potential of an economy; hence, it is important to examine whether or not there exists fiscal space for inclusive growth in terms of the fiscal profile. This involves looking at the potential for securing incremental fiscal space that may be necessary to improve inclusion; it also means that the size of the government–gross domestic product (GDP) ratio, whether tax or debt financed, should not increase to an extent and at a pace such that it crowds out growth-generating private sector activity.

When inclusive growth is the objective of national development strategies, the focus is on securing economic growth through investing in the social and human resources that enable such growth to be resilient. This is a sharp break from the growth mantras of the 1980s and 1990s that focused either on growth driven by an increase in exports based on static comparative advantage or on import substituting industrialization that, for lack of physical and social infrastructure and human capital, faltered in its execution.

This important change in thinking about development strategy is epitomized in the centrality of policy interventions to scale up investments that secure the achievement of the Millennium Development Goals (MDGs). Considerable progress has been made in many developing countries in designing and implementing supply-side interventions to secure the MDGs. More recently, attention is being paid to ensuring that exposure to economic shocks and to asymmetries in access to the public goods necessary to secure the MDGs do not retard or even derail progress towards those goals.[2] It is here that specific fiscal measures assume an important role in the overall context of fiscal policy making.

From a fiscal perspective, there are two important issues pertinent to this strategic shift.[3] Many of the objects of public spending for inclusive growth – including health, education, and social welfare – are financed out of current expenditure. Macroeconomic prudence requires a zero current deficit except in times of temporary cyclical stress. However, increases in expenditures on social services are (i) largely current expenditures and (ii) permanent in the short to medium term (although, with increased incomes and improved employment performance, they decline as a proportion of total expenditure in the long term). For these reasons, finance ministries worldwide have been skeptical of arguments to enhance outlays on social spending.

The second issue is whether inclusion is expected to happen sooner or later. The Second Theorem of Welfare Economics[4] stipulates that the prior and prime objective must be to attain the maximum sustainable rate of steady state growth irrespective of the extent to which the compensation to different factors of production in the process of traversing to that steady state is consistent with the desired distribution expressed in a given social welfare function. Having achieved steady state growth, a suitable income distribution can then be attained without efficiency losses through neutral lump sum taxes and transfers. In effect, here, the role of fiscal policy is principally distributive, and it is redistributive transfers that secure such an optimal steady state.

An alternative policy stance is to ensure that growth maintains or improves inclusion by securing greater participation in the process. Essentially this is a question of choice of techniques and relative prices.[5] The role of fiscal policy here is not to actively intervene to secure a better income distribution but to provide a prudential environment that (i) allows fiscal space to exist for securing increases in economic growth including public investments in economic services that complement private investments without crowding them out; (ii) provides fiscal space for counter-cyclical fiscal policies to protect against exogenous shocks; and (iii) delivers merit and public goods, significantly health and education, that increase human capital and permanently enhance participation in growth.

Thus, the key questions in this chapter are the following:

• Have economies in developing Asia chosen to pursue inclusive growth through maximizing progress to a steady state growth path with redistributive income transfers as the main instrument to eventually secure desired inclusion outcomes?

OR

- Have economies in developing Asia tended to use fiscal policy to maintain a prudential environment for economic growth, to secure counter-cyclical stabilization of growth, and to deliver merit and public goods to increase human capital and to permanently enhance participation in growth?

B. Country groupings

Analyses of economic trends in developing Asia are typically undertaken on a subregional scale. When assessing fiscal impact, this tends not to be very informative because the structural and other features of the fiscal base of different economies in a subregion can vary immensely. The principal reason for this is differences in the income and consumption base; however, changes in economic structure at different points in development also matter.

When working with subregional classifications for this chapter, it was difficult to come up with interesting fiscal trends at a macro level. Different groupings were therefore devised clustering economies with similar incomes and consumption patterns together, but also allowing for economic size, special characteristics, and geopolitical situations. The groupings that proved to be the most pertinent are the following:

- **High-income economies (HIE):** Brunei Darussalam; Hong Kong, China; the Republic of Korea; Malaysia; and Singapore. These economies continue to be classified as part of developing Asia, and with the exception of small and resource rich Brunei Darussalam, exhibit trends typical of HIE globally in terms of their fiscal incidence.
- **Middle-income economies I (MIE I):** Azerbaijan, Kazakhstan, the Maldives, Turkmenistan, and Uzbekistan. With the exception of the Maldives, these countries are more or less subregionally coherent in their fiscal patterns.
- **Middle-income economies II (MIE II):** Pakistan, the Philippines, Sri Lanka, Thailand, and Viet Nam. This mix of countries from South and Southeast Asia also displays distinct middle-income patterns.
- **Small economies with special characteristics (SSC):** Armenia, Bhutan, Georgia, Mongolia, and Papua New Guinea.
- **Low-income economies (LIE):** Afghanistan, Bangladesh, Cambodia, the Kyrgyz Republic, the Lao People's Democratic Republic (Lao PDR), Nepal, Tajikistan, and Timor-Leste.
- **Emerging mega economies (EME):** the People's Republic of China (PRC), India, and Indonesia.

C. Overview of fiscal trends in developing Asia

On the basis of this revised grouping for comparing and examining trends in different fiscal indicators, growth, and savings–investment balance, a number of interesting inferences can be drawn.

1. *Fiscal stance: revenue and expenditure trends*

a. *Revenue trends*

Revenue trends and the consequent fiscal stance tended to be extremely similar within most groups though with some important outliers; however, there was considerable variation across groups. The emerging patterns were the following:

- The revenue stances of HIE with the exception of Brunei Darussalam have converged since about 2005 (Figure 2.1).
- This is also true of MIE I and II and SSC with the exception of Viet Nam, though MIE I and SSC display somewhat higher volatility (Figures 2.2, 2.3, and 2.4).
- There is also some convergence in the LIE (Figure 2.5) with revenues in all increasing over time, though the revenue efforts for the Kyrgyz Republic, Tajikistan, and more recently Timor-Leste are of a much higher order than those of the other LIE as is to be expected due to their high reliance on natural resource receipts. Revenue–GDP ratios have been rising in the LIE since 2006, and in some cases like Afghanistan, the Lao PDR, and Nepal, this rise has been quite dramatic.
- The EME as expected show no such congruence though trends individually are stable. The PRC records a steady rise in its revenue–GDP ratio, while India performs poorly on this score with temporary improvements in good years reversed in bad years (Figure 2.6).

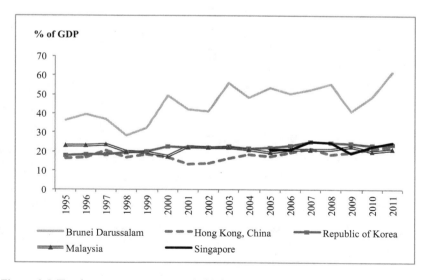

Figure 2.1 Total government revenue in high-income economies (% of gross domestic product)

GDP = gross domestic product.

Source: ADB Country Profiles Database of *Key Indicators for Asia and the Pacific.*

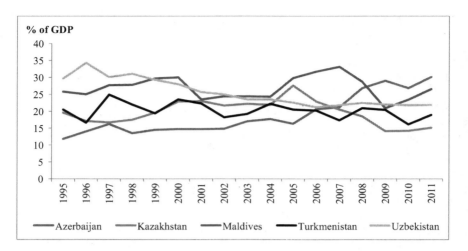

Figure 2.2 Total government revenue in middle-income economies I (% of gross domestic product)

GDP = gross domestic product.

Source: ADB Country Profiles Database of *Key Indicators for Asia and the Pacific*.

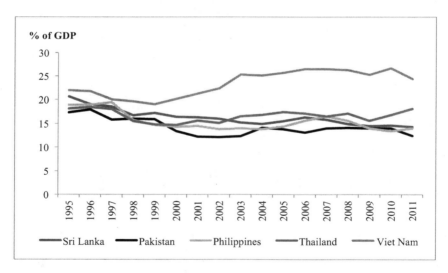

Figure 2.3 Total government revenue in middle-income economies II (% of gross domestic product)

GDP = gross domestic product.

Source: ADB Country Profiles Database of *Key Indicators for Asia and the Pacific*.

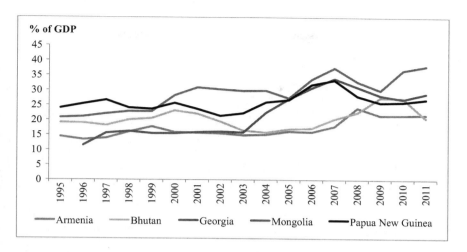

Figure 2.4 Total government revenue in small economies with special characteristics (% of gross domestic product)

GDP = gross domestic product.

Source: ADB Country Profiles Database of *Key Indicators for Asia and the Pacific.*

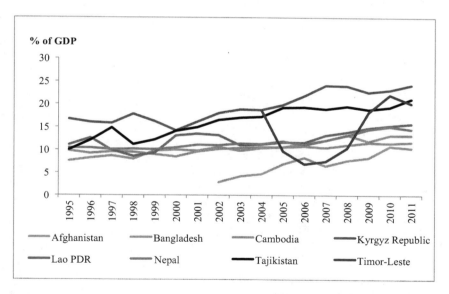

Figure 2.5 Total government revenue in low-income economies (% of gross domestic product)

GDP = gross domestic product, Lao PDR = Lao People's Democratic Republic.

Source: ADB Country Profiles Database of *Key Indicators for Asia and the Pacific.*

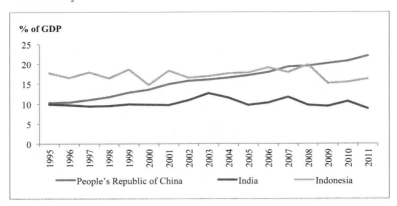

Figure 2.6 Total government revenue in emerging mega economies (% of gross domestic product)

GDP = gross domestic product.

Source: ADB Country Profiles Database of *Key Indicators for Asia and the Pacific.*

On the whole, developing Asia has a conservative revenue stance. In 2011, no HIE or MIE collected tax revenues in excess of 22% of GDP except Brunei Darussalam and Uzbekistan. Total revenue ratios in excess of that number are observed only in MIE I, chiefly due to high non-tax revenue receipts. These, in turn, tend to be volatile. Viet Nam is a possible exception though there too revenue–GDP ratios appear to have peaked at around 25% since 2004. On average, compared with high- and middle-income economies in other regions, this is indeed a fairly conservative effort particularly for the EME, where only the PRC exhibits a steady increase in its ratio.

b. Expenditure trends

Trends in total expenditures also converge. For the HIE, again with the exception of Brunei Darussalam, both the Republic of Korea and Malaysia spend a stable amount of GDP (around 20%) on public expenditures (Figure 2.7).

The MIE I are more heterogeneous (Figures 2.8 and 2.9). The government of the Maldives increased public expenditures from 35% to more than 40% of GDP in 2005 and has spent about the same proportion since then. Kazakhstan has seen a sharp rise in public expenditures since 2005, while in Uzbekistan, the ratio has steadily fallen since 1997. The SSC, on the other hand, have displayed remarkable convergence in recent times with spending in all cases around 30% of GDP. This convergence has meant both spending cuts in Bhutan and increases in Georgia and Mongolia (Figure 2.10). The LIE are again heterogeneous with all but Bangladesh showing increases in the total expenditure–GDP ratio with some dramatic increases occurring post 2006 in some (Figure 2.11). In the EME, the PRC has matched increased revenue–GDP ratios with increases in public spending; the ratio has stayed more or less constant in India and has fallen since 2008 in Indonesia (Figure 2.12).

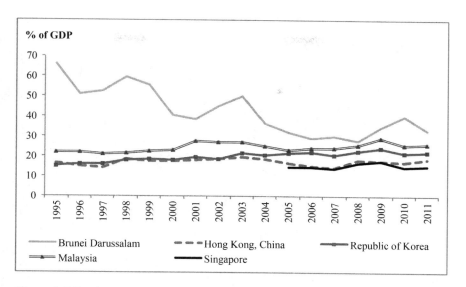

Figure 2.7 Total government expenditure in high-income economies (% of gross domestic product)

GDP = gross domestic product.

Source: ADB Country Profiles Database of *Key Indicators for Asia and the Pacific*.

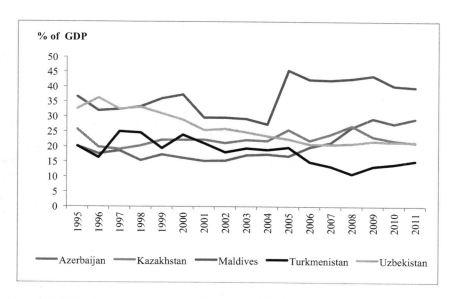

Figure 2.8 Total government expenditure in middle-income economies I (% of gross domestic product)

GDP = gross domestic product.

Source: ADB Country Profiles Database of *Key Indicators for Asia and the Pacific*.

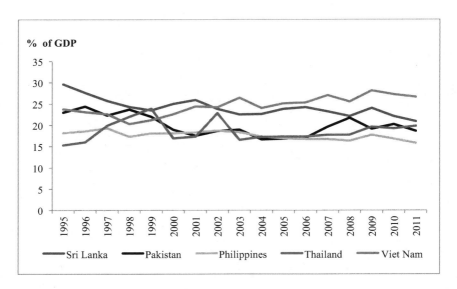

Figure 2.9 Total government expenditure in middle-income economies II (% of gross domestic product)

GDP = gross domestic product.

Source: ADB Country Profiles Database of *Key Indicators for Asia and the Pacific*.

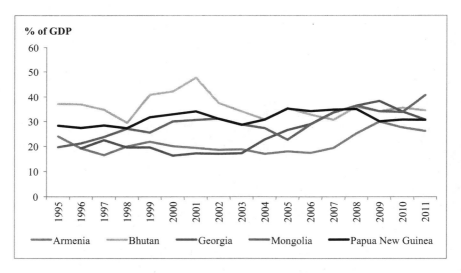

Figure 2.10 Total government expenditure in small economies with special characteristics (% of gross domestic product)

GDP = gross domestic product.

Source: ADB Country Profiles Database of *Key Indicators for Asia and the Pacific*.

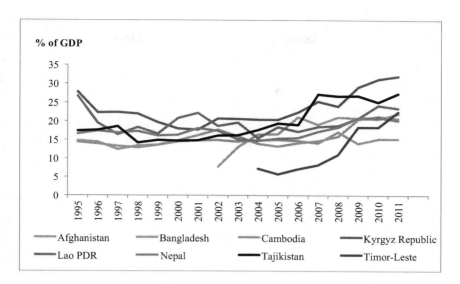

Figure 2.11 Total government expenditure in low-income economies (% of gross domestic product)

GDP = gross domestic product, Lao PDR = Lao People's Democratic Republic.

Source: ADB Country Profiles Database of *Key Indicators for Asia and the Pacific*.

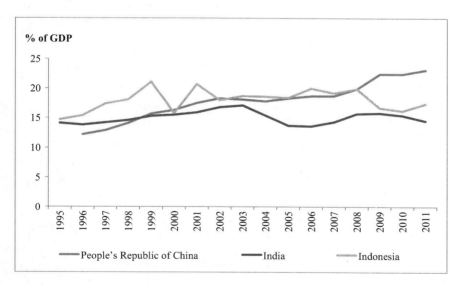

Figure 2.12 Total government expenditure in emerging mega economies (% of gross domestic product)

GDP = gross domestic product.

Source: ADB Country Profiles Database of *Key Indicators for Asia and the Pacific*.

Thus, developing Asia exhibits a generally prudent and conservative fiscal stance whether assessed in terms of the share of revenue in national income or the share of public expenditure. There is considerable convergence within different groups in revenue shares. Non-tax revenues do cause some volatility in the MIE I. For expenditures, the HIE exhibit stable and by global standards conservative public expenditure ratios indicating that there has been no recourse to redistributional policies over the period. The same is true for the MIE groups with the exception of Kazakhstan. Remarkably, the SSC also show convergence with respect to public spending at around 30% of GDP. The LIE have recorded increases in their expenditure–GDP ratios, but with the exception of the Kyrgyz Republic and Timor-Leste, shares continue to be low at around 20% of GDP.

Inference. Revenue and expenditure shares in developing Asia indicate that the region has not resorted to redistributive fiscal policies in the pursuit of inclusive growth. The endeavor is to pursue inclusion through improving human capital and maintaining a prudent macro-fiscal stance.

2. Public expenditure trends and spending on inclusive growth

When it comes to the incidence of public expenditure by functional outlay, several interesting trends can be discerned. The Republic of Korea and Malaysia have significant outlays on defense (Figure 2.13); however, Malaysia deploys almost double its GDP on education compared with the former, and its health expenditures are also significantly higher (Figures 2.14 and 2.15). Other than

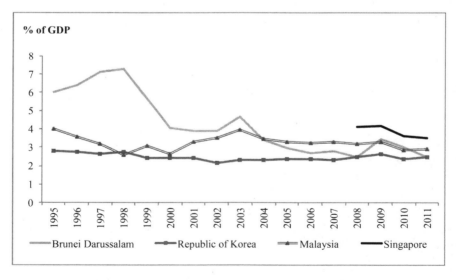

Figure 2.13 Defense spending in the high-income economies (% of gross domestic product)

GDP = gross domestic product.

Source: ADB Country Profiles Database of *Key Indicators for Asia and the Pacific*.

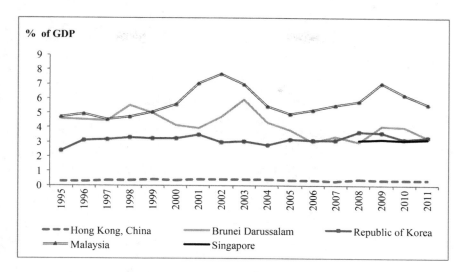

Figure 2.14 Education spending in the high-income economies (% of gross domestic product)

GDP = gross domestic product.

Source: ADB Country Profiles Database of *Key Indicators for Asia and the Pacific.*

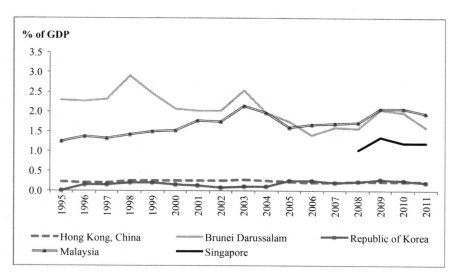

Figure 2.15 Health spending in the high-income economies (% of gross domestic product)

GDP = gross domestic product.

Source: ADB Country Profiles Database of *Key Indicators for Asia and the Pacific.*

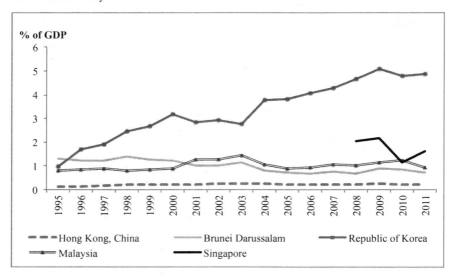

Figure 2.16 Social welfare spending in the high-income economies (% of gross domestic product)

GDP = gross domestic product.

Source: ADB Country Profiles Database of *Key Indicators for Asia and the Pacific*.

defense, the Republic of Korea has major and growing social welfare expenditures that perhaps account for the persistently and significantly low levels of inequality there (Figure 2.16).

The MIE for which data are available all seem to spend about the same as the HIE on defense; their outlays on education are comparable to those of the Republic of Korea, while their health spending is somewhat greater. Other than in Sri Lanka, social welfare spending has always been low in the MIE, and in Sri Lanka too, it has been consistently falling since 1995. With the exception of the Kyrgyz Republic, the LIE spend moderately on defense. Cambodia – the other historically high spender – has sharply moderated its defense spending. At the same time, spending on social welfare, education, and health as a pro-portion of GDP was low in all except the Kyrgyz Republic notwithstanding a sharp rise in the allocation to social welfare expenditures by Tajikistan in this decade. Among EME, the PRC and India spend moderately on defense, but India has not managed to significantly increase GDP allocations to health and education. It appears, therefore, that by and large developing Asia spends mod-erately on defense in relation to GDP; however, health and education outlays are low in the SSC, LIE, and the EME.

Inference. While developing Asia has historically not been a significant spender on defense (though data gaps for this indicator mean that this must be inter-preted with caution especially for countries like Pakistan and Indonesia), spending on education, health, and social welfare remains low, except in the HIE. The

MIE has increased outlays on education in recent years, but health and social welfare outlays are still low, and there is considerable scope to increase these expenditures, especially given generally conservative levels of revenue mobilization if macro-fiscal balances are sound.

An examination of the shares of health, education, and social welfare, respectively, in total government expenditures (as opposed to GDP) affords some interesting insights to nuance the above inference. Table 2.1 shows whether expenditures on social welfare and security were greater or less than combined

Table 2.1 Comparison of expenditures on social welfare and security with those on health and education, 1995–2011

	1995	2000	2005	2008	2011
High-Income Economies					
Singapore	less than	less than	less than	less than	less than
Hong Kong, China	less than	less than	less than	less than	less than
Brunei Darussalam	less than	less than	less than	less than	less than
Republic of Korea	less than	less than	less than	greater than	greater than
Malaysia	less than	less than	less than	less than	less than
Middle-Income Economies I					
Kazakhstan					
Maldives	less than	less than	less than	less than	less than
Uzbekistan					
Azerbaijan	less than	less than	less than	less than	less than
Turkmenistan					
Middle-Income Economies II					
Viet Nam					
Sri Lanka	greater than	less than	less than	less than	less than
Philippines	less than	less than	less than	less than	less than
Thailand	less than	less than	less than	less than	less than
Pakistan					
Small Economies with Special Characteristics					
Armenia	less than	less than	less than	greater than	greater than
Georgia	greater than	greater than	greater than	less than	greater than
Bhutan			less than	less than	less than

(*Continued*)

Table 2.1 (Continued)

	1995	2000	2005	2008	2011
Mongolia	less than	less than	less than	greater than	greater than
Papua New Guinea	less than	less than			
Low-Income Economies					
Lao People's Democratic Republic					
Timor-Leste			less than	less than	less than
Cambodia	less than	less than	less than	less than	less than
Kyrgyz Republic	less than	less than	less than	less than	less than
Bangladesh	less than	less than	less than	less than	less than
Nepal	less than	less than	less than	less than	less than
Tajikistan	less than	less than	less than	less than	less than
Afghanistan					
Emerging Mega Economies					
People's Republic of China	less than	less than	less than	less than	less than
India		less than	less than	less than	
Indonesia					

Source: Author's estimates using ADB database on inclusive growth indicators. *Framework of Inclusive Growth Indicators: Key Indicators for Asia and the Pacific.*

expenditures on health and education from 1995 to 2011. Table 2.2 compares them with expenditures on health, and Table 2.3 compares them with expenditures on education over time.

Table 2.1 shows that developing Asia continued to favor expenditures on health and education over expenditures on social welfare and security with the exception of Armenia and Georgia possibly due to transition legacy effects. The Republic of Korea is the only economy that has seen a change in the relative importance of welfare spending which is to be expected as it approaches a steady state. However, when it comes to social welfare expenditures compared with health expenditures (Table 2.2), most MIE and SSC do indeed prioritize the former as surprisingly do several LIE and as both the PRC and India do. The same is not true for education.

Inference. While redistributive social welfare transfers are not in general prioritized over expenditures on health and education in a typical developing Asian expenditure portfolio, it appears that there is some scope to increase the focus on health either through raising total current expenditures (if possible) due to reasonable current fiscal surpluses, or in the case of economies with low or negative current surpluses, by switching expenditures to health.

Table 2.2 Comparison of expenditures on social welfare and security with those on health, 1995–2011

	1995	2000	2005	2008	2011
High-Income Economies					
Singapore	less than	less than	less than	greater than	greater than
Hong Kong, China	less than	less than	greater than	greater than	less than
Brunei Darussalam	less than	less than	less than	less than	less than
Republic of Korea		greater than	greater than	greater than	greater than
Malaysia	less than	less than	less than	less than	less than
Middle-Income Economies I					
Kazakhstan					
Maldives	less than	less than	less than	less than	greater than
Uzbekistan					
Azerbaijan	greater than	greater than	greater than	greater than	greater than
Turkmenistan					
Middle-Income Economies II					
Viet Nam					
Sri Lanka	greater than	greater than	greater than	greater than	greater than
Philippines	less than	greater than	greater than	greater than	greater than
Thailand	less than	less than	greater than	less than	less than
Pakistan					
Small Economies with Special Characteristics					
Armenia	less than	greater than	greater than	greater than	greater than
Georgia	greater than	greater than	greater than	greater than	greater than
Bhutan			less than	less than	less than
Mongolia	greater than	greater than	greater than	greater than	greater than
Papua New Guinea	less than	less than			

(*Continued*)

Table 2.2 (Continued)

	1995	2000	2005	2008	2011
Low-Income Economies					
Lao People's Democratic Republic					
Timor-Leste			less than	greater than	greater than
Cambodia	greater than	less than	less than	less than	less than
Kyrgyz Republic	greater than	less than	greater than	greater than	greater than
Bangladesh	less than	less than	less than	less than	less than
Nepal	less than	less than	less than	less than	less than
Tajikistan	less than	greater than	greater than	greater than	greater than
Afghanistan					
Emerging Mega Economies					
People's Republic of China				greater than	greater than
India		greater than	greater than	greater than	
Indonesia					

Source: Author's estimates using ADB database on inclusive growth indicators. *Framework of Inclusive Growth Indicators: Key Indicators for Asia and the Pacific.*

Table 2.3 Comparison of expenditures on social welfare and security with those on education, 1995–2011

	1995	2000	2005	2008	2011
High-Income Economies					
Singapore	less than	less than	less than	less than	less than
Hong Kong, China	less than	less than	less than	less than	less than
Brunei Darussalam	less than	less than	less than	less than	less than
Republic of Korea	less than	less than	greater than	greater than	greater than
Malaysia	less than	less than	less than	less than	less than
Middle-Income Economies I					
Kazakhstan					
Maldives	less than	less than	less than	less than	less than

	1995	2000	2005	2008	2011
Uzbekistan					
Azerbaijan	less than	less than	less than	less than	less than
Turkmenistan					
Middle-Income Economies II					
Viet Nam					
Sri Lanka	greater than	greater than	greater than	less than	greater than
Philippines	less than	less than	less than	less than	less than
Thailand	less than	less than	less than	less than	less than
Pakistan					
Small Economies with Special Characteristics					
Armenia	less than	less than	less than	greater than	greater than
Georgia	greater than	greater than	greater than	less than	greater than
Bhutan			less than	less than	less than
Mongolia	less than	less than	greater than	greater than	greater than
Papua New Guinea	less than	less than			
Low-Income Economies					
Lao People's Democratic Republic					
Timor-Leste			less than	less than	greater than
Cambodia	less than	less than	less than	less than	less than
Kyrgyz Republic	less than	less than	less than	less than	less than
Bangladesh	less than	less than	less than	less than	less than
Nepal	less than	less than	less than	less than	less than
Tajikistan	less than	less than	less than	less than	
Afghanistan					
Emerging Mega Economies					
People's Republic of China	less than	less than	less than	less than	less than
India		less than	less than	less than	
Indonesia					

Source: Author's estimates using ADB database on inclusive growth indicators. *Framework of Inclusive Growth Indicators: Key Indicators for Asia and the Pacific.*

3. *Macro-fiscal stability: fiscal space for inclusive growth*

The story of macro-fiscal stability is at first told by the extent to which revenues cover public expenditures. A golden rule of fiscal policy is that current expenditures should, at least, be covered by current revenues. It is clear that in much of developing Asia this rule is meticulously followed. There are a few clear exceptions clustered mainly in South and Central Asia. India, Kazakhstan, the Kyrgyz Republic, the Maldives, Pakistan, and Sri Lanka consistently ran current deficits from 1995 to 2011. In the Kyrgyz Republic, the economic downturn reversed an earlier trend of current deficits, and the country recorded current surpluses from 2003 to 2008 and deficits before and after. Armenia, Georgia, Tajikistan, and Thailand recorded current deficits during the 2009 to 2011 downturn but appear to have reverted to compliance with the golden rule in 2011.

As far as overall fiscal balance goes, while fiscal deficit limits are determined by national characteristics and policy limits such as fiscal rules, it is interesting to note that much of developing Asia in fact operated at reasonable levels of fiscal prudence from 1995 to 2011. The HIE, with the exception of Malaysia, quite routinely incurred fiscal surpluses. The MIE II routinely ran fiscal deficits, but there is a distinction between the Association of Southeast Asian Nations MIE and the South Asian MIE as in the latter the fiscal deficits were of a much greater magnitude. What marked the SSC was high volatility in fiscal balances with large deficits and also significant surpluses in different phases since 2003 and 2004. The LIE tended to be prudent as a whole; in recent times, only Tajikistan consistently faced fiscal deficits of any significant magnitude. In the EME, again the PRC and Indonesia ran moderate fiscal deficits, but India was unable to reduce its deficits to its own Fiscal Responsibility and Budget Management Act targets in the 16-year period.

The EME and LIE are at opposite ends of the economic size spectrum but tend to finance their deficits domestically thus limiting concerns regarding spillovers. This is also true of the MIE with the exception of Kazakhstan and the Maldives with the MIE II significantly reducing external debt over the past 8 years to less than 50% of gross national income (GNI). The opposite is true of the SSC that have witnessed a spike in external debt since the 2008 crisis with Mongolia currently the only exception.

Remarkably, across all of developing Asia, most debt is long term in nature, which bodes well for fiscal prudence. The two exceptions are the PRC and Thailand where there appears to have been a deliberate policy initiative to switch to short-term debt. With these overall debt patterns, general government gross debt is also low enough to be called prudent in most of developing Asia with the exception of the Maldives, Singapore, and Sri Lanka (where it fell consistently until 2008).

Inference. There is fiscal space to invest in inclusive growth in developing Asia; however, there are some important exceptions especially in South and Central Asia where the golden rule is consistently violated. Until the tax effort improves there, there is extremely limited room to increase spending. The debt patterns both in terms of size and composition are remarkably stable and low across most of developing Asia and are not a constraint to inclusive growth.

4. Comparison of selected economies with developing Asian economies

This section compares the performance of the economies of Organisation for Economic Co-operation and Development (OECD) members Canada, Japan, and Turkey, and the emerging economies of non-OECD members Brazil and South Africa with those of developing Asia on similar parameters of interest. The OECD and non-OECD economies showed an increased convergence in revenue efforts from 2002 to 2011 (Figure 2.17). Canada, however, was an exception with a declining trend since 2000, yet converging to the broader trend of the group as a whole, possibly due to the continuous decline in the tax–GDP ratio. While Japan and Turkey showed somewhat stable trends in their tax–GDP ratios since 2004, South Africa and Brazil showed an increasing tax effort during the same period (Figure 2.18).

Thus, while developing Asia on the whole collected relatively lower tax revenues, these OECD and non-OECD members showed higher shares of tax revenues even when compared with HIE and MIE. An interesting thing to notice in this group is the composition of taxes. Both Canada and Japan relied more on direct taxes (i.e., on incomes and profits) though the trend for direct and indirect taxes (i.e., on goods and services) declined and was stable respectively (Figure 2.19). Brazil and Turkey both showed more reliance on indirect taxes, and the trend for both direct and indirect taxes increased. The rate of increase in indirect taxes was much faster and almost doubled for Turkey from 1995 to 2011 (Figure 2.20).

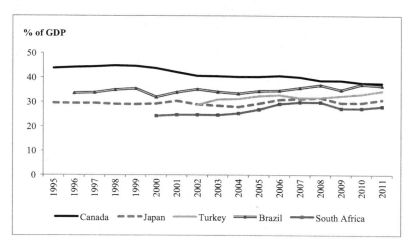

Figure 2.17 Total government revenue in selected OECD and non-OECD economies (% of gross domestic product)

GDP = gross domestic product.

OECD = Organisation for Economic Co-operation and Development.

Sources: ADB Country Profiles Database of *Key Indicators for Asia and the Pacific* and World Bank's World Development Indicators.

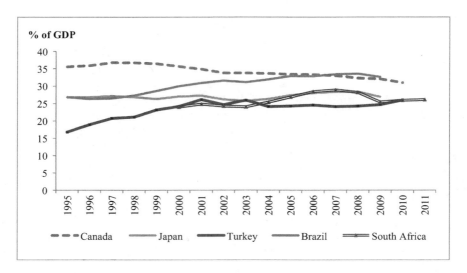

Figure 2.18 Tax revenue in selected OECD and non-OECD economies (% of gross domestic product)

GDP = gross domestic product, OECD = Organisation for Economic Co-operation and Development.

Note: Data for South Africa refer to central government.

Sources: ADB Country Profiles Database of *Key Indicators for Asia and the Pacific* and World Bank's World Development Indicators.

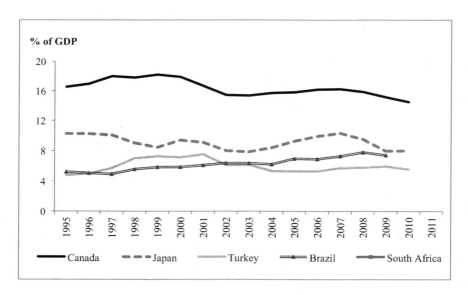

Figure 2.19 Direct taxes in selected economies (% of gross domestic product)

GDP = gross domestic product, OECD = Organisation for Economic Co-operation and Development.

Source: World Bank's World Development Indicators.

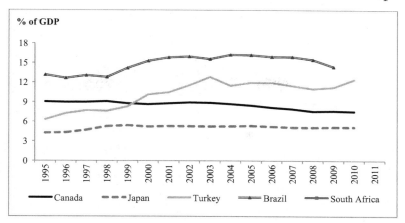

Figure 2.20 Indirect taxes in selected economies (% of gross domestic product)

GDP = gross domestic product, OECD = Organisation for Economic Co-operation and Development.

Source: World Bank's World Development Indicators.

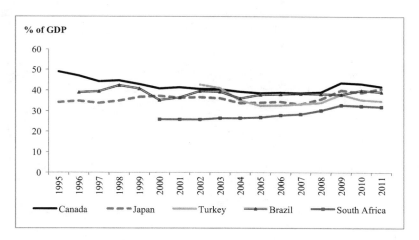

Figure 2.21 Total government expenditures in selected economies (% of gross domestic product)

GDP = gross domestic product, OECD = Organisation for Economic Co-operation and Development.

Source: World Bank's World Development Indicators.

These trends are quite different from those in developing Asia and particularly in the PRC, India, and Indonesia where the share of direct taxes has risen dramatically.[6]

Trends in total expenditures show a mixed pattern (Figure 2.21). Canada had a continuous and sharp decline in total expenditures with a spurt in 2008

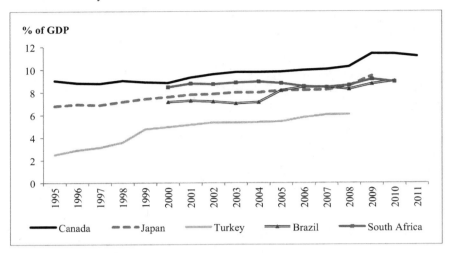

Figure 2.22 Expenditures on health in selected economies (% of gross domestic product)

GDP = gross domestic product, OECD = Organisation for Economic Co-operation and Development.

Source: World Bank's World Development Indicators.

and 2009 followed by declines once again, while expenditures in South Africa and Japan remained nearly stable with a marginal increase in the former. The trend in Brazil was cyclical, stabilizing from 2004 till 2009.

Health expenditures in this group increased from 1995 to 2011 and were always greater than 6% of GDP, except in Turkey (Figure 2.22). Canada spent the most on health at an average of 8%–10% till 2008 and then at more than 10% of GDP until 2011. Brazil, Japan, and South Africa spent around 8% starting in 2006. Although, Turkey had the lowest expenditure on health as a percentage of GDP, it remained steady and was on track to converge with the rest of the group. In contrast, developing Asia spent much less on health and needs to increase public expenditures on it.

After 2008, fiscal deficits were less than 5% of GDP in most of the group. Japan was a strong outlier with consistently higher fiscal deficits of more than 5% till 2007 that peaked to 10% in 2009 (Figure 2.23). This explains the similarly volatile net lending/borrowing patterns for Japan (Figure 2.24). Another issue of great concern for Japan is the excessive increase in the government debt from just below 100% in 1995 to around 230% of GDP in 2011 (Figure 2.25).

Japan saw a sharp decline in both savings and investment ratios as percentages of GDP from 1995 to 2011 (Figures 2.26 and 2.27). The share of Japan in the global pool of savings dropped significantly from 10.5 % in 2005 to 6.5% in 2011. Canada and Turkey showed a mixed trend over the period, though

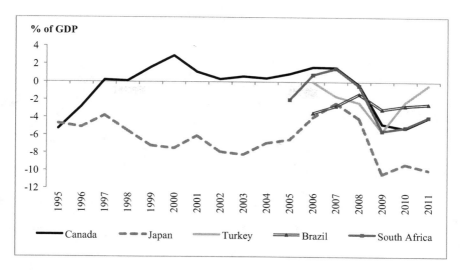

Figure 2.23 Fiscal balance in selected economies (% of gross domestic product)

GDP = gross domestic product, OECD = Organisation for Economic Co-operation and Development.

Source: World Bank's World Development Indicators.

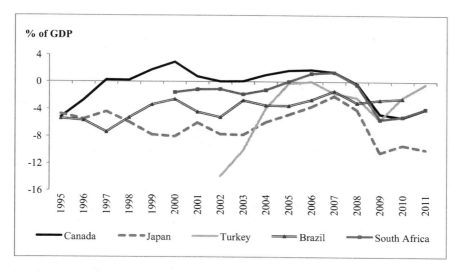

Figure 2.24 General government net lending/borrowing in selected economies (% of gross domestic product)

GDP = gross domestic product, OECD = Organisation for Economic Co-operation and Development.

Source: World Bank's World Development Indicators.

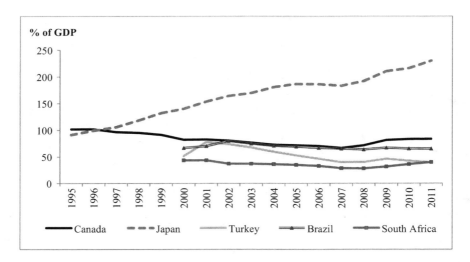

Figure 2.25 General government gross debt in selected economies (% of gross domestic product)

GDP = gross domestic product, OECD = Organisation for Economic Co-operation and Development.

Source: World Bank's World Development Indicators.

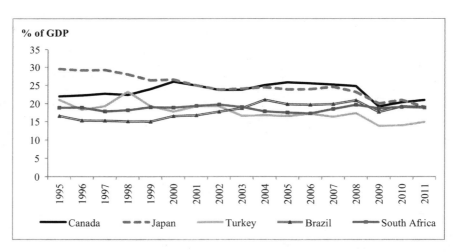

Figure 2.26 Gross domestic savings in selected economies (% of gross domestic product)

GDP = gross domestic product, OECD = Organisation for Economic Co-operation and Development.

Source: World Bank's World Development Indicators.

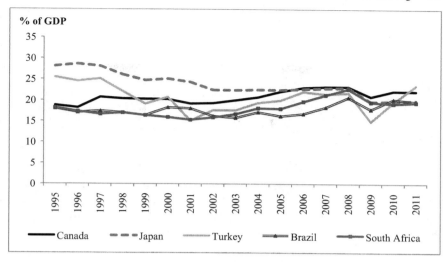

Figure 2.27 Total investment in selected economies (as a percentage of gross domestic product)

GDP = gross domestic product, OECD = Organisation for Economic Co-operation and Development.

Source: World Bank's World Development Indicators.

the shares of the global pool of savings in both declined as well. The trends in Brazil and South Africa, on the other hand, steadily increased by 15%–20%. An interesting comparison between the two is that if Brazil had a higher savings–GDP ratio, South Africa had a higher investment–GDP ratio for the same period and vice versa. Nevertheless, both converged to similar levels after 2009 and at the same time, the global share of savings in both rose marginally.

Inference. Comparing developing Asia with selected emerging non-OECD economies and with OECD members in other regions, it is clear that there is comparative fiscal space in developing Asia. Fiscal space exists because

- tax revenue–GDP ratios are lower in developing Asia compared to both selected OECD members and emerging non-OECD economies (Brazil and South Africa);
- both total revenue and total expenditure shares are lower in developing Asia;
- developing Asia in general maintains fiscal prudence more consistently and to a greater degree; and
- the tax structure in developing Asia is more progressive in nature.

A comparison of revenue and expenditure shares in developing Asia and in the selected OECD and non-OECD members indicates that the latter had higher tax revenues, while developing Asia on the whole had relatively lower tax revenue–GDP ratios. This was true both for HIE and MIE and even for the EME where the ratios were much lower than those of Brazil and South Africa (Figure 2.18). Government expenditures in OECD and non-OECD members were greater than those in the HIE and MIE. For instance, total government expenditure in Brazil has been 35%–40 % of GDP (Figure 2.21) since 1995, which was much greater than any economy in developing Asia. South Africa also spent more than any EME (Figures 2.12 and 2.21). Thus, the government–GDP ratio was much larger in these economies compared with that in developing Asia.

A comparison of fiscal balance indicates that developing Asia has consistently followed a prudent fiscal stance (with a few notable exceptions discussed in section 5). In recent years, most of the HIE and MIE have maintained either fiscal surpluses or moderate fiscal deficits (below 5%) except Malaysia, Maldives, Pakistan, and Tajikistan.[7] Even the PRC and Indonesia performed better than Brazil, South Africa, and Turkey during the recent financial crisis (India is an exception here for different reasons stated in Part E). Thus, the fiscal stance of developing Asian economies allowed them to weather the aftermath of the recent financial crisis better than many OECD members and emerging economies in other regions.

The tax structure of developing Asia also seems to be relatively progressive. The share of direct taxes showed a significant rise in MIE, LIE, and the EME, whereas in Brazil and Turkey, there has been a significant rise in the share of indirect taxes since 1998 and 1995, respectively (Figures 2.19 and 2.20).

5. *The Asian growth story and the inclusive growth story*

As highlighted in the Introduction (page 26), for growth to be inclusive, it must be sustained and of a magnitude sufficient to allow for targeted public spending to improve human capital and to provide the necessary economic and social infrastructure to improve inclusivity. Prudent fiscal policies may act as a constraint on growth if they do not sufficiently stimulate economic activity. Furthermore, if growth is volatile then scarce fiscal resources can be diverted to stabilization and can act as a constraint on the fiscal space for inclusive growth.

For the past 30 years, Asian growth rates have been phenomenal compared with those of other regions. Whether or not such growth has been inclusive, it would be instructive to first discern what the Asian growth story has been in recent times. Other than the well-known rise of the PRC and India and the continued importance of countries like the Republic of Korea and Singapore as growth poles, what else do the numbers show?

- In the HIE, growth in the Republic of Korea and Malaysia appears to be cyclical. It is difficult to judge whether indeed the recent growth story approximates a scenario of steady state growth. Yet, even if this were to be the case, the steady state level would be somewhere between 4% and 5%

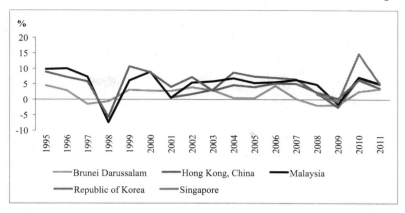

Figure 2.28 Real gross domestic product growth in the high-income economies, 1995–2011

Source: ADB Country Profiles Database of *Key Indicators for Asia and the Pacific*.

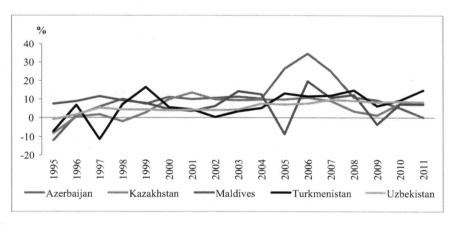

Figure 2.29 Real gross domestic product growth in the middle-income economies I, 1995–2011

Source: ADB Country Profiles Database of *Key Indicators for Asia and the Pacific*.

for both, a level significantly higher than that reported for similar economies in other regions (Figure 2.28).

- The MIE I display volatile growth trends with pronounced cyclical features. The exception in this group is Uzbekistan which has recorded steady high growth over the past 8 years (Figure 2.29).
- The MIE II present a mixed picture. Other than in Viet Nam, growth is volatile with the last economic slowdown causing a pronounced drop in all of them (Figure 2.30).

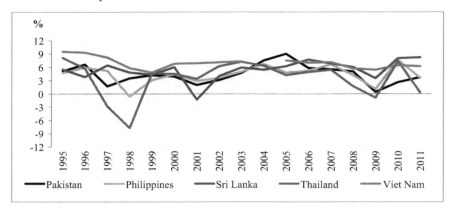

Figure 2.30 Real gross domestic product growth in the middle-income economies II, 1995–2011

Source: ADB Country Profiles Database of *Key Indicators for Asia and the Pacific*.

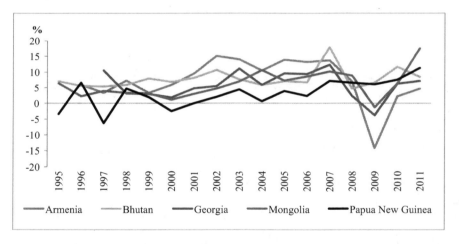

Figure 2.31 Real gross domestic product growth in the small economies with special characteristics, 1995–2011

Source: ADB Country Profiles Database of *Key Indicators for Asia and the Pacific*.

- Between 2008 and 2009, the economies of the SSC did not grow except in Papua New Guinea (Figure 2.31).
- The EME, on the other hand, displayed remarkable resilience in growth in the same period though India and Indonesia both faced slowdowns in 2011 (Figure 2.32).

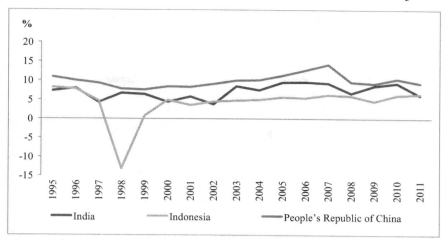

Figure 2.32 Real gross domestic product growth in the emerging mega economies, 1995–2011
Source: ADB Country Profiles Database of *Key Indicators for Asia and the Pacific.*

Inference. Examining trends and looking at median growth figures across the groupings reveals that growth rates have not been low in the medium term notwithstanding a prudent fiscal stance; thus, prudent fiscal policies have not obviously retarded growth in developing Asia. However, the MIE and the SSC face a challenge from volatility requiring greater attention to using fiscal policy as an instrument for stabilization.

The main interest here is to see whether there are any sharp changes in inclusion within and across economies in developing Asia that can in any reasonable way be linked to the design and articulation of fiscal policies. Here, the lack of adequate comparable data is a problem.

One of the critical indicators of inclusive growth discussed in the Introduction is the extent to which people are participating in the business of delivering growth. The obvious indicator to use for this is employment, and indeed there has been a lot of emphasis placed on this by many authors.[8] However, it is difficult to see how employment can be influenced by fiscal policy unless governments decide to provide incentives in the form of selective taxes and subsidies to enhance wage shares and/or the intensity of labor output. This would be both inefficient – in the sense that other policy instruments would achieve this with far greater efficacy – and highly distortionary.

One can, however, gauge how well developing Asia is doing on this score by examining employment–population ratios. While this is an imperfect measure as national demographics vary widely, it is the only measure for which some time-related data are available.[9] These indicate that median employment–population ratios tend to be fairly stable; in fact the ratio has tended to be fairly stable across all groupings except in the MIE I where it has risen possibly due to the stabilizing of the economic transition.

The trend in most of developing Asia is for declining infant mortality rates.[10] In economies in which data on health spending are available, it appears that there is no clear correlation between increased (or reduced) health spending and infant mortality results. Such declines appear to be linked with the growth effect if anything.

Income and consumption inequality is another popular measure of the extent to which growth is inclusive. The Gini coefficient is a measure of income and consumption inequality. Inclusion, on the other, is better measured by changes in the income shares of the highest versus the lowest quintiles on the assumption that given the virtual absence of redistributive welfare measures in the fiscal policies of most economies in developing Asia; changes in this ratio would be influenced by changes in the intensity of use of factor endowment and/or factor prices of those factor endowments that belong to populations in the lowest quintiles.[11] Again, this ratio appears to have been quite stable across the medium term (Table 2.4), and many economies have recorded mild improvements. The most striking cases of worsening ratios are in the EME. These are also the fastest-growing and most dynamic economies in Asia; it would be imprudent to draw any conclusions about the link between this and the conduct of fiscal policy. More detailed research would be required to establish any correlations.

Inference. For the bulk of developing Asia, trends in the limited number of variables for inclusive growth examined do not indicate any dramatic, first-order link between performance in individual measures of inclusion and the conduct of fiscal policy. In the EME, it is clear that there is a need for redistributive measures to address the increase in top–bottom inequity in consumption. In the case of India, there is limited fiscal space to undertake such an exercise though some room may exist for enhancing the magnitude of redistributive policies consistent with fiscal prudence in the PRC and Indonesia. Otherwise, it appears that inclusion is best served by making fiscal policy an instrument to secure rapid progress to steady state growth rather than to attempt a break with the extant model by resorting to redistributive measures.

D. Fiscal space, savings, and inclusive growth

The Asia and Pacific region has historically been thought of as one with high savings. The traditional story of development has not, therefore, been tied to aid or to large financial transfers from other regions with the exception of US aid to Japan and the early underwriting of defense budgets in the PRC; Hong Kong, China; the Republic of Korea; and Taipei,China. Rather, savings – both domestic and cross border – have been successfully mobilized to accelerate investment. There are two dimensions to this story that are of specific interest for this chapter.

The global pool of savings – not the savings–GDP ratio which is the stock-flow counterpart that measures the size of the savings flow compared to GDP – is

Table 2.4 Ratio of income or consumption of the highest quintile to the lowest quintile, 1995–2011 (%)

	1995	1996	1997	1998	1999	2000	2001	2002	2003	2004	2005	2006	2007	2008	2009	2010	2011
High-Income Economies																	
Singapore[a]				12.3					12.0					14.5			
Hong Kong, China[a]		9.6															
Brunei Darussalam																	
Korea, Republic of[b]												5.4	5.4			5.7	5.7
Malaysia[a]	12.0		12.4							6.9			11.0		11.3		
Middle-Income Economies I																	
Kazakhstan		6.2					8.5	5.9	5.6	5.1		4.5	4.6	4.2	4.2		
Maldives				46.6													
Uzbekistan				12.7				5.5	6.2	6.8							
Azerbaijan	6.1						5.9							5.3			
Turkmenistan				7.7													
Middle-Income Economies II																	
Viet Nam				5.5				6.1		6.2		6.0		5.9			
Sri Lanka		5.5						7.2					6.9			5.8	
Philippines			9.8			9.7			9.3			9.0			8.3		
Thailand		8.1		7.6				7.7				8.1		7.2		6.9	
Pakistan			3.9		4.8			4.3			4.4	4.7		4.2			
Small Economies with Special Characteristics																	
Armenia	9.2				5.8		5.8	5.5	5.0	6.1	5.6	4.9	4.5	4.5		4.6	
Georgia	7.1	9.4		7.1	8.8	8.9	8.4	8.2	8.4		8.7	8.5	7.6	8.9	8.8	9.5	

(Continued)

Table 2.4 (Continued)

	1995	1996	1997	1998	1999	2000	2001	2002	2003	2004	2005	2006	2007	2008	2009	2010	2011
Bhutan									9.9				6.8				
Mongolia	5.5			4.9				5.4						6.2			
Papua New Guinea		12.5															
Low-Income Economies																	
Lao PDR			5.4					4.9						5.9			
Timor-Leste							7.0						4.6				
Cambodia										7.2			7.9	6.1	5.6		
Kyrgyz Republic				6.1				4.8		5.6	7.7	6.1	4.8	6.9	6.4	6.5	5.4
Bangladesh		4.9				4.9					4.8					4.7	
Nepal		5.5							7.8							5.0	
Tajikistan					4.5				5.2	5.4			5.5		4.7		
Afghanistan														4.0			
Emerging Mega Economies																	
China, People's Republic of[c]		6.0			7.2			8.9			9.6			10.0	10.1		
											4.9					5.0	
Indonesia[c]		4.5			4.1			4.2			5.1			5.3		5.7	

Lao PDR = Lao People's Democratic Republic.

[a] Data derived from income share of the highest quintile to lowest quintile.

[b] Data for the Republic of Korea are derived from income share of the highest quintile to lowest quintile. Income is defined as disposable household income.

[c] Data derived from the consumption share of the highest quintile to lowest quintile. Combines the urban and rural distributions weighted by share of urban and rural population to total population.

Note: Data for all other economies are derived from consumption share of the highest quintile to lowest quintile.

Source: ADB Financial Inclusion Indicators Database.

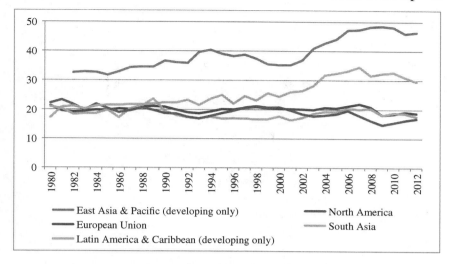

Figure 2.33 Savings–gross domestic product ratios by region
Source: World Bank's World Development Indicators.

pertinent in assessing Asia's role and contribution to the future of global development. The fact that the global pool of savings is sufficient to address development challenges after the 2015 deadline for achieving the MDGs is well recognized by those tasked to think about development financing.[12] The United Nations[13] too asserts that, "The money is there – world savings this year will likely be over $18 trillion."

Figure 2.33 shows that from 1980 to 2012, the high-savings regions of the world have been East and South Asia. One could quite legitimately conclude that Asia has always dominated global savings mobilization, but this, of course, is not true.

The reason is that historically the share of developed country savings in total savings has been of a far higher magnitude than that of developing countries. Thus, international public finance was an instrument to reassign these savings from deployment in developed economies to developing economies through a public sector process when markets failed to do so or failed to do so in a magnitude sufficient to address the needs for public goods.

This logic held until at least 2005. Figure 2.34(a) shows that the United States and the Group of 7 (G7) Eurozone (France, Germany, and Italy) collectively generated more than 30% of global savings in 2005. Adding in Japan, more than half of global savings was generated within the G7 as recently as 2005 despite the rise of the PRC and more recently Brazil, the Russian Federation, India, and the PRC (BRIC).

This picture has changed dramatically in recent years, see Figure 2.34(b). In 2011, the PRC accounted for the highest share in world savings followed by

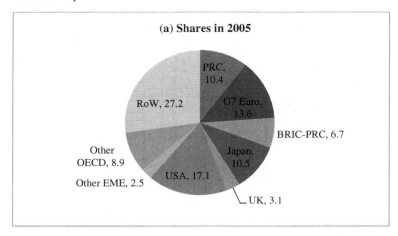

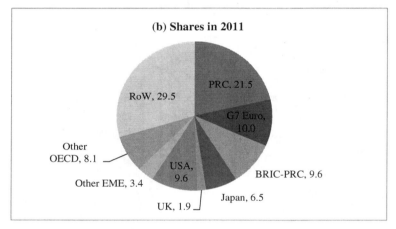

Figure 2.34 Shares of world savings in 2005 and 2011

BRIC = Brazil, the Russian Federation, India, and the People's Republic of China; EME = emerging mega economies; Euro = Eurozone; OECD = Organisation for Economic Co-operation and Development; PRC = People's Republic of China; RoW = Rest of the World; UK = United Kingdom; USA = United States.

Source: World Bank's World Development Indicators.

the United States, and the other BRIC economies contributed savings comparable to the G7 Eurozone and exceeding those of Japan.

This affects developing Asia quite dramatically (Figure 2.35). While the bulk of the rise in the share of developing Asia in global savings was accounted for by the PRC, there was also a non-trivial increase in the share of the rest of developing Asia as well. Furthermore, among developed economies, only Australia has seen an increase in its share of global savings. If private sector and World Bank research is credible, then this reversal is likely to continue over the

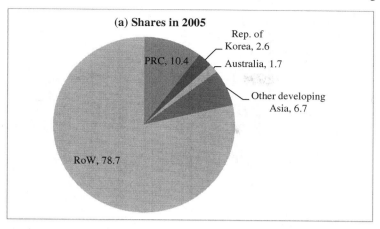

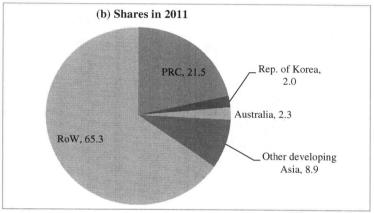

Figure 2.35 Shares of savings in Asia in 2005 and 2011
PRC = People's Republic of China, RoW = Rest of the World.
Source: World Bank's World Development Indicators.

next 5 years, but existing institutions for mobilizing savings for international public financing continue to operate as if the world were what it was in 2005.

This new trend presents perhaps the greatest challenge to international public financing architecture. The Asia and Pacific region has ample use for savings for domestic investment as most economies are not (with the possible exception of the HIE) anywhere near their maximum possible steady state growth paths. At the same time, these economies have proactively sought to explore ways in which their savings could be deployed to reinforce mutual gains through growth in South–South development relationships. The available pool of domestic savings in Asia is now of an order of magnitude that is highly conducive to regional arrangements to mobilize these resources for investments in key economic services and other capital expenditures. Thus domestic savings will relax the fiscal constraints in developing Asia to increase current expenditures on health, education, and other outlays conducive to inclusive growth.

In other words, with the appropriate institutional arrangements in place, Asia has enough savings to finance the growth requirements of the region. Regional cooperation to maximize the disposition of these savings for public and private investment then opens up fiscal space to prudently utilize current revenues for spending on merit and public goods for inclusive growth that require increases in current expenditures.

Inference. The phenomenon of Asian dominance in savings has two important implications for developing Asia.

- The scope for coordination to channel resources for public and private investments across developing Asia is now significant.
- This provides a significant pool of resources for public and private investments in inclusive growth. Coordinated fiscal (and monetary) actions across developing Asia could be key to optimizing the pool of available resources for such investments.

The rapid increase in the share in global savings of developing Asia is already having a beneficial impact on fiscal stability. Thus even in the HIE, investment–GDP ratios are high and stable at between 25% and 30%. The MIE I, traditionally considered low savers in the 1990s, have seen very sharp increases in their savings–GDP ratios and in total investment–GDP ratios over the past decade. In the MIE II, low savings continue to constrain the investment outlays of Pakistan and the Philippines. In the SSC too, high savings–GDP ratios have led to increased investment–GDP ratios. In Bhutan's case, it marks a shift from aid-financed investments to domestically resourced investments in a significant measure. The LIE exhibit higher investment ratios notwithstanding low savings ratios, chiefly due to access to highly concessional investment finance, yet the fact that savings are higher in Asian LIE than in LIE in other regions means that the overall investment–GDP ratio for most Asian LIE is also higher. Given the fact that the region as a whole follows sound public financing principles, the only countries where the "draft" of public sector spending on domestic savings is high are India, Pakistan, and Sri Lanka. These three countries are also remarkable for their extent and magnitude of borrowing to finance government consumption measured by the current fiscal deficit, a phenomenon they have failed to address in recent years.

Inferences. (i) There have been important recent changes in the incidence of global savings favoring developing Asia. (ii) An examination of savings behavior and debt deficit patterns indicates that fiscal space exists both for public investment and for expanding current expenditures in most of developing Asia. (iii) These two trends together indicate that there is scope for enhancing fiscal space for public investment, though tax effort would need to increase if the provisioning of merit goods is to be enhanced.

E. The impact of counter-cyclical fiscal policy on growth and inclusion

There is constant tension for governments between (i) securing fiscal prudence and maintaining predictability in the course of fiscal policy and (ii) the pressure to expand spending on public goods and to moderate tax burdens to secure inclusive growth. That pressure is particularly pronounced in times of fiscal stress. When there is an exogenous shock that threatens a recession, there is pressure on governments to run expansionary counter-cyclical fiscal policies and to suspend fiscal rules and other prudential commitments until the crisis is weathered.

All governments in developing Asia face such pressures, but in particular, the emerging economies of developing Asia have to craft fiscal policies very carefully when expansionary demands arise. The argument for such expansionary counter-cyclical fiscal policies became more forceful after the 1997 Asian financial crisis when it was felt that governments that followed fiscal compression suffered in contrast to those that took active steps to counter the recessionary impact of the crisis using fiscal instruments.

An analysis by Adams, Ferrarini, and Park (2010)[14] in an early finding on counter-cyclical fiscal stimuli across Asia indicated that public finances were in relatively good shape prior to the crisis and therefore, fiscal stimuli were sustainable. They warned, however, that failure to unwind the anti-crisis stimulus would erode the region's fiscal stability; this would in turn seriously restrict medium-term fiscal space for inclusive growth. From the vantage of the present, the experience of the PRC, India, Indonesia, and Malaysia with counter-cyclical policies following the 2008 crisis provides interesting insights on this issue.

In the case of India, the global economic crisis coincided with national elections, so a fiscal expansion had already been undertaken just prior to its onset. A fiscal stimulus equivalent to 4% of GDP was introduced in the central government's 2008 budget. The crisis also impacted state finances with the result that the combined fiscal deficit grew to 11.4% of GDP that year. While this had serious implications in future years for India's sovereign ratings, given its high and rising current account deficit and poor growth performance, the immediate fiscal sustainability implications in terms of debt dynamics were not negative as feared by some commentators at the time.[15] Thus, India's public debt–GDP ratio actually declined from 73% in 2008–2009 to 66.36% in 2011–2012.

Why was this the case? To some extent, it was because the tradition of fiscal prudence for both central and state governments set in place by the 12th Finance Commission in 2004 and reinforced by the 13th Finance Commission in 2010 led to increased fiscal discipline at the state level. State deficits thus declined to more manageable levels shortly after the crisis. On the other hand, with inflation at around 10%, the nominal value of GDP continued to rise faster than the nominal value of debt. Thus, debt sustainability ratios stayed under control. In addition, the low ratio of external debt to total debt in India and the extremely high proportion of long-term debt in total debt meant that debt management was relatively easy. So debt sustainability did not threaten India's macroeconomic fundamentals; rather, the fact that the fiscal stimulus did not result in the expected growth response – India underperformed on growth compared to the other EME and indeed compared to the other BRIC economies – led to increasing macroeconomic difficulties for India and the consequent pressure to reduce deficits and therefore fiscal space.

In the case of the PRC, the government provided a massive fiscal stimulus equivalent to 14% of GDP for fiscal year (FY) 2008 and FY2009.[16] This included a fiscal stimulus that was expected to result in a fiscal deficit of 3% of GDP in 2009; however, the PRC had plenty of fiscal space to begin with. Fiscal deficits had fallen to below 2% of GDP by 2004 and to less than 0.5% of GDP in 2008; the highest fiscal deficit incurred was therefore just 2.3% of GDP in 2009. The 9.6% median growth rate from 1995 to 2011 was maintained, thus fiscal expansion was accompanied by the requisite growth payback ensuring fiscal sustainability.

In Malaysia, there was an extremely short-term fiscal response to the crisis equivalent to an increase in the fiscal deficit from 4.6% of GDP in 2007 to 6.7% in 2009, but this was a 1-year expansion. Deficits were then reduced to 4.8% of GDP in 2011 equivalent to the median fiscal deficit from 1995 to 2011. To some extent this was necessitated by worsening debt dynamics, both an increase in the debt–GDP ratio to over 50% of GDP post crisis which was well above the 1995–2011 median, and an increase in the ratio of relatively more expensive external debt to total debt. This limited stimulus had little impact on growth or medium-term macro-fiscal policy.[17]

Indonesia went through a fairly long process of fiscal reforms that included reforms in public financial management as well as significant structural changes in intergovernmental fiscal relations following the 1997 Asian financial crisis. The fiscal deficit–GDP ratio declined continuously. The median fiscal deficit from 1995 to 2011 was therefore a very low 1.1% of GDP with a concomitant decline in the debt–GDP ratio over time. Indonesia also had in place a fiscal rule that limits the fiscal deficit to 3% of GDP and the ceiling debt–GDP ratio to 60% of GDP.[18]

Indonesia's 2009 fiscal stimulus package involved an expansionary fiscal policy as well as tax cuts. Over two-thirds of the stimulus came from tax cuts and the rest through increased public spending and subsidies;[19] however, this increase did not breach the fiscal rules. Chiefly due to the government's inability to increase public spending, the 2010 fiscal deficit was 0.7% of GDP against a target of 1.3%.[20] As a consequence, both revenues and expenditures fell as a percentage of GDP from 2008. Thus in Indonesia's case, the fiscal stimulus was not expansionary but rather involved stimulating the private sector through tax cuts and a fall in the government–GDP ratio.

These four economies followed very different strategies with very different outcomes after the 2008 financial crisis. The chief impact on inclusive growth seems to have been driven by the impact of the fiscal stimulus on growth. There was little impact on the disposition of public spending with no marked increase (relative to trends) in functional outlays on health, education, and social welfare post crisis. All four maintained fiscally prudent policies in administering the fiscal stimulus, even India. It was the failure of the fiscal stimulus to maintain growth that resulted in concomitant pressures on economic activity chiefly through inflation, high nominal interest rates, and rising current account deficits. Debt sustainability was not impaired by fiscal expansion.

F. Concluding observations

Developing Asia is diverse; however, several common trends can be observed if similar economic circumstances are looked at together. In general, it can be said that given the exigencies of economic structure and history, most developing Asian economies have elected to maintain a prudent rather than an activist fiscal stance. Taxation and revenue mobilization instruments have not in general been used to alter the economic structure such that the tax burden is relatively high. Public spending, too, tends to be of an order of magnitude that generates a stable government–GDP ratio. Given this fiscal stance what has been the approach to ensuring that there is inclusive growth?

The overall finding from examining trends is that developing Asia in general has little resorted to redistributive measures in the pursuit of inclusive growth. Rather they have relied on fiscal policies to secure counter-cyclical stabilization of growth or to enhance human capital. At the same time, the macro-fiscal structure and the composition of revenue are not regressive overall, and there is evidence of appreciable spending when required to protect growth against external shocks. This is found to be largely the case with the HIE and MIE as well as the SSC and the EME. The share of spending on defense is controlled in most cases, and in some important cases like Cambodia has even declined over time.

Given that this conclusion emerges from an examination of trends, it marks a significant departure from historical stories in other regions that have undergone development. The "welfare state" model of Western Europe to which many middle-income and rapidly growing countries in Latin America and the Middle East have aspired is one that developing Asia has eschewed to date. Growth and productive inclusion have been at the center of the development story. A prudent fiscal stance, macroeconomic stability, and protecting growth from external shocks have been typical features of fiscal policies in the region.

A prudential environment for economic growth has been secured through the maintenance of the golden rule of fiscal policy, which is to finance current expenditure out of current revenue. If the rule is followed, there is scope to increase spending on merit and public goods to increase human capital; governments in developing Asia have elected to prioritize expenditures on health and education to that end. There are, however, important exceptions to this in South Asia, namely in India, the Maldives, Pakistan, and Sri Lanka. In these countries, there is limited incremental room to invest in human capital without paying considerable attention either to improving the tax effort or to reducing expenditures on subsidies and defense.

In most of developing Asia, there is some scope to increase public expenditures on health consistent with the overall fiscal stance by raising current expenditures where the scope to do so is afforded by medium-term positive fiscal balances together with mild efforts to increase the tax effort. In economies with low or no current surpluses, policies switching expenditures to increase the share of health spending relative to that on food subsidies, social welfare (subject to maintaining a safety net), and fuel subsidies affords scope for a reprioritization that would be consistent with the overall fiscal stance.

A prudent fiscal stance has not impeded growth which has progressed reasonably and at a stable pace across the economic groupings (though the levels obviously vary), but fluctuations do impact growth when there are global shocks such as in 1997 and 2008. However, many MIE and SSC continue to be challenged by the volatility of growth relative to the rest of the region necessitating the need for more attention to using fiscal policy for stabilization.

The EME show that counter-cyclical fiscal policies have been deployed, have been tailored to individual circumstances, and have been mindful of prudential limitations thus alleviating the fear that persistence with such policies would jeopardize fiscal prudence. Even in the case of India which has been going through some recent macroeconomic difficulties, it is supply-side constraints and balance of payment difficulties that have caused problems in macroeconomic management rather than the inability to speedily tone down counter-cyclical fiscal policies.

As far as inclusion goes, this overview does not find any dramatic, first-order link between performance on individual measures of inclusion and the conduct of fiscal policy. In the EME, there is an apparent case for redistributive measures to address the increase in top–bottom inequity in consumption, and this may be feasible consistent with fiscal prudence for the PRC and Indonesia, though not for India. Otherwise, in the absence of a first-order link, inclusion is best served by using fiscal policy as an instrument to maximize public spending on merit goods and to secure a growth maximizing macro-fiscal environment rather than by resorting to income redistributive fiscal measures.

There is considerable fiscal room for increasing public or publicly funded investment to remove infrastructural barriers to growth. This is especially so looking at two factors together: (i) the important recent changes in the incidence of global savings favoring developing Asia and (ii) the savings behavior and debt-deficit patterns examined in this chapter. Taken together, these two trends indicate that there is scope for enhancing the fiscal space for public investment, and there is an increased scope for pan-Asian coordination to channel resources for public and private investment. This provides a significant pool of resources for public and private investments in inclusive growth. Coordinated fiscal (and monetary) actions across developing Asia could be key to optimizing the pool of available resources for such investment if renewed attention is paid to fostering a regional institutional architecture and improved fiscal coordination.

Notes

Unless otherwise noted, the data used in this chapter are from the Asian Development Bank's Country Profiles Database of the *Key Indicators for Asia and the Pacific*.

1 Roy, Heuty, and Letouze (2009).
2 International Monetary Fund (2011).
3 Roy, Heuty, and Letouze (2009).
4 Hicks (1939); Kaldor (1939).
5 Roy (2011).
6 World Bank. World Development Indicators (WDI) database.
7 WDI.
8 For example, Felipe (2009).
9 WDI.
10 WDI.
11 See, Roy (2011).
12 For example, Sheng (2013).
13 United Nations (2013).
14 Adams, Ferrarini, and Park (2010).
15 Kumar and Vashisht (2009).
16 Yongdin (2010).
17 Lim and Goh (2012).
18 Basri and Rahardja (2011).
19 Hur, Jha, Park, and Quising (2010).
20 Basri and Rahardja (2011).

Bibliography*

Adams, C., B. Ferrarini, and D. Park. 2010. Fiscal Sustainability in Developing Asia. *ADB Economics Working Paper Series*. No. 205. Manila: Asian Development Bank (ADB).

ADB. 2013a. *Framework of Inclusive Growth Indicators 2013: Key Indicators for Asia and the* Pacific. Database on Financial Inclusion Indicators. http://www.adb.org/publications/framework-inclusive-growth-indicators-2013-key-indicators-asia-and-pacific (accessed 23 November 2013)

———. 2013b. *Key Indicators for Asia and the Pacific 2013*. Country Profile Database. http://www.adb.org/publications/key-indicators-asia-and-pacific-2013 (accessed 23 October 2013)

Basri, M.C. and S. Rahardja. 2011. Mild Crisis, Half Hearted Fiscal Stimulus: Indonesia during the GFC. In Ito, T. and F. Parulian, eds. *Assessment on the Impact of Stimulus, Fiscal Transparency and Fiscal Risk*. ERIA Research Project Report 2010, No. 01. Jakarta: Economic Research Institute for ASEAN and East Asia (ERIA). pp. 169–211. http://www.eria.org/publications/research_project_reports/assessment-on-the-impact-of-stimulus-fiscal-transparency-and-fiscal-risk.html (accessed 5 November 2013)

Felipe, J. 2009. *Inclusive Growth, Full Employment, and Structural Change: Implications and Policies for Developing Asia*. Manila: ADB and New Delhi: Anthem Press.

*The Asian Development Bank recognizes China by the name People's Republic of China.

Hicks, J. R. 1939. The Foundations of Welfare Economics. *The Economic Journal.* 49 (196). pp. 696–712.

Hur, S.-K., S. Jha, D. Park, and P. Quising, 2010. Did Fiscal Stimulus Lift Developing Asia out of the Global Crisis? A Preliminary Empirical Investigation. *ADB Economics Working Paper Series.* No. 215. Manila: ADB.

International Monetary Fund (IMF). 2011. Managing Volatility: A Vulnerability Exercise for Low-Income Countries. *IMF Policy Paper.* 9 March. Washington, DC. https://www.imf.org/external/pp/longres.aspx?id=4540 (accessed 5 November 2013)

Kaldor, N. 1939. Welfare Propositions of Economics and Interpersonal Comparisons of Utility. *The Economic Journal.* 49 (195). pp. 549–552.

Kumar, R. and P. Vashisht. 2009. The Global Economic Crisis: Impact on India and Policy Responses. *ADBI Working Paper Series.* No. 164. Tokyo: ADB Institute.

Lim, M. and S. Goh. 2012. *How Malaysia Weathered the Financial Crisis: Policies and Possible Lessons.* Ottawa, Canada: The North–South Institute.

Roy, R. 1994. *The Politics of Fiscal Policy.* Cambridge: Cambridge University Press.

———. 2011. Intersections between Social Protection, Inclusive Growth and Fiscal Space. Issues Paper for G20 Development Working Group on Growth with Resilience. New York and Brasilia: United Nations Development Programme.

Roy, R., A. Heuty, and E. Letouze. 2009. Fiscal Space for Public Investment: Towards a Human Development Approach. In Roy, R. and A. Heuty, eds. *Fiscal Space: Policy Options for Financing Human Development.* London: Earthscan.

Sheng, A. 2013. Outlook for Global Development Finance – Excess or Shortage? Background Paper for the High-Level Panel of Eminent Persons on the United Nations Post-2015 Millennium Development Goals Agenda. Hong Kong, China and Penang, Malaysia. 22 May.

United Nations. 2013. *A New Global Partnership: Eradicate Poverty and Transform Economies through Sustainable Development.* Report of the High-Level Panel of Eminent Persons on the Post-2015 Development Agenda. New York. http://www.post2015hlp.org/wp-content/uploads/2013/05/UN-Report.pdf (accessed 5 November 2013)

World Bank. World Development Indicators Database (WDI). http://data.worldbank.org/indicator/all (accessed 05 November 2013).

Yongdin, Y. 2010. Asia: China's Policy Response to the Global Financial Crisis. *Journal of Globalization and Development.* 1 (1). pp. 1–10.

3 Fiscal policy and growth in developing Asia

Arnelyn Abdon, Gemma Estrada, Minsoo Lee, and Donghyun Park

A. Introduction

Fiscal policy can play a significant role in economic growth. In the short term, counter-cyclical fiscal expansion can help support aggregate demand and growth during cyclical downturns. Conversely, fiscal contraction can cool down an economy that is growing at an unsustainable pace and thus faces the risk of overheating. Advanced economies in particular have a long history of using taxes and government spending to smooth the business cycle. At the same time, fiscal policy can also have a major impact on medium- and long-term economic growth. This is especially true in developing economies where the private sector is relatively weak and underdeveloped. Public spending on physical infrastructure such as roads, ports, and power plants affects the productivity of all firms and industries and the entire economy. Likewise, public spending on education fosters human capital, a vital ingredient in long-term growth. Taxes can harm growth because they distort economic incentives and behavior; for example, corporate income taxes have a negative impact on investment. More generally, different taxes differ in the extent to which they distort incentives and behavior.

In developing Asia, as in the rest of the world, fiscal policy can influence both short- and long-term growth. The region has more limited experience in using fiscal policy for counter-cyclical purposes than the advanced economies have; nevertheless, during the global financial and economic crisis of 2008–2009, developing Asia's governments forcefully unleashed large fiscal stimulus programs that helped the region stave off recession. More broadly, in much of the region the primary strategic objective of fiscal policy – and of public policy in general – has been to foster long-term economic growth. The prioritization of growth was perfectly understandable in light of developing Asia's low-income levels in the past. A tradition of fiscal prudence laid the foundation for macroeconomic stability in large parts of the region, which combined with large public investments in physical infrastructure and human capital laid the foundation for sustained rapid growth. Different components of public spending will likely have different impacts on growth; for example, public spending on health care is likely to have a bigger growth effect than public spending on military equipment.

The central objective of this chapter is to take a closer look at the role of fiscal policy in economic growth in developing Asia. To do so, we first review the literature on fiscal policy and economic growth before taking a look at the overall trends in taxation and government spending in the region. We then empirically analyze the effect of a change in the composition of taxes on growth and do the same for a change in the composition of government spending before concluding with a few observations.

B. Review of literature

The question of whether changes in fiscal policy – both taxation and expenditure – can affect growth has been widely explored in the literature. Endogenous growth models (e.g., Barro 1990) predict that fiscal policy will have effects on growth, both temporary and permanent. Empirical studies on whether taxation or government spending fosters economic growth, however, have yielded mixed results.

On the link between taxes and growth, there are studies that show weak or non-robust relationships such as those by Easterly and Rebelo (1993) and Agell, Lindh, and Ohlsson (1997), and studies that reveal strong associations such as those by Skinner (1987); Arnold et al. (2011); and Gemmell, Kneller, and Sanz (2011). Skinner (1987) showed that the increase in tax effort in Sub-Saharan countries was predicted to have reduced output growth, even accounting for the positive effects of additional government spending. Comparing various taxes, Skinner (1987) found that personal income and corporate tax rates had a negative direct effect on output growth, that trade taxes had little direct effect, and that sales and excise taxes were neutral with respect to both output growth and investment. King and Rebelo (1990) showed that tax policy can have a potentially large impact on long-term growth. Public policies can exert a significant influence on economic growth rates by affecting private incentives for accumulating physical and human capital. Even relatively small changes in tax rates can lead countries to stagnate or even regress if these policies eliminate incentives for growth.

In contrast, earlier studies found a weak relationship between tax policy and growth. To examine this relationship, Easterly and Rebelo (1993) used cross-section data for 100 countries from 1970 to 1988 and a panel of annual data for 28 countries from 1870 to 1988. They applied different approaches to measuring tax rates namely (i) statutory tax rates; (ii) tax revenue as a fraction of gross domestic product (GDP); (iii) income-weighted marginal income tax rates that combine information on the lowest and highest statutory tax rates; and (iv) marginal tax rates obtained by regressing the revenue from each type of tax to its tax base. Still, they found that the effects of taxation are difficult to isolate empirically. In the same way using data for 23 Organisation for Economic Co-operation and Development (OECD) members, Agell, Lindh, and Ohlsson (1997) found no firm evidence regarding the relationship between growth and tax share. In his review of studies consisting mostly of cross-country evidence for advanced economies, Slemrod (1995) concluded that there was no compelling evidence that the extent of government spending had either a positive or negative impact on growth owing to weaknesses in the estimation models used in these studies.

According to Gemmell and Au (2012), much has changed since Slemrod's review with cross-section studies giving way to panel analyses across or within countries and to country-specific, time-series evidence. Theory on output effects has also developed substantially, and improvements in econometric methods and new datasets have been noted. Thus, aggregated studies have produced more robust results and reliable magnitudes of fiscal impacts. Gemmel and Au (2012) also indicated that recent studies, mainly done after 2000, have taken into account testing the government budget constraint, have allowed for potential growth differences from tax or spending decompositions, and have used panel or time-series rather than cross-section methods.

Kneller and Misch (2011) categorized recent literature broadly into two groups: one mostly dealing with medium- and long-run relationships and employing panel methods, and the other relying on time series for particular countries and mainly applying vector autoregressions and referring to shorter-run effects. Their review suggests that the direction of the long-run impacts of tax changes can be predicted with some degree of certainty and are mainly in line with theory (i.e., increases in non-distortionary taxation offset by declines in distortionary taxation have positive growth effects). Different magnitudes of the estimated long-run effects are often due to varying measurements of tax burdens or the offsetting factors considered. However, they found that predicting short-run effects is associated with greater uncertainty as most tax measures used are rather broad and the estimated output effects can be difficult to interpret for policy purposes.

Fairly recent studies that have focused on long-term growth impacts while considering both short-run and long-run dynamics in their models include those by Arnold et al. (2011); Gemmell, Kneller, and Sanz (2011); and Acosta-Ormaehea and Yoo (2012). A key feature of recent estimations is having revenue-neutral tax changes in which more use of a given type of tax entails lesser amounts of revenue to be raised from other taxes. Applying data on 69 countries from 1970 to 2009, Acosta-Ormaechea and Yoo (2012) found that lowering income taxes while raising consumption taxes (i.e., value-added and sales tax) can be favorable to growth. Based on a panel of 21 OECD countries over 34 years, results from Arnold et al. (2011) suggest a "tax and growth ranking" with recurrent taxes on immovable property the least harmful (or most beneficial) to growth followed by consumption taxes and other property taxes, personal income taxes, and corporate income taxes. Applying data for 17 OECD countries from the early 1970s to 2004, Gemmell, Kneller, and Sanz (2011) found that those taxes predicted by theory to be distortionary (i.e., income and profit, payroll and manpower, property taxes, and social security contributions) tended to have persistent effects on GDP growth. Still, the largest fiscal policy impacts on growth were relatively short-lived and might persist as long as the relevant fiscal policy changes were in effect.

On government spending, varying results have also been reported regarding its relationship with economic development, that is, whether Wagner's Law[1] holds. Some found a significant and positive association between public expenditure and growth (e.g., Ram 1986; Wu, Tang, and Lin 2010), while others recorded a negative relationship (e.g., Alfonso and Furceri 2010; Landau 1983). In addition, there are studies that found no relationship (e.g., Durevall and Henrekson 2011). In a survey, Bergh and Henrekson (2011) explained that the conflicting results were due to inconsistency in definitions and variations in the countries studied.

Using a panel Granger causality test on data from 1950 to 2004, Wu, Tang, and Lin (2010) found that government expenditure promoted economic growth even across different levels of development except for low-income countries (with per capita gross national income less than $936) which, according to the authors, was most likely due to generally poor institutions and high levels of corruption. Bose, Emranul, and Osborn (2007) examined the growth effects of government expenditure using a panel of 30 developing countries from 1970 to 1990 and found that the size of government capital expenditure with respect to GDP was positively and significantly correlated with economic growth but that the same did not hold for current expenditure. This was in contrast to Devarajan, Swaroop, and Zou (1996) who found a positive relationship between the share of current expenditure and per capita income growth in developing countries but a negative relationship between capital public expenditure and growth. The authors showed that there are certain conditions under which a change in expenditure composition leads to higher steady state growth. This includes the productivity of the various expenditure components and the level of initial shares.

At the disaggregated level of expenditure, Bose Emranul, and Osborn (2007) found a robust, positive relationship between investments and spending on education and economic growth. Similarly, using annual data from 1970 to 2005 on 10 developing countries in Asia (Bangladesh, India, Indonesia, the Republic of Korea, Malaysia, Pakistan, the Philippines, Singapore, Sri Lanka, and Thailand), Alam, Sultana, and Butt (2010) found evidence that greater social expenditure – on education, health, and social welfare – enhanced productivity thereby fostering economic growth.

Some studies have focused on the effects of changing the composition of government expenditure or reallocating spending on long-term growth and on understanding which elements of public expenditure have the most significant impact on growth and development. Results consistently point to the importance of reallocating funds to education and infrastructure for long-term growth (e.g., Acosta-Ormaechea and Morozumi 2013; Baffes and Shah 1998; Gemmell, Kneller, and Sainz 2011). These findings are consistent in the context of endogenous growth theory that the main contributors to cross-country differences in the level of development and growth are investment in human capital, physical capital, and infrastructure, and knowledge spillovers. Along these lines, the theoretical work of Barro (1990) predicted that increasing "utility-enhancing" public consumption while reducing "production-enhancing" public spending would reduce growth regardless of the level of total spending, and that of Agenor (2010) showed that re-allocating expenditures from "unproductive" public spending to infrastructure spending would lead to higher steady state growth.

C. Overall trends

In this section, we examine the overall trends in taxation as well as in government expenditures in developing Asia.

1. *Taxation*

Tax revenues vary widely across economies in developing Asia; still, compared to other regions, they tend to have lower tax revenues relative to GDP as well as in terms of actual tax collections relative to potential tax revenues (Figure 3.1). On average, taxes in the region were less than one-half those of OECD members in the 1990s, although the gap narrowed somewhat in the 2000s (Figure 3.2).

Given its level of development, developing Asia may be expected to have lower tax revenues compared to advanced economies. This is consistent with Wagner's Law which supports the notion that the size of government tends to increase with per capita income. Since economic development can bring in higher government revenues thereby enabling greater public spending, then Wagner's Law is plausible. Furthermore, as economies get richer, people tend to demand better and more varied public services.

While there has been no discernable change in overall taxes in the region during the past decades, the structure of taxes has generally evolved. In the 1990s, trade taxes were still a substantial part of overall taxation and were about one-half that of consumption taxes (Figure 3.3). However, since 2000, as economies around the region – especially those in East and Southeast Asia – rapidly expanded external trade and continued to post robust growth, the importance of trade taxes has greatly diminished. Indeed, other studies have noted the declining importance of trade taxes as economies develop (Acosta-Ormaechea and Yoo 2012; IMF 2011).

While trade taxes have fallen in developing Asia, other types of taxes have increased. In particular, income taxes rose in the 2000s compared to the 1990s (Figure 3.4). With the increase, corporate income tax rates have remained close to OECD levels, but the gap in personal income taxes remains huge. There has been no noticeable increase in consumption taxes, which are just about half those of OECD. Still, consumption taxes account for the bulk of the region's taxes at 44% followed by corporate taxes at 25%. In contrast, in developed economies consumption and personal income taxes are almost equally important and account for a large part of total taxes.

In Asia, indirect taxes are more important than direct taxes. Indirect taxes, that is, consumption and trade taxes, account for over one-half of total taxes in the region.

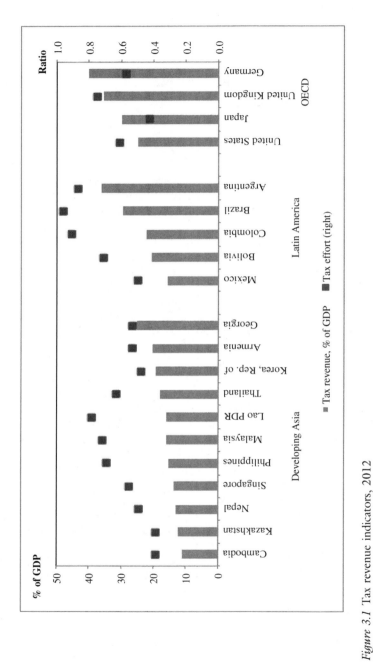

Figure 3.1 Tax revenue indicators, 2012

GDP = gross domestic product, Lao PDR = Lao People's Democratic Republic, OECD = Organisation for Economic Co-operation and Development.

Note: Tax effort is defined as ratio of actual tax collection to potential tax revenue.

Source: International Monetary Fund 2013a.

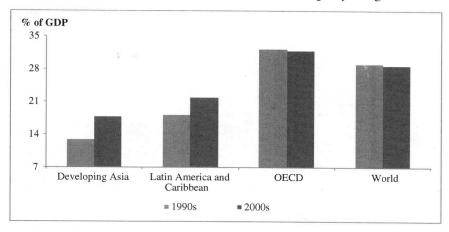

Figure 3.2 Tax revenues

GDP = gross domestic product.

Source: Authors' estimates based on data from International Monetary Fund's *Government Financial Statistics* and World Development Indicators (accessed 30 October 2013).

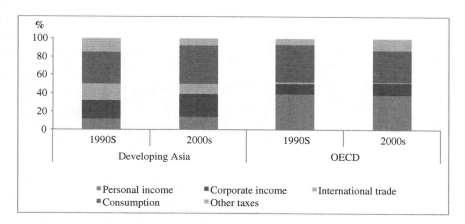

Figure 3.3 Share of components to overall taxes in developing Asia

OECD = Organisation for Economic Co-operation and Development.

Note: Data are based on simple averages. Other taxes include social security contributions and other taxes.

Sources: Acosta-Ormaechea and Yoo 2012, International Monetary Fund's Government Financial Statistics, and OECD Stat.Extracts (databases accessed 29 October 2013).

Taxes covering social security contributions and property taxes may be substantial in developed economies, but this is not the case in developing Asia.

Tax ratios have increased in some economies, but in others, taxes have fallen especially in those with relatively high tax ratios in the 1990s. For example,

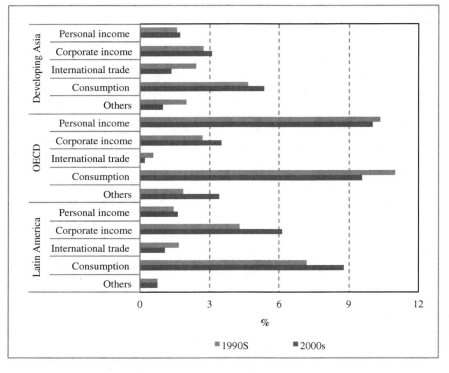

Figure 3.4 Taxation by type (% of gross domestic product)

OECD: Organisation for Economic Co-operation and Development.

Note: Data are based on simple averages.

Sources: Acosta-Ormaechea and Yoo 2012, IMF Government Financial Statistics, and OECD. StatExtracts (databases accessed 29 October 2013).

Indonesia, Malaysia, and Singapore were among those with the highest tax ratios in the 1990s but have since seen their tax revenues fall (Figure 3.5). The source of changes in the tax ratios differs across countries and appears to reflect government policy objectives. Further investigation reveals that in Indonesia, the source of the decline was income taxes which may be linked to tax amendments in the recent decade. In Malaysia, it was due to falling trade taxes. For Singapore, the decline was primarily due to income taxes although other taxes also fell.[2] Efforts had already been made to accelerate tax cuts in the 1990s, and after that, the government continued to lower income tax rates consistent with the policy to boost in-migration and to increase the workforce.

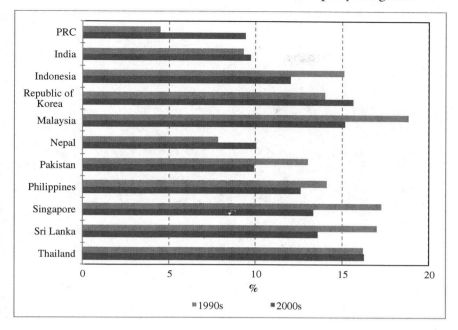

Figure 3.5 Tax revenue (% of gross domestic product)

OECD = Organisation for Economic Co-operation and Development, PRC = People's Republic of China.

Sources: Acosta-Ormaechea and Yoo 2012, International Monetary Fund's Government Financial Statistics, and OECD.StatExtracts (databases accessed 29 October 2013).

2. Government expenditure

Public expenditures of developing Asian economies with unweighted average incomes per capita of purchasing power parity (PPP) $6,000 averaged around 20% of GDP between 1990 and 2011, while those of OECD members with unweighted average incomes per capita of PPP $29,000 were 30% of GDP. The size of government generally rises as income increases (Wagner's Law), but at a certain level of income the size of government expenditure flattens and then slightly declines. Acosta-Ormaechea and Morozumi (2013) show that this non-monotonic relationship between the level of development and public expenditure happens at about a per capita income of $20,000 in PPP terms.

Figure 3.6 shows the evolution of average total government expenditure as a share of GDP of developing Asia and OECD members between 1990 and 2011. There is a marked shift in the trend beginning in 2004 for developing Asia and in 2007 for the OECD. Government size was gradually declining with

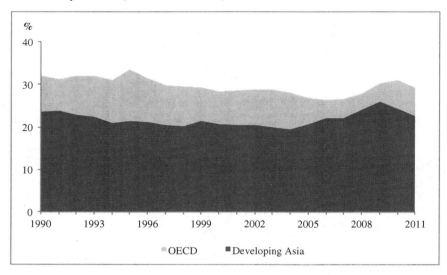

Figure 3.6 Total expenditure, 1990–2011 (% of gross domestic product)

OECD = Organisation for Economic Co-operation and Development.

Note: Unweighted average.

Source: Authors' estimates based on International Monetary Fund's Government Financial Statistics (accessed 15 October 2013).

respect to the size of economy prior to the shift. In the case of high-income economies, the decline was generally due to waning spending on general public services as a share of GDP and on social protection. The shift in the trend in the expenditure–GDP ratio of high-income economies beginning in 2009 is associated with the rebound in spending on these two components. For developing Asia, the declining trend from 1990 to around 2004 was driven by lower expenditures as a share of GDP on economic affairs and education. The shift in the trend that peaked around 2009 was due to an increase in all expenditure components in developing Asia.

D. Quantifying the impact on growth of fiscal policy changes

1. Tax structure

Figure 3.7 plots the relationship between tax ratios and GDP per capita growth from 1970 to 2011 for 13 developing Asian economies, 25 high-income OECD economies, and 33 economies from other regions. The trend in all indicates no clear association between GDP per capita growth and changes in tax ratios given the presence of outlying observations, but the trend in developing Asian economies indicates that there may be a positive association between growth and

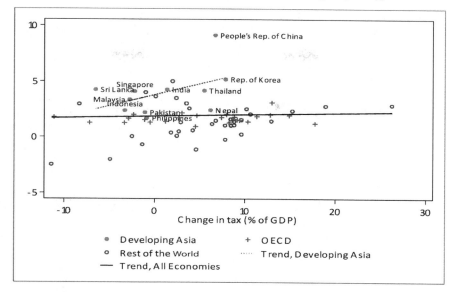

Figure 3.7 Gross domestic product per capita growth versus change in tax ratio

GDP = gross domestic product, OECD = Organisation for Economic Co-operation and Development.

Note: The period ranges between 1970 and 2011 depending on the availability of country data.

Sources: Acosta-Ormaechea and Yoo 2012, International Monetary Fund's Government Financial Statistics online database, and OECD.StatExtracts (databases accessed 29 October 2013).

taxation. It is, however, difficult to model the relationship between the two given that it is likely endogenous. While government taxation may impact growth, higher growth may also lead to higher taxes.

Kneller and Misch (2011) provide a summary of panel estimates of growth effects by type of taxation for OECD members. In general, results indicate that raising the proportion of personal and corporate income taxation tends to decrease growth, although the magnitude of effects differs across studies. Another common result is the positive effects on growth of higher shares of consumption and property taxes.

In contrast to most studies that focused on only advanced economies, a recent study that examines the fiscal policy and growth relationship across income groups is that by Acosta-Ormaechea and Yoo (2012). In particular, they analyzed the impact of changes in tax composition on long-run economic growth for low-, middle-, and high-income economies. Their estimation also corrected for possible endogeneity arising from the simultaneous relationship between tax burden and growth. While tax burden affects growth, changes in growth may also lead to changes in the tax level or structure.

This chapter uses the estimates from Acosta-Ormaechea and Yoo (2012) to examine the impact of changing the composition of taxation on long-run economic

Table 3.1 Estimation coefficients on the impact of changes on tax composition on per capita gross domestic product growth

Tax structure	Omitted tax variable	Impact on growth (percentage points)		
		High-income	Middle-income	Low-income
Income tax	Consumption and other taxes[a]	−0.119	−0.089	Insignificant
Personal income tax	Consumption and other taxes[a]	−0.207	−0.327	0.475
Corporate income tax	Consumption and other taxes[a]	Insignificant	−0.084	Insignificant
Property tax	Income tax	0.278	0.427	Insignificant

[a]Includes taxes on property, goods and services, international trade and transactions, and other consumption and property taxes.

Source: Acosta-Ormaechea and Yoo 2012.

growth for selected Asian economies. Table 3.1 shows their results by income class on changing the shares of income and property taxes. Their estimation assumes that altering one given tax instrument requires an offsetting change in other taxes, thus the tax-policy change occurs in a context of revenue neutrality. In the table, changes in income taxes are offset by changes in consumption and other taxes thus keeping the overall tax revenue unchanged. The coefficients for income tax are significant and negative for high- and middle-income economies indicating a negative relationship between changes in income tax share and growth; however, the result is insignificant for low-income economies. Disaggregating by type of income tax, the results on personal income tax are significant for all income groups, that is, negative for high- and middle-income economies and positive for low-income economies. For corporate income tax, the impact is significant only for middle-income economies. They also found that increasing property taxes and reducing income taxes increased long-term growth.

Table 3.2 shows the results for developing Asian economies in terms of the growth impacts of changing the tax structure. Included are 2 high-income economies – the Republic of Korea and Singapore – and 11 middle-income economies: Armenia, Azerbaijan, Bhutan, the People's Republic of China, India, Indonesia, Kazakhstan, Malaysia, the Philippines, Sri Lanka, and Thailand. Since there tends to be a negative relationship between income tax share and growth, the first exercise deals with the likely impact on growth of reducing the income tax to OECD levels. Column 1 shows that the shares of income taxes of 9 economies are higher than the average for OECD. Reducing the proportion of their income taxes to OECD levels may raise GDP per capita growth on average by about 1 percentage point (column 2) in the long run. The impact is relatively substantial for Bhutan, Indonesia, and Malaysia given their huge

Table 3.2 Impact of changing tax structure on growth in selected developing Asian economies

Economy	Initial income tax (% of tax)	Percent point-change in GDP per capita growth due to reduction in income tax[a]	Initial personal income tax (% of tax)	Percent point-change in GDP per capita growth due to reduction in personal income tax[b]	Initial corporate income tax (% of tax)	Percent point-change in GDP per capita growth due to reduction in corporate income tax[b]	Initial property tax (% of tax)	Percent point-change in GDP per capita growth due to increase in property tax[c]
	(1)	(2)	(3)	(4)	(5)	(6)	(7)	(8)
Armenia	26.7	NA	12.1	1.0	14.6	NA	2.4	2.6
Azerbaijan	44.7	0.8	11.4	0.7	33.4	1.0	2.4	2.6
Bhutan	58.0	2.0	6.9	NA	51.2	2.5	–	–
China, People's Republic of	22.7	NA	6.2	NA	16.5	NA	10.0	NA
India	35.5	NA	11.8	0.9	23.6	0.2	0.4	3.5
Indonesia	54.1	1.6	0.4	NA	53.7	2.7	3.8	2.1
Kazakhstan	41.1	0.5	5.5	NA	35.6	1.2	2.3	2.7
Korea, Republic of	39.6	0.5	21.3	2.5	18.3	NA	12.9	NA
Malaysia	70.3	3.1	15.0	1.9	55.3	2.9	–	–
Philippines	45.7	0.9	16.7	2.4	29.1	0.6	–	–
Singapore	44.6	1.1	14.9	1.2	29.7	0.0	8.5	0.0

(Continued)

Table 3.2 (Continued)

Economy	Initial income tax (% of tax)	Percent point-change in GDP per capita growth due to reduction in income tax[a]	Initial personal income tax (% of tax)	Percent point-change in GDP per capita growth due to reduction in personal income tax[b]	Initial corporate income tax (% of tax)	Percent point-change in GDP per capita growth due to reduction in corporate income tax[b]	Initial property tax (% of tax)	Percent point-change in GDP per capita growth due to increase in property tax[c]
	(1)	(2)	(3)	(4)	(5)	(6)	(7)	(8)
Sri Lanka	15.9	NA	3.2	NA	12.7	NA	–	NA
Thailand	42.4	0.6	10.7	0.5	31.8	0.9	2.5	2.6
Developing Asia	30.5	0.9	8.7	1.4	21.7	0.9	7.8	2.8
OECD	35.8		26.7		8.9		8.6	

– = data not available, GDP = growth domestic product, NA = not applicable, OECD=Organisation for Economic Co-operation and Development.

[a]Tax share is brought down to OECD average.

[b]Tax share is brought down to regional average.

[c]Tax share is raised to OECD average.

Note: Data on initial tax structures are between 2009 and 2011.

Source: Authors' estimates using data from Acosta-Ormaechea and Yoo (2012).

discrepancies from OECD levels. Disaggregating income tax, shares of personal income tax among developing Asian economies are already lower than those of OECD; thus, the benchmark used for examining the impact of reducing the proportion of personal income tax is the average for Asian economies instead of OECD. Column 4 shows that this applies to 8 economies, and the impact averages 1.4 percentage points for GDP per capita growth. On corporate income tax shares, column 5 shows that there is a huge gap between developing Asian economies and OECD economies. While the average for Asia is 21.7%, that for OECD is only 8.9%. Among those with the highest shares are Bhutan, Indonesia, and Malaysia. Similar to personal income tax, corporate income tax is reduced to the regional average. Results indicate that reducing the proportion of corporate income tax while raising that of consumption and other taxes can raise long-run GDP per capita growth by 0.9 percentage points (column 6). Considering the negative relationship between property taxes and growth, columns 7 and 8 show the impact of raising the shares of property taxes to OECD levels. This was done for 7 economies with India having the largest gains at a more than 3 percentage point rise in long-term GDP per capita growth.

Corporate income taxes are expected to be harmful to growth because they discourage investment in capital and productivity improvements in addition to reducing foreign direct investment (Arnold et al. 2011; Hajkova et al. 2006; Myles 2009). Owing to their progressive nature, personal income taxes can discourage growth more per unit of tax revenue than consumption taxes which are generally flat. In addition, they can discourage savings by taxing both the return on savings and the income from which the savings originated. While consumption taxes raise the prices of goods, they are not expected to discourage saving and investment as long as they remain constant over time. Property taxes are preferred over income taxes since they can help shift investment from housing into higher-return activities and thus increase the rate of growth.

The above exercise has shown which changes in tax structure are more beneficial to economic growth. For example, raising consumption tax rather than personal or corporate income tax can have better effects on long-term growth. Still, the projected growth rates from altering tax structures should be interpreted with caution. There are other factors that need to be considered such as revenue sufficiency, equity, simplicity, and compliance (Arnold et al. 2011). It would be insufficient, for example, to recommend reducing corporate taxes alone without considering other critical factors. A key benefit from the exercise is that it can help provide a basis for the direction of tax reforms.

If public spending reforms are implemented alongside changes in tax structures, then it is possible that a rise in long-run GDP growth due to productive spending will be offset by the impact of distortionary taxes resulting in negligible or no long-run growth (Gemmell and Au 2012). Hence, there is a need to carefully measure the growth impacts of fiscal reforms involving both tax and spending reform.

2. Composition of government expenditures

Reallocating spending to infrastructure (usually transportation and communication) and education has been shown to have a positive impact on long-term growth. Looking at expenditure components in developing Asia by decade, however, public expenditures on transportation and communication and education, on average, have dropped (Figure 3.8). In some economies, education spending has been consistently low. India's and Pakistan's spending on education, for example, has been less than 1% of GDP (Figure 3.9). Between the 1990s and 2000s, expenditures on education in the region as a share of GDP dropped to 2.9% from 3.1% on average. It is interesting to quantify the impact on growth of reallocating spending to these components, particularly to education. The focus on education is based on empirical studies (e.g., Acosta-Ormaecha and Morozumi 2013; Bose, Emranul, and Osborn 2007) that show the robustness of expenditures on education across different estimation specifications.

Following a similar exercise on tax structure, we use estimates from existing studies to simulate the effect of increasing the share of education expenditures on growth in income per capita in developing Asian economies. Table 3.3 presents estimates obtained by Acosta-Ormaecha and Morozumi (2013) across different compensating factors and specifications. The results show that the magnitude of the effects of reallocating spending toward education is not trivial. In specification (1) for example, a 1 percentage point increase in education spending offset by a 1 percentage point drop in spending on the other components results in a 1.098 percentage points increase in growth over a 5-year period or around 0.2 percentage points annually.

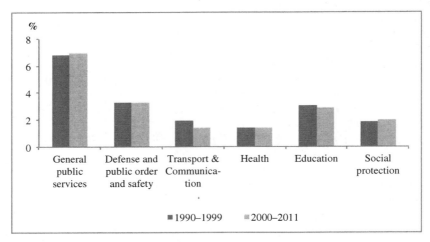

Figure 3.8 Expenditure components (% of gross domestic product)

Note: Unweighted average.

Source: Authors' estimates based on International Monetary Fund's Government Financial Statistics (accessed 15 October 2013).

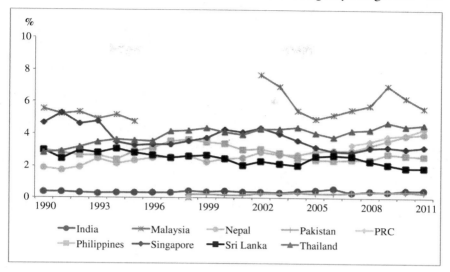

Figure 3.9 Education spending, 1990–2011 (% of gross domestic product)
PRC = People's Republic of China.
Source: International Monetary Fund's Government Financial Statistics (accessed 15 October 2013).

Table 3.3 Estimated effects of education spending on growth

Compensating factor	(1)	(2)	(3)	(4)
All others	1.098*	1.278*	0.741	
Defense	0.539	0.761	0.811	1.417**
Health	1.553**	1.423	1.154	0.594
Social protection	1.090**	1.234**	0.804*	1.380**
Transportation and communication	−0.816	0.785	−0.601	1.555***

(1) to (4) represents estimates from different specifications done by Acosta-Ormaechea and Morozumi (2013) to check for robustness. See Tables 3, 5, 6, and 7 in Acosta-Ormaechea and Morozumi (2013).

*** $p < 1\%$; ** $p < 5\%$; * $p < 10\%$

Source: Acosta-Ormaechea and Morozumi 2013.

We estimate that the average education spending (as a percentage of total expenditure) in developing Asia is 13.6%. The seven countries in Table 3.4 – Azerbaijan, Georgia, India, Kazakhstan, the Kyrgyz Republic, Pakistan, and Sri Lanka – have expenditure ratios below this average. The table presents the simulated impact on annual GDP and GDP per capita growth if the level of public expenditure on education in these economies were to be increased to the average in the region.

Table 3.4 Simulated impact on gross domestic product and gross domestic product per capita growth of increasing expenditure on education

	Education expenditure (% of total)	Impact (annual, percentage points)	
		GDP per capita growth	GDP growth
Azerbaijan	8.6	1.1	1.4
Georgia	7.7	1.3	1.4
India	2.7	2.4	2.7
Kazakhstan	7.0	1.5	1.8
Kyrgyz Republic	11.9	0.4	0.6
Pakistan	1.8	2.6	2.9
Sri Lanka	9.1	1.0	1.1

Source: Authors' estimates.

E. Concluding observations

Developing Asia stands at a crossroads in the aftermath of the global financial and economic crisis. After decades of sustained, rapid economic growth that has lifted general living standards and sharply reduced poverty, the region's growth is slowing down noticeably. To some extent, the deceleration is the consequence of a less favorable external environment due to the weakening of the advanced economies since the global economic crisis, and there are also a number of homegrown issues that have contributed to moderating the growth momentum. For example, India continues to suffer from an infrastructure deficit and a difficult business environment, while the People's Republic of China is in the midst of a strategic transition toward a more sustainable growth paradigm in which domestic demand and private consumption play a bigger role. While the magnitude and the cause of the deceleration differ across economies, sustaining rapid growth after the global crisis remains a difficult yet urgent challenge for the whole region.

Fiscal policy can help developing Asia meet this challenge. Fiscal policy contributed to the region's growth in the past, and it can continue to do so in the future. Our analysis indicates that in developing Asia the composition of taxes and government spending matters for economic growth. In theory, different types of taxes and public spending have different effects on growth. In line with theory, we find that in developing Asia property taxes are more conducive for growth than personal and corporate income taxes. Therefore, when the region improves fiscal revenue mobilization efforts across all revenue categories to expand its relatively limited revenue base, governments would do well to pursue a mix of taxes and other fiscal revenues that minimize adverse growth effects. We find that the composition of government spending also has a significant effect on economic growth. More specifically, our analysis indicates that shifting public spending to education will yield a sizable growth dividend. To sum up, developing Asia's governments must pay attention to the mix of both their revenues and expenditures in order to maximize the contribution of fiscal policy to growth.

Finally, in light of growing popular demand for more inclusive growth which benefits the broadest possible swathes of the Asian population, Asian governments must explore ways to leverage fiscal policy for inclusive growth. That is, while sustaining growth must be a key objective of fiscal policy, making sustained growth more inclusive should be an important additional consideration. The two objectives need not be mutually exclusive; public investments in education and health can augment overall human capital and thus foster growth, while augmenting the productive capacity of the poor.

Notes

1 This is also known as the law of increased state spending and states that as an industrial economy grows, it will be accompanied by an increased share of public expenditure in gross national product.
2 Due to lack of data, it cannot be determined whether the decline in income taxes was due to a decline in corporate or personal income taxes.

Bibliography

Acosta-Ormaechea, S. and A. Morozumi. 2013. Can a Government Enhance Long-Run Growth by Changing the Composition of Public Expenditure? *IMF Working Paper*. No. 13/162. Washington, DC: International Monetary Fund.

Acosta-Ormaechea, S. and J. Yoo. 2012. Tax Composition and Growth: A Broad Cross-Country Perspective. *IMF Working Paper*. No. 12/257. Washington, DC: International Monetary Fund.

Agell, J., T. Lindh, and H. Ohlsson. 1997. Growth and the Public Sector: A Critical Review Essay. *European Journal of Political Economy*. 13 (1). pp. 33–52.

Agenor, P.-R. 2010. A Theory of Infrastructure-led Development. *Journal of Economic Dynamics & Control*. 34 (5). pp. 932–950.

Alam, S., A. Sultana, and M. Butt. 2010. Does Social Expenditure Promote Economic Growth? A Multivariate Panel Cointegration Analysis for Asian Countries. *European Journal of Social Sciences*. 14 (1). pp. 44–54.

Alfonso, A. and D. Furceri. 2010. Government Size, Composition, Volatility, and Economic Growth. *European Journal of Political Economy*. 26 (4). pp. 517–532.

Arnold, J.M., B. Brys, C. Heady, A. Johansson, C. Schwellnus, and L. Vartia. 2011. Tax Policy for Economic Recovery and Growth. *The Economic Journal*. 121 (February). pp. F59–F80.

Baffes, J. and A. Shah. 1998. Productivity of Public Spending, Sectoral Allocation Choices and Economic Growth. *Economic Development and Cultural Change*. 46 (2). pp. 291–303.

Barro, R. 1990. Government Spending in a Simple Model of Endogenous Growth. *Journal of Political Economy*. 98 (5). pp. S103–S125.

Bergh, A. and M. Henkerson. 2011. Government Size and Growth: A Survey and Interpretation of the Evidence. *Journal of Economic Surveys*. 25 (5). pp. 872–897.

Bose, N., H. M. Emranul, and D. R. Osborn. 2007. Public Expenditure and Economic Growth: A Disaggregated Analysis for Developing Countries. *The Manchester School.* 75 (5). pp. 533–556.

Devarajan, S., V. Swaroop, and H. Zou. 1996. The Composition of Public Expenditure and Economic Growth. *Journal of Monetary Economics.* 37 (2). pp. 313–344.

Durevall, D. and M. Henrekson. 2011. The Futile Quest for a Grand Explanation of Long-run Government Expenditure. *Journal of Public Economics.* 95 (7–8). pp. 708–722.

Easterly, W. and S. Rebelo. 1993. Fiscal Policy and Economic Growth: An Empirical Investigation. *NBER Working Paper.* No. 4499. Cambridge, MA: National Bureau of Economic Research.

Gemmell, N. and J. Au. 2012. Government Size, Fiscal Policy and the Level and Growth of Output: A Review of Recent Evidence. Working Paper in Public Finance 10/12. Wellington: Victoria Business School.

Gemmell, N., R. Kneller, and I. Sanz. 2011. The Timing and Persistence of Fiscal Policy Impacts on Growth: Evidence from OECD countries. *Economic Journal,* 121 (550). F33–F58.

———. 2012. Does the Composition of Government Expenditure Matter for Economic Growth. Manuscript. Nottingham: University of Nottingham. http://www. victoria.ac.nz/sacl/about/cpf/research/pdfs-research/1GKSOECDPubExp-and-Growth.pdf (accessed 15 October 2013).

Hajkova, D., G. Nicoletti, L. Vartia, and K.Y. Yoo. 2006. Taxation and Business Environment as Drivers of Foreign Direct Investment in OECD countries. *OECD Economic Studies.* 43. pp. 8–38.

International Monetary Fund. 2011. *Revenue Mobilization in Developing Countries.* Washington, DC.

———. 2013a. Fiscal Monitor: Taxing Times. *World Economic and Financial Surveys.* Washington, DC.

———. 2013b. Government Financial Statistics online database (accessed 29 and 30 October 2013).

King, R. G. and S. Rebelo. 1990. Public Policy and Economic Growth: Developing Neoclassical Implications. *Journal of Political Economy.* 98 (5). Part 2: The Problem of Development: A Conference of the Institute for the Study of Free Enterprise Systems. pp. S126–S150.

Kneller, R. and F. Misch. 2011. What Does Ex-post Evidence Tell Us about the Output Effects of Future Tax Reforms? Mannheim: Centre for European Economic Research.

Landau, D. 1983. Government Expenditure and Economic Growth: A Cross-Country Study. *Southern Economic Journal.* 49 (3). pp. 783–792.

Myles, G. D. 2009. Economic Growth and the Role of Taxation – Disaggregate Data. *OECD Economics Department Working Paper.* No. 715. Organisation for Economic Co-operation and Development Publishing. http://dx.doi.org/10.1787/222775817802

Organisation for Economic Co-operation and Development. 2013. OECD StatExtracts. http://stats.oecd.org (accessed 29 October 2013).

Ram, R. 1986. Government Size and Economic Growth: A New Framework and some Evidence from Cross-section and Time-series Data. *American Economic Review.* 76 (1). pp. 191–203.

Skinner, J. 1987. Taxation and Output Growth: Evidence from African Countries. *NBER Working Paper Series*. No. 2335. Cambridge, MA: National Bureau of Economic Research.

Slemrod, J. 1995. What Do Cross-country Studies Teach about Government Involvement, Prosperity, and Economic Growth? *Brookings Papers on Economic Activity*. 2. pp. 373–431.

World Bank. 2013. World Development Indicators Database. http://databank. worldbank.org/data/views/variableSelection/selectvariables.aspx? (accessed 30 October 2013).

Wu, S.-Y., J.-H. Tang, and E. Lin. 2010. The Impact of Government Expenditure on Economic Growth: How Sensitive to the Level of Development. *Journal of Policy Modeling*. 32 (6). pp. 804–817.

4 Government spending and inclusive growth in developing Asia

Seok-Kyun Hur

A. Introduction

Inclusive growth refers to long-term, sustained economic growth that is broad based and includes a large part of the labor force, thereby reducing unemployment and income inequality significantly. Policies that encourage inclusive growth tend to emphasize removing constraints to growth, creating opportunities, and creating equal treatment for investment. Ranieri and Ramos (2013) compare various definitions of inclusive growth and demonstrate that there is no standard one, although there is a certain consensus. According to Rauniyar and Kanbur (2010), "Inclusive growth is that which is accompanied by lower income inequality, so that the increment of income accrues disproportionately to those with lower incomes." This chapter follows that definition and explores how government spending can better serve the goal of inclusive growth.

Compared with revenue policies, spending programs are more likely to have direct effects on specific groups. For example, social transfers and the free or subsidized provision of public services are often directed to low-income families. In this sense, it would be meaningful to discuss whether and/or how government expenditures contribute to economic growth, while alleviating income inequality and maintaining social cohesion.

Figure 4.1 identifies the three key variables in this chapter and their relationships; confirming or refuting any of the arrows would be a worthy research endeavor. Actually, many studies have dealt with one or more of the arrows, and one very popular debate issue is how equity and economic growth are linked to each other (the two arrows at the top). Some economists claim there is a tradeoff between the two, while others favor co-movement. In addition, there are studies that examine the causality between equity and growth, but in my opinion, there is no dominant theory as arguments that are supported in one theory are refuted by changing the empirical evidence.

For example, in his seminal paper, Kuznets (1955) argued that there was an inverted U-shaped relationship between the Gini coefficient and economic growth, and the resulting Kuznets curve is well supported by data from western European and Latin American countries. On the other hand, it is also known that extending the dataset to include more economies, especially those in East Asia, weakens

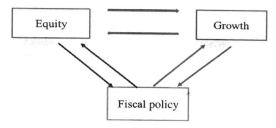

Figure 4.1 Three key variables and their links
Source: Author.

the validity of the curve. Acemoglu and Robinson (2002) point out that the discrepancy between so-called East Asian miracles and the Kuznets curve may be reconciled by introducing political factors and redistributive mechanisms through political competition.

Recently, Berg and Ostry (2011) reported that the trade-off between efficiency and equality may not exist in the long run. They provide empirical findings that greater inequality may shorten the duration of growth; however, they are very cautious about suggesting a policy recommendation because poorly designed efforts to reduce inequality could be counterproductive.

Various empirical results on the relationship between growth and equity have been reported using different scopes and time data. Those results are sometimes consistent or conflicting, and have been interpreted by emphasizing specific policy or transmission channels. Regardless of such differences, however, the existing literature seems to reach a minimal consensus that equity and economic growth closely interact with each other.

Another avenue of research is to explore the effectiveness of fiscal policy as a countercyclical measure and/or to examine the responsiveness of fiscal policy to business cycle fluctuations. The two arrows at the right in Figure 4.1 represent this research. Studies in this area do not reach unanimous decisions. Recently, Jha et al. (2010) estimated the fiscal multipliers for tax cuts and spending expansion for 10 Asian economies using the sign restriction estimations of Mountford and Uhlig (2002). They reported that tax cuts tend to have greater and more persistent growth effects than spending increases which, however, may not be valid for economies in other areas. It is not so surprising considering that governments have different fiscal management systems and different mind sets in policy making, not to mention different national priorities.

Though results diverge from one economy to another or by period, most of the research in this area adopts a structural vector autoregression (SVAR) setup. According to de Castro and Hernandez (2006), the literature using SVAR can be categorized into the four groups in Table 4.1 by differences in fiscal shock identification strategies.[1]

Table 4.1 Relevant literature using structural vector autoregression

Study	Shock Identification Strategy
Ramey and Shapiro (1998), Edelberg, Eichenabum, and Fisher (1999)	Vector autoregression (VAR) models with dummy variables specifying certain episodes (such as wars and drastic changes in fiscal stance)
Mountford and Uhlig (2002)	VAR with sign restrictions on the impulse response functions
de Castro (2004), Fatas and Mihov (2000), Favero (2002)	Structural vector autoregression (SVAR) (Cholesky Decomposition)
Blanchard and Perotti (2002), Perotti (1999), Hoppner (2002)[a]	SVAR using institutional information and quarter dependence.

[a]Hoppner (2002), following the shock representation by Blanchard and Perotti (2002), concentrates on distinguishing the direct effects of fiscal shock from the indirect effects of automatic stabilization mechanisms.

Source: Hur 2007.

The popularity of SVAR lies in that it is less dependent on existing economic theory and is less susceptible to endogeneity and co-integration[2] among the variables of interest. Using SVAR is, however, more challenging for analyzing fiscal policy than for analyzing monetary policy for several reasons such as the existence of uncertain or unidentifiable policy lags and automatic stabilization mechanisms. These factors combined with the low frequency of fiscal data (mostly quarterly) cause technical difficulties in identifying sources of correlations or causalities among the disturbances of the vector autoregression (VAR) system and disentangling the contributions of built-in stabilization mechanisms. Recent developments in analyzing fiscal policy using VAR naturally have concentrated on dealing with those problems.

In estimating SVAR, it is crucial to track down the fiscal stance and see how it varies in a business cycle. Fiscal policy could influence the dynamics of an economy through automatic stabilizers as well as through discretionary measures. Thus, we need to separate the portion contributed by automatic stabilizers from that contributed by discretionary policy. Though conceptually clear, it is quite intriguing to empirically decompose changes in fiscal variables into those two categories. It also explains why shock identification is critical in estimating SVAR as shown in Table 4.1.

In policy circles, fiscal impulse and fiscal stance indicators are commonly used as proxies for discretionary fiscal policies (Heller, Haas, and Mansur 1986). With these indicators, the interaction between fiscal stance and the business cycle can be approached more simply than using SVAR. The time series of fiscal impulse and/or fiscal stance in a business cycle can be assessed jointly with that of real gross domestic product (GDP) growth in terms of efficacy and timing.

Obviously, VAR is not the only option; many studies have adopted a single equation approach linking real GDP growth and fiscal variables with other control variables. Fiscal impulse and fiscal stance are variables frequently used in the single equation approach.

Still another avenue of research is to assess the distribution effects of fiscal policy (the two arrows at the left in Figure 4.1). Compared with the other two avenues, this one is relatively new. In the most recent study,[3] Ball et al. (2013) estimated the distributional effects of fiscal consolidation. Using a sample of 17 Organisation for Economic Co-operation and Development (OECD) members, they showed that fiscal consolidation increases inequality. They also showed that spending-based adjustments tend to have greater distributional impacts than tax-based adjustments. Woo et al. (2013) also focused on the effects of fiscal consolidation and/or fiscal policy on equity and reported qualitatively the same results as Ball et al. (2013). Using a larger dataset, Woo et al. (2013) estimated equations with variables representing several fiscal items and reported that progressive taxation and targeted social benefits and subsidies reduced income inequality. Many other studies on the same issue provide empirical findings that some spending items (such as transfers and welfare, education, health, and housing) tend to have greater effects on reducing income inequality than other spending items or even specific taxes (Cubero and Hollar 2010; Joumard, Pisu, and Bloch 2012; Martinez-Vazquez, Moreno-Dodson, and Vulovic 2012).

This chapter distinguishes itself from the existing literature in that it examines the effects of fiscal policy on both equity and growth,[4] specifically whether it is possible to design fiscal spending so that it enhances equity without sacrificing economic growth and vice versa. Generally, it is agreed that greater spending on health, education, and public infrastructure, as long as it is efficiently administered, is one key to more inclusive growth. A well-known survey by Lopez (2004) on economic growth concludes that macroeconomic stability, low inflation rates, and appropriate education and infrastructure-related policies have positive effects on growth and reduce inequality. Hence, fiscal policy is not the only policy vehicle to rely on, but undoubtedly, it is a crucial one. In this context, this chapter examines the contribution of fiscal expenditure to sustaining an inclusive growth path. Keeping in mind that poorly designed efforts to reduce inequality could be counterproductive (Berg and Ostry 2011), I decompose fiscal spending into several subgroups and evaluate their relative contributions to inclusive growth.

B. Data and key variables

As mentioned previously, this chapter analyzes the effects of fiscal policy on both equity and growth. For that purpose, I created a cross-country panel by combining data from the Standardized World Income Inequality Database (SWIID) and the World Bank's World Development Indicators (WDI). I specifically chose SWIID for an inequality measure because the dataset provided by

Solt (2014) is better than the Luxemburg Income Study and the World Income Inequality Database in terms of coverage and quality.

1. Key variables

Government spending (expense) was classified into the following subgroups from WDI; each was converted to a percentage of GDP:[5]

- Government final consumption expenditure[6]
- Gross capital formation, public
- Health expenditure, public
- Military expenditure
- Social transfer and subsidy
- Public spending on education

Next, two Gini coefficients – Gini_net and Gini_market (Gini_gross) – were gathered from SWIID. Gini_net is a coefficient calculated after subtracting taxation and adding public transfers, while Gini_market uses income before taxation and transfers. For this study, I used the Gini_market coefficients because it would be more interesting to examine the distributional and the growth effects of fiscal spending excluding direct and contemporaneous effects. For example, some fiscal items such as social subsidies, transfers, and progressive income tax tend to have direct distributional effects by construction. The difference between Gini_market and Gini_net is mainly explained by the direct influences of those fiscal items.

In addition, the following variables were collected from WDI, some of which were used as control variables if necessary:

- Real GDP growth
- Revenue (% of GDP)
- Tax revenue (% of GDP)
- Taxes on income, profits, and capital gains (% of GDP)
- Social contributions (% of GDP)
- Literacy rate
- Labor force with primary (secondary or tertiary) education
- Unemployment rate
- Labor force with primary (secondary or tertiary) education
- Market capitalization (% of GDP)
- Standard & Poor's Global Equity Indices (annual % change)
- Life expectancy at birth, total (years)
- Cash surplus/deficit (% of GDP)
- Central government debt, total (% of GDP)
- Poverty gap at the national poverty line (%)[7]

Table 4.2 provides the abbreviations and definitions for these variables.

Table 4.2 Definitions and abbreviations for key variables

Abbreviations	Definitions
cap_exp	Gross fixed capital formation, public (% of GDP)
edu_exp	Public spending on education (% of GDP)
expense	Expense (% of GDP)
fiscal_debt	Central Government debt, total (% of GDP)
fiscal_surplus	Cash surplus/deficit (% of GDP)
gfce	Government final consumption expenditures (% of GDP)
gini_diff	Difference between the two gini coefficients (gini_gross–gini_net)
gini_gross	Gini before taxation and transfers
gini_net	Gini after taxation and transfers
global_equity_index	S&P Global Equity Indices (annual % change)
health_exp	Health expenditure, public (% of GDP)
income_tax	Taxes on income, profits, and capital gains (% of GDP)
life_exp	Life expectancy at birth, total (years)
literacy	Literacy rate, adult total (% of pop ages 15 and above)
market_cap	Market capitalization (% of GDP)
mil_exp	Military expenditure (% of GDP)
poverty_gap	Poverty gap at national poverty line (%)
primary_edu	Labor force with primary education (% of total pop ages 15–64)
r_gdp_growth	Real GDP growth
revenue	Revenue excluding grants (% of GDP)
secondary_edu	Labor force with secondary education (% of total pop ages 15–64)
social_contribution	Social contributions (% of GDP)
tax_revenue	Tax revenue (% of GDP)
tertiary_edu	Labor force with tertiary education (% of total pop ages 15–64)
transfer_exp	Subsidies and other transfers (% of GDP)
unemployment	Unemployment, total (%)

GDP = gross domestic product, pop = population, S&P = Standard and Poor's.
Source: Author.

2. Coverage

The dataset covers 34 OECD members and 33 out of 48 Asian Development Bank (ADB) regional members (the 15 missing are Afghanistan; Brunei Darussalam; the Cook Islands; Kiribati; the Marshall Islands; the Federated States of Micronesia; Myanmar; Nauru; Palau; Samoa; Solomon Islands; Taipei,China;

Tonga; Tuvalu; and Vanuatu) for a total 63 economies in the panel data. Of the four that overlap the two groups, Australia, Japan, and New Zealand are treated as OECD members, while the Republic of Korea is included in the ADB group.

In WDI, there are approximately 100 countries that are neither OECD nor ADB regional members; the observations for them are also used if necessary.[8] All the economies in the dataset are classified into one of five income groups based on per capita GDP (constant $2005) in 2010. Income group 1 has a per capita income less than $1,000; group 2 is between $1,000 and $5,000; group 3 is between $5,000 and $10,000; group 4 is between $10,000 and $20,000; and group 5 is more than $20,000.

3. Summary statistics

Summary statistics of the key variables are reported in the Appendix. Separate tables are provided depending on membership in ADB or OECD or on income group. The following anticipated patterns can be noted.

(i) **The real GDP growth rate is lower for high-income economies.** The higher growth momentum in developing economies is consistent with the so-called beta convergence theory. The first graph in Figure 4.2 confirms that such a phenomenon has been consistently observed over time between OECD and ADB members with the exception of the 1997 Asian financial crisis. On the other hand, the second graph in Figure 4.2 shows that economies in income groups 2 or 3 tend to have greater growth rates than those in the other income groups indicating that catching up may begin in those growth stages.

(ii) **Both Gini coefficients are higher in developing economies.** Figure 4.3 confirms that the Gini coefficients are higher in developing economies with a few exceptions. Furthermore, the differences between ADB and OECD members, or between income groups 1 and 3, and 4 and 5 are magnified for the Gini_net coefficients. As expected, fiscal policy in developed economies puts more emphasis on redistribution.

Another notable point is that the Gini coefficients cannot be ordered by income groups. For example, in the Gini_gross graphs in Figure 4.3, the income inequalities in income group 3 are greater than or almost equal to those of income group 1. Though consistent with the traditional Kuznets curve, the pattern still needs further explanation.

(iii) **Government spending takes a smaller fraction of GDP in developing economies, and the percent of GDP (expense) is also smaller** (Figure 4.4). The pattern is the same with the ratio of government final consumption expenditures to GDP. It indicates that developing economies are likely to hold more fiscal capacity than developed ones. The recent global financial crisis made people aware how critical it is to maintain room for fiscal expansion in difficult times. Furthermore, in the next 2 decades, most developing economies are expected to experience demographic aging, which will also be a heavy fiscal burden. On the other hand, this implies that governments in developing economies may

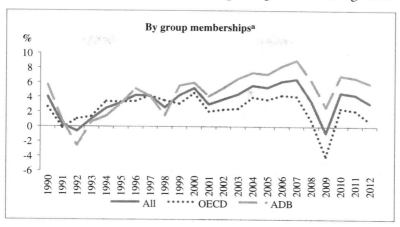

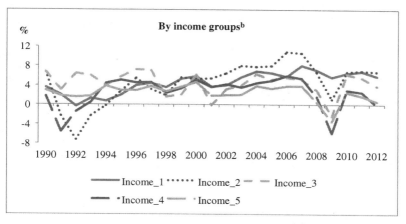

Figure 4.2 Time trends of real gross domestic product growth rates

ADB = Asian Development Bank, OECD = Organisation for Economic Co-operation and Development, r_gdp_growth = real gross domestic product growth rate.

[a]ADB covers 33 of its 48 members, while OECD has its 34 members.

[b]Income group 1 has a per capita income less than $1,000; group 2 is between $1,000 and $5,000; group 3 is between $5,000 and $10,000; group 4 is between $10,000 and $20,000; and group 5 is more than $20,000.

Source: Author's estimates.

provide fewer public services than those in developed ones and/or may do less redistributing.

(iv) **With the exception of gross fixed capital formation (public, % of GDP), the ratios of all the other fiscal items to GDP are smaller in developing economies.** Since 2000, the average ratio of gross fixed capital formation (public) to GDP in ADB members has been 7.68, which is much higher than the 4.33 for OECD members. Developing economies tend to allocate their

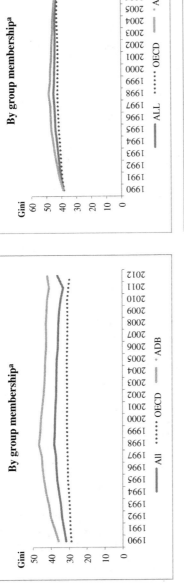

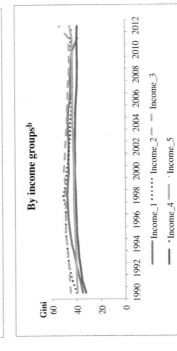

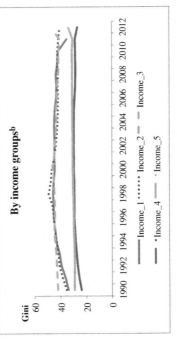

Figure 4.3 Time trends of Gini coefficients

ADB = Asian Development Bank, Gini_gross = Gini coefficient before taxation and transfers, Gini_net = Gini coefficient after taxation and transfers, OECD = Organisation for Economic Co-operation and Development.

[a] ADB covers 33 of its 48 members, while OECD has its 34 members.

[b] Income group 1 has a per capita income less than $1,000; group 2 is between $1,000 and $5,000; group 3 is between $5,000 and $10,000; group 4 is between $10,000 and $20,000; and group 5 is more than $20,000.

Source: Author's estimates.

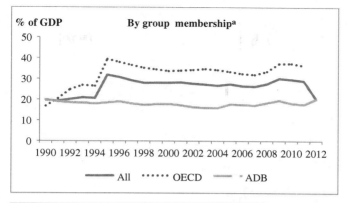

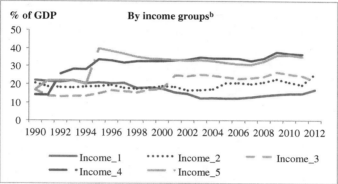

Figure 4.4 Time trends of expense

ADB = Asian Development Bank, OECD = Organisation for Economic Co-operation and Development.

[a]ADB covers 33 of its 48 members, while OECD has its 34 members.

[b]Income group 1 has a per capita income less than $1,000; group 2 is between $1,000 and $5,000; group 3 is between $5,000 and $10,000; group 4 is between $10,000 and $20,000; and group 5 is more than $20,000.

Source: Author's estimates.

limited fiscal resources intensively to building social overhead capital which supports economic activities in the private sector and improves quality of life. This is reflected in the high proportions of government final consumption expenditures to GDP in Asian economies.

(v) **The role of fiscal policy in redistribution is emphasized in developed economies.** Figure 4.5 provides scatter plots between the Gini_gross (Gini_market) and Gini_net coefficients and demonstrates how close the fitted line between the two is to 45 degrees. Compared with ADB members, the Gini_net coefficients of OECD members tend to lie below the 45 degree line with respect to the Gini_gross coefficients. These two figures confirm the conjecture that developed economies pay more attention to redistribution.

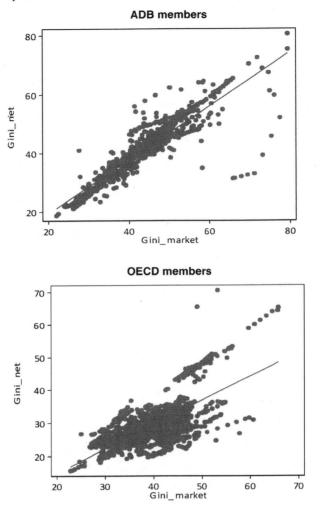

Figure 4.5 Relationship between Gini_net and Gini_market coefficients

ADB = Asian Development Bank, OECD = Organisation for Economic Co-operation and Development

Source: Author's estimates.

C. Empirical strategies

This chapter focuses on estimating the effects of spending composition on both equity and economic growth. I used mainly panel vector autoregression (PVAR) for calculations in light of the close interaction among those three key variables as well as the panel structure of the dataset. Compared with VAR, PVAR has the relative advantage that it can complement short-time coverage with more cross-section samples. The time coverage differs from one economy to another in the dataset, so PVAR was used. As a complement, the results from single equation estimations are also provided.

1. Panel vector autoregression

The PVAR estimates the interactions among the growth rate, the Gini coefficient, and fiscal variables, and includes four variables. With the GDP growth rate and Gini coefficient fixed, government expense (spending) and a selected component of the expense are included.

In a four-variable PVAR, a change in one individual fiscal spending item can influence the other variables through two separate channels – first by changes in gross spending (magnitude effect) and second by changes in the composition of spending (composition effect). In contrast with the magnitude effect, the composition effect is based on substituting different fiscal items. In other words, increasing the share of a fiscal expenditure item can be done only by decreasing the shares of others. The four-variable PVAR was adopted to separate the two effects.

All the fiscal variables are measured as a percentage of GDP. By including expense and its components together, we can compare the effects from the two fiscal variables and assess whether a change in the fiscal spending component has a bigger impact on economic growth and the Gini coefficient than the other spending components.

The PVAR are specified as follows.

$$X_{it} = A(L)X_{it} + f_i + \varepsilon_{it} \ , \ i = \text{country}, \ t = \text{year}, \ f_i \text{ fixed effects}$$

$$X_{it} \equiv \begin{bmatrix} growth_{it} \\ \Delta gini_{it} \\ \Delta B_{it} \end{bmatrix} \tag{1}$$

In (1), B_{it} is a vector or a scalar of the fiscal items covering all types of expenditures and tax revenues and fiscal balance (deficit or surplus). All these numbers are counted as a percentage of GDP. Considering that the length of the time series may vary from one economy to another, I did not consider the case that the dimension of the vector X_{it} was greater than 5. Maintaining the dimension of PVAR below 5 is acceptable in the following sense.

$$\sum_{j=1}^{n} \Delta B_{it}^{j} = 0, \ B_{it} \equiv \left(B_{it}^{1}, B_{it}^{2}, \dots, B_{it}^{j}, \dots, B_{it}^{n} \right) \tag{2}$$

In (2), the superscript j classifies fiscal expenditure, tax revenues, and fiscal deficit (or surplus) into smaller groups. Their sum should be equal to zero by construction. Hence, equation (1) using n-itemized fiscal variables combined with this restriction can be always transformed into a new equation with $(n - 1)$ fiscal variables (Kneller, Bleaney, and Gemmell 1999).

$$X_{it}^* = A^*(L)X_{it}^* + f_i + \varepsilon_{it} \ , \ i = \text{country}, \ t = \text{year}$$

$$X_{it} \equiv \begin{bmatrix} growth_{it} \\ \Delta gini_{it} \\ \Delta E_{it} \end{bmatrix} \tag{3}$$

In (3), E_{it} is a vector or a scalar of itemized government spending, and the dimension of E_{it} is smaller than B_{it} by 1. Of course, the coefficients should be differently interpreted in consideration of substitutions. In other words, $A(L) \neq A^*(L)$.

Estimating (3) and drawing impulse response functions was done using the Stata code of Love and Zicchino (2006). Gini coefficients and fiscal variables are differenced in order to control non-stationarity. Lags of 4 were given, and shocks were assumed to occur in the order of real GDP growth, Gini coefficient, and fiscal spending.[9] It was also assumed that a contemporaneous shock would affect expense first and would later affect an individual component of expense. This ordering is consistent with the prior belief that fiscal policy is responsive to the state of the economy.

2. The single equation approach

Depending on the utilization of the panel structure of the data, the single equation approach can use either ordinary least squares (OLS) or panel regression. In this study, OLS measure how government spending influences GDP growth and the Gini coefficient respectively while controlled by other socioeconomic variables. The free use of control variables especially distinguishes this approach from PVAR. OLS will take the form of either (4) or (5).

$$growth_{it} = \gamma_1 E_{it-1} + \sum_{k=1}^{m} \beta_k Z_{it}^k + \varepsilon_{it}^1 , \tag{4}$$

$$gini_{it} = \gamma_2 E_{it-1} + \sum_{k=1}^{m} \alpha_k Z_{it}^k + \varepsilon_{it}^2 , \ i = \text{country}, \ t = \text{year}$$

$$growth_{it} = \gamma_1 E_{it} + \sum_{k=1}^{m} \beta_k Z_{it}^k + \delta D_i + \varepsilon_{it}^1 , \tag{5}$$

$$gini_{it} = \gamma_2 E_{it} + \sum_{k=1}^{m} \alpha_k Z_{it}^k + \delta D_i + \varepsilon_{it}^2 , \ i = \text{country}, \ t = \text{year}$$

In the above, D_i is a dummy variable representing income group or membership in ADB or OECD.

In the panel regression allowing fixed heterogeneity among economies (f_i), I estimated the following equations one by one. Furthermore, lagged dependent variables were used for explanatory ones. Only lagged fiscal variables (E_{it-1}) as well as control variables (Z_{it}^k) were used as regressors. Therefore, the estimation required the use of instrumental variables, and the equations in (6) are estimated by the Arellano and Bond (1991) method.

$$growth_{it} = \beta_1(L)\, growth_{it-1} + \gamma_1 E_{it-1} + \sum\nolimits_{k=3}^{m+2} \beta_k Z_{it}^k + f_i + \varepsilon_{it}^1 , \qquad (6)$$

$$gini_{it} = \alpha_1(L)\, gini_{it-1} + \gamma_2 E_{it-1} + \sum\nolimits_{k=3}^{m+2} \alpha_k Z_{it}^k + f_i + \varepsilon_{it}^2 , \quad i = \text{country}, \; t = \text{year}$$

D. Results

This section presents results from estimating (3)–(6) in the following order. To begin with, results from PVAR are provided in the form of impulse response functions (IRFs). Next, the results from OLS and the panel regression are shown in tables. Finally, long-term correlations of various fiscal expenditure items are reported with the GDP growth rate and the Gini coefficient.

1. Results from panel vector autoregression

The IRFs are drawn and interpreted in this section. Each of them is generated by Monte Carlo simulations with 500 repetitions. Areas between the upper and lower lines have a 90% confidence interval for IRFs over the next 6 years.

a. Estimation of the whole sample

The four-variable PVARs consist of government expense and a selected component of the expense as well as Gini_gross and real GDP growth.[10] First, Figure 4.6 draws the IRFs for expense and public spending on education. As for economic growth, public education spending is expected to have persistent and positive effects on GDP growth whereas the effect of expense is insignificant. On the other hand, increases in the two spending items are likely to raise the Gini coefficient temporarily. The negative effect of education spending on income inequality is almost negligible.

Second, Figure 4.7 draws the IRFs for expense and public health spending. The results are qualitatively the same as the three-variable PVAR. Hence, public health spending is likely to have a greater effect on growth than expense while its negative effect on the Gini coefficient is either insignificant or transient, just like expense.

Third, according to Figure 4.8, public gross fixed capital formation seems to have a significant positive effect on economic growth in the first year, while

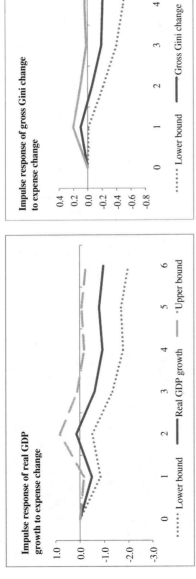

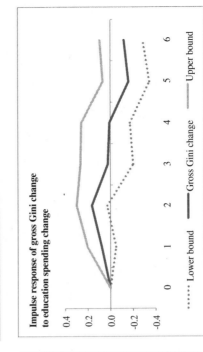

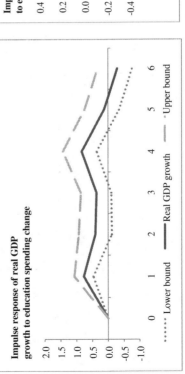

Figure 4.6 Four-variable panel vector autoregression for changes in expense and public education spending (% of GDP)

GDP = gross domestic product.

Source: Author's estimates.

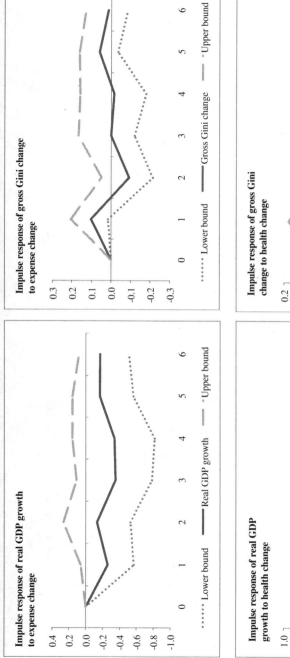

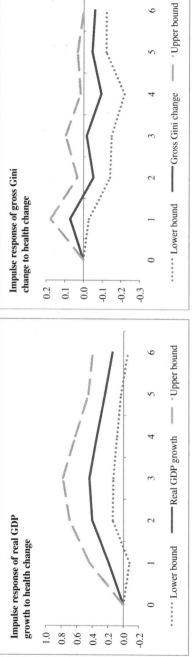

Figure 4.7 Four-variable panel vector autoregression for changes in expense and public health spending

GDP = gross domestic product.

Source: Author's estimates.

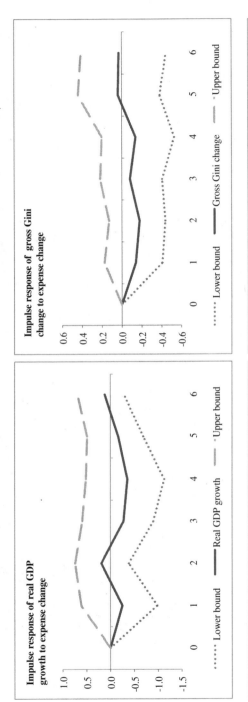
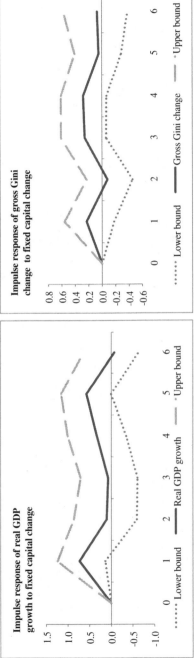

Figure 4.8 Four-variable panel vector autoregression for changes in expense and public gross fixed capital formation

GDP = gross domestic product.

Source: Author's estimates.

expense does not make any visible contributions to growth; however, neither has a significant effect on the Gini-coefficient.

Fourth, the effects from a change in social subsidies and transfers are quite similar to public health expenditure and public education spending (Figure 4.9). Social subsidies and transfers seem to have persistent and positive effects on GDP growth whereas they are likely to raise the Gini coefficient temporarily. This result is qualitatively the same as in the corresponding three-variable PVAR estimation.

The results of the four-variable PVARs are quite appealing in that gross fixed capital formation as well as public health spending, education spending, and social subsidies and transfers have significant positive effects on economic growth even temporarily; however, they still do not give a definitive answer on the effects of those items on income inequality. Some expenditures naturally tend to have a significant effect on the Gini-coefficient, but even so, the effects turn out to be short lived or positive, which is contrary to expectations.[11]

In this regard, I suspect two possibilities. The first one is that the distribution effects of fiscal spending items may accrue either contemporaneously or over the long term. For example, social subsidies and transfers or progressive income taxation have direct effects on income inequality. In contrast, public spending on education contributes to the income growth of a recipient only when she or he finishes school and earns income. Considering that it usually takes longer than 10 years to graduate from secondary educational institutions, the effect of public spending on education can be assessed over a decade or so. As previously stated, I chose the Gini_gross (Gini_market) coefficient in order to exclude contemporaneous effects. Furthermore, the current PVAR setup of yearly frequency does not allow a time frame long enough to observe the long-run effects of fiscal spending items on the Gini coefficients. In this context, I focus on measuring long-term effects using simple correlations between fiscal spending items and the Gini coefficient with lags. This issue will be covered in section 3.

The second possibility is that the PVAR setup and the variables included may not represent the uniqueness of the situation in which each economy is positioned. OLS and panel regressions with control variables could complement PVAR in this aspect. The results from running OLS and panel regression are provided and interpreted in section 2. I divided the dataset into the two groups (ADB members and OECD members) and ran four-variable PVAR separately in part (b).

b. Results from panel vector autoregression estimations by groups

The results are summarized in Figures 4.10, 4.11, and 4.12. Compared with using whole sample, I noticed that the growth effects of public health spending, public education spending, and social subsidies and transfers[12] were greater for OECD members. In contrast, increases in public health and public education spending seemed to alleviate income inequality significantly in ADB members, which is not supported in the previous PVAR estimation. Although insignificant, the IRF of the Gini_gross coefficient to transfers for ADB members is lower than that for OECD members (Figure 4.12).

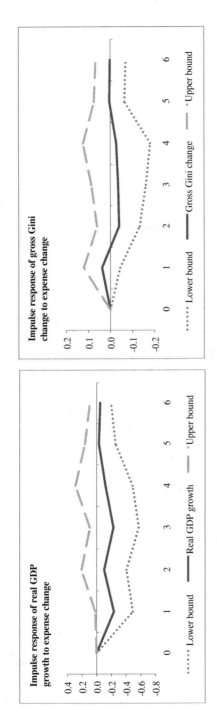

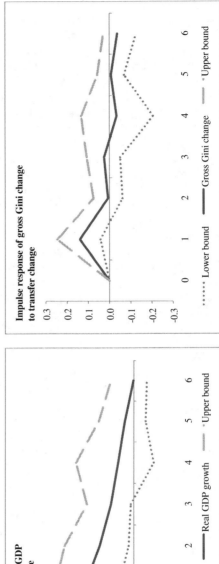

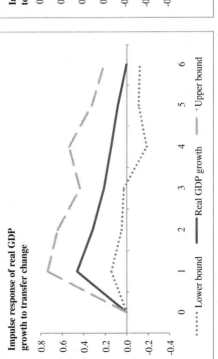

Figure 4.9 Four-variable panel vector autoregression for changes in expense and social subsidies and transfers

GDP = gross domestic product.

Source: Author's estimates.

(i) Organisation for Economic Co-operation and Development Members

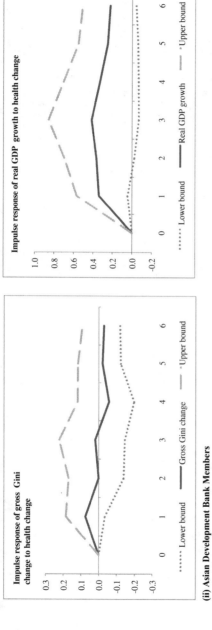

(ii) Asian Development Bank Members

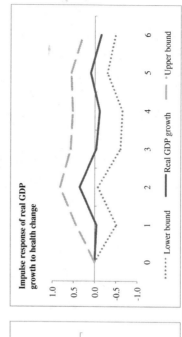

Figure 4.10 Four-variable panel vector autoregression for changes in expense and public health spending

gross Gini change = change in Gini before taxation and transfers.

Source: Author's estimates.

(i) Organisation for Economic Co-operation and Development Members

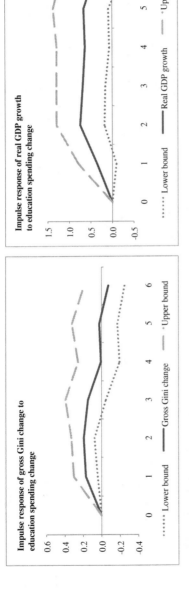

(ii) Asian Development Bank Members

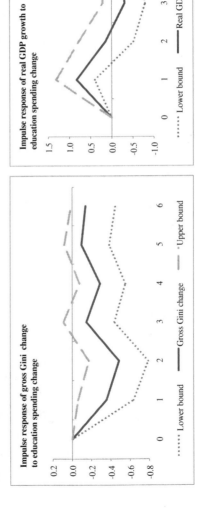

Figure 4.11 Four-variable panel vector autoregression for changes in expense and public education spending

gross Gini change = change in Gini before taxation and transfers.

Source: Author's estimates.

(i) Organisation for Economic Co-operation and Development Members

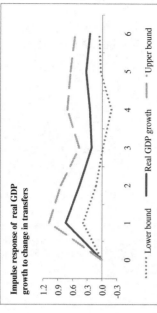

Impulse response of gross Gini change to change in transfers

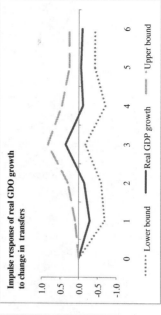

Impulse response of real GDP growth to change in transfers

(ii) Asian Development Bank Members

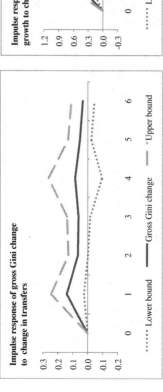

Impulse response of gross Gini change to change in transfers

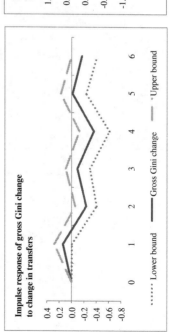

Impulse response of real GDO growth to change in transfers

Figure 4.12 Four-variable panel vector autoregression for changes in expense and transfers.
gross Gini change = change in Gini before taxation and transfers.
Source: Author's estimates.

These results are consistent with the reality in which developing economies allocate smaller portions of fiscal resources to health and education. Low-income households tend to have greater demand for public health and education and appreciate even a small increase in the shares of those fiscal spending items. Hence, positive distribution effects are more expected in developing economies.

c. Comparisons[13]

In this section the PVAR results from using the whole economy sample are compared with those from the ADB and OECD groups. To begin with, I report the sums of the impulse responses separately for ADB and OECD members.

The numbers in Table 4.3 are both significant and insignificant and thus tend to exaggerate effects. In contrast, Table 4.4 reports rather conservative estimates by summing only significant impulse responses.

Tables 4.5 and 4.6 report the sums of the estimated impulse responses for the whole economy sample.

Compared with public health and education spending, the effect of gross fixed capital formation on GDP growth seems slightly smaller; however, in the WDI data, gross fixed capital formation is available only for ADB members, whereas public health and education spending include both ADB and OECD members. Considering this limitation, the numbers marked with an "a" in Tables 4.5–4.8 could be compared with the numbers for ADB members in Table 4.3 and Table 4.4.

Summarizing Tables 4.7 and 4.8, gross fixed capital formation seems to have a greater positive effect on economic growth in ADB members than other fiscal spending items do. On the other hand, its negative impact on the Gini coefficient can be diluted by increasing spending on other items such as health and

Table 4.3 Estimates of cumulative impulse responses over 7 years (all responses included)

Gini_gross	health_change	edu_change	transfer_change
ADB	−1.004	−1.518	−0.735
OECD	−0.01	0.466	0.438
GDP growth	health_change	edu_change	transfer_change
ADB	0.109	0.476	−0.343
OECD	1.924	3.424	2.238

ADB = Asian Development Bank, GDP = gross domestic product, Gini_gross = Gini before taxation and transfers, edu_change = change in public education spending, health_change = change in public health spending, OECD = Organisation for Economic Co-operation and Development, transfer_change = change in social subsidies and transfers.

Note: ADB covers 33 of its 48 members, while OECD has its 34 members.

Source: Author's estimates.

Table 4.4 Estimates of cumulative impulse responses over 7 years (significant responses only)

Gini_gross	health_change	edu_change	transfer_change
ADB	−0.288	−1.13	−0.6
OECD	0	0.363	0.141
GDP growth	health_change	edu_change	transfer_change
ADB	0	0.827	0
OECD	0.338	2.708	1.776

ADB = Asian Development Bank, GDP = gross domestic product, Gini_gross = Gini before taxation and transfers, edu_change = change in public education spending, health_change = change in public health spending, OECD = Organisation for Economic Co-operation and Development, transfer_change = change in social subsidies and transfers.

Note: ADB covers 33 of its 48 members, while OECD has its 34 members.

Source: Author's estimates.

Table 4.5 Estimates of cumulative impulse responses over 7 years (whole economy, all responses included)

	health_change	edu_change	cap_change[a]	transfer_change
GDP growth	1.760	2.204	**1.735**	1.217
Gini_gross	−0.198	−0.011	**0.799**	0.093

cap_change = change in gross fixed capital formation, public; edu_change = change in public education spending; GDP = gross domestic product; Gini_gross = Gini before taxation and transfers; health_change = change in public health spending; transfer_change = change in social subsidies and transfers.

[a]Can be compared with Asian Development Bank results in tables 4.3 and 4.4.

Source: Author's estimates.

Table 4.6 Estimates of cumulative impulse responses over 7 years (whole economy, significant responses only)

	health_change	edu_change	cap_change[a]	transfer_change
GDP growth	1.428	1.597	**1.302**	0.986
Gini_gross	−0.059	0.164	**0**	0.139

cap_change = change in gross fixed capital formation, public; edu_change = change in public education spending; GDP = gross domestic product; Gini_gross = Gini before taxation and transfers; health_change = change in public health spending; transfer_change = change in social subsidies and transfers.

[a] Can be compared with Asian Development Bank results in tables 4.3 and 4.4.

Source: Author's estimates.

Table 4.7 Estimates of cumulative impulse responses over 7 years (ADB members, all responses included)

	health_change	edu_change	cap_change	trans_change
GDP growth	0.109	0.476	**1.735**[a]	−0.343
Gini_gross	−1.004	−1.518	**0.799**	−0.735

ADB = Asian Development Bank; cap_change = change in gross fixed capital formation, public; edu_change = change in public education spending; GDP = gross domestic product; Gini_gross = Gini before taxation and transfers; health_change = change in public health spending; transfer_change = change in social subsidies and transfers.

[a]Can be compared with Asian Development Bank results in Tables 4.3 and 4.4.

Source: Author's estimates.

Table 4.8 Estimates of cumulative impulse responses over 7 years (ADB members, significant responses only)

	health_change	edu_change	cap_change	trans_change
GDP growth	0	0.827	**1.302**[a]	0
Gini_gross	−0.288	−1.13	0	−0.6

ADB = Asian Development Bank; cap_change = change in gross fixed capital formation, public; edu_change = change in public education spending; GDP = gross domestic product; Gini_gross = Gini before taxation and transfers; health_change = change in public health spending; transfer_change = change in social subsidies and transfers.

[a]Can be compared with Asian Development Bank results in Tables 4.3 and 4.4.

Source: Author's estimates.

education. In this regard, gross fixed capital formation and public health and education spending complement each other in pursuing inclusive growth policies at least in developing countries.

2. Results from the single equation approach

The single equation approach is complementary to PVAR in that it is easy to implement and allows the free inclusion of control variables. On the other hand, it requires extra caution to eliminate endogeneity or misspecification from which PVAR is relatively free. The results were obtained by using observations from 164 countries. The extension of the dataset was somewhat necessary to prevent sample losses that might occur as more variables were added.

Tables 4.9–4.13 were obtained from running a pooled regression. Tables 4.10 and 4.13 differ from the rest in that they use one period–lagged variables for regressors in order to avoid endogeneity. Unlike PVAR, OLS allows not only control variables but also any number of fiscal expenditure items. In order to exploit the advantage of OLS, I included as many fiscal spending items as possible in the regression.

Table 4.9 shows consistently that public gross fixed capital investment contributes to growth better than any other fiscal spending item; however, that significant contribution disappears when all the regressors are lagged by one period (Table 4.10).

As for the distributional effect of fiscal expenditure items, social subsidies and transfers (transfer_exp) seem to significantly reduce income inequality regardless

Table 4.9 Real gross domestic product growth and fiscal expenditure items (pooled regression)

Variables	r_gdp_growth			
	(1)	(2)	(3)	(4)
health_exp	−1.091***	−0.792***	−0.224	
	(0.346)	(0.296)	(0.181)	
edu_exp	0.454*	0.171		
	(0.260)	(0.218)		
cap_exp	0.236**	0.222**	0.210***	0.148**
	(0.110)	(0.101)	(0.0723)	(0.0656)
transfer_exp	0.000456			
	(0.00106)			
expense	−0.0791			
	(0.101)			
fiscal_surplus	0.436***	0.425***	0.315***	0.345***
	(0.107)	(0.104)	(0.0753)	(0.0641)
fiscal_debt	−0.0148	−0.0246**	−0.0191***	−0.0178***
	(0.0121)	(0.0103)	(0.00643)	(0.00590)
OECD member	4.804**	0.875	0.581	0.789
	(2.079)	(1.458)	(1.075)	(1.023)
ADB member	−0.132	0.478	1.515***	2.477***
	(0.738)	(0.700)	(0.530)	(0.474)
Constant	7.503***	6.758***	5.258***	4.115***
	(1.455)	(1.254)	(0.779)	(0.502)
Observations	195	211	332	427
R-squared	0.216	0.186	0.162	0.181

ADB = Asian Development Bank; cap_exp = gross fixed capital formation, public (% of GDP); edu_exp = public spending on education (% of GDP); expense = expense (% of GDP); fiscal_debt = Central Government debt, total (% of GDP); fiscal_surplus = cash surplus/deficit (% of GDP); health_exp = health expenditure, public (% of GDP); OECD = Organisation for Economic Co-operation and Development; r_gdp_growth = real gross domestic product growth; transfer_exp = subsidies and other transfers (% of GDP).

Notes: Standard errors are in parentheses; *** $p < 0.01$, ** $p < 0.05$, * $p < 0.1$.

Source: Author's estimates.

Table 4.10 Real gross domestic product growth and lagged fiscal expenditure items (pooled regression)

VARIABLES	(1)	(2)	(3)	(4)
	r_gdp_growth	r_gdp_growth	r_gdp_growth	r_gdp_growth
health_exp (−1)	−0.473 (0.371)	−0.417 (0.352)	−0.0923 (0.211)	
edu_exp (−1)	0.231 (0.279)	0.287 (0.254)		
cap_exp (−1)	0.122 (0.118)	0.135 (0.115)	0.192** (0.0820)	0.0795 (0.0711)
transfer_exp (−1)	0.00101 (0.00114)	0.00141* (0.000799)	0.000333 (0.000508)	0.000522 (0.000447)
expense (−1)	0.0534 (0.109)			
fiscal_surplus (−1)	0.167 (0.115)	0.156 (0.113)	0.110 (0.0789)	0.195*** (0.0677)
fiscal_debt (−1)	−0.000279 (0.0130)	0.00117 (0.0126)	−0.00406 (0.00736)	−0.000382 (0.00706)
OECD member	2.259 (2.232)	2.351 (2.219)	0.979 (1.402)	1.342 (1.507)
ADB member	2.006** (0.792)	1.929** (0.775)	1.583*** (0.565)	2.618*** (0.521)
Constant	2.170 (1.562)	2.426 (1.469)	3.740*** (0.945)	3.067*** (0.807)
Observations	195	195	311	392
R-squared	0.088	0.087	0.070	0.090

ADB = Asian Development Bank; cap_exp = gross fixed capital formation, public (% of GDP); edu_exp = public spending on education (% of GDP); expense = expense (% of GDP); fiscal_debt = Central Government debt, total (% of GDP); fiscal_surplus = cash surplus/deficit (% of GDP); health_exp = health expenditure, public (% of GDP); OECD = Organisation for Economic Co-operation and Development; r_gdp_growth = real gross domestic product growth; transfer_exp = subsidies and other transfers (% of GDP).

Notes: Standard errors are in parentheses; *** p < 0.01, ** p < 0.05, * p < 0.1.

Source: Author's estimates.

of inequality measures. Table 4.11 is based on Gini_gross coeffcients, while Table 4.12 uses Gini_net coefficients. In both cases, the coefficients to transfer_exp turn out to be significantly negative.

Table 4.13 estimates the contribution of each fiscal expenditure item on income inequality using one period lagged explanatory variables, and it still

Table 4.11 Gini_gross coefficient and fiscal expenditure items (pooled regression)

Variables	gini_gross			
	(1)	*(2)*	*(3)*	*(4)*
health_exp	0.559	0.581	0.626**	−0.158**
	(0.674)	(0.620)	(0.254)	(0.066)
edu_exp	−0.433	−0.419	−0.305	
	(0.446)	(0.412)	(0.228)	
cap_exp	0.104	0.108		
	(0.202)	(0.197)		
transfer_exp	−0.0039**	−0.0038***	−0.0013***	−0.002***
	(0.002)	(0.001)	(0.000)	(0.000)
expense	0.0155			
	(0.187)			
fiscal_surplus	−0.0790	−0.0837	−0.158**	−0.170***
	(0.199)	(0.190)	(0.066)	(0.057)
fiscal_debt	−0.0190	−0.0187	0.000900	0.00377
	(0.0217)	(0.0212)	(0.008)	(0.007)
OECD member	−0.391	−0.368	−1.587*	−1.183
	(3.528)	(3.506)	(0.926)	(0.820)
ADB member	0.964	0.942	2.260**	2.728***
	(1.343)	(1.312)	(0.882)	(0.752)
Constant	46.46***	46.54***	43.79***	44.50***
	(2.729)	(2.558)	(1.224)	(0.878)
Observations	177	177	536	782
R-squared	0.115	0.115	0.077	0.121

ADB = Asian Development Bank; cap_exp = gross fixed capital formation, public (% of GDP); edu_exp = public spending on education (% of GDP); expense = expense (% of GDP); fiscal_ debt = Central Government debt, total (% of GDP); fiscal_surplus = cash surplus/deficit (% of GDP); gini_gross = Gini before taxation and transfers; health_exp = health expenditure, public (% of GDP); OECD = Organisation for Economic Co-operation and Development; transfer_ exp = subsidies and other transfers (% of GDP).

Notes: Standard errors are in parentheses; *** $p < 0.01$, ** $p < 0.05$, * $p < 0.1$.

Source: Author's estimates.

confirms that social subsidies and transfers (transfer_exp) reduce income inequality significantly.

The results from the dynamic panel regression are reported in Table 4.14 and Table 4.15. Table 4.14 confirms that public education spending contributes the most to real GDP growth. In contrast, according to Table 4.15, there is no significant fiscal expenditure item that affects the Gini coefficient.

Table 4.12 Gini_net coefficient and fiscal expenditure items (pooled regression)

Variables	gini_net			
	(1)	*(2)*	*(3)*	*(4)*
health_exp	0.656	−0.126	−0.126	
	(0.650)	(0.226)	(0.226)	
edu_exp	−0.353	−0.908***	−0.898***	−0.927***
	(0.430)	(0.213)	(0.203)	(0.174)
cap_exp	0.0324			
	(0.194)			
transfer_exp	−0.00788***	−0.00340***	−0.00334***	−0.00341***
	(0.00180)	(0.000503)	(0.000357)	(0.000356)
expense	0.163	0.00665		
	(0.180)	(0.0434)		
fiscal_surplus	−0.0387	−0.234***	−0.236***	−0.139**
	(0.192)	(0.0608)	(0.0591)	(0.0579)
fiscal_debt	−0.0161	0.00661	0.00709	0.00837
	(0.0209)	(0.00815)	(0.00751)	(0.00748)
OECD member	−3.564	−5.966***	−5.964***	−6.688***
	(3.400)	(0.825)	(0.824)	(0.639)
ADB member	2.479*	1.393*	1.376*	0.832
	(1.294)	(0.793)	(0.785)	(0.713)
Constant	43.24***	47.23***	47.27***	47.39***
	(2.630)	(1.110)	(1.089)	(1.027)
Observations	177	536	536	589
R-squared	0.312	0.630	0.630	0.617

ADB = Asian Development Bank; cap_exp = gross fixed capital formation, public (% of GDP); edu_exp = public spending on education (% of GDP); expense = expense (% of GDP); fiscal_debt = Central Government debt, total (% of GDP); fiscal_surplus = cash surplus/deficit (% of GDP); gini_net = Gini after taxation and transfers; health_exp = health expenditure, public (% of GDP); OECD = Organisation for Economic Co-operation and Development; transfer_exp = subsidies and other transfers (% of GDP).

Notes: Standard errors are in parentheses; *** $p < 0.01$, ** $p < 0.05$, * $p < 0.1$.

Source: Author's estimates.

3. Long-term relationships among key variables

In this section, I measure the long-run effects of itemized fiscal spending on growth and income inequality using simple correlations. First, I calculated correlations with 10-year lags. In the upper half of Table 4.16, no fiscal spending items (in differences) have significant positive effects on real GDP growth. On

Table 4.13 Gini coefficients and lagged fiscal expenditure items (pooled regression)

Variables	gini_gross	gini_net
	(1)	(2)
health_exp (−1)	0.503	0.518
	(0.691)	(0.652)
edu_exp (−1)	−0.558	−0.550
	(0.471)	(0.444)
cap_exp (−1)	0.123	0.0661
	(0.211)	(0.199)
transfer_exp (−1)	−0.00347*	−0.00779***
	(0.00198)	(0.00186)
expense (−1)	0.0528	0.231
	(0.199)	(0.187)
fiscal_surplus (−1)	0.0156	0.0468
	(0.211)	(0.199)
fiscal_debt (−1)	−0.0170	−0.0192
	(0.0228)	(0.0215)
OECD member	−1.613	−4.670
	(3.598)	(3.395)
ADB member	0.698	2.073
	(1.417)	(1.337)
Constant	45.65***	42.75***
	(2.926)	(2.761)
Observations	166	166
R-squared	0.091	0.297

ADB = Asian Development Bank; cap_exp = gross fixed capital formation, public (% of GDP); edu_exp = public spending on education (% of GDP); expense = expense (% of GDP); fiscal_debt = Central Government debt, total (% of GDP); fiscal_surplus = cash surplus/deficit (% of GDP); gini_gross = Gini before taxation and transfers; gini_net = Gini after taxation and transfers; health_exp = health expenditure, public (% of GDP); OECD = Organisation for Economic Co-operation and Development; transfer_exp = subsidies and other transfers (% of GDP).

Notes: Standard errors are in parentheses; *** $p < 0.01$, ** $p < 0.05$, * $p < 0.1$.

Source: Author's estimates.

the other hand, with the exceptions of public gross capital formation and military spending, all fiscal expenditure items have negative and significant effects on the Gini_gross (Gini_market) coefficient and are thus likely to reduce income inequality.

Next, I get the bottom half of Table 4.16 by taking 10-year averages of the variables for the 1990s and 2000s. The results confirm the effect of fiscal

Table 4.14 Real gross domestic product growth and lagged fiscal expenditure items (dynamic panel regression)

Variables	r_gdp_growth		
	(1)	*(2)*	*(3)*
r_gdp_growth (−1)	0.0475	0.0511	0.0516
	(0.0998)	(0.0951)	(0.0521)
r_gdp_growth (−2)	−0.219**	−0.214**	−0.281***
	(0.0962)	(0.0928)	(0.0502)
health_exp (−1)	−3.025**	−2.183*	−1.091***
	(1.371)	(1.298)	(0.350)
edu_exp (−1)	1.509*	1.201	1.131**
	(0.859)	(0.770)	(0.462)
cap_exp (−1)	−0.213	0.0967	
	(0.309)	(0.254)	
transfer_exp (−1)	0.000171		
	(0.00390)		
expense (−1)	0.161		
	(0.270)		
fiscal_surplus (−1)	0.122	0.0238	0.144
	(0.262)	(0.241)	(0.0914)
fiscal_debt (−1)	0.0869**	0.0627	0.0348*
	(0.0421)	(0.0383)	(0.0181)
Constant	1.990	3.457	2.223
	(6.063)	(5.306)	(2.864)
Observations	122	135	439
Number of countries	35	38	72

cap_exp = gross fixed capital formation, public (% of GDP); edu_exp = public spending on education (% of GDP); expense = expense (% of GDP); fiscal_debt = Central Government debt, total (% of GDP); fiscal_surplus = cash surplus/deficit (% of GDP); health_exp = health expenditure, public (% of GDP); r_gdp_growth = real gross domestic product growth; transfer_exp = subsidies and other transfers (% of GDP).

Notes: Standard errors are in parentheses; *** $p < 0.01$, ** $p < 0.05$, * $p < 0.1$.

Source: Author's estimates.

spending items on the Gini coefficient again but with a low significance level; however, correlations with real GDP growth become negative except for public gross capital formation and military spending (in differences). By construction, the two period panel data in the bottom half take an average lag of 5 years. I suspect that the time frame of 5 years may not be long enough to see the long-run effect accrue and the short-run effect dissipate.

Table 4.15 Gini coefficient and lagged fiscal expenditure items (dynamic panel regression)

Variables	gini_gross			
	(1)	*(2)*	*(3)*	*(4)*
gini_market (−1)	0.501***	0.789***	0.798***	0.779***
	(0.0908)	(0.0447)	(0.0436)	(0.0409)
gini_market (−2)	0.189*	−0.147***	−0.150***	−0.115***
	(0.104)	(0.0411)	(0.0404)	(0.0382)
health_exp (−1)	−0.384	0.107	0.117	
	(0.389)	(0.102)	(0.100)	
edu_exp (−1)	−0.396	−0.215	−0.274*	−0.221
	(0.261)	(0.155)	(0.150)	(0.138)
cap_exp (−1)	−0.0900			
	(0.0972)			
transfer_exp (−1)	−0.00173	−5.70e-06		
	(0.00123)	(0.000273)		
expense (−1)	0.203**	0.0466**	0.0447**	0.0457**
	(0.0840)	(0.0228)	(0.0184)	(0.0181)
fiscal_surplus (−1)	−0.113	−0.0733***	−0.0770***	−0.0872***
	(0.0803)	(0.0277)	(0.0274)	(0.0248)
fiscal_debt (−1)	−0.00894	−0.0333***	−0.0323***	−0.0335***
	(0.0118)	(0.00614)	(0.00573)	(0.00553)
Constant	13.73***	16.13***	16.21***	15.86***
	(4.118)	(1.309)	(1.292)	(1.206)
Observations	103	396	409	452
Number of countries	32	64	67	72

cap_exp = gross fixed capital formation, public (% of GDP); edu_exp = public spending on education (% of GDP); expense = expense (% of GDP); fiscal_debt = Central Government debt, total (% of GDP); fiscal_surplus = cash surplus/deficit (% of GDP); gini_gross (or gini_market) = Gini before taxation and transfers; gini_net = Gini after taxation and transfers; health_exp = health expenditure, public (% of GDP); transfer_exp = subsidies and other transfers (% of GDP).

Notes: Standard errors are in parentheses; *** $p < 0.01$, ** $p < 0.05$, * $p < 0.1$.

Source: Author's estimates.

Summing up, there are significant long-term correlations between lagged fiscal spending items and the current Gini coefficient. In contrast, any correlation with real GDP growth is insignificant. Combined with the results from the previous sections, Table 4.16 indicates that the contributions of individual spending items to economic growth and income inequality should be measured over different time frames.

Table 4.16 Correlations between key variables and their notations

Spending Items (t years)	Real GDP growth (t + 10 years)	Gini_market (t + 10 years)
education_exp	0.012 (0.745)	–0.083**(0.013)
cap_exp	–0.030 (0.559)	0.165***(0.002)
health_exp	–0.010(0.841)	–0.152***(0.003)
transfer_exp	0.016 (0.779)	–0.289*** (0.000)
mil_exp	–0.043 (0.246)	0.043 (0.256)
gfce	–0.019 (0.402)	–0.172***(0.000)
Spending Items (during 1990~1999)	Real GDP growth (during 2000~2010)	Gini_market (during 2000~2010)
education_exp	–0.538***(0.000)	–0.196+(0.155)
cap_exp	0.082 (0.718)	0.276(0.215)
health_exp	–0.672*** (0.000)	–0.198+(0.125)
transfer_exp	–0.721*** (0.000)	–0.308* (0.053)
mil_exp	0.154 (0.248)	0.066 (0.624)
gfce	–0.382***(0.002)	–0.256**(0.045)

cap_exp = gross fixed capital formation, public (% of GDP); edu_exp = public spending on education (% of GDP); expense = expense (% of GDP); GDP = gross domestic product; gfce = government financial consumption expenditures (% of GDP); health_exp = health expenditure, public (% of GDP); transfer_exp = subsidies and other transfers (% of GDP).

Notes: The numbers in ( ) are significance levels of the correlation coefficients.

*** $p < 0.01$, ** $p < 0.05$, * $p < 0.1$, and + $p < 0.15$.

Source: Author's estimates.

4. Contemporaneous relationships among key variables

VAR, by construction, is useful for evaluating contemporaneous effects among endogenous variables depending on shock identification strategies; however, contemporaneous effects on income inequality cannot be precisely estimated by PVAR because the Gini_gross coefficients are used. Hence, in this section, I estimate the contemporaneous effects of fiscal composition on income inequality separately.

a. Difference between gini_gross and gini_net

First, I define Gini_diff to be Gini_gross minus (–) Gini_net. Accordingly, the greater the Gini_diff is, the more redistributive the fiscal system is. The scatter plots in Figure 4.13 exhibit the relationships between the Gini_diff and various components of fiscal expenditure. Keeping in mind that these scatter plots detect contemporaneous relationships between any pair of variables, we see that all the

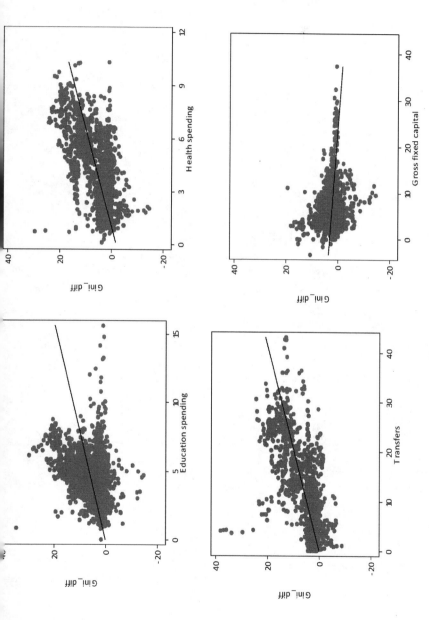

Figure 4.13 Gini_diff and government expense (% of gross domestic product)

Gini_diff = difference between Gini_gross (Gini before taxation and transfers) and Gini_net (Gini after taxation and transfers).

Source: Author's estimates.

Table 4.17 Correlation of poverty gap with Gini coefficients

Correlation with Gini coefficients	Poverty gap at the national poverty line (%)	Gini_net	Gini_market
Poverty gap at the national poverty line (%)	1.000		
Gini_net	0.441 (0.000)	1.000	
Gini_market	0.348 (0.000)	0.854 (0.000)	1.000

Gini_market = Gini before taxation and transfers, Gini_net = Gini after taxation and transfers.

Source: Author's estimates.

fiscal spending components tend to work for redistribution with the exception of public gross capital formation.

The subplots in Figure 4.13 are regressed on various fiscal expenditure items. For a dependent variable, Gini_diff (Gini_gross–Gini_net) is used, and the estimated slope coefficients measure the contemporaneous effects of fiscal spending items on economic inequality. Here the positive coefficients indicate that the corresponding fiscal expenditure items tend to alleviate economic inequality.

b. The poverty gap at the national poverty line

As mentioned previously, the poverty gap is not a precise measure for income inequality. The two are, however, closely related and complementary as proxies for social cohesion. Table 4.17 demonstrates that the poverty gap has significant and positive correlations with the two Gini coefficients, but the correlations are less than 1. Furthermore, some definitions of inclusive growth (Ranieri and Ramos 2013) include poverty reduction. In this context, I substituted poverty gap at the national poverty line (%) for the Gini_diff and examined its relationships with fiscal spending composition.

As with Gini_diff, the scatter plots in Figure 4.14 show that all the fiscal spending components tend to work for redistribution with the exception of public gross capital formation.

E. Policy implications

This chapter examines the effects of fiscal policy on income inequality and growth with an emphasis on the composition of fiscal expenditure using cross-country panel data. The results were the following:

- Gross fixed capital formation, public health spending, and education spending have significant positive effects on economic growth.

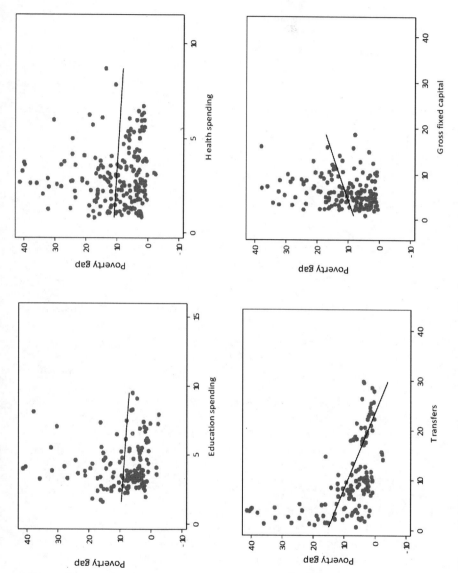

Figure 4.14 Poverty gap and government expense (% of gross domestic product)
Source: Author's estimates.

- The positive effects of health and education spending on growth tend to be more persistent than those of gross fixed capital formation.
- The effects of fiscal spending items on the Gini coefficient are either temporarily positive or negligible in the annual frequency with the exception of social subsidies and transfers.
- Compared with OECD members, public health spending and public education spending seem to alleviate income inequality significantly. This implies that fiscal expenditure policy may contribute more to inclusive growth in developing economies than in advanced ones.
- The distributional effects of fiscal expenditure items occur in the long run. All the fiscal expenditure items have negative and significant effects on the Gini coefficient with the exceptions of public gross capital formation and military spending with 10-year lags. An examination of contemporaneous distribution effects confirms a similar pattern.

Based on these results, I recommend that the following should be implemented in designing fiscal expenditures for inclusive growth.

- Estimate multipliers of individual fiscal spending items using a time series of a single economy, then order them according to their magnitudes. This study uses a panel dataset and cannot consider economy-specific factors thoroughly. For example, PVAR reflects the heterogeneity of each economy only by fixed effect and ignores differences in transmission channels across economies. In this respect, it would be more useful to use the time series data of a single economy to estimate various fiscal multipliers.[14] In the meantime, we should also be cautious about interpreting the results from the cross-country data and applying them to policy making.
- Reducing income inequality is not a goal that can be achieved in the short term; hence, a solution is to increase the portion of fiscal spending items that have substantial direct effects on the Gini coefficient. Items such as social subsidies and transfers and public health spending are known to have greater direct effects on alleviating income inequality. Another solution is to increase the size of a spending program that has greater potential to reduce inequality in the long run. Compared with the first option, the latter seems not to be feasible in that the time frame of most politicians will be definitely shorter than a decade.
- In pursuing inclusive growth, coordination with tax policy is crucial. Matched with adjustments in the composition of fiscal spending, changes in the composition of various tax items could be considered and vice versa. In reality, however, spending is more flexible than taxation in most countries. Thus, adjustments in fiscal spending should be made after considering tax policies and other social and macroeconomic needs. An approach by Cournède, Goujard, and Pina (2013) is a good example of how an understanding of the multipliers of various fiscal items over time can be applied to find an optimal mix of expenditures and tax revenues.

- Note that the government may replace the private sector in some fiscal spending areas. For example, spending on education and health and public investment are shared by both entities, private and public. In other words, public spending in an area may crowd out (or crowd in, though this is less likely) its private counterpart. In the case of crowding out, expansionary fiscal spending could result in lower or ineffective fiscal multipliers. Crowding in is also a concern because it may lead to excessive government supported resource allocations.

Table 4.18 confirms that crowding out is likely between public and private contributions in gross fixed capital formation, while in contrast, the public and private sectors appear complementary in health expenditure. Careful examination is thus required as part of "the science of delivery" to assess the consequences of crowding out or crowding in in every fiscal activity. Improving the delivery of public programs will help governments design fiscal programs so that both public and private spending may contribute to inclusive growth. Without an enhanced delivery system, increased fiscal activity cannot achieve what it is intended for. In this context, micro-level program evaluation could be useful.

- Fiscal programs with different targets and means can be compared in terms of both efficiency and equity; such an assessment, of course, should be based on a complete understanding of the entire delivery system of those programs. Program evaluation has been recently highlighted as a means for enhancing the efficiency of fiscal programs, mostly on the expenditure side. In principle, program evaluations should measure the effectiveness and the efficiency of any public program, and as with others, any fiscal programs intended for inclusive growth should be assessed thoroughly.

For this purpose, policy targets should be defined properly. For example, poverty, inequality, gender inequality, social protection, and basic social services are targets of inclusive growth and are especially related to inclusiveness. On the other hand, barriers for investment and access to infrastructure are linked with economic growth. Productive employment serves both. Next, those targets should be matched with proper proxies. Finding a good proxy is key in program evaluation because selecting a bad proxy may lead to incorrect conclusions. Additionally, the proxies should take the form of indices because quantifiable indices allow the application of statistical methods in assessing the performance of individual programs.

- As mentioned previously, coordination with tax policy is critical in pursuing fiscal policies for inclusive growth, especially when the size of government debt matters. In this context, it would be worthwhile to discuss how public–private partnership (PPP) investments could replace fiscal resources and contribute to inclusive growth. Developing economies are likely to be constrained by narrow tax bases and low levels of capital accumulation

Table 4.18 Crowding out versus crowding in

Changes in the Share of Gross Fixed Capital Formation to GDP	Whole Sample (WDI)	Per capita GDP less than $5,000	Per capita GDP greater than $5,000	Public Sector		
				~1997	1998~2008	2008~
Private sector	-0.1684***	-0.1675***	-0.2277*	-0.1336***	-0.2026***	-0.3102***
	(0.000)	(0.000)	(0.062)	(0.000)	(0.000)	(0.000)

Changes in the share of Health Expenditure to GDP	Whole Sample (WDI)	Per capita GDP less than $5,000	Per capita GDP greater than $5,000	Public Sector		
				~1997	1998~2008	2008~
Private sector	0.0874***	0.0857***	0.3513+	0.3371***	0.0563**	0.0734+
	(0.000)	(0.000)	(0.1089)	(0.000)	(0.018)	(0.1092)

GDP = gross domestic product, WDI = World Development Indicators.

Note: Correlations are calculated with the whole-country data in WDI.

Source: Author's estimates.

whereas they have higher demand for investment in social overhead capital. In this context, public–private infrastructure investment has been widely recommended. Investment in transportation infrastructure (road, railways, and ports); electricity networks (generation facilities, transmission and distribution systems); and water supply (drinking water and irrigation for agriculture) is a key determinant of economic growth. Furthermore, developing economies can get greater benefits from building social overhead capital thanks to the higher rate of returns. Therefore, financing such investments is considered to be a crucial condition for a developing economy in pursuing long-term growth; however, their domestic financial markets have yet to mature. They cannot afford the domestic demand for infrastructure investment without government guarantees. In these circumstances, PPPs allow a government to meet fiscal demands – especially for social overhead capital – by mobilizing private funds. That explains why public–private infrastructure investment attracts the attention of public officials in developing economies.

Using PPPs cannot be limited to building social overhead capital. The results in previous sections confirm that public health expenditure and public education spending are more likely to alleviate income inequality in ADB members. What if a government were to allocate financial resources to those areas through PPPs instead of using tax money? Building new public schools and hospitals and installing proper equipment represents a substantial fiscal burden. It would be beneficial to mobilize private funds for those purposes.

Still the question of whether private investors are willing to take on this role remains. In this sense, a key to successfully introducing PPPs in these areas lies in the profitability of the project and the assurance that private investors will be paid as agreed initially. In practice, the government provides a certain form of payment guarantee (including minimum revenue guarantees) in order to attract private investors. Substantial guarantees, however, may become fiscal burdens. Thus, the government needs to restrict PPPs to areas with a certain level of profitability anticipated. For example, forecasting demand for local medical services is relatively easier with socioeconomic data, and the willingness to pay can also be calculated. Based on those estimates, the profitability of building a new hospital in a region can be assessed. In building infrastructure, demand forecast is affected by various factors, some of which are neither directly observable nor perceivable. Compared with social overhead capital, PPPs in health and education tend to be smaller in size and easier to implement; their creative use in pursuing inclusive growth could lighten the public fiscal burden substantially.

Appendix: Summary statistics

Table A4.1 All economies

Variable	Observations	Mean	Standard deviation	Minimum	Maximum
cap_exp	628	7.01	4.7	–1.58	38.57
edu_exp	1,373	4.5	1.64	0	11.9
expense	852	27.5	11.16	7.59	62.82
gfce	2,670	15.59	5.97	1.38	43.41
gini_gross	2,242	41.58	8	21.98	79.36
gini_net	2,242	34.28	9.97	15.71	80.41
global_equity_index	869	10.85	36.24	–78.76	254.5
gs_expense	836	4.04	3.01	0.95	25.87
health_exp	1,049	4.28	2.44	0.27	10.31
income_tax	898	6.85	4.36	0.26	22.15
life_exp	3,272	68.14	9.78	19.5	85.16
literacy	153	84.37	18.66	20.57	99.8
market_cap	1,221	60.88	67.81	0.04	606
mil_exp	1,347	2.2	1.67	0.13	17.96
primary_edu	659	29.58	17.21	0	80.4
r_gdp_growth	2,633	4.06	4.88	–44.90	42.41
revenue	899	25.96	10.57	2.94	51.12
secondary_edu	653	44.24	16.67	2.9	80.2
social_contribution	622	8.01	5.79	0	20.46
tax_revenue	900	16.87	6.43	2.5	35.78
tertiary_edu	659	23.67	9.78	2.1	57.1
transfer_exp	826	14.34	9.47	0.03	39.17
unemployment	1,324	6.89	4.13	0.1	36.4

cap_exp = gross fixed capital formation, public (% of GDP); edu_exp = public spending on education (% of GDP); expense = expense (% of GDP); GDP = gross domestic product; gfce = government final consumption expenditures (% of GDP); gini_gross = Gini before taxation and transfers; gini_net = Gini after taxation and transfers; global_equity_index = S&P Global Equity Indices (annual % change); gs_expense = goods and services expense (% of GDP); health_exp = health expenditure, public (% of GDP); income_tax = taxes on income, profits, and capital gains (% of GDP); life_exp = life expectancy at birth, total (years); literacy = literacy rate, adult total (% of pop ages 15 and above); market_cap = market capitalization (% of GDP); mil_exp = military expenditure (% of GDP); primary_edu = labor force with primary education (% of total pop ages 15–64); r_gdp_growth = real GDP growth; revenue = revenue excluding grants (% of GDP); secondary_edu = labor force with secondary education (% of total population ages 15–64); social_contribution = social contributions (% of GDP); tax_revenue = tax revenue (% of GDP); tertiary_edu = labor force with tertiary education (% of total population ages 15–64); transfer_exp = subsidies and other transfers (% of GDP); unemployment = unemployment, total (%).

Source: Author's calculations based on the World Development Indicators online database (accessed 7 September 2013).

Table A4.2 Organization for Economic Co-operation and Development members

Variable	Observations.	Mean	Standard Deviation	Minimum	Maximum
cap_exp	64	5.14	2.04	2.79	12.09
edu_exp	907	5.07	1.39	0	8.98
expense	492	34.57	8.87	13.35	62.82
gfce	1,563	17.92	5.32	5.64	43.41
gini_gross	1,340	40.36	6.44	22.83	65.79
gini_net	1,340	29.84	7.12	15.71	70.53
global_equity_index	646	10.25	33.1	−69.94	254.5
gs_expense	492	3.5	2.35	0.95	15.55
health_exp	561	6.1	1.55	1.94	10.27
income_tax	492	8.97	4.14	2.29	22.15
life_exp	1,712	73.81	4.94	45.38	85.16
literacy	57	92.91	7.97	61.63	99.8
market_cap	778	62.16	52.97	0.17	479.81
mil_exp	783	2.07	1.78	0.13	17.96
primary_edu	558	28.75	17.22	0	80.4
revenue	492	33	8.17	11.22	51.12
r_gdp_growth	1,480	3.24	3.41	−14.57	42.41
secondary_edu	552	45.72	16.16	2.9	80.2
social_contribution	469	10.19	4.94	0.02	20.46
tax_revenue	493	20.16	6.03	7.84	35.78
tertiary_edu	558	24.6	9.39	7.1	57.1
transfer_exp	481	20.84	6.71	6.18	39.17
unemployment	908	7.55	3.88	0.6	23.9

cap_exp = gross fixed capital formation, public (% of GDP); edu_exp = public spending on education (% of GDP); expense = expense (% of GDP); GDP = gross domestic product; gfce = government final consumption expenditures (% of GDP); gini_gross = Gini before taxation and transfers; gini_net = Gini after taxation and transfers; global_equity_index = S&P Global Equity Indices (annual % change); gs_expense = goods and services expense (% of GDP); health_exp = health expenditure, public (% of GDP); income_tax = taxes on income, profits, and capital gains (% of GDP); life_exp = life expectancy at birth, total (years); literacy = literacy rate, adult total (% of pop ages 15 and above); market_cap = market capitalization (% of GDP); mil_exp = military expenditure (% of GDP); primary_edu = labor force with primary education (% of total pop ages 15–64); r_gdp_growth = real GDP growth; revenue = revenue excluding grants (% of GDP); secondary_edu = labor force with secondary education (% of total population ages 15–64); social_contribution = social contributions (% of GDP); tax_revenue = tax revenue (% of GDP); tertiary_edu = labor force with tertiary education (% of total population ages 15–64); transfer_exp = subsidies and other transfers (% of GDP); unemployment = unemployment, total (%).

Source: Author's estimates.

Table A4.3 Asian Development Bank members

Variable	Observations	Mean	Standard Deviation	Minimum	Maximum
cap_exp	564	7.22	4.87	−1.58	38.57
edu_exp	466	3.41	1.52	0.83	11.9
expense	360	17.85	5.09	7.59	36.55
gfce	1,107	12.29	5.25	1.38	35.78
gini_gross	902	43.39	9.6	21.98	79.36
gini_net	902	40.87	9.95	18.76	80.41
global_equity_index	223	12.57	44.13	−78.76	147.18
gs_expense	344	4.81	3.63	1.13	25.87
health_exp	488	2.18	1.33	0.27	10.31
income_tax	406	4.29	3.04	0.26	14.49
life_exp	1,560	61.92	9.99	19.5	83.42
literacy	96	79.31	21.22	20.57	99.76
market_cap	443	58.63	88.04	0.04	606
mil_exp	564	2.38	1.49	0.23	9.36
primary_edu	101	34.21	16.47	2.9	68.7
revenue	407	17.45	5.81	2.94	37.69
r_gdp_growth	1,153	5.13	6.12	−44.90	35.38
secondary_edu	101	36.15	17.14	7.2	76.1
social_contribution	153	1.35	1.54	0	6.66
tax_revenue	407	12.87	4.27	2.5	28.71
tertiary_edu	101	18.51	10.33	2.1	50
transfer_exp	345	5.29	3.33	0.03	15.17
unemployment	416	5.46	4.31	0.1	36.4

cap_exp = gross fixed capital formation, public (% of GDP); edu_exp = public spending on education (% of GDP); expense = expense (% of GDP); GDP = gross domestic product; gfce = government final consumption expenditures (% of GDP); gini_gross = Gini before taxation and transfers; gini_net = Gini after taxation and transfers; global_equity_index = S&P Global Equity Indices (annual % change); gs_expense = goods and services expense (% of GDP); health_exp = health expenditure, public (% of GDP); income_tax = taxes on income, profits, and capital gains (% of GDP); life_exp = life expectancy at birth, total (years); literacy = literacy rate, adult total (% of pop ages 15 and above); market_cap = market capitalization (% of GDP); mil_exp = military expenditure (% of GDP); primary_edu = labor force with primary education (% of total pop ages 15–64); r_gdp_growth = real GDP growth; revenue = revenue excluding grants (% of GDP); secondary_edu = labor force with secondary education (% of total population ages 15–64); social_contribution = social contributions (% of GDP); tax_revenue = tax revenue (% of GDP); tertiary_edu = labor force with tertiary education (% of total population ages 15–64); transfer_exp = subsidies and other transfers (% of GDP); unemployment = unemployment, total (%).

Source: Author's estimates.

Notes

1 Perotti (2004) classifies SVAR literature into three groups. De Castro and Hernandez (2006) add an additional group that includes Blanchard and Perotti (2002) and Perotti (2004).
2 Even when co-integrated relations exist among the key variables, the use of basic VAR can be still advocated on the grounds that the parameters are estimated consistently and the estimates have the same asymptotic distribution as those of differenced data (Hamilton 1994).
3 Refer to Woo et al. (2013) for other studies on similar topics.
4 "One reasonably firm conclusion is that it would be a big mistake to separate analyses of growth and income distribution" Berg and Ostry (2011).
5 The proportion is easily converted to a percent of expense if multiplied by expense (percent of GDP).
6 According to the World Bank, "General government final consumption expenditure (formerly general government consumption) includes all government current expenditures for purchases of goods and services (including compensation of employees). It also includes most expenditures on national defense and security, but excludes government military expenditures that are part of government capital formation."
7 "Poverty gap at the national poverty line" is the mean shortfall from the poverty line (counting the non-poor as having zero shortfall) as a percentage of the poverty line. This measure reflects the depth of poverty as well as its incidence.
8 I use the whole-country WDI data in Tables 4.5–4.11 and in Table 4.14 to prevent the loss of observations due to the inclusion of control variables. Other than in these tables, results from PVAR are based on the dataset covering OECD and ADB members as previously specified.
9 Sometimes results from VAR estimations are quite sensitive to shock ordering. Luckily, however, this PVAR seems robust with respect to different orders.
10 Of the four variables, three are used in differences. Real GDP growth is not.
11 Based on the existing literature, Cournède, Goujard, and Pina (2013) conjecture that education and health spending would reduce income inequality.
12 The impulse responses of public gross fixed capital formation are not compared here due to data problems. In the WDI dataset, gross fixed capital formation is available only for ADB members whereas public health spending, education spending, and transfers and social subsidies include the observations from both OECD and ADB members.
13 Note that numbers in the tables of this section answer either of the following questions: (1) If the share of a certain expenditure item to GDP increases by 1 percentage point, then what percentage of GDP will grow in response in the next 7 years? (2) If the share of a certain expenditure item to GDP increases by 1 percentage point, then how much will Gini_gross (0~100 scale) grow in response in the next 7 years?
14 In the case of SVAR, shock identification restrictions can vary depending on institutional arrangements as in Blanchard and Perotti (2002).

Bibliography*

Acemoglu, D. and J.A. Robinson. 2002. The Political Economy of the Kuznets Curve. *Review of Development Economics.* 6 (2). pp. 183–202.

*The Asian Development Bank recognizes Korea by the name Republic of Korea.

Arellano, M. and S. Bond. 1991. Some Tests of Specification for Panel Data: Monte Carlo Evidence and an Application to Employment Equations. *Review of Economics Studies.* 58 (2). pp. 277–297.

Ball, L., D. Furceri, D. Leigh, and P. Loungani. 2013. The Distributional Effects of Fiscal Consolidation. *IMF Working Paper.* No. 13/151. Washington, DC: Internal Monetary Fund.

Berg, A. and J. Ostry. 2011. Equality and Efficiency: Is there a Trade-off between the Two or Do They Go Hand in Hand? *Finance and Development.* 48 (3). pp. 12–15.

Blanchard, O. J. and R. Perotti. 2002. An Empirical Characterization of the Dynamic Effects of Changes in Government Spending and Taxes on Output. *Quarterly Journal of Economics.* 117 (4). pp. 1329–1368.

Cournède, B., A. Goujard, and A. Pina. 2013. How to Achieve Growth and Equity Friendly Fiscal Consolidation? A Proposed Methodology for Instrument Choice with an Illustrative Application to OECD Countries. *OECD Working Paper Series.* No. 1088. Paris: Organisation for Economic Co-operation and Development.

Cubero, R. and I. V. Hollar. 2010. Equity and Fiscal Policy: The Income Distribution Effects of Taxation and Social Spending in Central America. *IMF Working Paper.* No. 10/112. Washington, DC: International Monetary Fund.

de Castro, F. 2004. The Macroeconomic Effects of Fiscal Policy in Spain. *Banco de España Working Paper.* No. 0311. Madrid: Banco de España.

de Castro, F. and P. Hernandez de Cos. 2006. The Economic Effects of Exogenous Fiscal Shocks in Spain: A SVAR Approach. *European Central Bank Working Paper.* No. 647. Frankfurt: European Central Bank.

Edelberg, W., M. Eichenbaum, and J. Fisher. 1999. Understanding the Effects of Shocks to Government Purchases. *Review of Economic Dynamics.* 2 (1). pp. 166–206.

Fatas, A. and I. Mihov. 2000. The Effects of Fiscal Policy on consumption and Employment: Theory and Evidence. Mimeo. Fountainebleau: INSEAD.

Favero, C. 2002. How do European Monetary and Fiscal Authorities Behave? *CEPR Working Paper.* No. 3426. Washington, DC: Center for Economic and Policy Research.

Hamilton, J. 1994. *Time Series Analysis.* Princeton: Princeton University Press.

Heller, P., R. Haas, and A. Mansur. 1986. A Review of the Fiscal Impulse Measure. *IMF Occasional Paper.* No. 44. Washington, DC: International Monetary Fund.

Hoppner, F. 2002. *Fiscal Policy and Automatic Stabilizers: A SVAR Perspective.* University of Bonn Lennestr.

Hur, S.-K. 2007. Measuring the Effectiveness of Fiscal Policies in Korea. In Ito, T. and A. Rose, eds. *Fiscal Policy and Management in Asia.* National Bureau of Economic Research-East Asia Seminar on Economics Book Series Volume 16. Chicago: University of Chicago Press.

Jha, S., S. Malick, D. Park, and P. Quising. 2010. Effectiveness of Countercyclical Fiscal Policy: Time Series Evidence from Developing Asia. *ADB Economics Working Paper.* No. 211. Manila: ADB.

Joumard, I., M. Pisu, and D. Bloch. 2012. Less Income Inequality and More Growth – Are They Compatible? Part 3. Income Redistribution via Taxes and Transfers across OECD Countries. *OECD Economics Department Working Paper.* No. 926. Paris: Organisation for Economic Co-operation and Development.

Kneller, R., M. Bleaney, and N. Gemmell. 1999. Fiscal Policy and Growth: Evidence from OECD Countries. *Journal of Public Economics.* 74 (2). pp. 171–190.

Kuznets, S. 1955. Economic Growth and Income Inequality. *American Economic Review*. 45 (1). pp. 1–28.

Lopez, H. 2004. Pro-Poor Growth: A Review of What We Know (and of What We Don't). Mimeo. Washington, DC: World Bank.

Love, I. and L. Zicchino. 2006. Financial Development and Dynamic Investment Behavior: Evidence from Panel VAR. *Quarterly Review of Economics and Finance*. 46 (2). pp. 190–210.

Martinez-Vazquez, J., B. Moreno-Dodson, and V. Vulovic. 2012. The Impact of Tax and Expenditure Policies on Income Distribution: Evidence from a Large Panel of Countries. *Review of Public Economics*. 200 (1). pp. 95–130

Organisation for Economic Co-operation and Development (OECD). 2011. *Divided We Stand: Why Inequality Keeps Rising*. Paris: Organisation for Economic Co-operation and Development.

Mountford, A. and H. Uhlig. 2002. What are the Effects of Fiscal Policy Shocks? *CEPR Working Paper* No. 3338. Washington, DC: Center for Economic and Policy Research.

Perotti, R. 1999. Fiscal Policy in Good Times and Bad. *Quarterly Journal of Economics*. 114 (4). pp. 1399–1436.

———. 2004. Estimating the Effects of Fiscal Policy in OECD countries. *IGIER Working Paper*. No. 276. Milan: Innocenzo Gasparini Institute for Economic Research.

Ramey, V. and M. Shapiro. 1998. Costly Capital Reallocation and the Effects of Government Spending. *Carnegie–Rochester Conference Series on Public Policy*. 48. pp. 145–194.

Ranieri, R. and R.A. Ramos. 2013. Inclusive Growth: Building up a Concept. *International Policy Centre for Inclusive Growth Working Paper*. No. 104. Brasilia.

Rauniyar, G. and R. Kanbur. 2010. *Inclusive Development: Two Papers on Conceptualization, Application, and the ADB Perspective*. Manila: ADB.

Solt, F. 2014. The Standardized World Income Inequality Database. http://myweb.uiowa.edu/fsolt/swiid/swiid.html (accessed 14 September 2014).

Woo, J., E. Bova, T. Kinda, and S. Zhang. 2013. Distributional Consequences of Fiscal Consolidation and the Role of Fiscal Policy: What Do the Data Say? *IMF Working Paper*. No. 13/195. Washington, DC: International Monetary Fund.

World Bank. 2013. World Development Indicators Database. http://data.worldbank.org/data-catalog/world-development-indicators (accessed 7 September 2013).

5 Benefit incidence of public transfers

Evidence from the People's Republic of China

Ke Shen and Sang-Hyop Lee

A. Introduction

Three decades of virtually uninterrupted hyper economic growth have propelled the People's Republic of China (PRC) into the ranks of middle-income countries; however, this rapid economic growth has been accompanied by an equally rapid increase in levels of inequality. The official Gini coefficient reached 0.47 in 2012 (*Xinhua News* 2013), which is greater than the international alert line of 0.4 set by the United Nations (UN-HABITAT 2008). In response to the great concerns about inequality, the government has been paying close attention to redistributive goals through a wide variety of instruments. Public transfers targeting vulnerable groups to promote equality and improve the welfare of the population serve as one of these instruments. In the past decade, the government has made great strides in instituting and improving public sector programs to provide public education, health care, and pensions for its citizens. For example, in 2005, textbook and miscellaneous fees were waived for one-third of students enrolled in compulsory education in western and central rural areas of the country, reaching all students in primary and junior high school by 2008. In addition to broader coverage, it is essential to know whether disadvantaged groups such as rural dwellers, females, or the poor benefit more from public transfers in order to justify them as a rationale for public spending.

A second distinctive feature of public transfers is to reallocate resources from the working-age population to both children and the elderly in terms of education, health care, and pensions (Lee 2003). This suggests that public transfers are unevenly distributed across generations. Downward transfers from older to younger cohorts such as education might crowd out upward transfers such as pensions and health care; however, less attention has been paid to this area. One notable study by Bommier et al. (2010) shows that all generations born from 1950 to 2050 in the United States are net gainers in combined public transfers net of taxes, while many of today's older people are net losers. With the accelerated aging occurring in the PRC, the old-age dependency ratio will increase rapidly in the coming years, thus the lack of balance in benefits across generations will become even more pronounced. For example, pension reform is hotly debated in the PRC just as it is in industrialized nations. The necessity to reform social security is undisputed, but there is strong disagreement about how that reform should be designed. The dilemma is that either future generations are unfairly saddled with the burden of a large public debt or current generations are unfairly treated especially those nearing retirement age (Bommier et al. 2010).

Measuring how government spending is distributed is a matter of long-standing concern in economics literature (Meerman 1979; Selowsky 1979; van de Walle and Nead 1995). A more recent study in Latin American countries (Turra, Holz, and Cotlear 2011) showed that the distribution of public transfers across income groups and the distribution of these transfers across generations are not independent; instead, they are closely related to each other. They found that much of the regressive nature of public expenditures across income groups in Brazil and Chile was due to generational allocations as public spending was almost neutral in education, lightly progressive in health care, and strongly regressive in public pensions. Following the framework of Turra, Holz, and Cotlear (2011), we extended our analyses to look into the distribution of public spending by residence, by gender, and by income, and to figure out its link with distribution across generations in the PRC. Part B introduces the methods used to estimate the benefit incidence of public transfers, Part C describes the age patterns of public spending by sector and by residence, Part D presents the age patterns of public spending by sector and by gender, Part E shows the age distributions of public spending by sector and by income, Part F shows the age distributions of combined public spending by socioeconomic groups, and Part G concludes.

B. Methodology

To understand and appreciate the benefit incidence of public spending, we used the method of the National Transfer Accounts (NTA) Project. NTA captures a fundamental feature of all societies: the economic life cycle. The life-cycle deficit generated by the mismatch between consumption and labor income across age groups should be financed through intergenerational transfers, asset income, or dissavings. Essentially, the national transfer flow account is based on the following identity:

$$C(x) - \Upsilon^l(x) = \tau^+(x) - \tau^-(x) + \Upsilon^A(x) - S(x)$$

The left-hand side represents life-cycle deficit at age x, the difference between consumption $C(x)$ and labor income $\Upsilon^l(x)$. The right-hand side is the age reallocation system that consists of two economic mechanisms: net transfers $\tau^+(x) - \tau^-(x)$, and asset-based reallocations equal to asset income $\Upsilon^A(x)$ net of savings $S(x)$. Except for labor income, the other components can be distinguished by public or private sector. This chapter focuses on public transfers through which the government tries to fill the gap between consumption and labor income across generations. Public transfers are comprised of two components: in-kind transfers such as public education and public health-care consumption and cash transfers such as public pensions.

Using the framework of the NTA, the analyses are based on micro-level household data from the 2010 wave of China Family Panel Studies (CFPS), which collected data on consumption, income, and other information in 2009, and macro-level data from the System of National Accounts and government administrative records. The CFPS is a nationally representative household survey that has been collected every year since 2010. The 2010 survey covered 25 out of 31 provinces and targeted about 16,000 households including adults and children under the age of 16. The CFPS provides detailed information on household structure, income, and expenditures which facilitated our estimates. CFPS data collection is under strict quality control (Yan et al. 2012). A comparison of income data between the 2010 wave of CFPS and the 2010 wave of the China General Social Survey showed that the income distributions were quite similar (Xu et al. 2012).

The first step was to estimate age profiles of public expenditures on education, health care, and pensions. To estimate the age profile of public education consumption, administrative data from the *Educational Finance Statistical Yearbook 2010* were used to input the cost per student enrolled by level of education, and CFPS data were used to estimate the age-specific enrollment rates in each level of education (Chen 2010). The age profile of public pension expenditures was based on survey responses on pension benefits received in 2009; however, CFPS provides pension benefits on a household basis only; therefore, pension benefits were assumed to be equally distributed among the elderly[1] living in the household.

The age profile of public health-care consumption is more complex. The macro control for public health consumption in NTA is comprised of two parts: medical expenditures reimbursed by public health insurance and government health-care spending. The age-specific, reimbursed health consumption originates directly from the responses on the CFPS survey; however, the CFPS has no information on inpatient and outpatient utilization rates, which is essential to estimate the age profile of government health-care spending as was done in Brazil and Chile (Turra, Holz, and Cotlear 2011). Instead, we calculated out-of-pocket medical expenditures based on CFPS data as a substitute for utilization rates with the assumption that medical expenditures are proportional to utilization rates. Finally, we combined the age profile of reimbursed health consumption and the age profile of out-of-pocket medical expenditures to formulate the age profile of public health consumption.

The second step was to estimate age profiles of public transfers across socioeconomic groups. We split the CFPS household data into urban and rural residence, gender, and income quartiles and estimated the above-mentioned age profiles using each sub-sample. Subsequently, most age profiles were smoothed except for education[2] as age patterns of public education spending have too many discontinuities that are not random but are the product of specific ages of entering and leaving school (United Nations 2013).

The last step was to adjust the smoothed and non-smoothed profiles to macro controls. As the NTA method imputes only macro controls for pubic transfers by purpose for the whole nation, we further needed to calculate corresponding macro controls for each sub-sample. Taking public education spending as an example, we used the ratio of average value of spending per capita in urban areas to the value in rural areas to divide the macro control for public education spending. These macro controls were then used to scale the NTA age profiles so that the NTA aggregate estimates matched the estimates from the System of National Accounts.

C. Benefit incidence of public spending by residence

In this section, we investigate the urban–rural differentials in the age distributions of public expenditures in three categories: public education, health care, and pensions. The analysis is based on a comparison of per capita values and aggregate values across ages between urban and rural areas.

1. Education

Education has long attracted government subsidies in the PRC because of the equity considerations and high externalities involved. The government is the main provider of education with over 90% of students in primary and secondary education attending public schools. Government spending per student normally increases with the level of education. According to the *Educational Finance Statistical Yearbook 2010*, the outlays for college education are nearly three times the amount spent on primary schools (Chen 2010).

As shown in Figure 5.1, most public education spending targeted students under age 25, while some also reached urban adults in their 30s who were

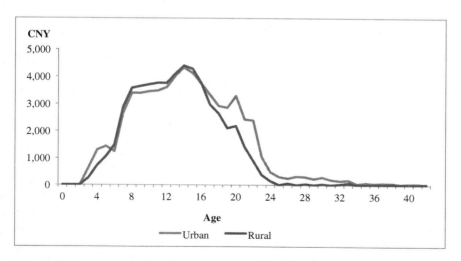

Figure 5.1 Per capita public education spending by residence

CNY = yuan.

Source: Authors' estimates.

receiving post-graduate education or adult education. Public education expenditure for the age group 6–16 was equal in urban and rural areas due to the government's endeavor to promote the balanced development of compulsory education. The government has mandated public funding for 9 years of compulsory education since 2001, and as mentioned previously, by 2005 textbook and miscellaneous fees were waived for about one-third of students in western and central rural areas. This program was extended to all rural students in primary and junior high school by 2007 and further covered all urban students by 2008. Compulsory education is now virtually universal. In 2009, the crude enrollment rate in primary school was over 100% and in junior high school was about 99% (Chen 2010).

Two distinctions between the urban and rural populations also emerge in Figure 5.1. First, public spending on pre-primary education was less in rural areas due to lower enrollment rates in kindergartens. In recent years, many local governments have been expanding rural kindergartens, but the urban–rural gap cannot be fully eliminated in the short term. Second, public spending on college education was much greater for the urban population. Per capita education spending at age 20 reached 3,890 yuan (CNY) in urban areas, while the figure in rural areas was only CNY2,380, about 40% less. The PRC has seen the fastest expansion in higher education in its history. According to *The People's Republic of China Yearbook 2011,* in the 10 years since 2000, annual enrollment in college education tripled from 2.2 million to 6.6 million. This expansion has been more beneficial for urban youths. The 2010 census revealed that of the population aged 20–29, only 20% had college or higher education in the nation as a whole, but nearly 40% of those aged 20–24 and 32.5% of those aged 25–29 in urban areas were college educated. In addition, the share of rural students in the top universities has shown an evident downward trend in recent years.[3] On one hand, low enrollment rates in the countryside are indicators of poor performance as college enrollment is generally determined by how students do on national examinations. On the other hand, low enrollment also reflects income constraints faced by poor rural households as tuition fees rise.

Figure 5.2 presents age distributions of aggregate public education expenditure. Aggregate public spending on education in urban areas was 16% higher than that in rural areas. Unlike per capita values, more aggregate public funding was allocated to rural children under the age of 16 because of the larger population size. With the 3-decade long enforcement of family planning policies, urban couples strictly follow the one child per couple rule, while rural couples in a majority of provinces are allowed to have a second child if the first is a female. Hence, the number of children in rural areas is larger than that in urban areas. In contrast, public education funding for urban youth older than 17 years was much greater than that for rural people. In addition to higher per capita values, the greater number of young people in cities due to frequent and massive rural-to-urban migration also accounts for the differences in aggregate values.

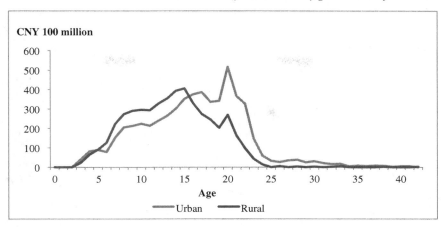

Figure 5.2 Aggregate public education spending by residence

CNY = yuan.

Source: Authors' estimates.

2. Health care

Public health-care institutions dominate the PRC's health-care system. In 2009, person–time patients treated by public institutions amounted to 1.8 billion in contrast to only 153 million in private institutions, as indicated in the *Public Health Statistical Yearbook 2012*. The number of patients hospitalized in public facilities was 78 million, while the number in private organizations was only 6.8 million.

As shown in Figure 5.3, the age profile of per capita public health-care spending has a J-shape in both urban and rural areas: per capita spending is high in infancy then decreases in the teenage years and increases again at middle age. The peak of public health spending occurs around age 80 in urban and rural areas, while the peak value in urban areas is almost twice that of rural areas. Urban dwellers benefit more from public health-care funding than rural dwellers at all ages, in particular after age 60.

One major reason for this differential is the segregated public health insurance system in the PRC. There are two major types of insurance in urban areas: employees are covered by the Urban Employees Basic Medical Insurance established in 1998, and unemployed residents are under the Urban Residents Basic Medical Insurance piloted since 2007. In rural areas, nearly 80% of residents (about 640 million) did not have any health insurance in 2003 (Government of the People's Republic of China 2004). To address this problem, the government launched the New Cooperative Medical Scheme in 2003 which dramatically expanded coverage to about 96% (836 million) of the rural population in 2010 (Sheng 2011). Benefit packages differed substantially among these three programs. For example, the average inpatient reimbursement rate for urban employees was 65% in 2008 and for urban residents was 45% in 2007, while the figure

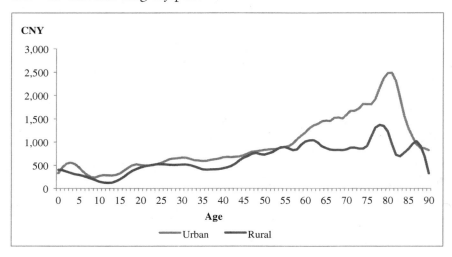

Figure 5.3 Per capita public health-care spending by residence

CNY = yuan.

Source: Authors' estimates.

for the New Cooperative Medical Scheme was only 41% in 2009 (Barber and Yao 2010). More generous health insurance benefits encouraged urban dwellers to make intensive use of public health services. In particular, public health-care spending on urban retirees increased sharply as the deductibles and reimbursements are more favorable for retirees than for employees. This gap between urban and rural areas in public health-care spending is expected to shrink in the coming years as the government raised its subsidy to the New Cooperative Medical Scheme from CNY40 per enrollee annually in 2006 to CNY280 in 2013.

A second reason is the concentration of health-care facilities and personnel in urban areas. According to the *China Social Statistical Yearbook 2013* in 2009, the number of beds in health institutions per thousand persons in urban areas was 5.54 in contrast to 2.41 in rural areas, and there were 2.1 million health-care personnel in urban areas, but only 1.3 in the countryside (Li 2013). Consequently, urban dwellers have better access to public health resources.

The age profiles in urban PRC were closer to the pattern in developed countries, while in other newly emerging countries such as Brazil and Chile, the increase in public health-care expenditure at old ages is less evident (Turra, Holz, and Cotlear 2011).

For aggregate values, public health-care spending in urban areas was about 30% greater than that in rural areas, which was a larger gap than that in public education spending. As presented in Figure 5.4, the age distributions of aggregate public health-care consumption exhibited an inverted U-shape, reflecting the age composition of the population. For instance, there is a notch at around age

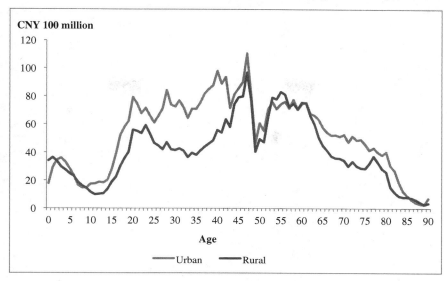

Figure 5.4 Aggregate public health-care spending by residence

CNY = yuan.

Source: Authors' estimates.

50 due to birth deficits during the great famine from 1959 to 1961, while the bump at age 47 reflects the baby boom generation after the famine. Rapid population aging will significantly elevate the fiscal burden of health care given the greater per capita spending at older ages.

3. Pensions

As shown in Figure 5.5, there were huge differences in the age profiles of per capita pensions between urban and rural areas. Per capita annual pensions in urban areas increased quickly peaking around age 75 with a value of CNY8,300.[4] In contrast, per capita pensions in rural areas were roughly flat at age 60 and older at a much lower level of CNY1,500. The urban–rural gap in pension benefits mainly results from the fragmentation of the emerging public old-age support system in the PRC, an arrangement that dates back to the socialist years with a social and economic system that separated the urban and rural populations and urban populations working in different types of organizations. The most prestigious group is government employees (including military personnel) who do not need to pay into the system but receive up to 100% of pre-retirement income (Pozen 2013). By comparison, rural people trail far behind in social security benefits, though the government has recently made great strides in expanding pension coverage for them. The new rural pension scheme was piloted in 2009 and covered roughly 72.8 million individuals, 10.2% of the

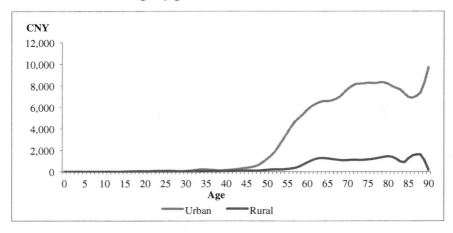

Figure 5.5 Per capita public pension spending by residence

CNY = yuan.

Source: Authors' estimates.

rural population. Under this insurance scheme, the individual contribution amount is currently set at up to CNY1,000 annually, and the monthly payout is CNY55 (roughly $9).

The pension systems not only differ in values of benefits per beneficiary but also in qualifying ages for pensions. For example, the retirement age is set at 50 or 55 years for urban female workers and at 60 years for urban male workers, while the qualifying age for pensions is 60 years in rural areas. This explains why per capita pension payments in urban areas pick up in the early 50 age group, while they do not start to increase in rural areas till the late 50s. The vast differences in pension systems between urban and rural dwellers also affect the models of elderly support. According to the 2010 census, up to 70% of the urban elderly relied on public pensions as their main income source in contrast to only about 10% in the countryside. The weak pension system in rural areas increases income uncertainty at older ages, especially in the context of declining fertility and extended life expectancy, which could also lead to meager consumption.

As presented in Figure 5.6, both age profiles of aggregate pension spending exhibit an inverted U-shape with the peak at around age 60. The urban–rural gap in pension benefits is more pronounced than that in public education and health-care consumption. In aggregate terms, public pension expenditure in cities is almost five times greater than in the countryside. The urban elderly aged 60 received CNY356 billion in pension benefits in total in contrast to only about CNY64 billion in the countryside. This indicates that population aging and rapid urbanization will put severe strains on the government-run pension system in the coming years.

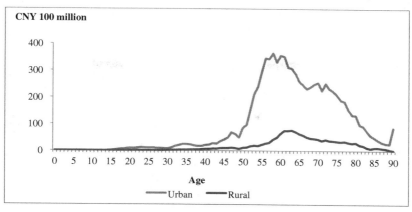

Figure 5.6 Aggregate public pension spending by residence

CNY = yuan.

Source: Authors' estimates.

D. Benefit incidence of public spending by gender

1. Education

As indicated in Figure 5.7, per capita spending on public education is nearly identical for males and females younger than 17 as enrollment rates in primary school and high school are almost the same. Lee (2012) indicated that the 3-decade long enforcement of the one-child policy inadvertently promoted educational gender equality in the PRC. Females aged 18 to 23 received even more public education transfers than their male counterparts due to higher college enrollments. In 1999, the government made a strategic decision to expand higher education in order to increase human capital and to relieve employment pressure in the urban sector. The number of new students admitted to college increased by more than 40% in 1999, and the expansion continued in subsequent years (Li, Whalley, and Xing 2013). By 2005, annual enrollment had more than quadrupled compared with the level in 1998. Meanwhile, many studies have demonstrated a growing female dominance in school performance in recent decades in the PRC and in other countries (e.g., Buchmann and DiPrete 2006; Lai 2010). Lai (2010) found that girls outperformed boys throughout both primary and middle schools; hence, the radical expansion in higher education has mainly benefited females. The gap in college enrollments has even reversed to favor women recently (Wu and Zhang 2010).

Aggregate public education expenditure was roughly balanced between males and females. As shown in Figure 5.8, the aggregate profiles bulge at age 20 for both due to higher tuition fees for college and the larger cohort size. The total fertility rate in the PRC hit replacement level (2.1 children per couple) in 1990 and has decreased ever since. Thus the cohort aged 20 in 2010 is larger than the younger cohorts.

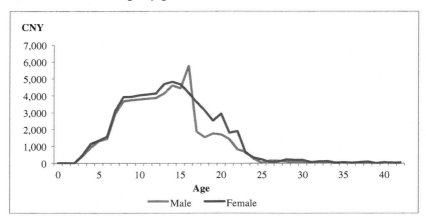

Figure 5.7 Per capita public education spending by gender

CNY = yuan.

Source: Authors' estimates.

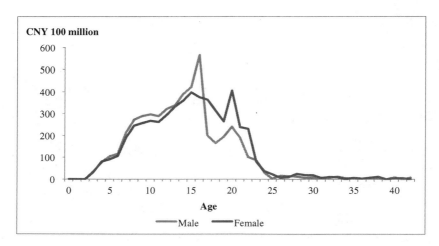

Figure 5.8 Aggregate public education spending by gender

CNY = yuan.

Source: Authors' estimates.

2. Health care

As shown in Figure 5.9, there were no major differences in per capita public health consumption between males and females aged 10 to 60. At very young ages, boys received more health care than girls, which might arise from higher male infant mortality and the son preference in traditional PRC families. At older ages, men also consumed more public health resources than women. In general, the urban health insurance scheme is directly tied to employment status before

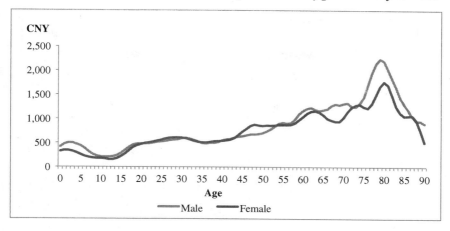

Figure 5.9 Per capita public health-care spending by gender

CNY = yuan.

Source: Authors' estimates.

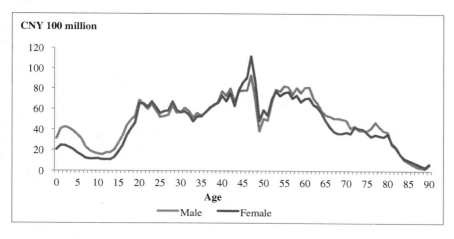

Figure 5.10 Aggregate public health-care spending by gender

CNY = yuan.

Source: Authors' estimates.

retirement for the elderly with coverage for other family members not provided (Strauss et al. 2012). Higher male employment rates in past decades – especially employment in government and public institutions – means that older men are more likely to be insured or to benefit from generous health insurance packages. At the peak age of 80, per capita public health spending for women was about CNY1,764 in contrast to CNY2,238 for men.

Aggregate public health-care consumption for men was only 7.6% higher than that for women. As shown in Figure 5.10, the escalating number of live male births per 100 female live births since the mid-1980s, which reached 118.1 in 2010 exacerbated the differences in aggregate spending between males and females younger than 13. In contrast to higher per capita public health-care spending for older men, the aggregate expenditure was roughly gender neutral for older people as female life expectancy is longer than male life expectancy.

3. Pensions

Figure 5.11 shows gender differentials in per capita pension benefits. Pension benefits for women in their late 50s were higher than those for men as urban female workers are entitled to pensions at the age of 50 or 55, while urban male workers have to wait until the age of 60, but benefits for males increased substantially with age. For instance, annual pension benefits were CNY2,652 for men aged 60 but more than double that for men aged 80. Compared with men, per capita pension benefits for women increased much more slowly with age, and decreased drastically after age 80 because of lower coverage rates and lower benefits per beneficiary. The 2010 census data showed that only 20% of women aged 80 cited public pensions as their major source of income in contrast to nearly 40% of men that age. Hence, public support programs currently still play a minor role in elderly livelihoods, especially among very elderly females.

In terms of aggregate pension benefits, the age profiles for men and women both peaked around age 60 and then declined (Figure 5.12). A noticeable difference from per capita pension benefits is that aggregate pension spending was almost equal for men and women older than 60 as women have lower per capita pension benefits but a better possibility of surviving into older age.

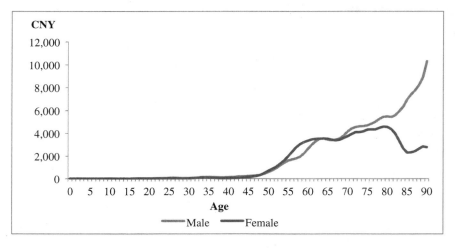

Figure 5.11 Per capita public pension spending by gender

CNY = yuan.

Source: Authors' estimates.

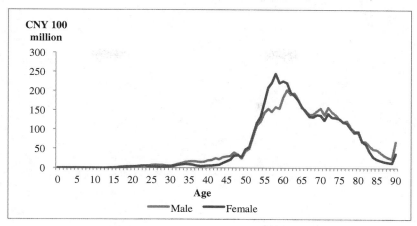

Figure 5.12 Aggregate public pension spending by gender
CNY = yuan.
Source: Authors' estimates.

E. Benefit incidence of public spending by per capita household income

This section estimates the benefit incidence of government spending across income groups to examine whether public transfers attenuate income inequalities. The CFPS sample was divided into four income quartiles by per capita household income in the last year.

1. Education

As shown in Figure 5.13, the age pattern of per capita public education spending was similar for the lower-income quartiles. Their peak education consumption occurred at age 15, the age for enrolling in senior high school. There are, however, several distinctive differences among the lower three quartiles and the top quartile. First of all, the top quartile got more public education resources for children under age 5 indicating that children from better-off families were more likely to be enrolled in kindergarten. Pre-primary education has not yet been included in compulsory education and thus charges higher tuition fees.

Second, children in the top quartile have a much higher probability of entering college compared with the other income groups. Under the earlier central planning regime, higher education was heavily subsidized (Li et al. 2013). College students were not only exempted from tuition fees but also received monthly allowances. With the expansion of higher education, the government gradually reduced the subsidies. From 1995 to 2004, college tuition fees increased sharply from CNY800 per person per year to CNY5,000 on average (Yang 2006). Education expenditures ranked first in total household expenditures in the Tenth

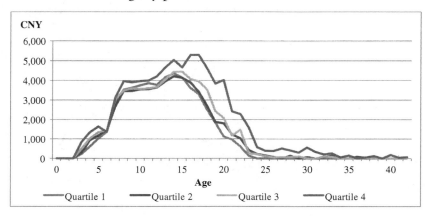

Figure 5.13 Per capita public education spending by income quartiles
CNY =
Source: Authors' estimates.

Five-Year Plan. The ever increasing tuition fees have intensified the financial constraints of lower-income families, and some poor students might give up the
opportunity to enter college. Students from wealthier families therefore benefit
more from the recent expansion of higher education (Li 2007).

Third, adults older than 25 in the top quartile received public education funds
indicating that they were pursuing post-graduate education or adult education,
but this was not true in lower-income quartiles where funding covered children
and adults younger than 25 only. The resulting differences in educational attain-
ment in turn become a source of income inequality.

The ratio of public education spending in the top three quartiles to that in the
bottom quartile is presented in Figure 5.14. Public spending on education appears
to be neutral with respect to income as it was almost the same for all quartiles; this
finding is misleading, however, as the share of school-age children in the poorer
quartiles is much greater. This difference in population distribution explains why
children aged 6–16 from wealthier families received less public education funding
as shown in Figure 5.15. The concentration of children in lower-income groups has
several complementary reasons. First, per capita income in our analyses was estimated by dividing household income by the number of household members. Thus
households with more dependent children are more likely to be in lower-income
quartiles. Second, poorer families tend to have higher fertility, especially as family
planning policies differ by region and ethnicity in the PRC. As mentioned previously, rural couples in a majority of provinces are allowed to have a second child if
the first birth is female, and minority couples are allowed to have two children in
any case. Urban couples, on the other hand, follow the strict one child per couple
rule. Over age 20, young people in the higher-income quartiles consume more
education resources in total due both to the larger share of young people among
higher-income groups and higher per capita public education consumption.

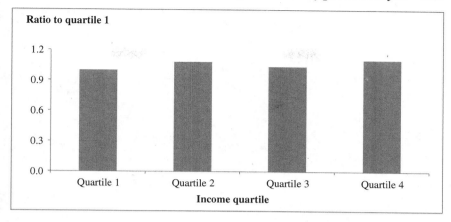

Figure 5.14 Distribution of aggregate public education consumption by income quartile
Source: Authors' estimates.

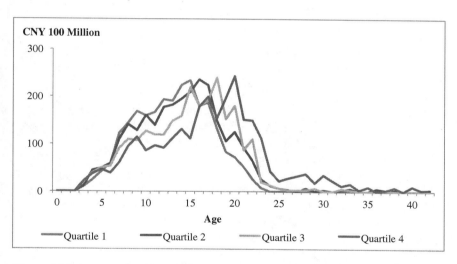

Figure 5.15 Aggregate public education spending by income quartile
Source: Authors' estimates.

2. Health care

Figure 5.16 conveys two messages. First, public health-care consumption is equally distributed across income groups under age 60. Though higher-income groups might be covered by more generous public health insurance, they may also be in better health and thus utilize fewer public resources. Second, per capita spending is targeted to the richer groups and is highly skewed in favor of the top quartile over the age of 60, which is the opposite of the pattern in Brazil and Chile (Turra, Holz, and Cotlear 2011). In both those countries, the poor make more

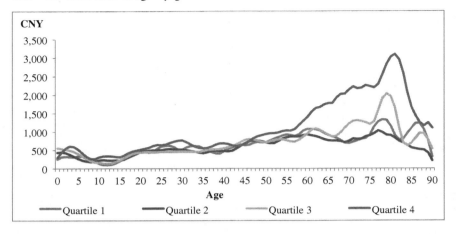

Figure 5.16 Per capita public health-care consumption by income quartile

CNY = yuan.

Source: Authors' estimates.

intensive uses of public health-care services than the rich at all ages because the rich are inclined to use private services. African countries in which public health facilities dominate and private institutions are generally poorly developed show a pattern similar to that of the PRC (Castro-Leal et al.1999).

Three principal factors affect the use of public health services by the elderly poor: health insurance, income, and access. First, enrollment in health insurance has significantly improved access to health care for older people (Cheng et al. 2013) as they are more susceptible to health problems (Levy and Meltzer 2008) and have more elastic demand for health care (Ringel et al. 2002) than young people. The health insurance status of the elderly is linked to previous employment in urban PRC. The top quartile always served in formal sectors prior to retirement and is thus covered by generous health insurance benefits and more inclined to seek public health care.

Second, health care is a normal good which means that use will increase as income increases. In rural areas, for example, enrollment in the New Rural Cooperative Medical Insurance program significantly increased inpatient service utilization among high-income groups but had no impact on low-income groups because low reimbursement rates and high out-of-pocket medical expenses discouraged poor people from going to hospitals.

Third, poor families often live far away from quality public health institutions so face long journeys and high opportunity costs to obtain health care (Castro-Leal et al. 1999). Distance constraints are especially serious for older people.

Figure 5.17 presents the incidence of aggregate public health-care consumption by income quartile. Consumption is equally distributed among the three lower-income quartiles, but the transfer to the top quartile is about 60% higher than that to the other three. Figure 5.18 shows the incidence of aggregate health-care

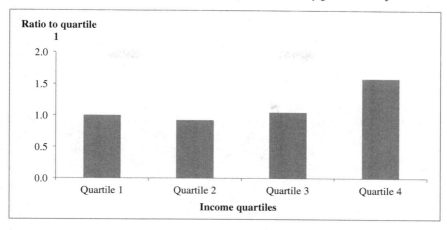

Figure 5.17 Distribution of aggregate public health-care spending by income quartile
Source: Authors' estimates.

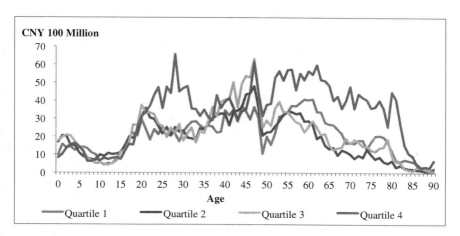

Figure 5.18 Aggregate public health-care consumption by income quartile
CNY = yuan.
Source: Authors' estimates.

spending by age and by income group. Consumption by people in their 20s in the top quartile is much higher than that of the other quartiles mainly because there is a concentration of young people in the richest group. In addition, public health spending on the elderly in the top-income quartile ranks first, followed by spending on the bottom quartile. This pattern is partly due to the high fraction of older people in the richest and poorest groups. In Brazil and Chile, however, the elderly are more concentrated in the top-income groups due to high life-cycle savings and the wide coverage of the pension system.

3. Pensions

As shown in Figure 5.19, per capita public pension benefits were strongly regressive with older people at the top of the income distribution enjoying much greater benefits. The concentration of public transfers in pension benefits in the top quartile is particularly striking compared with public education and health care. For instance, people aged 75 in the top quartile received a pension of CNY11,793 on average, while those in the second quartile received approximately CNY4,000, and the elderly in the bottom quartile received less than CNY250. Because the pension system in the PRC is a combination of pay-as-you-go and a funded system, the highest paid workers made greater contributions during their working lives and are thus entitled to bigger pensions. On the other hand, as shown in Figure 5.5, the vast majority of pension benefits were received by urban residents, and the average per capita income of urban residents was more than three times that of rural residents in 2009.[5] Therefore, the top-income quartile was predominately from urban areas and also enjoyed greater pension benefits.

Figure 5.20 indicates a huge inequality in aggregate pension benefits. Aggregate benefits delivered to the top quartile were 55 times those delivered to the bottom quartile; hence, pension benefits did not favor the poor but rather increasingly rewarded the rich. Gao, Evans, and Garfinkel (2012) compared the distribution of pension benefits in the PRC and Viet Nam and found that the system in the PRC was much more regressive. As shown in Figure 5.21, the age profiles of aggregate pension spending show an inverse U-shape for each income group with higher-income quartiles peaking at a much higher level.

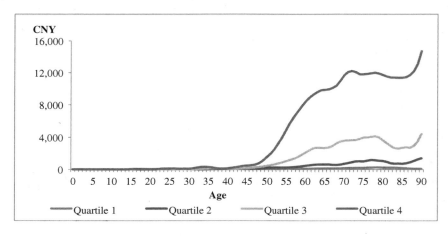

Figure 5.19 Per capita public pension spending by income quartile
CNY = yuan.
Source: Authors' estimates.

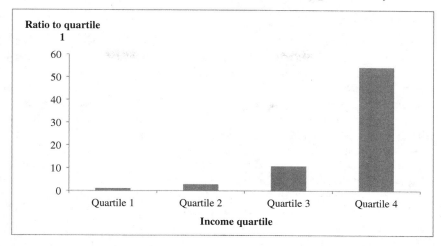

Figure 5.20 Distribution of aggregate public pension spending by income quartile
Source: Authors' estimates.

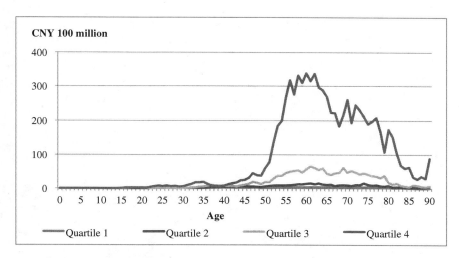

Figure 5.21 Aggregate public pension spending by income quartiles
CNY = yuan.
Source: Authors' estimates.

F. Benefit incidence of total public transfers

This section examines whether total public transfers (education, health care, and pensions) are targeted to disadvantaged groups and which generations benefit more from them.

1. Residence

Figure 5.22 shows the distribution of per capita total public transfers by age and by residence. Transfers peaked in the teenage years in both urban and rural areas at around CNY4,000 and were nearly equal in urban and rural areas before middle age due to equally distributed education and health-care spending. The urban–rural difference in per capita public spending gets increasingly larger after the age of 45 as urban dwellers received much higher pension benefits and made more intensive use of public health services.

The tilt in public transfers toward the elderly was pronounced in urban areas; public spending on them averaged more than CNY9,000 per person aged over 65, while public spending on children was only CNY2,891 per child under the age of 19 on average.[6] In contrast, public spending in rural areas was more targeted to children as rural health insurance and the pension system provide limited support for the elderly.

As shown in Figure 5.23, public spending on children accounted for only 23% of total spending in urban areas, while the share amounted to 47% in rural areas partially

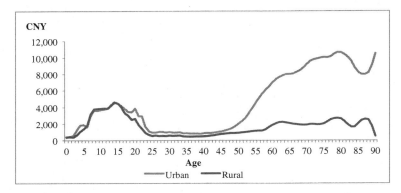

Figure 5.22 Per capita total public transfers by residence
Source: Authors' estimates.

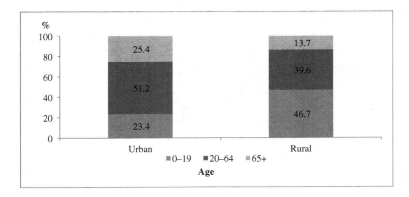

Figure 5.23 Aggregate public transfers to different age groups by residence
Source: Authors' estimates.

due to the higher proportion of children in the countryside. In absolute terms, aggregate spending on urban elderly is 3.5 times the spending on rural elderly.

2. Gender

As shown in Figure 5.24, per capita profiles of total public transfers coincide for males and females under the age of 65 indicating they equally take advantage of public education and health-care resources. There is, however, a tilt toward men over age 65 – especially over age 80 – due to greater pension benefits for men. The government spent nearly CNY7,000 per male 65 years and older, which was nearly 50% higher than the CNY4,800 per capita for females.

The older generations gained more from public spending than the younger generations did. Despite the strong interest most people in the PRC have in the well-being of children, per capita public spending on children was relatively modest, while the amount spent on health care and pensions for the elderly was greater. Note that the age bias was much greater for men than for women.

As shown in Figure 5.25, male children accounted for 33.6% of total public spending, and the male elderly accounted for 23.4%. The distribution of public spending to different age groups among the female population was similar with a greater share spent on working-age people.

3. Income quartiles

As presented in Figure 5.26, per capita public spending was equally distributed across income groups among the young and middle aged but was highly regressive over age 50. For the bottom quartile, public spending per child amounted to

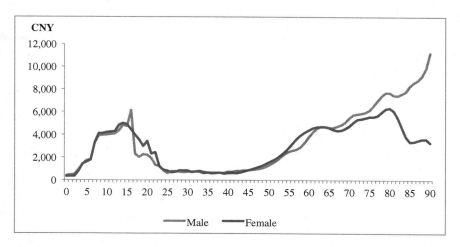

Figure 5.24 Per capita total public transfers by gender

CNY = yuan.

Source: Authors' estimates.

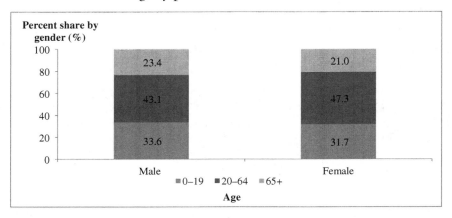

Figure 5.25 Aggregate public transfers on different age groups by gender
Source: Authors' estimates.

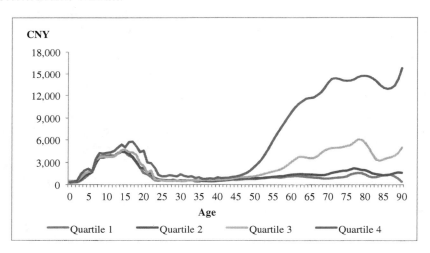

Figure 5.26 Per capita total public transfers by income quartile
CNY = yuan.
Source: Authors' estimates.

CNY2,689, which was more than twice the public spending per elderly person of CNY1,107. On the contrary, in the top quartile, public spending per elderly person was almost three times greater than public spending per child. This suggests that among higher income groups, the public sector is responsible for the sustenance of the elderly and families remain responsible for childrearing.

The share of public spending devoted to the elderly was less than 20% in the second and third quartiles. In contrast, spending on the elderly in the top quartile was 34% due both to the high proportion of older people and to high levels of per capita spending (Figure 5.27).

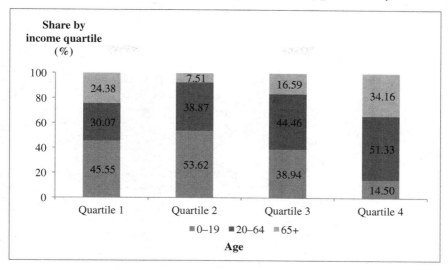

Figure 5.27 Aggregate public transfers on different age groups by income quartile
Source: Authors' estimates.

4. Incidence of total public transfers

Figure 5.28 presents the benefit incidence of public spending across generations in the whole population. Per capita public spending averaged CNY5,619 on people 65 years and older compared with only CNY2,841 on children under the age of 19. This suggests that public transfers favored the elderly by a factor of 1.98 to 1. A bias toward the elderly was observed not only in other developing countries such as Brazil and Chile (Turra, Holz, and Cotlear 2011) but also in developed countries. Based on the estimates by Isaacs (2009), per capita public spending on the elderly was 2.4 times the amount on children in the United States in 2004 due to heavy government investment in Social Security and in Medicare.

According to the estimates, public spending in the PRC on children under the age of 19 totaled CNY931 billion, which was 32% of total public spending. As a share of the total economy, 2.7% of GDP was spent on public support for children in 2009, while the share amounted to 6% in the United States in 2004 (Isaacs 2009). In comparison, public spending on people over the age of 64 totaled CNY646.5 billion and accounted for 22.1% of total public transfers. The share of public spending of the GDP on the elderly was thus 1.9% in contrast to 6.9% in the United States in 2004 (Isaacs 2009). These comparisons suggest that pubic transfers played a less important role in supporting dependent children and elderly people in the PRC than in the United States though the tax structure in the United States is different from that in the PRC.

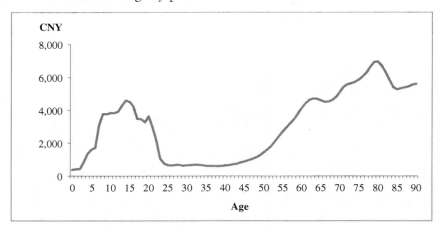

Figure 5.28 Per capita total public transfers

CNY = yuan.

Source: Authors' estimates.

G. Conclusion

Utilizing the NTA framework, we systematically analyzed the benefit incidence of public transfers across generations and across socioeconomic groups in the PRC in 2009. Education and health care are basic services essential to combating poverty and are often subsidized with public funds to help achieve that goal. Public education spending was equally distributed by region, gender, and income group at the primary and secondary levels but favored urban residents, females, and the rich at the tertiary level as they have much better chances of going to college. The public health-care program equally benefited people from different socioeconomic groups among the young and middle aged; however, there was a tilt toward urban dwellers, males, and higher-income groups at older ages due to higher utilization rates and more generous reimbursements. Public pensions are an important public cash transfer and are expected to provide livelihood support for the elderly. Our results show that pension benefits strongly favored higher-income groups as rural residents, females, and lower-income groups received much less in the way of benefits. For instance, the top quartile received almost 80% of public pension funding in 2009 in contrast to only 1.5% for the bottom quartile. The regressive nature of public pension spending mainly arises from the fragmented pension system in the PRC.

Our results also indicate that public transfers were unevenly distributed across generations. Total public spending per person aged 65 and older was twice the spending per child aged 19 or younger. Though public education spending was almost equivalent to public pension spending in the NTA in 2009, the elderly consumed many more public health resources than teenagers, so total public transfers significantly favored the elderly. Generational imbalances in benefit incidence are closely related to population aging which is occurring at an unprecedented pace. As shown in the 2010 census, the population aged 60 and older totaled over 178 million accounting for 13.26% of the entire population which was 2.93 percentage points more compared with the 2000 census. The United Nations projection under the medium fertility variant scenario shows that the population aged 60 and older in the PRC will increase to 340 million by 2030 accounting for 24% of the total population and to 440 million by 2050 accounting for 34% of the total population (United Nations 2011). The expansion of the elderly population combined with high levels of spending on the elderly will exert heavy pressure on the government budget in the coming years.

Distributions of public transfers across generations are also connected with distributions of public transfers by socioeconomic groups. For instance, per capita public spending is greater on children than on the elderly in rural areas and among lower-income groups, while public spending is evidently targeted to elderly persons and to high-income groups in urban areas. Per capita public transfers were equally distributed across socioeconomic groups among the young and middle aged; however, they were highly regressive at older ages favoring urban dwellers, males, and rich people.

Our results have provided important insights into the problems facing the PRC government that is struggling to deliver essential and equitable social services to its citizens. In the next 10 or 20 years, the government should endeavor to improve and strengthen public support systems. Public transfers including education, health care, and pensions accounted for 8.6% of GDP in 2009, while Social Security, Medicare, and Medicaid combined accounted for almost 9% of GDP in the United States in 2008 without taking into account public education (Isaacs 2009). In addition to increasing government investments, the currently fragmented health insurance system and pension system should move toward a unified system to reduce inequalities in benefit incidence across socioeconomic groups. In the past decade, the PRC government has been dedicated to targeting the poor with programs like those that extend public health insurance and pensions to the rural population, but regional and socioeconomic disparities are still evident. At present, the elderly living in rural areas and those in low-income groups rely heavily on transfers from their children to cover living expenses and medical care. With declining fertility and frequent migration, the large, strong family network is weakened or even collapses. If the disadvantaged elderly are not well targeted by government programs, the level of inequality will be greater.

While we present abundant evidence on the benefit incidence of public transfers, our findings should be interpreted with caution. First, the nature of the data and of the NTA method necessitates making a variety of assumptions in the calculations; the results should be taken as indicative rather than definitive. For instance, as public education spending in urban and rural areas is not available from government financial statistics, the estimated urban and rural differentials in the age distribution of public education spending mainly reflect differentials in enrollment rates. Our results might underestimate urban–rural gaps if government spending on rural schools is less than that on urban schools.

Second, due to price differentials by urban and rural residence and across regions, the differences in real values of public spending would be smaller than the differences in nominal values by place of residence; thus those in rural areas and in less developed regions might be better targeted than was done in our estimation.

Third, CFPS data do not indicate whether a child is in public school or private school. We assumed that all children were enrolled in public schools given the dominance of public education in the PRC. For instance, the *China Education Yearbook 2009* indicates that the share of public school students of all students was 95% for primary education, 92% for middle school education, and almost 80% for tertiary education in 2009. Children in urban areas or from wealthier families are more likely to attend private schools, which might bias our estimates. Further investigation into this issue is needed.

Fourth, we divided the urban and rural population based on current residence instead of *hukou* status, that is, the registered residency status of a particular individual. This division is also adopted in measuring the urbanization level in the country. This suggests that the urban population in our definition includes the floating population, namely rural migrant workers who reside and work in the cities without an urban *hukou*. The floating population in the PRC was estimated to be over 260 million in 2012 accounting for 36.9% of the urban population (Government of the People's Republic of China 2013).[7] Our division alleviates some confusion raised by the division of urban *hukou* and rural *hukou*. For instance, rural *hukou* children are likely to attend school and go to hospital in cities thus consuming urban public resources. Furthermore, some indicators such as pension benefits are household amounts in CFPS data and need to be split among household members, some of whom may have urban *hukou*, while others hold rural *hukou*. In this circumstance, the split among household members cannot present the real distinction between the urban *hukou* and the rural *hukou* populations.

Fifth, we focused on whether disadvantaged groups received more public transfers than well-off groups. Another important question is how much the poor received compared with what they paid. This is especially important for public pension spending as some pension benefits are earning (tax) related. For instance, the average labor income of adults aged 30 to 49 in the top quartile was 7.3 times (CNY48,816) of that of the bottom quartile (CNY6,701), which should affect the size of the pension an individual receives. The figures in the Appendix show public pension spending divided by the average labor income of adults aged 30–49 by residence, by gender, and by income quartiles in 2009. The results still show that public pensions strongly favored urban and high-income groups; however, the previous results changed as the lowest-income groups received more pension benefits than the bottom 50% income percentiles. Furthermore, it appears that most women received more pension benefits than their male counterparts compared with their labor income. This result should, however, be interpreted with care as the analysis requires detailed tax payment profiles that are beyond the scope of this chapter.

Appendix: Per capita public pension spending normalized by labor income of people aged 30–49

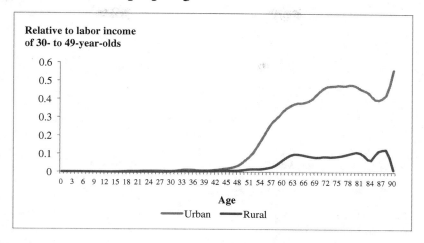

Figure A.1 By residence

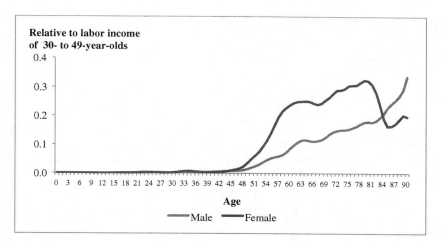

Figure A.2 By gender

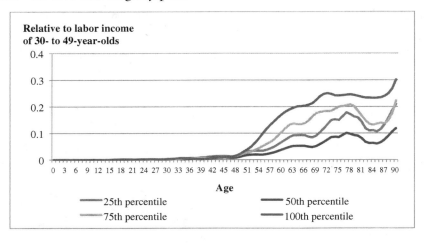

Figure A.3 By income quartile

Source: Authors' estimates.

Notes

1   The elderly in urban areas are defined as women older than 55 years and men older than 60 as those are the normal retirement ages in urban areas. In rural areas, the elderly are defined as people older than 60 years as they are entitled to pension benefits. If there are no elderly individuals in the household and household pension benefits are positive, the household amounts are allocated to the oldest individual living in the household.
2   We used locally weighted scatterplot smoothing (LOWESS) with a bandwidth of 0.1. The default bandwidth in a LOWESS command is 0.8. The smaller the number of the bandwidth, the less smoothing.
3   *People's Daily* (2009).
4   There is a sharp increase in urban pension benefits over age 85, which may arise from a few outliers and the small sample size at very senior ages.
5   In 2009, the average income per capita in urban areas was CNY17,174.7 and was only CNY5,153.2 in rural areas (He 2013).
6   We define the population under 19 years of age as children for two reasons. First, the enrollment rate in senior high school reached 82.5% in 2010 indicating most students younger than 19 received public education transfers. Second, Isaacs (2009) also adopted this definition in comparing public spending on children and the elderly in the United States.
7   The urban population reached 711.8 million in 2012.

Bibliography*

Barber, S. L. and L. Yao. 2010. Health Insurance Systems in China: A Briefing Note. *World Health Report Background Paper* 37. Geneva: World Health Organization. http://www.who.int/healthsystems/topics/financing/healthreport/37ChinaB_YFINAL.pdf (accessed 1 October 2013).

*The Asian Development Bank recognizes China by the name People's Republic of China and Vietnam by the name Viet Nam.

Bommier, A., R. Lee, T. Miller, and S. Zuber. 2010. Who Wins and Who Loses? Public Transfer Accounts for US Generations Born 1850 to 2090. *NBER Working Paper Series.* No. 10969. Cambridge, MA: National Bureau of Economic Research (NBER).

Buchmann, C. and T. A. DiPrete. 2006. The Growing Female Advantage in College Completion: The Role of Family Background and Academic Achievement. *American Sociological Review.* 71 (4). pp. 515–541. http://asr.sagepub.com/content/71/4/515.abstract (accessed 1 October 2013).

Castro-Leal, F., J. Dayton, L. Demery, and K. Mehra. 1999. Public Social Spending in Africa: Do the Poor Benefit? *The World Bank Research Observer.* 14 (1). pp. 49–72. http://wbro.oxfordjournals.org/content/14/1/49.abstract (accessed 1 October 2013).

Chen, W., ed. 2010. *China Educational Finance Statistical Yearbook.* Beijing: China Statistics Press.

Cheng, L., H. Liu, K. Shen, Y. Zhang, and Y. Zeng. 2013. *The Impact of Health Insurance on Health Outcomes and Spending of the Elderly: Evidence from China's New Cooperative Medical Scheme.* http://papers.ssrn.com/sol3/papers.cfm?abstract_id=2280202 (accessed 1 October 2013).

Gao, Q., M. Evans, and I. Garfinkel. 2012. Social Benefits and Income Inequality in Post-Socialist China and Vietnam. http://umdcipe.org/conferences/policy_exchanges/conf_papers/Papers/gao-evans-garfinkel.pdf (accessed 1 October 2013).

Government of the People's Republic of China, Ministry of Health. 2004. Report on China's Health Care Development. Beijing.

———. 2012. *China Public Health Statistical Yearbook.* Beijing: Peking Union Medical College Publishing House.

Government of the People's Republic of China, National Bureau of Statistics. 2010. Sixth National Population Census. Beijing: China Statistics Press.

Government of the People's Republic of China, National Health and Family Planning Commission. 2009. *China Education Yearbook.* Beijing: People's Education Press.

———. 2012. *The People's Republic of China Yearbook 2011.* Beijing: China Yearbook Press.

———. 2013. Monitoring Report on China's Rural Migrant Workers. Beijing.

He, J., ed. 2013. *China Financial Yearbook.* Beijing: Financial Magazine of China.

Institute of Social Science Survey. 2010. *China Family Panel Studies.* Beijing: Peking University.

Isaacs, J. B. 2009. *How Much Do We Spend on Children and the Elderly?* Washington, DC: Brookings Institution.

Lai, F. 2010. Are Boys Left Behind? The Evolution of the Gender Achievement Gap in Beijing's Middle Schools. *Economics of Education Review.* 29 (3). pp. 383–399.

Lee, M.-H. 2012. The One-Child Policy and Gender Equality in Education in China: Evidence from Household Data. *Journal of Family and Economic Issues.* 33 (1). pp. 41–52.

Lee, R. 2003. The Demographic Transition: Three Centuries of Fundamental Change. *The Journal of Economic Perspectives.* 17 (14). pp. 167–190.

Levy, H. and D. Meltzer. 2008. The Impact of Health Insurance on Health. *Annual Review of Public Health.* 29. pp. 399–409. Li, S., ed. 2013. *China Social Statistical Yearbook.* Beijing: China Statistics Press.

Li, S., J. Whalley, and C. Xing. 2013. China's Higher Education Expansion and Unemployment of College Graduates. *China Economic Review.* In Press.

Li, W. 2007. Family Background, Financial Constraints and Higher Education Attendance in China. *Economics of Education Review.* 26 (6). pp. 724–734.

Meerman, J. 1979. *Public Expenditures in Malaysia: Who Benefits and Why?* New York: Oxford University Press.

People's Daily. 2009. Let's Talk: Focus on Fewer and Fewer Rural Students in Universities (in Chinese). 15 January. http://edu.people.com.cn/GB/1053/8676707. html (accessed 1 October 2013).

Pozen, R. C. 2013. Tackling the Chinese Pension System. *Paulson Policy Memorandum.* Chicago: The Paulson Institute.

Ringel, J. S., S. D. Hosek, B. A. Vollaard, and S. Mahnovski. 2002. The Elasticity of Demand for Health Care: A Review of the Literature and Its Application to the Military Health System. http://www.rand.org/pubs/monograph_reports/ MR1355.html (accessed 1 October 2013).

Selowsky, M. 1979. *Who Benefits from Government Expenditure?: A Case Study of Colombia.* New York: Oxford University Press.

Sheng, L., ed. 2011. *China Statistical Yearbook.* Beijing: China Statistics Press.

Strauss, J., H. Hong, X. Lei, L. Li, A. Park, L. Yang, and Y. Zhao. 2012. Health Care and Insurance among the Elderly in China: Evidence from the CHARLS Pilot. http://ihome.ust.hk/~albertpark/papers/NAS_health.pdf (accessed 1 October 2013).

Turra, C. M., M. Holz, and D. Cotlear. 2011. Who Benefits from Public Transfers? Incidence across Income Groups and across Generations in Brazil and Chile. In Cotlear, D., ed. *Population Aging: Is Latin America Ready?* Washington, DC: World Bank.

United Nations, Department of Economic and Social Affairs Population Division. 2011. *World Population Prospects: The 2010 Revision.* New York.

———. 2013. *National Transfer Accounts Manual: Measuring and Analysing the Generational Economy.* New York.

United Nations Human Settlements Programme (UN-HABITAT). 2008. *State of The World's Cities 2010/2011: Bridging the Urban Divide.* Nairobi.

van de Walle, D. and K. Nead, eds. 1995. *Public Spending and the Poor: Theory and Evidence.* Baltimore: Johns Hopkins University Press.

Wu, X. and Z. Zhang. 2010. Changes in Educational Inequality in China, 1990–2005: Evidence from the Population Census Data. In Hannum, E., H. Park, and Y. G. Butler, eds. *Globalization, Changing Demographics, and Educational Challenges in East Asia (Research in the Sociology of Education, Volume 17).* Bingley, UK: Emerald Group Publishing Limited.

Xinhua News. 2013. China Gini Coefficient at 0.474 in 2012. 18 January. http:// news.xinhuanet.com/english/china/2013–01/18/c_132111927.htm (accessed 1 October 2013).

Xu, Q., C. Zhang, X. Zhou, and Y. Xie. 2012. Comparison in Income Data among CGSS, CHIP, CFPS and CFPS Surveys. http://www.isss.edu.cn/cfps/d/file/wd/ jsbg/2010jsbg/a29e71f54de2f5dcd71c6284e4eed017.pdf (accessed 1 October 2013).

Yan, J., X. Sun, X. Teng, L. Ren, and Y. Sun. 2012. Report on Quality Control of 2010 China Family Panel Studies Survey. http://www.isss.edu.cn/cfps/d/file/ wd/jsbg/2010jsbg/bc8d67c159ff99efdde945137191b133.pdf (accessed 1 October 2013).

Yang, D. 2006. *Transition and Development of China's Education.* Beijing: Social Science Academic Press (in Chinese).

6 Fiscal resources for inclusive growth

Arindam Das-Gupta

A. Conceptual framework

1. Inclusive growth

This chapter looks at the economic growth and income distribution effects of fiscal policy instruments for raising resources. Very broadly, inclusive economic growth can be taken to encompass income growth in which no socioeconomic group is deprived of growth benefits. Economically weak groups can include the poor, the handicapped, the illiterate, children, indigenous peoples, and some women. Also included are unemployed workers and victims of war and natural disasters. Fiscal policy is inclusive if it deploys instruments promoting inclusion in addition to promoting its traditional goals of growth and macroeconomic stability. Here, non-income dimensions of inclusion are ignored, so inclusive economic growth is growth with static or falling poverty and inequality. Furthermore, this chapter looks only at instruments used to raise fiscal resources.

2. Fiscal resource categories

Resources can be classified into six categories: debt, non-debt capital receipts, foreign aid and other unilateral grants, non-tax revenue including resource rents, seigniorage, and taxes. (See the following box for a potential seventh category.) Of these, a government's own fiscal revenue sources include taxes, non-tax revenue, and seigniorage. In most economies, the most widely used taxes are domestic and international taxes on good and services followed by individual and corporate income taxes. In addition to these, many diverse taxes are levies.[1] A few resource-rich economies where the resources are publicly owned, however, do not levy taxes and rely mainly on income from the sale of resources or their use rights. Non-tax revenues arise mainly from the sale of government goods or resources and income from publicly owned assets. Seigniorage is the increase in the government's command over goods and services due to its issuing money.[2] Unfortunately, statistics on the flow of seigniorage income to the government are not easily available.[3] In addition to own sources, other revenue sources are foreign aid and other unilateral grants. The other fiscal resource category is capital receipts, including domestic and foreign borrowing and proceeds from the sale of public assets.

Since non-tax revenues are not widely discussed, a brief overview of their composition may be useful. In the United Nations System of National Accounts, taxes are defined as: "compulsory, unrequited payments, in cash or kind made by institutional units to government units." From this it follows that non-tax revenues are payments made to the government that are (i) voluntary and requited, (ii) compulsory and requited, or (iii) voluntary and unrequited. "Revenue" implies that both tax and non-tax revenue excludes "capital receipts" such as government borrowing, money creation, receipts from asset sales, and foreign aid or other grants. The most important sources of non-tax revenue are voluntary, requited payments including revenue from asset exploitation (fees, charges, royalty, dividends, tolls, interest, auction proceeds); sales of goods and services (fees, user charges); and sales of licenses for regulated activities (license fees, permits, registration fees). Fines and penalties are among other widely used non-tax revenue sources. Most non-tax revenue instruments, including those listed here, are typically underutilized.[4]

The seventh fiscal resource category: curbing fiscal waste

While it is obvious that reducing wasteful fiscal expenditure can free up resources for useful public services (or tax reductions), what is surprising is that measurements of fiscal waste and policies to systematically identify and tackle fiscal waste are not part of the fiscal policy armory of any country.[a] What is fiscal waste? What are policies to reduce it?

Fiscal waste has four dimensions:

- The public sector is too large. Private resources pre-empted for fiscal spending exceed the value of public services financed by pre-empted resources.
- Public sector resource allocation is unbalanced. Benefits (marginal) from some public services are much greater than others. Fiscal budgets should be reallocated to the more beneficial public services.
- Some outputs cannot help to achieve intended outcomes. For example, tertiary health-care spending has a limited impact if the targeted outcome is reduced infant mortality. This calls for redesigning public expenditure programs.
- The economic cost per unit of output is too high. For this dimension of fiscal waste, possibly the most important, monitoring bodies (such as audit institutions) exist in many countries.

The first step in tackling fiscal waste is for the term to become part of the fiscal policy lexicon. Waste consciousness itself should lead to fiscal gains.

Except in the most blatant cases, to identify and reduce fiscal waste systematically, institutional reform is needed (i) to identify the actual government goods and services (or public outputs) and (ii) to measure the unit economic cost of each public output. For accurate measurement of economic resource costs, government accounts should be kept on an accrual basis with full recognition of capital costs. These institutional reforms will permit costs of public outputs to be measured. By comparing measured costs across time and different government divisions, fiscal waste can be identified and then reduced and measured.

[a] Some countries, for example Australia and Singapore, impose spending cuts but require the level of public services to remain unchanged. These cuts create an incentive to identify and reduce waste and are sometimes termed "efficiency dividends."

Source: This box is based on unpublished work by the author.

3. Growth and distribution effects of resource categories

There are four possible types of growth and distribution effects of resources. First and most importantly, resources are a source of finance for growth- and distribution-promoting expenditure. In this role, resources do not directly promote growth or inclusion. The main issue here is, therefore, the economic cost of raising resources. Slemrod and Yitzhaki (1996) identify five components of the economic cost of taxation: (i) deadweight or efficiency costs due to induced resource misallocation, (ii) compliance costs, (iii) administrative costs, (iv) the excess burden of tax evasion, and (v) avoidance costs. Conceptually, these costs can be understood by comparing situations with and without taxation. Taxes themselves merely transfer purchasing power from the nongovernment sector to the government. The Slemrod and Yitzhaki (1996) classification seeks to capture the economic costs of making this transfer. An important example of efficiency costs is when economic activity is driven to the informal or underground sector to escape taxes.[5] Slemrod and Yitzhaki (1996) focused on the costs of taxation; however, similar costs can also be identified for sources of fiscal funds. Clearly, less costly sources are to be preferred and should be used first.

The efficiency costs of raising resources arising from their negative impact on individual incentives or on governance institutions can be difficult to identify or measure. For example, there is some evidence that unilateral transfers such as foreign aid can reduce economic efficiency by weakening work incentives or institutions, but there is also evidence that weakened institutions are present where public resources are available without public accountability, such as in resource-rich economies where resources are legally owned by the government. Lack of accountability can lead to the "natural resource curse" of poor governance adversely impacting both growth and inclusion.[6] Efficiency may also be negatively affected if funds from any source are volatile thus reducing the ability of fiscal agencies to predict the level of fiscal spending.

In principle, the economic costs of funds from any source vary with the extent of the use of the source. So when multiple sources of funds are used, the appropriate rule is to equate the marginal cost of funds across sources. For some sources of funds at initially low levels of usage, there may be efficiency benefits rather than costs. A good example is seigniorage where the government is the monopoly supplier of money and when non-inflationary additions to the money supply satisfy increased money demand without any adverse impact on investment. A second example is a "green" tax on a polluting activity in which the direct economic cost of the tax may be more than offset by the efficiency gain from reduced pollution.

The second effect of resources is if the resource is itself an instrument of redistribution integral to the redistribution strategy. Progressive individual income tax rates and consumption tax thresholds are good examples. The main issue here is the trade-off between growth costs and redistribution benefits. In general, the tax systems of most developing economies make a limited contribution to the overall redistributive impact of fiscal policy (Bird and Zolt 2012). The incidence of broad-based taxes both on income and consumption is estimated to be at best mildly progressive. There is also a consensus that the value-added tax (VAT) that has recently replaced taxes on international trade and some excise duties is more progressive than the taxes it replaced. Specific features of resource instruments such as income tax rates and VAT thresholds may, however, be tailored to enhance their redistributive potential.

Evidence on the overall redistributive impact of taxes and fiscal transfers in Latin America (Argentina, Bolivia, Brazil, Mexico, Peru, and Uruguay) for sample periods during 2008 and 2009 is available in Lustig et al. (2012), Lustig, Pessino, and Scott (2013), and Lustig (2013). For inequality, Gini coefficients are reported for "market income" and "final income."[7] In terms of fiscal policy, final income largely captures the impact of raising and spending fiscal resources. The market income/final income Gini coefficients that the study[8] found were the following: Argentina 0.497/0.369; Bolivia 0.503/0.446; Brazil 0.574/0.438; Mexico 0.504/0.429; Peru 0.503/0.463; and Uruguay:0.492/0.393. Fiscal policy does appear to have a substantial net impact on income distribution taking account of both the resource and spending sides.[9]

Regarding poverty, the study compares the headcount ratio for market income with that for post fiscal income. Post fiscal income is final income plus co-payments and user fees minus in-kind transfers, so the comparison is less comprehensive than the inequality comparison. The headcount ratios reported were Argentina 13.0/5.5; Bolivia 9.6/9.4; Brazil 15.4/14.3; Mexico 12.6/10.2; Peru 15.2/14.3; and Uruguay 5.1/2.3.[10] So although fiscal policy did reduce poverty, except in Argentina and Uruguay, the impact is not as significant as the inequality impact.[11]

Third, some resource instruments are deployed to curb undesirable activities that harm growth such as the tax on a polluting activity; the fiscal funds raised are an incidental "double dividend." Examples range from "sin" taxes on demerit goods, environmental levies, information-oriented transaction taxes, and selective tariffs on imports to prevent excessive balance of payments deterioration.

The fourth effect covers the diverse ways in which the process or administration of resource raising affects inclusive growth. The effects included here are not intrinsic to the resource instrument unlike the other three effects but depend on rules for deployment in practice. Some important examples are the following:

- Weak tax administrations that impose heavy bookkeeping and return filing obligations on taxpayers burden small businesses relatively more than big businesses. This adds to tax regressivity.[12]
- Complex or frequently changed tax laws add to taxpayer costs and may lead to excessive tax disputes and litigation. This affects business costs and therefore growth.[13]
- Greater use of information technology, web-based portals, and banking channels tends to reduce taxpayer and tax administration costs and also the scope for tax evasion. This promotes growth and efficiency and also reduces the compliance cost burden, especially of small taxpayers.
- Revenue leakage through capital flight and international tax avoidance is of importance where weak administrations are unable to cope with unfamiliar tax avoidance and evasion strategies associated with globalization.[14] This can be mitigated by international tax coordination and information sharing between national tax administrations.
- To the extent that inflation tends to have a greater impact on the poor, inflationary finance (or overuse of seigniorage) can be regressive.
- Printing currency notes, the basis of seigniorage, requires technology to prevent forgery and counterfeiting. Otherwise, seigniorage benefits can be diluted, while excessive money creation can be inflationary.
- The auctioning of public resource–use rights such as spectrum bandwidth increases their revenue potential, while reducing opportunities for corruption and nepotism. Given the fixed supply of bandwidth, properly designed auctions permit governments to extract a significant portion of the rents associated with bandwidth usage without any negative efficiency impact.[15]
- User charges for publicly provided private goods targeted at the poor can have positive or negative distributional consequences depending on the size of the implicit subsidy reflected in these charges.[16]
- The use of "large taxpayer units" for collecting taxes from, for example, the top 1% of taxpayers, enhances the revenue potential of broad-based taxes in many developing economies.
- Tax withholding is another method that is thought to be effective for reducing revenue leakage from broad-based taxes.

This review suggests that the resources that should first be used to raise fiscal funds are those with either little or no economic costs or with benefits that outweigh costs.[17] Of the sources looked at, non-inflationary seigniorage appears, therefore, to be the most attractive source of funds followed by corrective taxes and non-tax revenue from the sale of government provided goods, services, and asset-use rights.[18] Broad-based taxes like income and commodity taxes should be resorted to only if and only to the extent that other sources fail to yield adequate fiscal revenue.[19] Among broad-based taxes, evidence of their ranking according to their growth impact finds property taxes the least harmful followed by consumption taxes and personal income taxes with corporate income taxes the most harmful.[20] Since property taxes are also likely to be progressive and the corporate tax possibly regressive, this also suggests that among taxes to promote inclusive growth, property taxes should be looked to first and corporate taxes last.

Regarding capital receipts, the equal marginal-cost-of-funds rule suggests that some use of debt finance may be useful; however, no quantitative guidance is available, so the standard advice against deficit finance is also appropriate here.[21]

Table 6.1 lists various resource instruments according to their growth and distribution effects.[22] Major resource categories for which comparative data are likely to be available are in capital letters. The important point made by the table is that non-tax sources of revenue can be the least costly in terms of growth without adversely impacting inclusion. On the other hand, for major taxes there is a growth-inclusion trade-off. This may also be true of capital receipts if they are overused or are available without adequate safeguards.

4. Notes on some major revenue instruments

Value-added tax (VAT). In the past 50 years, the VAT has been extensively adopted replacing cascading domestic taxes and taxes on imports. While widely welcomed, many best practice VAT design principles have not been followed in implementation.[23] While most VATs do have a broad base covering sales of goods and all but a few services (education, health, and financial services) by firms to other firms and to final consumers, few are levied at a single rate above a threshold that excludes small businesses. Furthermore the base is seldom limited only to consumption since tax credits for capital goods purchases and the zero rating of exports with prompt payment to firms of resulting input tax credits are often implemented only partially. Since the administrative cost of taxing small taxpayers is high per dollar of revenue, low VAT thresholds reduce VAT efficiency. There is also evidence that tax compliance costs are regressively distributed and are particularly burdensome for small businesses (Barbone, Bird, and Vázquez-Caro 2012). A major advantage of the VAT is that it indirectly taxes the informal sector, thus reducing the incentive for informalization in an economy (Keen 2012).

Individual income taxes. Though expert advice to have low and few individual income tax rates is mostly heeded, most governments provide a variety of exemptions or deductions, for example for savings, allowances such as child allowances, and medical and education expenses. They also tax some income sources – especially capital income – at different rates. Although such "schedular" taxation results in the horizontally inequitable treatment of taxpayers, it may be administratively more effective (Bird and Zolt 2011). A common design feature is presumptive taxation of hard-to-observe business expenses and unincorporated businesses. There is little evidence that such tax provisions are positively related to real business margins or that they reduce administrative and compliance costs.

Table 6.1 Properties of major fiscal resources[a]

No.	Fiscal Resource	Growth Impact	Distribution Impact	Advantages and Disadvantages	Key Risk Areas	Other Observations
1	TAXES	Negative. For corrective taxes negative impact may be outweighed by corrective benefits (below).	No uniform impact	Taxation promotes accountable government. Economic cost tends to be higher than other revenue sources.	Tax evasion, corruption, informal and underground activity	Hard-to-tax groups pay proportionately less taxes than other groups.
1.1	TAXES ON INCOME	Negative	No uniform impact	Regressive compliance costs for business	Evasion prone especially for cross-border income flows. Corruption prone. Can lead to relatively high informal sector growth and limit formal sector.	Revenue importance is next to taxes on goods and services in most developing countries.
1.1.1	Individual income tax	Negative especially if economic activity is driven into the informal sector that has limited-scale economies	Generally progressive but not uniformly so	Usually also imposes high and possibly regressive compliance costs on business and self-employment income	Most prone to tax evasion and official corruption except possibly where subject to tax withholding	Evidence suggests individual income tax has a lower growth impact than corporate tax but more than commodity taxes (McBride 2012).
1.1.2	Social security taxes	Negative	Generally regressive, especially if tax deductible for individuals paying these taxes. Regressivity limited to taxpayers who do not include informal sector workers.	Reduces private saving and investment in pay-as-you-go systems if workers covered by social security save less		

(Continued)

Table 6.1 (Continued)

No.	Fiscal Resource	Growth Impact	Distribution Impact	Advantages and Disadvantages	Key Risk Areas	Other Observations
1.1.3	Corporate tax	Negative	Possibly progressive since poor will not have corporate shares. However international tax competition and shifting on to immobile factors including labor may reverse this.	Few taxpayers so low cost of collection and compliance per unit of revenue collected. Lowered further if administration is through efficient large taxpayer units.	Can cause greater informality. Subject to competitive pressure in countries seeking foreign investment.	Tax shifting impact and incidence on domestic and foreign labor is not a settled issue (Clausing 2011).Evidence suggests it has a larger growth impact than income, property or commodity taxes (McBride 2012).
1.1.4	Capital gains tax	Limited if taxed on realization, but negative	Similar to the corporation tax except for capital gains on immobile capital such as real estate where progressivity is more likely	Relatively easily avoided or evaded but can adversely impact investment	Subject to competitive pressure in countries seeking foreign investment	
1.2	TAXES ON GOODS AND SERVICES	Negative	No uniform impact			Usually the most important revenue source in developing countries
1.2.1	Value-added tax (VAT)	Possibly negative	Depends on VAT threshold. Possibly distributionally neutral (Bird and Zolt 2012, Keen 2012)	Costly to administer and comply with. Compliance costs tend to be regressive depending on how high the tax threshold is.If properly administered can reduce tax evasion avenues and the informal sector.	Tax administration in developing countries tends to be weak leading to revenue leakage but less leakage than taxes it usually replaces.	VAT usually has a lower growth impact than the commodity taxes and international trade taxes that it has replaced.Evidence suggests it has a lower growth impact than income or corporation taxes (McBride 2012).

1.2.3	Selective excises	Negative	Regressive if shifted forward to final consumers	Can control economically and socially undesirable activity yielding a double dividend		Fuel taxes can have large growth costs in the short run. In the long run, if they reduce overuse of non-renewable resources growth impact may be positive. Their distribution impact is not clear.
1.2.3	Domestic commodity taxes other than VAT and selective excises (including sales taxes)	Negative	Regressive	Distort relative prices via tax cascading	Evasion prone compared to the VAT	
1.3	TAXES ON INTERNATIONAL TRADE	Negative	No uniform impact	Negative impact on international trade. Easy to administer revenue source for countries with easily controlled boundaries (e.g., islands) (Keen 2012).		Subject to World Trade Organization (WTO) agreements. Of limited revenue importance except among poorer countries with controllable boundaries.
1.3.1	Import duties	Negative	No uniform impact	Lead to excessive import substitution if protective	Evasion prone and can give rise to smuggling	Subject to WTO agreements. May help growth by improving the current account and preventing an adverse macroeconomic impact due to currency depreciation.

(*Continued*)

Table 6.1 (Continued)

No.	Fiscal Resource	Growth Impact	Distribution Impact	Advantages and Disadvantages	Key Risk Areas	Other Observations
1.3.2	Export duties	Negative	No uniform impact	Allow countries to exploit international monopoly power		Subject to WTO agreements
1.4	ASSET TAXES					
1.4.1	Individual wealth taxes	Limited but negative	Generally progressive	Limited source of revenue	Can cause hardship for income poor but asset rich individuals	
1.4.2	Land taxes	As with wealth taxes				
	Asset taxes other than land and property taxes (including resource taxes)	Negative unless it is a tax on pure rents	Generally progressive		Resource taxes may lead to illegal resource extraction and environmental costs	
1.4.2	Stamp duties and transaction taxes	Negative	No uniform impact	Distort prices reducing market efficiency and may reduce transaction volume (e.g., for financial transactions)	May lead to under-declaration of property sales prices	
1.5	OTHER TAXES					
1.5.1	Property Taxes (further discussion is after the table)	Negative	Progressive if rates are proportional to property values		Can be evasion prone unless levied using presumptive valuation norms	Evidence suggests it has a lower growth impact than income, corporation, or commodity taxes
1.5.2	Betting and gambling taxes	Not clear	No uniform impact			
1.5.3	Corrective taxes	Gross effect negative, may be positive with corrective impact	No uniform impact	May yield a double dividend		
2	NON-TAX REVENUE	Positive or neutral if rates are not excessive	No uniform impact		Generally more volatile than tax revenue	Possibly underexploited by most countries

2.1	Resource rents	Positive if not overexploited. Can be negative if overexploited.	No direct impact	Permits allocation of resources in line with development objectives leading to faster growth and inclusion	Natural resource curse if governance is poor as funds may be misused	Generally underexploited in most countries
2.2	User charges	Positive if set at the economically (marginal cost) efficient level	Can be positive (Balestrino 1999)	Can help reduce externality causing consumption or production and give rise to a double dividend	May be costly to administer and so impractical for goods and services targeted at the poor	Generally underexploited in most countries
2.3	Fines and penalties	Positive if they reduce economically undesirable activity	No uniform impact	If well designed, can help reduce external harmful activity and give rise to a double dividend. Proper penalty design is not very common. Revenue importance will be limited if very effective in deterring harmful activity.	May be costly to administer.	Generally under exploited in most countries
2.4	Non-tax revenue other than resource rents, user charges and penalties	No direct impact	No direct impact	Using prices to ration availability of goods can improve resource allocation. Some sources can be tailored to have a positive distribution impact via price discrimination.	Corruption in supply of priced goods or in allocation of resources. Revenue leakage due to large decentralized administration of some goods (e.g., public school fees and hospital charges).	Sources such as spectrum auction fees can exploit public monopoly power.
2.5	Seigniorage[b]	Positive if non-inflationary	Negative if overexploited causing inflation	Efficiency benefits if non-inflationary	Moral hazard due to temptation to resort to inflationary finance	Data not generally included in fiscal budgets. May be accounted for as income of money issuing authority and not the fiscal budget.

(*Continued*)

Table 6.1 (Continued)

No.	Fiscal Resource	Growth Impact	Distribution Impact	Advantages and Disadvantages	Key Risk Areas	Other Observations
3	OTHER REVENUE SOURCES					
3.1	Domestic gifts	No uniform impact	No uniform impact	No efficiency costs. Not a significant revenue source.	Lower accountability	Can generate additional resources during wars and natural disasters
3.2	Foreign aid and other unilateral foreign transfers	Can be negative or positive	No uniform impact	Can give rise to domestic policy irresponsibility.Donor priorities may distort domestic policy goals.	Corruption and lack of adequate donor accountability	
4	SALE OF PUBLIC ASSETS	No uniform impact	No uniform impact	Since public assets are limited, not a sustainable source of fiscal resources.		
5	DEFICIT FINANCE	Positive if not overexploited else possibly negative	Regressive if inflationary or unsustainable	Useful if not overused. Otherwise can adversely impact financial market development.	Relative lack of accountability leads to risk of overuse leading to debt crises.	For external debt crises, multilateral institutions have been important lenders who also impose fiscal rules on debtors.
5.1	External debt	Negative, especially if unsustainable (e.g., Eurozone crisis)	No direct impact. Negative if unsustainable.	Can make additional market-based resources available for development	Financial market instability; vulnerability to currency movements	Multilateral institutions have been important lenders during crises and natural disasters.
5.2	Internal debt	Positive if debt servicing cost is low or else possibly negative	No uniform impact	Can help domestic financial development.Inflationary if excessive.	Growing pre-emption of public resources to pay interest on debt	War and natural disasters

[a] This table has benefited from detailed comments by Iris Claus though any errors are still the responsibility of the author.

[b] Money creation is normally reckoned as a part of government debt; however, since it does not require repayment, it is included here as a source of revenue.

Source: Author.

Their impact on revenue, efficiency, and distribution is unknown (Bird and Das-Gupta 2014).

Corporate taxes. Overall, these taxes are the second highest source of revenue in developing economies after taxes on goods and services.[24] This is partly because of the low administrative costs given relatively few corporate taxpayers and the widespread recent use of large taxpayer units. The ability of corporations to shift taxes on to labor continues to be debated with globalization adding a further dimension to the ability of firms to insulate themselves from international tax differences.[25]

Auctioning of spectrum and other licenses. This non-tax revenue source has helped several governments to raise fiscal revenue. These auctions have been carefully designed following several lapses in the early days of auctioning in the 1980s.[26]

Property taxes. Since property taxes have been identified as important for inclusive fiscal policy, the discussion here is more elaborate than for other revenue sources.[27] Taxes levied on immoveable property are widely advocated as a source of fiscal funds especially for local governments; however they are generally underused, offering scope for strengthening fiscal resources particularly for local governments.[28]

Taxes on property include annual taxes on land and property (LPT) but also stamp duties on property transfer taxes, development fees, betterment levies, estate duties or inheritance taxes, and capital gains taxes on property transfers.[29] The most widely levied tax is the LPT. The United Nations Human Settlement Programme (UN-Habitat 2011) provided a convenient formula for property tax revenue to facilitate the discussion of property tax issues:

Revenue = Base x Rate x Coverage x Valuation x Collection

The base of the LPT varies depending on the nature of property rights or ownership; the types of properties included in the base (rural or urban, vacant or built-up plot); the area of the property; and the per-unit area value. Where property rights are based on traditional systems or are informal, legally identifying taxable properties is often a challenge.[30] The LPT rate can be *ad valorem* or more typically specific but tied to property characteristics. Coverage refers to the proportion of taxable properties actually taxed, varying between 30% in some developing economies to as high as 98% (Norregaard 2013). In rapidly expanding cities, identifying new properties to keep the fiscal cadaster up to date is a challenge but one that can increasingly rely on technology such as satellite imagery. The valuation of a property is ideally at its market value but may be difficult if there are few property sales or if market values are not easily observed. Instead, many property tax systems base property values on a combination of area and property characteristics often via a prescribed and periodically updated valuation formula.[31] Actual tax collection requires that a tax administration be in place. To mention only one example of what this implies, the administration could be centralized and be part of an existing tax administration or decentralized to the local government.

B. Fiscal resource systems in developing Asia

1. *Data sources and limitations*

Data sources with information on most of the resources identified in Table 6.1 are not available for many economies, including those in developing Asia. For the broad resource position of developing Asia, data from 2005 to 2011 (or available years within this period) from the Asian Development Bank (ADB) Statistical Database were used. Despite gaps in coverage, this enabled documentation of the resource pictures for 41 developing Asian economies (Tables 6.2 and 6.4 and Figure 6.1). The most serious limitation is that the level of government – central or consolidated – is not the same in all. For example, for India information is for the central government though states collect substantial additional revenue.

Supplementary data from the World Bank's World Development Indicators (WDI) were used to look at shares of major tax groups for 26 economies in developing Asia for the same period, again with some gaps (Table 6.5). WDI data on per capita income, inequality, poverty, and governance were also used (Figures 6.2 to 6.5). These data are also the source of a comparison of revenue sources in developing Asia with those in Latin America and in the world as a whole (Table 6.6). Finally, data from the International Finance Corporation (IFC) and World Bank's *Doing Business Survey 2012* on the burden of tax administration and the tax payment process were used (Figures 6.6 and 6.7). Significant data gaps include disaggregated non-tax data and data on seigniorage.

2. *Resource systems*

Relative to gross domestic product. In Table 6.2, resources as a percentage of gross domestic product (GDP) are divided into current revenue and capital receipts with grants, including foreign aid, and the budgetary deficit or surplus. Current revenue consists of taxes and non-tax revenue. Columns 11 and 12 of the table provide information respectively on the share of current revenue in total resources, including fiscal deficits if any, and the share of non-tax revenues in current revenue.

Total available resources reflected in total revenue and grants vary between 10% of GDP in India (central government only) to over 100% in Kiribati which depends heavily on external grants. On average, fiscal resources in developing Asia are less than expected. Data in Bahl and Bird (2008) show that revenue for the past 2 decades exceeded 24% of GDP in developing economies, which is greater than the 21% of GDP (excluding grants) found here. On average, therefore, for adequate spending, greater revenue effort appears to be needed in developing Asia.

Table 6.2 also shows that capital receipts are a minor source of revenue except in some Pacific island economies, while deficit (debt) finance is most important in South Asia. Instead, the bulk of receipts in developing Asia consist prudently of current revenue. Current revenue is least important in some South Asian countries (Afghanistan) and the Pacific (the Federated States of Micronesia) where grants contribute substantial resources. Since grants, deficits, and other

Table 6.2 Average resource positions in developing Asia, 2005–2011 (% of gross domestic product)

1	2	3	4	5	6	7	8	9	10	11	12
	Government Level	Total Revenue and Grants	Total Revenue Current and Capital	Current Revenue	Taxes(% of Current Revenue)	Non-Taxes	Capital Receipts	Grants	Overall Budgetary Surplus/Deficit	(5) as a % of (3)+ Deficit	(7) as a % of (5)
Developing Asia		**29.6**	**21.6**	**22.4**	**15.7**	**6.7**	**1.7**	**6.7**	**-0.5**	**74.6**	**29.7**
Central Asia	Central	**24.1**	**22.5**	**21.5**	**15.7 (73)**	**3.2**	**0.6**	**7.3**	**-1.7**	**83.4**	**14.8**
Armenia	Central	20.4	19.7	19.2	17.9	1.2	0.6	0.7	-2.5	83.6	6.5
Azerbaijan	Central	24.6	24.6	24.6	15.0	9.6	0.0	0.0	-0.2	99.2	39.0
Kazakhstan	Central	22.6	19.0	18.6	17.9	0.7	0.4	3.6	-1.4	77.5	3.9
Kyrgyz Republic	Consolidated	25.0	23.0	22.7	18.1	4.6	0.2	2.0	-1.5	85.9	20.3
Georgia	Consolidated	31.2	29.6	26.5	23.9	2.6	3.1	1.6	-2.0	79.8	9.7
Tajikistan	Consolidated	20.5	20.0	19.4	17.9	1.6	0.0	0.6	-5.0	76.0	8.1
Uzbekistan	Central	22.0	22.0	22.0	20.5	1.4	0.0	0.0	0.6	100.0	6.6
East Asia		**22.5**	**22.1**	**21.2**	**16.8 (79)**	**4.4**	**0.9**	**0.2**	**0.2**	**93.9**	**20.6**
PRC	Central	19.6	19.6	19.6	17.3	2.3	0.0	0.0	-1.0	95.2	11.6
Hong Kong, China	Central	20.4	20.4	16.5	13.4	3.2	3.8	0.0	3.2	81.2	19.2
Korea, Republic of	Central	23.6	23.6	23.4	15.6	7.9	0.2	0.0	1.0	99.2	33.6
Mongolia	Central	34.4	34.1	34.1	28.9	5.2	0.1	0.2	-1.0	96.4	15.3
Taipei,China	Central	12.8	12.8	12.2	8.9	3.3	0.6	0.0	-1.3	86.4	27.0
South Asia		**18.8**	**15.1**	**15.0**	**10.2 (68)**	**4.8**	**0.1**	**4.3**	**-4.2**	**64.8**	**32.1**
Afghanistan	Central	17.3	8.1	8.1	5.4	2.6	0.0	9.2	-2.6	40.6	32.4

(Continued)

Table 6.2 (Continued)

	Government Level	Total Revenue and Grants	Total Revenue Current and Capital	Current Revenue	Taxes(% of Current Revenue)	Non-Taxes	Capital Receipts	Grants	Overall Budgetary Surplus/Deficit	(5) as a % of (3)+ Deficit	(7) as a % of (5)
Bangladesh	Consolidated	11.4	11.2	11.0	8.9	2.1	0.0	0.6	-3.9	72.2	19.0
Bhutan	Central	34.3	21.0	20.7	11.2	9.5	0.4	13.2	2.4	60.3	45.8
India	Central	10.1	10.1	9.7	7.7	2.0	0.4	0.0	-4.7	65.4	20.4
Maldives	Central	31.5	28.1	27.9	13.5	14.4	0.2	3.4	-10.7	66.1	51.5
Nepal	Central	15.8	13.1	13.1	10.9	2.2	0.0	2.7	-2.0	73.7	16.7
Pakistan	Consolidated	14.5	14.2	14.2	10.2	4.0	0.0	0.3	-5.0	72.7	28.2
Sri Lanka	Central	15.8	15.1	15.1	13.4	1.7	0.0	0.7	-7.5	64.7	11.1
Southeast Asia		**21.8**	**21.2**	**20.5**	**13.9 (69)**	**6.6**	**0.8**	**0.7**	**1.4**	**94.1**	**32.1**
Brunei Darussalam	Central	50.6	50.6	50.6	23.3	27.4	0.0	0.0	21.2	100.0	54.0
Cambodia	Central	14.9	12.1	11.8	9.8	2.0	0.4	2.8	-2.2	68.8	16.8
Indonesia	Central	17.4	17.4	17.4	12.1	5.3	0.0	0.0	-0.9	94.9	30.2
Lao PDR	Central	16.3	13.4	13.4	11.6	1.8	0.0	2.9	-3.0	69.5	13.2
Malaysia	Central	20.8	20.8	20.8	14.6	6.2	0.0	0.0	-4.3	82.7	29.6
Myanmar	Central	15.7	15.7	15.3	3.6	11.7	0.4	0.0	-3.9	78.3	76.5
Philippines	Central	14.8	14.8	14.5	12.9	1.6	0.3	0.0	-2.0	86.5	11.4
Singapore	Central	21.9	21.9	18.4	12.7	5.7	3.5	0.0	6.8	84.1	30.9
Thailand	Central	16.9	16.9	16.9	14.9	2.0	0.0	0.0	-1.4	92.1	11.6
Viet Nam	Central	28.5	28.1	25.9	23.6	2.4	2.1	0.5	-1.6	86.1	9.1
The Pacific		**46.9**	**27.4**	**32.5**	**19.0 (59)**	**13.8**	**0.2**	**16.4**	**1.1**	**69.3**	**42.4**

Cook Islands	Central	34.7	27.9	25.9	23.9	2.0	2.0	6.8	2.1	74.6	7.9
Fiji	Central	25.2	25.1	24.9	21.8	3.0	0.2	0.1	-2.3	90.2	12.2
Kiribati	Consolidated	111.0	80.3	80.3	21.5	58.7	0.0	30.8	16.4	72.3	73.2
Marshall Islands	Central	67.8	25.4	25.4	17.0	8.4	0.0	42.5	1.3	37.4	33.0
FSM	Consolidated	59.3	21.2	21.2	11.4	9.8	0.0	38.1	-1.9	34.7	46.2
Papua New Guinea	Central	33.6	28.6	28.5	26.4	2.0	0.1	5.0	0.5	84.7	7.2
Samoa	Central	34.0	26.0	26.0	22.2	3.8	0.0	8.0	-2.7	70.9	14.4
Solomon Islands	Central	38.1	32.3	32.3	28.8	3.5	0.0	5.8	1.5	84.8	10.9
Timor-Leste	Central	12.5	12.5	12.5	1.2	11.3	0.0	0.0	1.0	100.0	90.7
Tuvalu	Central	76.8	54.3	54.3	18.2	36.2	0.0	22.5	-4.1	67.1	66.6
Vanuatu	Central	23.0	18.8	18.8	16.8	1.9	0.0	4.2	0.3	81.6	10.4

FSM = Federated States of Micronesia, Lao PDR = Lao People's Democratic Republic, PRC = People's Republic of China.

Note: For economies for which data are not available for the entire period 2005–2011, the average is for available years.

Source: Author's estimates using data from ADB Statistical Database and World Bank's World Development Indicators except the gross domestic product for Malaysia (both accessed 14 August 2013).

184   *Arindam Das-Gupta*

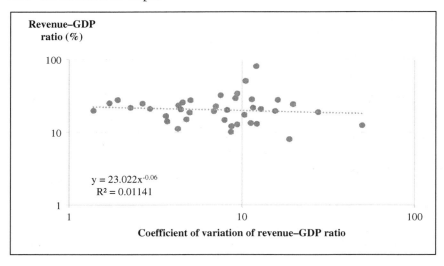

Figure 6.1 Revenue–gross domestic product ratio and its volatility, 2005–2011

Source: Author's estimates using data from ADB Statistical Database and World Bank's World Development Indicators (both accessed 14 August 2013).

capital receipts cannot provide sustainable resources for inclusive growth, the finances of South Asian and Pacific governments appear to be most in need of strengthening.

In Table 6.2, the importance of non-tax revenue in current revenue is also discernable. This picture here is mixed with substantial non-tax revenue present in all Asian regions, but for different reasons. Resource dependence, for example, is clearly the reason for the high non-tax revenue share in Brunei Darussalam – a low tax economy – and also in some Pacific island economies. On the other hand, conscious policy is likely the cause of the relatively high non-tax revenue share in Singapore compared, for example, to Indonesia.[32]

The economies in Table 6.2 can be cross-classified according to whether they are above or below the median in terms of (i) their reliance on current revenue and (ii) within this, their reliance on non-tax revenue. Roughly a quarter of the sample falls into each quadrant of this cross classification with no region showing a distinct revenue pattern for all group members. Economies above the median for both current and non-tax revenue include Azerbaijan and the Kyrgyz Republic; Hong Kong, China; the Republic of Korea; and Taipei,China; Brunei Darussalam, Indonesia, Malaysia, and Singapore; and Timor-Leste. Economies that are below the median for both revenue sources and need to improve include Kazakhstan, Georgia, and Tajikistan; Nepal and Sri Lanka; the Lao People's Democratic Republic and Cambodia; and Cook Islands and Samoa.

To measure if a country has the minimum resources needed to achieve inclusive growth, Ravallion (2009) looks at the marginal tax the rich would have to bear for sufficient funds to become available to finance transfers to the poor to raise them to the poverty line. His sample consisted of 89 developing countries. One

exercise he carried out was with a poverty line of $1.25 a day and a "rich" line of
$13 a day, both in terms of 2005 purchasing power parity (PPP). Since $13 was
then the US poverty line, anyone there with at least this income would not have
been poor.

His findings for the 21 developing Asian economies in his sample are in
Table 6.3. The table shows that in at least 12 economies including India and the

Table 6.3 Capacity for redistribution, Ravallion's measure at $1.25 purchasing power
parity

	Marginal Tax Rate on the Rich Needed to Provide $1.25 in 2005 $ Purchasing Power Parity per Poor Person per Day	Gross Domestic Product per Capita (2005 $ Purchasing Power Parity)
Central Asia		
Armenia	100.0	5,083
Azerbaijan	23.9	7,469
Georgia	84.6	4,307
Kazakhstan	62.7	10,253
Kyrgyz Republic	8.8	1,943
Tajikistan	100.0	1,632
Uzbekistan	100.0	2,448
East Asia		
China, People's Republic of	100.0	5,732
Mongolia	9.0	3,485
South Asia		
Bangladesh	100.0	1,337
India	100.0	2,740
Nepal	100.0	1,125
Pakistan	100.0	2,321
Sri Lanka	69.7	4,195
Southeast Asia		
Cambodia	100.0	1,808
Indonesia	41.4	3,579
Lao People's Democratic Republic	100.0	2,015
Malaysia	2.7	13,200
Philippines	100.0	3,341
Thailand	2.9	7,474
Viet Nam	100.0	2,597

Source: Ravallion 2009.

Table 6.4 Revenues as a percentage of gross domestic product: volatility (coefficients of variation), 2005–2011

Region	Total Revenue and Grants	Total Revenue Current, and Capital	Current Revenue	Taxes	Non-taxes	Capital Receipts	Grants	Overall Budgetary Surplus/ Deficit
Developing Asia	11.4	9.6	9.4	12.3	26.4	63.0	41.6	126.3
Central Asia	11.6	11.8	11.8	17.9	25.8	72.0	54.6	137.5
East Asia	9.0	7.6	6.6	6.6	15.1	34.8	58.1	174.3
South Asia	13.7	10.1	10.0	14.5	22.6	73.5	38.5	66.6
Southeast Asia	9.1	7.8	7.6	12.4	19.4	94.7	36.9	66.6
The Pacific	12.7	10.2	10.2	9.3	41.7	44.5	38.2	195.1

Source: Author's estimates using ADB Statistical Database and World Bank's World Development Indicators (both accessed August 14, 2013).

Table 6.5 Contribution of major tax groups to revenue

Region	Taxes as a Percentage of Total Revenue	Taxes on Income (% of taxes)	Tax on International Trade (% of taxes)	Taxes on Goods and Services (% of taxes)	Other Taxes (% of taxes)
Developing Asia	76.93	32.30	12.40	39.20	16.10
Central Asia	83.64	28.14	7.47	43.92	20.47
East Asia	70.65	41.04	3.98	43.17	11.81
South Asia	72.17	23.65	20.90	33.20	22.26
Southeast Asia	79.27	39.54	9.79	39.66	11.02

Note: Central Asia covers Armenia, Azerbaijan, Georgia, Kazakhstan, and the Kyrgyz Republic. East Asia includes the People's Rep. of China; Hong Kong, China; the Republic of Korea; and Mongolia. South Asia consists of Afghanistan, Bangladesh, Bhutan, India, Maldives, Nepal, Pakistan, and Sri Lanka. Southeast Asia has Cambodia, Indonesia, the Lao People's Democratic Republic, Malaysia, Myanmar, the Philippines, Singapore, and Thailand.

Source: Author's estimates using World Bank's World Development Indicators (accessed 14 August 2013)

People's Republic of China (PRC), redistribution to achieve inclusion is not feasible as a marginal tax rate of 100% or more would be needed. To achieve inclusion, these countries cannot rely on internal resources alone till further income growth takes place. On the other hand, in the Kyrgyz Republic – a country with a relatively low per capita income – Malaysia, Mongolia, and Thailand, inclusion could be achieved.

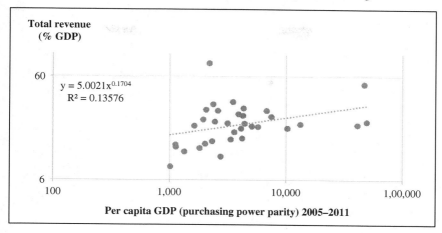

Figure 6.2 Total revenue vs per capita gross domestic product (log scales)

PPP = purchasing power parity.

Source: Author's estimates using World Bank's World Development Indicators (accessed 14 August 2013).

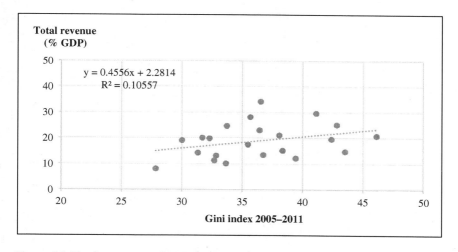

Figure 6.3 Total revenue vs Gini index

Source: Author's estimates using World Bank's World Development Indicators (accessed 14 August 2013).

Revenue volatility. Other things equal, a volatile revenue source is less attractive than a more predictable source. In Table 6.4 the coefficients of variation across years of resources relative to GDP are reported for the same data and period as in Table 6.2. Data are for averages across regional groupings of economies. The table shows that taxes are the least volatile source of revenue on average with non-tax revenue more than twice as volatile. Capital receipts, grants, and

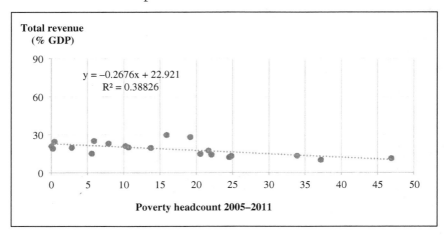

Figure 6.4 Total revenue vs poverty headcount

Source: Author's estimates using World Bank's World Development Indicators (accessed 14 August 2013).

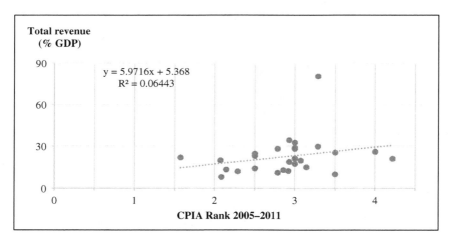

Figure 6.5 Total revenue vs Country Policy and Institutional Assessment (CPIA) Index

Source: Author's estimates using World Bank's World Development Indicators (accessed 14 August 2013).

deficit finance are far more volatile than current revenue, a further reason they do not contribute to a reliable fiscal resource base. Looking across regions, total revenues are least volatile in East and Southeast Asia and most volatile in South Asia, though economies in the top quarter by volatility are to be found in all

Table 6.6 A comparison of revenues in the world, developing Asia, and Latin America and the Caribbean (average percentage of revenue for available years, 2005–2011)

	Revenue Excluding Grants (% of Gross Domestic Product)	Tax Revenue (% of Gross Domestic Product)	Taxes on Goods and Services	Taxes on Income, Profits and Capital Gains	Taxes on International Trade	Other Taxes	Non-tax Revenue	Grants and Other Revenue
1	2	3	4	5	6	7	8	9
Developing Asia	18.15	13.64	30.08	25.04	9.60	3.50	20.50	29.62
Latin America and the Caribbean	22.42	17.54	34.23	24.49	12.68	5.61	21.43	18.46
World	23.52	14.51	32.18	21.80	4.49	1.99	37.50	15.61

Notes:

1: Data for Latin America and the Caribbean are for 21 countries: The Bahamas, Barbados, Belize, Bolivia, Brazil, Chile, Colombia, Dominican Republic, El Salvador, Grenada, Guatemala, Honduras, Jamaica, Nicaragua, Paraguay, Peru, St. Kitts and Nevis, St. Vincent and the Grenadines, Trinidad and Tobago, Uruguay, and Venezuela. Data for Developing Asia are averages for the same 26 economies in Table 6.5.

2: While World Bank's World Development Indicators (WDI) contain data on 214 economies, they provide no information on the actual number included in different (weighted) averages given that there are problems with missing data.

3: The non-tax revenue share was estimated by the author as (column 2 − column 3)/column 3)*(column 4 + column 5 + column 6 + column 7). Some non-tax revenue sources (such as fines and penalties) are included as "other revenue" in the WDI classification system.

Sources: WDI (accessed 23 December 2013) and author's estimates.

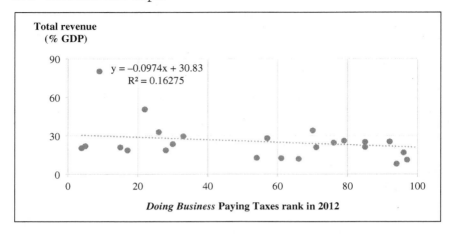

Figure 6.6 Total revenue vs *Doing Business'* Paying Taxes ranking, 2012

Sources: Author's estimates using World Bank's World Development Indicators (accessed 14 August 2013) and International Finance Corporation (2012).

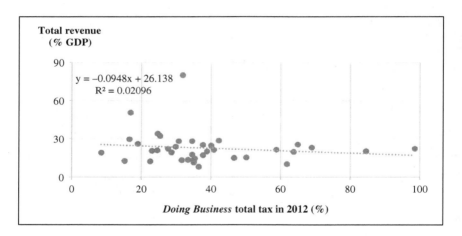

Figure 6.7 Total revenue vs *Doing Business* total tax (% in 2012)

Sources: Author's estimates using World Bank's World Development Indicators (accessed 14 August 2013) and International Finance Corporation (2012).

regions. There appears to be no link between the revenue-GDP ratio and its volatility (Figure 6.1).

Tax shares. The composition of tax revenues from 2005 to 2011 is in Table 6.5 for a sample of 26 economies in developing Asia. The ranking of taxes by major groups follows the expected pattern with taxes on goods and services contributing the major share and taxes on international trade the lowest share.

The latter property is relatively new following recent trade liberalization and tariff reductions in light of World Trade Organization (WTO) negotiations (Bahl and Bird 2008). Bahl and Bird document the share of personal income taxes at less than 50% of total income taxes with the share the lowest in Asian economies. In Table 6.5, the high shares of income taxes in India and Indonesia stand out, but this may be due to a reporting problem. For example, for India, only central taxes are covered and not the large amount of indirect taxes collected below the central level.

Overall, however, the limited share of income taxes, particularly individual income taxes, corroborates the observation by Bird and Zolt (2012) that taxes are likely to contribute little to income redistribution.[33] On the efficiency of raising resources, with corrective taxes, no disaggregated cross-section information is available on "other taxes," so they cannot be assessed. Neither is any cross-country information available on the cost of collecting taxes or other funds. There is, therefore, no scope to apply the criterion for marginal cost of funds to judge the efficiency of raising resources from this perspective.

International comparison. While the share of income taxes may be too small to make it a major tool of inclusive growth, Table 6.6 shows that in developing Asia the share of income taxes is higher than in Latin America and also in the world as a whole.[34] This suggests that further redistributive mileage from income taxes is even more limited in developing Asia than in the rest of the world. Table 6.6 also corroborates the low overall share of total taxes and revenues relative to GDP in developing Asia. Third, the table documents the relatively low share of non-tax revenue in developing Asia and the relatively high share of foreign aid and other receipts (column 9). Overall, however, the high average share of non-tax revenue in the world suggests that it is much too important a revenue source to be treated with the benign neglect usually accorded to it.[35]

3. Fiscal resources, per capita income, poverty, inequality, and governance

How fiscal resources are related to major national characteristics like per capita income, its distribution, and good governance in developing Asia is examined in Figures 6.2 through 6.5.[36] As the figures show, revenue is only mildly positively related to GDP per capita (PPP) and its inequality as measured by the Gini index. The positive link to per capita GDP is expected and replicates results in earlier studies.[37] The positive link to inequality suggests that taxes are mildly progressive in this cross section of economies. On the other hand, revenues are negatively related to the incidence of poverty in the economy, again as expected. The negative link to poverty is the strongest of the three correlations having an R-squared value of 0.38. No strong link is observed to good governance and the absence of corruption possibly due to data limitations; nevertheless, the link between good governance and revenue is, if anything, positive, again as expected.[38]

4. Compliance burden of taxes

The total economic burden of raising fiscal revenue discussed above includes resource misallocation costs and tax evasion and avoidance costs in addition to administration and compliance costs. No cross-section data are readily available on resource costs. Regarding administration and compliance costs, the IFC–World Bank's periodic *Doing Business* surveys are available, most recently for 2012. The "Paying Taxes" ranking from this survey measures the burden on businesses of paying taxes according to a number of indicators including the time it takes to make tax payments, the number of tax payments needed per year, and the actual tax paid as a percentage of profits. Combining these indicators in a single index yields the composite Paying Taxes rank. The survey covers 185 economies including 46 in developing Asia. The least burdensome system in developing Asia is that of Hong Kong, China (ranked 4) followed by Singapore (5) and Kiribati (9). The most burdensome tax system is that of Tajikistan (175) followed by Sri Lanka (169) and the Kyrgyz Republic (168). Figure 6.6 shows that there is a mildly negative relation between administrative and compliance costs and total fiscal revenues.[39] On the other hand, the tax rate has a much weaker link to fiscal revenue (Figure 6.7).

Overall, the analysis of developing Asia's revenue systems suggests that on average, governments do not raise adequate revenues and rely too much on taxation and not enough on non-tax revenue. Within taxes, the major share is that of indirect taxes on goods and services. According to Park (2012), this poor tax performance is caused by high tax evasion and large informal sectors. The other negative factors to raising more revenue tentatively identified in this analysis are poverty and most importantly high administrative and compliance costs.[40] Poor governance and low per capita incomes have less of a negative influence on raising fiscal revenue.

5. Diversity of resource systems in developing Asia

The resource systems in developing Asia display great diversity underscoring the often quoted maxim that there is no "one-size-fits-all" reform strategy. The following brief comments on different economies illustrate this diversity.

Cambodia's tax system is currently undergoing extensive reforms and modernization given its troubled past. Several elements of a modern tax system including a full corporate and non-corporate income tax are still missing, while the VAT is barely 5 years old. Much needs to be done to increase the strength of its medium and large taxpayer populations from the current 19,000. Furthermore, administrative capacity has to be augmented if the large volume of tax arrears is to be reduced.[41]

Contrasting sharply with Cambodia, Singapore's tax system is one of the simplest anywhere with full-fledged legislation with almost no gaps. Its tax administration, one of the most modern in the world, is highly automated and focused on excellence in taxpayer services.[42]

One of the major issues the PRC illustrates is the importance of well-designed resource transfer systems for potentially fiscally inclusive local government finances. It also points to the possibly greater importance of non-tax revenue sources for local governments.[43]

India illustrates the importance of political impediments to reforming fiscal resource systems. Subnational units (or states) have their own constitutional powers to raise resources, powers that they aggressively use. As a result, subnational tax reforms are subject to long, drawn-out negotiations and consensus building. For example, the subnational component of a country-wide VAT (or goods and services tax) first suggested in 1985 is still incomplete. Inefficiencies in raising resources persist for years after reforms are identified.[44]

The remote Pacific island of Kiribati depends crucially on external economic opportunities for its continued growth and development. The economy is currently highly reliant on foreign aid. Of internal resources, non-tax revenue from the sale of fishing licenses is the major revenue source, so future strategies for raising resources must strive to improve external economic relations and, to the extent possible, domestic economic activity.[45]

A landlocked Himalayan country with limited domestic industry, Nepal's revenue–GDP ratio (excluding grants) is lower than all its South Asian neighbors. Though partly because of poverty, tax collection is below even its limited potential due to a poorly designed and administered tax system. For Nepal and some other similarly placed countries, improving tax design and strengthening revenue administration should be a major element in the strategy to promote inclusive growth.[46]

The Philippines, like India, is a relatively open democracy with a free press. That both have similarly low tax–GDP ratios raises the possibility that democracy and relatively "free" societies cause low tax capacity. Parallels in their tax systems are striking and include sophisticated academic and research establishments for taxation; sophisticated and "modern" tax laws that, however, are riddled with tax concessions, some possibly due to political pressure groups; direct taxes predominating in their revenue structures, unusual for countries at their income levels; large-scale tax evasion; and allegedly deeply corrupt tax administrations.[47]

Finally, Georgia and Uzbekistan among former Soviet Union countries have sharply contrasting problems with their tax administrations.[48] The *Doing Business* Paying Taxes ranking places Georgia 33rd out of 185 economies; however, Georgia's tax administration, though allegedly free of corruption, has an adversarial attitude toward business taxpayers leading to uncertainty, high costs, and possibly growing informalization. Uzbekistan has a corrupt but inefficient tax administration that is being reformed and that as a result does not impose too high a cost on business. In Georgia, therefore, improving growth and revenue raising requires that the power of tax officials be curbed, while in Uzbekistan, better revenue performance should address corruption in the tax administration as is being done.

C. Overall assessment and suggested reform priorities

The following major conclusions about the resource systems of developing Asia appear warranted despite the limited information on which they are based.

- In developing Asia, economies rely too little on resources that have low economic costs and too much on broad-based taxes. Thus, the scope to raise resources more efficiently and inclusively exists by paying greater attention to non-tax revenues, property taxes, and corrective taxes. Within broad-based taxes, there is scope for some governments to enhance the productivity of the VAT.
- Poor and smaller economies have limited resource bases and lack the capacity to improve their strategies for raising resources unilaterally and so would benefit from external financial and technical support.
- The volatility of fiscal resource flows tends to be high for resource dependent economies, especially if global market prices fluctuate over time.
- The informal sector – to which tax administration may itself contribute – weakens fiscal resource bases.
- Tax administration effectiveness and efficiency can be improved by more effective information utilization and by the adoption of communication technology advances. Reforms of tax administrations need, however, to look at administrative institutions and incentives and cannot be limited to technical reforms alone.

These conclusions can also be taken as setting priorities for short-run reforms to strengthen resource systems in developing Asia.

Developing Asia displays a great deal of diversity in the nature of its fiscal resource bases and administrations with respect to the extent of reliance on direct taxes; VAT design and use; the number of taxes and the share of other taxes; the size and importance of subnational governments (if any); corruption in tax administration; and, on the other hand, business friendliness and lack of arbitrariness of tax administration.

For a more complete analysis, greatly improved data are needed particularly on the following:

- Seigniorage
- Effective rates for major taxes, the extent of revenue loss through tax concessions, and the taxpayer base
- Categories of non-tax revenues and their yield
- The administrative and compliance cost of collecting taxes so that the cost of funds from different sources can be computed and compared
- The effectiveness of institutions regarding fiscal accountability and anticorruption

Even this will not permit an analysis of the distribution impact of resource systems. For this, a combined incidence analysis of revenue and expenditures is required economy by economy.[49] Perhaps the way forward in the immediate future is to undertake case studies on those identified as fiscally the weakest.[50]

Notes

1 A useful overview of taxes and their classification is the classic textbook presentation in Musgrave and Musgrave (1984).
2 For an introduction and analysis, see Buiter (2007). For some empirical evidence, see Click (1998). When money supply is issued by a central bank or monetary authority that is not legally part of the government, resource transfers to fiscal authorities from the central bank or monetary authority rather than seigniorage itself are part of fiscal resources. This was pointed out by Joseph E. Zveglich, Jr.
3 For relatively recent cross-country data and analysis, see Aisen and Veiga (2005).
4 This paragraph is based on Das-Gupta (2005).
5 For a discussion of the importance of the informal sector in relation to taxation, see Keen (2012) and Bird and Zolt (2012). The value-added tax is claimed to be less hospitable to the informal sector than the sales taxes and excises it replaced.
6 Barma et al. (2012); Collier (2007); Collier and Hoeffler (2005); Gylfason, Herbertsson, and Zoega (1999); and Morrison (2010).
7 Final income is market income less personal and payroll taxes, indirect taxes, co-payments and user fees plus direct transfers, indirect subsidies, and in-kind (free) transfers.
8 The figures reported are from the more recent study in Lustig (2013).
9 Recent information on the impact of fiscal policy in Organisation for Economic Co-operation and Development (OECD) members in 2010 is reported by McCanne (2013). The Gini coefficients for income before taxes and transfers and income after taxes and transfers reported there are Canada 0.447/0.320 and United States 0.499/0.380. For the OECD, only the after-tax and transfer Gini is reported, and it is 0.316.
10 For Argentina, inequality and poverty figures are not strictly comparable with the other sample countries.
11 McCanne (2013) also reports headcounts (income poverty rates) for income before taxes and transfers and income after taxes and transfers. These are for Canada 26.0%/11.9% and for the United States 28.4%/17.4%. For the OECD as a whole, the after-tax and transfers poverty rate is reported to be 11.1%. See also OECD (2013) and Whiteford (2008).
12 A review of tax compliance cost studies of both individuals and business entities is in Evans (2003).
13 A particular case of this is tax legislation that applies retrospectively increasing the uncertainty of tax dues. India has had several instances of retrospective tax legislation.
14 See, for example, Asher and Rajan (2001).
15 For auction design principles see, for example, Klemperer (2004).
16 See Balestrino (1999), Besley (1991), and Sepehri and Chernomas (2001).
17 Unless there are drawbacks not discussed here. Examples are the citizen's opposition to the poll tax imposed by Margaret Thatcher and the collection of a land tax from poor farmers with small holdings where the collection cost has been found to exceed the revenue collected.
18 These sources can lose their sheen if effective accountability mechanisms preventing their overuse by governments are not available.
19 On the other hand, taxes, since they are salient, are held to generally be more accountable to citizens than other revenue sources.

20 See McBride (2012) for a review. He cites studies of OECD members by Arnold et al. (2011).
21 For a brief analysis of this and other resource issues, see Bird and Das-Gupta (2014) and references cited therein.
22 Recent reviews of taxation in developing countries are in Besley and Persson (2013), Bird (2012), Fjeldstad (2013), Fuest and Zodrow (2013), Keen (2012), Mogni (2012), and International Monetary Fund and World Bank (2013).
23 See Ebrill et al. (2001) and Keen (2012).
24 Data are presented in the next section.
25 See Clausing (2011).
26 Auction design theory is discussed in Klemperer (2004).
27 The discussion here mainly draws on Norregaard (2013) and UN-Habitat (2011). Information on Latin America's underutilization of property taxes and their suggestions for strengthening collection are in Corbacho, Cibils, and Lora (2013).
28 Information on property tax revenue for the year 2010 for a sample of countries including eight in developing Asia is in Norregaard (2013). He reports property tax contributions to revenue at less than 1% of GDP in all eight: Afghanistan: 0.23; Armenia: 0.24; Azerbaijan: 0.36; the People's Republic of China: 0.51; Georgia: 0.92; Kazakhstan: 0.56; Mongolia: 0.16; and Singapore: 0.90. In these countries, property taxes are recurrent (typically annual) levies on immoveable property.
29 Development fees are typically one-time charges on new constructions tied to public services that the new construction will have access to. Betterment levies are one-time or recurrent charges on existing properties to recover the cost of additional public services or infrastructure (UN-Habitat 2011).
30 Identifying ownership is also a challenge, for example in the PRC where property purchases are used to conceal illegal wealth, real estate markets are booming, and speculative trades are widespread. For recent attempts to strengthen or introduce property taxes and their impact on real estate see, for example, Century (2013). By levying property taxes, the government hopes to curb speculation and keep housing affordable in addition to reducing land grabbing from collectives by local governments. This tax can strengthen local government revenues since current local government land grabbing practices contribute to the real estate fever (Fung 2013, *The Economist* 2012, and Norregaard 2013).
31 See, for example, the computer-assisted mass appraisal (CAMA) system described by Norregaard (2013). A classification of property valuation systems is also in Norregaard (2013). Actual valuation in some countries is self-assessed with sample checks by tax officials to ensure that self-assessments are accurate. This is done, for example, in several Indian cities (UN-Habitat 2011).
32 Singapore is known for its sovereign wealth funds and particularly for road and automobile usage license fees and charges.
33 This point is also made in the context of Latin America's taxes by Corbacho, Cibils, and Lora (2013).
34 The reader should be cautioned that the simple averages and ranks reported in Table 6.6 could change if data for economies not in the WDI database were included.
35 The revenue contribution of non-tax revenue is underestimated here since some non-tax revenues such as fines and penalties are included in "grants and other revenue."
36 Data on variables used here are from WDI. Sample sizes of economies in developing Asia are 36 for per capita GDP, 23 for the Gini Index, 21 for the poverty headcount, and 27 for the Country Policy and Institutional Assessment Index.
37 See Bahl and Bird (2008). The link is stronger for tax revenues alone.
38 A discussion of various determinants of revenues from different sources is in Keen (2012).

39 The link to tax revenue alone is weaker.
40 Weak administration is also a factor identified by Park (2012).
41 See Chansopheak (2007), Puthipol (2011), and Um (2012).
42 See, for example, Araral (2009).
43 Wang and Herd (2013) point out that provinces are likely to soon introduce annual taxes on residential property to reduce their reliance on transfers. As pointed out previously, their likely incidence on the rich implies that these taxes could well promote inclusion in addition to contributing to raising resources. For additional relevant discussion see Wong and Bird (2005).
44 This paragraph is largely based on the author's interpretation of recent fiscal reforms and impediments. Also see for example De (2012) and Kelkar, Rajaraman, and Misra (2012).
45 See IMF (2013).
46 See Dahal (2009) and Dobrescu, Nelmes, and Yu (2011).
47 See Aldaba (2006), Blöndal (2010), Diokno (2010), Jeremias (2012), and World Bank (2013a).
48 Dekhanov (2011) and Tadjibaeva and Komilova (2009) for Uzbekistan, and Transparency International Georgia (2010).
49 As in the pioneering study by Devarajan and Hossain (1995).
50 Similar to the International Monetary Fund Article IV consultations but for fiscal resource systems.

Bibliography*

Aisen, A. and F. J. Veiga. 2005. The Political Economy of Seigniorage. *IMF Working Paper* 05/175. Washington, DC: International Monetary Fund.

Aldaba, R. M. 2006. FDI and Corporate Taxation: The Philippine Experience. http://www.econ.hit-u.ac.jp/~ap3/apppfdi6/paper/PHILIPPINES.pdf (accessed 10 September 2013).

Araral, E. 2009. Public Finance and Economic Development: The Case of Singapore. http://www.carecprogram.org/uploads/events/2009/Exec-Leadership-Devt-Program/Public-Finance-Case-Study-Singapore.pdf (accessed 15 August 2013).

Arnold J. M., B. Brys, C. Heady, Å. Johansson, C. Schwellnus, and L. Vartia. 2011. Tax Policy for Economic Recovery and Growth. *Economic Journal.* 121 (550). pp. F59–F80.

Asher, M. G. and R. S. Rajan. 2001. Globalization and Tax Systems: Implications for Developing Countries with Particular Reference to Southeast Asia. *ASEAN Economic Bulletin.* 18 (1). pp. 119–139.

Asian Development Bank (ADB). Statistical Database System Online. https://sdbs.adb.org/sdbs/index.jsp (accessed 14 August 2013).

Bahl, R. and R. M. Bird. 2008. Tax Policy in Developing Countries: Looking Back – and Forward. *National Tax Journal.* 61 (2). pp. 279–301.

Balestrino, A. 1999. User Charges as Redistributive Devices. *Journal of Public Economic Theory.* 1 (4). pp. 511–524.

Barbone, L., R. Bird, and J. Vázquez-Caro. 2012 The Costs of VAT: A Review of the Literature. *CASE Network Report* No. 106/2012. Warsaw: Center for Economic and Social Research.

*The Asian Development Bank recognizes China by the name People's Republic of China.

Barma, N. H., K. Kaiser, T. M. Le, and L. Viñuela. 2012. *Rents to Riches? The Political Economy of Natural Resource–led Development*. Washington, DC: World Bank.

Besley, T. 1991. Welfare Improving User Charges for Publicly Provided Private Goods. *Scandinavian Journal of Economics*. 93 (4). pp. 495–510.

Besley, T. and T. Persson. 2013. Taxation and Development. In Auerbach, A., R. Chetty, M. Feldstein, and E. Saez, eds. *Handbook of Public Economics*. Volume 5. http://sticerd.lse.ac.uk/dps/eopp/eopp41.pdf (accessed 20 January 2013).

Bird, R. M. 2012. Taxation and Development: What Have We Learned from Fifty Years of Research? *ICTD Working Paper* No. 1. Brighton, UK: International Centre for Tax and Development. http://www.ictd.ac/en/publications/taxation-and-development-what-have-we-learned-fifty-years-research (accessed 15 July 2013).

Bird, R. M. and A. Das-Gupta. 2014. Public Finance in Developing Countries. In Currie-Alder, B., R. Kanbur, D. M. Malone, and R. Medhora, eds. *International Development: Ideas, Experience and Prospects*. Oxford: Oxford University Press.

Bird, R. M. and E. M. Zolt. 2011. Dual Income Taxation: A Promising Path to Tax Reform for Developing Countries. *World Development*. 39 (10). pp. 1691–1703.

———. 2012. Redistribution via Taxation: The Limited Role of the Personal Income Tax in Developing Countries. *UCLA Law Review*. 52 (accessed 15 August 2013). http://www.uclalawreview.org/?p=761

Blöndal, J. R. 2010. Budgeting in the Philippines. *OECD Journal on Budgeting*. 2010/2. Paris: Organisation for Economic Co-operation and Development. http://www.oecd.org/gov/budgeting/48170279.pdf (accessed 10 September 2013).

Buiter, W. H. 2007. Seigniorage. *Economics: The Open-Access, Open-Assessment E-Journal*. 2007–2010.

Century, A. 2013. Property Taxes Hoped to Curb China's Real Estate Excesses. *The New York Times*. 20 November. http://sinosphere.blogs.nytimes.com/2013/11/20/property-taxes-hoped-to-curb-chinas-real-estate-excesses/? (accessed 18 December 2013).

Chansopheak, C. 2007. Cambodia's Government Revenues and Expenditures. 4 April. http://spheak.wordpress.com/2007/12/26/6/ (accessed 28 October 2013).

Clausing, K. A. 2011. In Search of Corporate Tax Incidence. A working paper. Portland: Reed College. http://www.americantaxpolicyinstitute.org/pdf/Clausing%20CTI%20paper.pdf (accessed 15 August 2013).

Click, R. W. 1998. Seigniorage in a Cross-Section of Countries. *Journal of Money, Credit and Banking*. 30 (2). pp. 154–171.

Collier, P. 2007. *The Bottom Billion: Why the Poorest Countries Are Failing and What Can Be Done about It*. Oxford: Oxford University Press.

Collier, P. and A. Hoeffler. 2005. *Democracy and Natural Resource Rents*. Oxford: Oxford University.

Corbacho, A., V. F. Cibils, and E. Lora. 2013. *More than Revenue: Taxation as a Development Tool*. New York: Inter-American Development Bank.

Dahal, M. K. 2009. Taxation in Nepal: Structure, Issues and Reforms. *Economic Journal of Nepal*. 32 (1). pp. 1–13.

Das-Gupta, A. 2005. Non-Tax Revenue in Indian States: Principles and Case Studies. Unpublished report prepared for the Asian Development Bank. http://www.academia.edu/8496509/Non-Tax_Revenues_in_Indian_States_Principles_and_Case_Studies (accessed 7 November 2013).

De, S. 2012. Fiscal Policy in India: Trends and Trajectory. A working paper of India's Ministry of Finance. http://finmin.nic.in/workingpaper/FPI_trends_Trajectory.pdf (accessed 28 October 2013).

Dekhanov, M. 2011. Taxation System of Uzbekistan: Influence of Tax Reforms on Small Enterprises. *European Journal of Business and* Economics. 3. (2011). pp. 23–28. http://ojs.journals.cz/index.php/EJBE/article/view/113 (accessed 28 October 2013).

Devarajan, S. and S. I. Hossain. 1995. The Combined Incidence of Taxes and Public Expenditures in the Philippines. *Policy Research Working Paper.* No. 1543. Washington, DC: World Bank. http://elibrary.worldbank.org/content/workingpaper/10.1596/1813-9450-1543. (accessed 10 September 2013).

Diokno, B. E. 2010. Philippine Fiscal Behavior in Recent History. *Philippine Review of Economics.* 47 (1). pp. 39–87. http://pre.econ.upd.edu.ph/index.php/pre/article/view/645/4 (accessed 10 September 2013).

Dobrescu, G., J. Nelmes, and J. Yu. 2011. Nepal: Selected Issues. *IMF Country Report.* No. 11/319. Washington, DC: International Monetary Fund. http://www.imf.org/external/pubs/ft/scr/2011/cr11319.pdf (accessed 28 October 2013).

Ebrill, L., M. Keen, J.-P. Bodin, and V. Summers. 2001. *The Modern VAT.* Washington, DC: International Monetary Fund.

Economist, The. 2012. Taxing China: Pay and Play. 4 February. http://www.economist.com/node/21546040 (accessed 18 December 2013).

Evans, C. 2003. Studying the Studies: An Overview of Recent Research into Taxation Operating Costs. *eJournal of Tax Research.* 1 (1). pp. 64–92.

Fjeldstad, O.-H. 2013. Taxation and Development: A Review of Donor Support to Strengthen Tax Systems in Developing Countries. *WIDER Working Paper.* No. 2013/010. Helsinki: United Nations University–World Institute for Development Economics Research (UNU–WIDER). http://www.wider.unu.edu/publications/working-papers/2013/en_GB/wp2013-010/ (accessed 15 August 2013).

Fuest, C. and G. R. Zodrow, eds. 2013. *Critical Issues in Taxation and Development.* The MIT Press. http://mitpress.mit.edu/books/critical-issues-taxation-and-development (accessed 15 August 2013).

Fung, E. 2013. China Policy Document Suggests More Property Tax Trials. *The Wall Street Journal.* 15 November. http://blogs.wsj.com/chinarealtime/2013/11/15/china-policy-document-suggests-more-property-tax-trials/ (accessed 18 December 2013).

Gylfason, T., T. T. Herbertsson, and G. Zoega. 1999. A Mixed Blessing: Natural Resources and Economic Growth. *Macroeconomic Dynamics.* 3. pp. 204–225.

International Finance Corporation and World Bank. 2012. *Doing Business 2012: Doing Business in a More Transparent World.* http://www.doingbusiness.org/reports/global-reports/doing-business-2012 (accessed 15 July 2013).

International Monetary Fund (IMF). 2013. Kiribati: 2013 Article IV Consultation – Staff Report; Informational Annex, Debt Sustainability Analysis, Public Information Notice on the Executive Board Discussion; and Statement by the Executive Director for Kiribati. *IMF Country Report.* No. 13/158. http://www.imf.org/external/pubs/ft/scr/2013/cr13158.pdf (accessed 28 October 2013).

International Monetary Fund and World Bank. 2013. Fiscal Policy, Equity, and Long-Term Growth in Developing Countries. Washington, DC. 21–22, April. http://www.imf.org/external/np/seminars/eng/2013/fiscalpolicy/ (accessed July 2013).

Jeremias, Jr., N. P. 2012. Revenue Mobilization and Current Tax Issues: The Case of the Philippines. Presentation for the IMF–Japan High Level Tax Conference for Asian and Pacific Countries seminar, in Tokyo, on 31 January–2 February.

https://www.imf.org/external/np/seminars/eng/2012/asiatax/pdf/
philippines.pdf (accessed 10 September 2013).

Keen, M. 2012. Taxation and Development – Again. *IMF Working Paper.* No.
12/2102. Washington, DC: International Monetary Fund.

Kelkar, V. J., I. Rajaraman, and S. Misra. 2012. *Report of the Committee on Roadmap
for Fiscal Consolidation.* India: Ministry of Finance. http://finmin.nic.in/reports/
Kelkar_Committee_Report.pdf (accessed 10 September 2013).

Klemperer, P. 2004. *Auctions: Theory and Practice.* Princeton: Princeton University Press.

Lustig, N. 2013. Taxes, Social Spending, and Income Redistribution in Latin America.
Presentation for the IMF–World Bank Fiscal Policy, Equity, and Long-Term
Growth in Developing Countries seminar, in Washington, DC, on 21–22 April.
http://www.imf.org/external/np/seminars/eng/2013/fiscalpolicy/pdf/lustig.
pdf (accessed 15 August 2013).

Lustig, N., G. Gray-Molina, S. Higgins, M. Jaramillo, W. Jiménez, V. Paz, C. Pereira,
C. Pessino, J. Scott, and E. Yañez. 2012. The Impact of Taxes and Social Spend-
ing on Inequality and Poverty in Argentina, Bolivia, Brazil, Mexico and Peru: A
Synthesis of Results. *CGD Working Paper.* No. 311. Washington, DC: Center for
Global Development. http://www.cgdev.org/sites/default/files/1426706_file_
Lustig_et_al_Impact_of_Taxes.pdf (accessed 18 December 2013).

Lustig, N., C. Pessino, and J. Scott. 2013. The Impact of Taxes and Social Spending
on Inequality and Poverty in Argentina, Bolivia, Brazil, Mexico, Peru and Uruguay:
An Overview. *ECINEQ Working Paper.* No. 315. Verona, Italy: Society for the
Study of Economic Inequality. http://www.ecineq.org/milano/WP/ECINEQ
2013-315.pdf (accessed 28 October 2013).

McBride, W. 2012. *What Is the Evidence on Taxes and Growth?* Tax Foundation.
Washington, DC. http://taxfoundation.org/article/what-evidence-taxes-and-
growth (accessed 15 August 2013).

McCanne, D. 2013. OECD Report on Income Inequality and Poverty. Physicians
for a National Health Program blog. 17 May. Chicago, Illinois. http://pnhp.
org/blog/2013/05/17/oecd-report-on-income-inequality-and-poverty/
(accessed 15 August 2013).

Mogni, A. 2012. The EU Position in Taxation and Development. *RSCAS Policy
Paper.* No. 2012/12. San Domenico di Fiesole, Italy: Robert Schuman Centre
for Advanced Studies. http://cadmus.eui.eu/bitstream/handle/1814/24555/
RSCAS_PP_2012_12.pdf (accessed 15 August 2013).

Morrison, K. M. 2010. What Can We Learn about the "Resource Curse" from
Foreign Aid? *World Bank Research Observer.* 27 (1). pp. 52–73. Washington, DC:
World Bank. http://elibrary.worldbank.org/doi/abs/10.1093/wbro/lkq013
(accessed 15 May 2012).

Musgrave, R. A. and P. B. Musgrave. 1984. *Public Finance in Theory and Practice.*
Fifth edition. McGraw-Hill.

Norregaard, J. 2013. Taxing Immovable Property: Revenue Potential and Implementation Challenges. *IMF Working Paper.* No. 13/129. Washington, DC: International Monetary Fund. http://www.imf.org/external/pubs/ft/wp/2013/
wp13129.pdf (accessed 30 December 2013).

Organisation for Economic Co-operation and Development (OECD). 2013. *Crisis
Squeezes Income and Puts Pressure on Inequality and Poverty.* Paris. http://www.
oecd.org/els/soc/OECD2013-Inequality-and-Poverty-8p.pdf (30 December
2013).

Park, C.-Y. 2012. Taxes, Social Transfers, and Inequality in Asia. Presentation for the IMF–Japan High-Level Tax Conference on Emerging Tax Issues in Asian Countries, in Tokyo, on 31 January–3 February. http://www.imf.org/external/np/seminars/eng/2012/asiatax/pdf/park.pdf (accessed 15 August 2013).

Puthipol, V. 2011. The Tax System of the Kingdom of Cambodia. Presentation for the 17th Pre-ASEAN Valuers Association Congress, in Siem Reap, Cambodia, on 20–21 July. http://www.aseanvaluers.org/PDF/The%20Tax%20System%20of%20 the%20Kingdom%20of%20Cambodia.pdf (accessed 15 August 2013).Ravallion, M. 2009. Do Poorer Countries Have Less Capacity for Redistribution? *Policy Research Working* Paper. No. 5046. Washington, DC: World Bank. http://elibrary. worldbank.org/doi/book/10.1596/1813-9450-5046 (accessed 28 October 2013).

Sepehri, A. and R. Chernomas. 2001. Are User Charges Efficiency- and Equity-Enhancing? A Critical Review of Economic Literature with Particular Reference to Experience from Developing Countries. *Journal of International Development.* 13 (2). pp. 183–209.

Slemrod, J. and S. Yitzhaki. 1996. The Cost of Taxation and the Marginal Efficiency Cost of Funds. *IMF Staff Papers.* 43 (1). Washington, DC: International Monetary Fund.

Tadjibaeva, D. and I. Komilova. 2009. The Influence of Tax Reforms on the Prosperity of Micro-Firms and Small Businesses in Uzbekistan. *Asia–Pacific Development Journal.* 16 (2). pp. 31–64. http://www.unescap.org/sites/default/files/apdj-16-2-2-Tadjibaeva_Komilova.pdf (accessed 28 August 2013).

Transparency International Georgia. 2010. *The Georgian Taxation System – An Overview.* Tbilisi. http://transparency.ge/sites/default/files/post_attachments/ Taxation%20in%20Georgia%20_ENG_final_0.pdf (accessed 28 August 2013).

Um, S. 2012. Cambodia: Tax Revenue Reform, Issues, Further Reforms. Presentation for the IMF High-Level Tax Conference for Asian and Pacific Countries, in Tokyo, Japan, on 31 January–3 February. http://www.imf.org/external/np/ seminars/eng/2012/asiatax/pdf/seiha.pdf (accessed 28 August 2013).

United Nations Human Settlement Programme (UN-Habitat). 2011. *Land and Property Tax – A Policy Guide.* Nairobi.

Wang, X. and R. Herd. 2013. The System of Revenue Sharing and Fiscal Transfers in China. *OECD Economics Department Working Paper.* No. 1030. Paris: Organisation for Economic Co-operation and Development.

Whiteford, P. 2008. How Much Redistribution Do Governments Achieve? The Role of Cash Transfers and Household Taxes. In OECD. *Growing Unequal: Income Distribution and Poverty in OECD* Countries. Paris: OECD.

Wong, C. and R. M. Bird. 2005. China's Fiscal System: A Work in Progress. *ITP Paper.* No. 0515. International Tax Program, Institute for International Business. Toronto: Joseph L. Rotman School of Management. http://www-2.rotman. utoronto.ca/iib/ITP0515.pdf (accessed 10 September 2013).World Bank. 2013a. *Philippine Economic Update: Accelerating Reforms to Meet the Jobs Challenge.* Washington, DC. http://www.worldbank.org/content/dam/Worldbank/document/EAP/Philippines/Philippine_Economic_Update_May2013.pdf (accessed 10 September 2013).

———. 2013b. World Development Indicators. http://databank.worldbank.org/ data/views/variableSelection/selectvariables.aspx?source=world-development-indicators# (accessed 14 August and 23 December 2013).

7 Are current tax and spending regimes sustainable in developing Asia?

Sang-Hyop Lee and Andrew Mason

A. Introduction

Changes in population age structure in Asia and the Pacific have been very dramatic over the last few decades and are certain to be so in the future. The changes in the People's Republic of China (PRC) have been particularly rapid but are nonetheless illustrative of the changes experienced elsewhere. In 1990, the population of the PRC was heavily concentrated at young ages with just over half of its people under the age of 25. Because of rapid fertility decline before and after 1990, the share of children in the population dropped to 35% in 2010. This will continue over the coming decades until by 2050 about 25% of the population will be under 25 years of age.

The decline in the share of children over the last 30 years was matched primarily by an increase in the population in the working ages of 25 to 59 that rose from 41% in 1990 to 52% in 2010. This had favorable implications for economic growth – referred to as the demographic dividend – but also favorable implications for public finances. A larger share of the population in the PRC was concentrated in high tax-paying ages and a smaller share at school-going ages. The share in the working ages is expected to peak during the current decade, however, and then begin decades of steady decline. By 2050, the percentage of the population between the ages of 25 and 59 is projected to be 42%, very close to the level in 1990.

The declines in the shares of the child and working-age populations over the coming decades will be offset by an increase in the share of the population 60 and older. In 2050, one-third of PRC's population is projected to fall into the 60 and older age range compared with 13% in 2010 and 9% in 1990 (United Nations [UN] 2013b).

The demographic changes in the PRC are part of a region-wide and a worldwide phenomenon as shown in the three snap shots of population age structure for the world in 1990, 2010, and projected in 2050 in Figure 7.1. In many rich and developing economies, the share of the working-age population has increased during the last few decades as the share of children has declined. Likewise, the future will be increasingly dominated by population aging. In most economies these changes have occurred more slowly than in the PRC, but in Hong Kong,

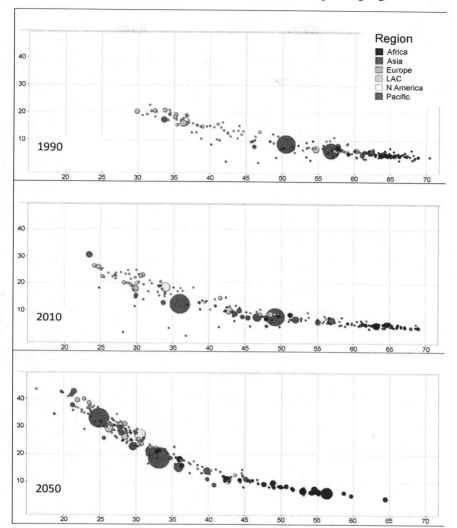

Figure 7.1 Percentage of population under 25 (horizontal axis) and 60 or older (vertical axis) of the world by region, 1990, 2010, 2050

LAC = Latin America and the Caribbean, N. America = North America.

Note: Size of bubble is proportional to the population.

Source: United Nations, Department of Economic and Social Affairs, Population Division. 2013b. *World Population Prospects: The 2012 Revision.* New York.

China; Japan; the Republic of Korea; Singapore; Taipei,China; and Thailand, rapid changes in population age structure have been the rule.

A clear understanding of the source of population aging is essential to understanding the kinds of policy responses that may be considered. One cause of population aging is that people are living longer and that gains in survival rates are increasingly concentrated at older ages. Life expectancy at birth for both sexes combined now exceeds 80 in Hong Kong, China; Japan; the Republic of Korea; and Singapore with steady increases expected in the coming decades. Other Asian economies lag to varying degrees with life expectancy at birth for both sexes in the mid-70s for the PRC and Viet Nam, around 70 in Bangladesh and Indonesia, and the mid-60s in India. As life expectancy rises in these countries, the share of the population concentrated at older ages will inevitably rise.

Lower fertility is the other major reason why populations are aging. Cohorts that bear fewer children during their reproductive ages will subsequently live out their old-ages in societies with relatively few members of the working-age population. In some East Asian economies fertility is particularly low. The total fertility rate – the average number of births per woman over her reproductive span – is less than 1.3 births per woman in Hong Kong, China; the Republic of Korea; Singapore; and Taipei,China; and 1.5 births per woman or fewer in Japan and Thailand and possibly in the PRC. Low fertility is leading to particularly rapid aging in these economies (UN 2013b).

Population aging can be slowed to some extent by immigration. Migrants tend to be relatively young and often their fertility is somewhat higher than the population of the receiving country. The effects of migration are relatively modest, however, except in a few places with expansive immigration policies. In very large countries like the PRC and India, immigration will never have an important impact on population age structure. The role of immigration as a moderating influence on aging is likely to diminish over time as the world as a whole becomes older. As can be seen in Figure 7.1, the current age structure is much more diverse now than it will be in 2050. This is particularly the case for Asia and the Pacific as the populations of Bangladesh, the PRC, India, and Indonesia age. In the future, young populations will increasingly be concentrated in Africa.

Changes in population age structure matter for public finances for a very simple reason: the beneficiaries of public programs are primarily children and the elderly. The age profiles of public transfer inflows are so central to the analysis in this chapter that they are shown for the Philippines in Figures 7.2 and 7.3. Figure 7.2 shows per capita public transfer inflows by age for education, health, pensions, and other purposes. The inflows are normalized by dividing the annual flows by the annual per capita labor income of persons 30–49 years of age, the prime working ages in most economies.

The inflow profiles for the Philippines shows two peaks. The first is for children driven primarily by public spending on education. The peak inflows occur at ages 9 to 11 and amounts to 16.5% of prime adult labor income. The second peak for transfer inflows occurs at older ages driven primarily by public pensions but also by rising publicly funded health-care spending. Public transfer inflows peak at ages 75 and 76 when they are equal to 27.1% of the labor income of a prime-age adult.

The aggregate flows by age are determined as the product of the per capita flows shown in Figure 7.2 and population by age. These values are shown for the Philippines in Figure 7.3. The influence of the Philippines' young population

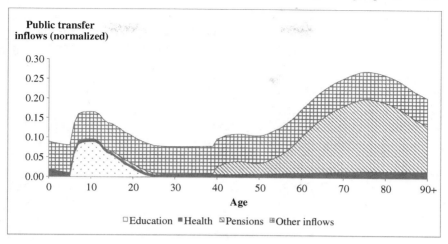

Figure 7.2 Per capita public transfer inflows by age and purpose in the Philippines, 1999

Source: National Transfer Accounts Project.

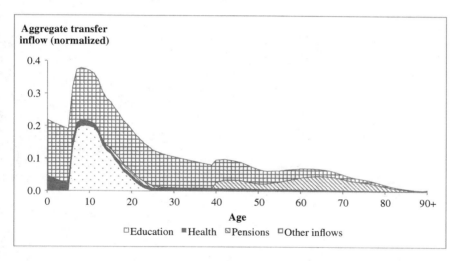

Figure 7.3 Aggregate public transfer inflows by age and purpose in the Philippines, 1999

Note: All flows are normalized by dividing them by the average of total labor income by single year of age for those 30 to 49.

Source: National Transfer Accounts Project.

age structure is clearly evident. Most public transfers go to children and not to seniors because there are many more Filipino children than seniors.

The age structure in the Philippines is changing relatively slowly, but it is changing. As the share of the population at young ages declines, it will push public spending on education lower relative to other public spending or to gross domestic product (GDP). For an extended period of time, the share of the population at young and old ages will be small so that the demographically related demand for public programs will be moderated. As the Philippines begins to age, however, public spending on health and pensions will begin to rise, and in the absence of other changes, public spending as a share of GDP will increase.

Lower-income economies in general and in Asia and the Pacific have low spending on public sector programs for reasons that are largely unrelated to demographic conditions. Public spending on education, health care, and pensions increases as economies prosper. This is very evident in Asia and the Pacific where the roles of the public sector are very different in high- and middle-income economies than in low-income economies. For the wealthier ones with well-developed public sectors, the key issue is whether those programs can be sustained as their populations age. As lower-income economies develop, the key issue for them is whether public programs can be expanded at the same time that their populations are aging.

B. Data

The analysis is based on two sources of data. The first is population projections by age produced by the United Nations Population Division of the Department of Social and Economic Affairs. The most recent population estimates and projections are *World Population Prospects 2012* (UN 2013b).

Data on public sector finances are based on National Transfer Accounts (NTA), a new set of economic accounts that document economic flows to and from ages in a manner consistent with the UN System of National Accounts. Research teams in 40 countries on 6 continents are currently collaborating in the construction of NTA, and 11 have been constructed for Asia–Pacific economies: Australia; Cambodia; the PRC; India; Indonesia; Japan; the Republic of Korea; the Philippines; Taipei,China; Thailand; and Viet Nam.

The theoretical foundations of the accounts build on Lee (1994a and 1994b), and some details and preliminary results are reported in Lee, Lee, and Mason (2008) and Mason et al. (2009). The most recent and comprehensive treatment is Lee and Mason (2011). Methods are fully documented and explained in UN (2013a) and on the NTA website (www.ntaccounts.org).

NTA estimates are constructed using household surveys, administrative data from government agencies, and data from the UN System of National Accounts. The NTA measure how much people at each age consume and produce through their labor, and how the gap between consumption and labor income is funded relying on public and private transfers and public and private asset-based reallocations. Public transfer inflows to each age distinguish in-kind and cash transfers for education, health, pensions, and other purposes. Public transfer outflows – the taxes and other public revenues that fund these transfers – are also classified by the age of those who pay the taxes.

NTA data are used to construct age profiles of public transfer inflows to each age group. These values are adjusted, however, to match aggregate values of public spending on education, health, and social security and welfare available in 2010 or earlier in some instances. More details are provided in Part C.

C. Methodology

The public transfer projections incorporate two factors: changes in population age structure and changes in age-specific transfers due to projected changes in per capita income.

1. Age profiles of education, health, and social protection

Public spending on education, health, and social protection is much lower in low-income economies in Asia than in high-income ones in not only per capita terms of course, but also relative to standards of living. As incomes grow in the region, public spending will become increasingly important. How governments adjust to higher incomes is a matter of policy and will be determined by political decisions, so there is little basis to make a long-term forecast of how public sector spending will rise. Consequently, the projections presented use current (or recent) spending in higher-income Asian economies as a guide to how spending is likely to change in lower-income Asian economies.

This is accomplished using age profiles of public spending by age on education, health, and social protection for Asian economies for which NTA profiles are available. All profiles are per capita flows to persons at each age expressed relative to the average of per capita labor income of adults 30–49 years of age. Thus given a particular profile, per capita spending by age rises at the same rate as projected per capita labor income for prime-age adults. In addition, we assume that as economies become members of higher-income groups, they will experience additional changes in their public spending profiles. The four model profiles constructed for varying levels of income shown in Table 7.1 are used to allow for the effects of income.

The profiles thus obtained for each income group are shown in Figure 7.4. The level of spending rises relative to income as per capita income reaches higher levels. There are also changes in the age patterns of transfers that are particularly notable for health. For low-income economies, spending on health care is only slightly elevated at older ages. For higher-income economies, health-care spending rises very sharply with age.

Table 7.1 Model public sector expenditure profiles by age

Income Range (per capita gross domestic product in $ 2005 prices)	Model Profiles
Under $5,000	Asian low-income economies for education and health (PRC 2002, India 2004, Indonesia 2005, the Philippines 1999, Thailand 2004, and Viet Nam 2008); for social protection PRC 2002, Philippines 1999, and Thailand 2004.
$5,000 to $10,000	Interpolated
$10,000 to $15,000	Republic of Korea 2000 and Taipei,China 1998
$15,000 to $20,000	Interpolated
$20,000 to $30,000	Interpolated
$30,000 to $35,000	Japan 1994
$35,000 or more	Japan 1999

PRC = People's Republic of China, $ = US dollar.

Source: Authors.

2. Gross domestic product growth

Long-term projections of real GDP are difficult to construct. Based on three sources, economies were classified into four groups.[1] The projection results are influenced by the GDP growth assumptions only when they graduate to a new income group. Many low-income economies do not exceed $5,000 per capita income throughout the entire projection, and many others reach a higher income level only near the end of the simulation.

3. Incorporating population

The size of the population has no direct effect on public spending as a percentage of GDP because the model age profiles of benefits are assumed to grow at the same rate as per capita income. Population age structure does have an important effect on public spending as a share of GDP, however, because benefits are concentrated at particular age groups – primarily the young for education and the old for health and social welfare spending.

One way to measure the effect of changes in age structure is to calculate the increase in benefits that would arise given the base-year age profile of benefits and the projected population age structure:

$$\frac{\sum \tilde{\tau}(x,t_0)\, N(x,t)/N(t)}{\sum \tilde{\tau}(x,t_0)\, N(x,t_0)/N(x)} \tag{1}$$

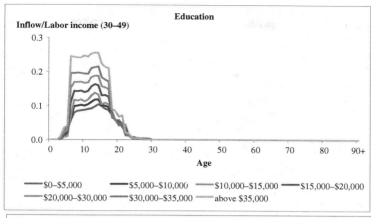

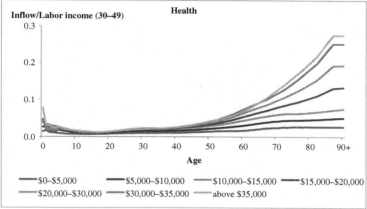

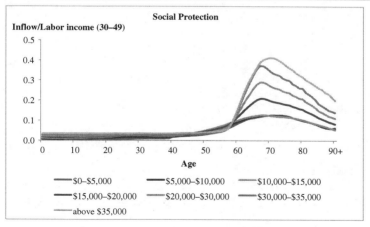

Figure 7.4 Model profiles of public sector spending in Asia by age of recipient
Source: Authors' estimates.

Table 7.2 Per capita gross domestic product growth rate assumptions

Group and Economy	Annual Rate of Real per Capita Gross Domestic Product Growth (%)	
	2010–2030	*2030–2050*
A: Bhutan, Cambodia, People's Republic of China, India, Lao People's Democratic Republic, Mongolia, Myanmar, Sri Lanka, Viet Nam	6.0	3.0
B: Bangladesh; Indonesia; Macau, China; Papua New Guinea; Solomon Islands; Thailand	4.0	2.5
C: Afghanistan; Armenia; Azerbaijan; Georgia; Hong Kong, China; Kazakhstan; Republic of Korea; Malaysia; Nepal; Pakistan; Philippines; Singapore; Taipei,China; Tajikistan; Turkmenistan; Uzbekistan	3.0	2.0
D: Brunei Darussalam, Japan, all others	1.0	1.0

Source: Authors' estimates using the data cited.

This expression has a simple interpretation. It is the ratio of per capita spending on a public program in year *t* relative to per capita spending on the program in the base year necessary to maintain the level of benefits per beneficiary at each age.

The United Nations' *World Population Prospects, 2012 Revision* prepared by the UN Population Division of the Department of Economic and Social Affairs was used for the analysis presented here. All projections are based on the medium fertility scenario. This scenario assumes that fertility will continue to decline in high-fertility economies and will recover towards replacement in low-fertility economies. Details are available on the UN Population Division website (www.un.org/en/development/desa/population/)

4. Aggregate controls

All projections are scaled – adjusted proportionately – to match observed values of public expenditure in 2010 as a percentage of GDP for each economy. The value of interest in all cases is general government spending for education, health, and social welfare.

For health spending, National Health Accounts (NHA) estimates of general government expenditure are available from the World Health Organization

Table 7.3 Public spending as a percentage of gross domestic product for Asia and the Pacific, 2010

	Health	*Education*	*Social Protection*
Average	3.0	3.5	3.4
High	12.6	6.7	17.0
Low	0.8	1.6	0.1

Source: Authors' estimates using the data cited.

(WHO). These data are quite complete and consistent over time. An alternative available from the Asian Development Bank (ADB) is for central government spending. In general, this will be lower than general government expenditure but inconsistently so because of differences in government organization and in some cases over time. For the Republic of Korea, for example, government expenditure on health in 2010 was 0.3% of GDP according to ADB as compared with 4.1% according to WHO. NHA/WHO data were used for country baseline values for health.

Education spending estimates from three sources were compared: the World Bank; the United Nations Educational, Scientific and Cultural Organization (UNESCO); and ADB. Generally, the World Bank and UNESCO data are slightly greater than ADB data, but there are many missing values for the World Bank and UNESCO as compared with ADB. The difference between ADB and World Bank data is small; hence, the more complete ADB data were used.

Our preference was to construct separate estimates for pension spending. Unfortunately, the availability of pension data is limited and inconsistently constructed when available. As a consequence, central government spending on social protection available from ADB was employed.

The simple average, the high, and the low for public spending for the region according to our aggregate estimates are reported in Table 7.3.

Health and social protection exhibit the greatest variation. The highest health-care spending as a percentage of GDP was in the Federated States of Micronesia (12.6%), Japan (7.4%), and Solomon Islands (6.9%). In lower-income economies, values of close to 1% of GDP were not uncommon (Bangladesh, Cambodia, India, Indonesia, and Pakistan). Spending on social protection was particularly high in Armenia (7.1%), Georgia (6.9%), Japan (17.0%), and Mongolia (12.9%).

Public spending on education was somewhat less variable across the region. Spending 6% of GDP or more on education was reported for Bhutan, Malaysia, and Maldives. Public spending in Japan and the Republic of Korea was about 3% of GDP.

5. *Projection method in brief*

Let per capita transfers to persons age x in year t in country z be designated by $b(z)\,\tau(x,t)$. For purposes of projection, we used a normalized support ratio equal to public transfers per person relative to per capita income, $y(t)$, so that public transfers per person age x in year t in country z is equal to $b(z)\tilde{\tau}(x,t)y(t)$, where $\tilde{\tau}(x,t) = \tau(x,t)/y(t)$. Thus, given the normalized transfer profile, per capita transfers are assumed to increase at the same rate as per capita income.

The normalized profile shifts upward in stepwise fashion as per capita income increases. In general, the normalized profile in year t is given by

$$\tilde{\tau}(x,t) = \sum_{k=1}^{K} D_k[y(t)]\tilde{\tau}(x,k) \qquad (2)$$

where $D_k[y(t)]$ is a dummy variable that takes the value of 1 if per capita income in year t falls in per capita income growth k (otherwise the dummy variable is zero) and $\tilde{\tau}(x,k)$ is the model profile for income group k. See the text for the income groups and the model profiles for each group.

Total transfers as a share of per capita gross national product (GNP) is computed as

$$\text{Transfers as a percentage of GNP} = \frac{b(z)y(t)\sum\tilde{\tau}(x,t)N(x,t)}{y(t)N(t)} \qquad (3)$$

$$= b(z)\sum\tilde{\tau}(x,t)\,N(x,t)/N(t)$$

The model is applied separately to education, health, and social welfare spending using transfer profiles estimated separately for each of those programs.

Several features of this specification should be noted. Growth in per capita income within income groups does not affect transfers as a percentage of GNP, all other things equal. It is assumed that governments increase spending as per capita income rises. Second, changes in age structure increase (reduce) transfers as a percentage of gross national product (GNP) if the population becomes increasingly concentrated in ages where public benefits are relatively large (small). Third, public transfers are scaled to match the initial level of spending in each economy. Those with large public sectors are projected to continue with their large public sectors.

The results should be interpreted as the cost (share of GNP) required to realize the model per capita transfers (indexed to per capita income) in the presence of changes in population age structure. As the effects of population age structure are anticipated or experienced, governments are likely to adjust benefits if growth in government is viewed as a problem.

D. Fiscal projections

Estimates of public spending on education as a percentage of GDP for selected years 1990 to 2010 and projections to 2050 are presented in Table 7.4. This is public spending only, and in some Asian economies (the PRC; Japan; the Republic of Korea; and Taipei,China for example) private spending on education is quite substantial. For a few (see table notes), spending at all levels of government are included, but in most the values refer to central government spending only. As noted in Table 7.3, in 2010 public spending averaged 3.5% of GDP (simple average of values) and ranged between 1.6% and 6.7%. Based on these summary values, the importance of education is projected to decline to an average value in 2050 of 2.7% of GDP with a range between 0.6% and 5.0% of GDP.

The projected decline in education spending is driven by fertility declines and the decline in the share of population in the school-going ages. This is analyzed in more detail below.

The declines are quite uniform in a qualitative way as in every economy, education spending as a percentage of GDP is projected to decline. The rate of decline does vary with the greatest declines projected for South and Southeast Asia. Very large declines are projected for Taipei,China as well.

Estimates and projections of health spending for 1995 to 2050 are provided in Table 7.5. The situation is very different than for education spending because demographic change and economic growth are mutually reinforcing when it comes to health care. Populations are aging so that the share at older ages with high health-care spending is increasing. At the same time, higher levels of per capita income should push per capita spending on health care higher, particularly at older ages. In no economy is the share of GDP devoted to health care projected to decline.

On average, the increase amounts to a 64% rise in the percentage of GDP spent on publicly funded health. The simple average increases from 2.8% of GDP in 2010 to 3.6% in 2030 and to 4.7% in 2050.

The rise in publicly funded health-care spending in East Asian economies is particularly dramatic with the average share of GDP rising from 3.4% of GDP in 2010 to 8.5% of GDP in 2050. In the PRC, the projected rise is from 2.7% to 9.8% of GDP, an increase of 264%. These increases reflect the particularly rapid aging anticipated for East Asia combined with high rates of economic growth anticipated for economies like the PRC. Outside of East Asia, the percentage devoted to health is projected to more than double in Azerbaijan, Bhutan, Brunei Darussalam, Cambodia, Kazakhstan, Malaysia, and Maldives. Health spending as a share of GDP is projected to triple in Thailand.

Health-care spending is already at relatively high levels in many Pacific island nations, but projected increases are relatively modest. By 2050 the regional average is projected to reach 6.4% compared with 5.5% in 2010.

Health-care spending in Pakistan, Bangladesh, and India is projected to reach 0.9%, 1.7%, and 2.0% of GDP, respectively, in 2050 because projected economic growth and projected population aging are quite small.

Table 7.4 Government expenditure on education (% of gross domestic product)[a]

Economy	1990	1995	2000	2005	2010	2020	2030	2040	2050
Developing Economies					3.5	3.1	3.1	2.8	2.7
Central and West Asia					3.7	3.3	3.4	2.9	2.8
Afghanistan	...	...	...	...	...	...	...	...	...
Armenia	...	...	2.8	2.7	2.8	2.5	2.3	2.0	1.9
Azerbaijan	7.7	3.5	3.9	3.0	2.8	2.3	2.5	2.1	2.0
Georgia	...	...	2.2	2.5	2.9	2.9	2.9	2.5	2.5
Kazakhstan	...	...	...	...	...	...	...	...	...
Kyrgyz Republic	7.5	6.6	3.5	4.9	5.8	5.2	5.6	4.8	4.4
Pakistan	...	...	...	...	...	...	...	...	...
Tajikistan	...	2.2	2.3	3.5	4.0	3.7	3.8	3.3	3.2
Turkmenistan	...	...	...	...	...	...	...	...	...
Uzbekistan	...	...	...	...	...	...	...	...	...
East Asia					3.5	3.1	3.4	3.2	3.2
China, People's Rep. of[b]	...	2.0	...	3.3	3.1	3.0	3.0	2.9	3.3
Hong Kong, China	2.8	3.0	3.9	3.8	3.4	3.4	3.9	3.5	3.3
Korea, Rep. of	2.9	2.4	3.2	3.2	3.2	2.4	3.3	3.2	3.0
Mongolia	11.5	3.6	6.7	4.9	5.9	5.4	5.5	4.6	4.9
Taipei,China	1.0	1.4	2.3	1.6	1.8	1.5	1.4	1.7	1.6
South Asia					3.8	3.3	3.2	2.7	2.5
Bangladesh	1.4	2.2	2.0	1.9	2.2	1.9	1.6	1.4	1.2
Bhutan	...	...	...	5.1	6.7	5.5	5.6	4.8	4.7
India	...	...	3.3	2.4	2.3	2.1	1.9	1.7	1.8
Maldives	...	4.8	7.4	6.7	6.0	4.9	5.1	4.1	3.5
Nepal	1.6	2.2	2.3	2.9	3.9	3.4	2.8	2.5	2.2
Sri Lanka	3.0	2.9	2.4	2.6	1.9	1.8	2.0	1.7	1.7

Southeast Asia

Brunei Darussalam	4.0	4.6	4.2	3.8	2.9	2.5	2.4	2.2	2.2
Cambodia	0.8	0.9	1.3	1.4	4.0	3.5	3.3	3.0	3.5
Indonesia	1.7	1.3	. . .	. . .	1.6	1.3	1.3	1.1	1.0
Lao PDR	0.5	0.1	1.0	. . .	1.1	1.1	0.9	0.8	0.9
Malaysia	5.5	4.8	5.6	4.9	6.3	5.1	5.2	4.8	5.0
Myanmar	. . .	. . .	. . .	. . .	. . .	. . .	. . .	. . .	. . .
Philippines	3.1	3.2	3.3	2.3	2.5	2.3	2.1	2.0	1.8
Singapore	4.0	2.9	3.9	3.2	3.1	2.5	2.3	2.2	2.0
Thailand	2.7	3.4	3.9	3.5	4.0	3.3	3.1	2.9	3.1
Viet Nam	. . .	. . .	. . .	. . .	. . .	. . .	. . .	. . .	. . .

The Pacific

Fiji	3.5	4.0	4.2	3.7	3.8	3.8	3.4	3.2	3.1
Micronesia, Fed. States of	. . .	. . .	. . .	. . .	3.4	3.3	3.1	2.8	3.0
Papua New Guinea	7.3	4.7	5.1	. . .	5.1	4.9	4.5	4.3	4.0
Samoa	. . .	4.4	4.9	4.4	4.8	4.9	4.4	4.1	4.0
Solomon Islands	. . .	. . .	. . .	. . .	. . .	. . .	. . .	. . .	. . .
Timor-Leste	. . .	. . .	. . .	0.9	1.7	1.6	1.5	1.5	1.3
Tonga	3.9	3.8	4.4	3.7	3.7	3.8	3.3	3.1	3.1
Vanuatu	5.0	5.2	4.9	4.5	4.2	4.1	3.7	3.4	3.2

Developed Economy

Japan	3.5	3.7	3.9	3.0	3.1	2.9	2.9	2.8	2.9

. . . = data not available.

a Data refer to central government, except for Bangladesh, Georgia, Kiribati, the Kyrgyz Republic, Pakistan, and Tajikistan, where data refer to consolidated government or general government.
b Prior to 2006, includes health data.

Sources: ADB Key Indicators and projections by authors.

Table 7.5 Government expenditure on health (% of gross domestic product)[a]

Economy	1995	2000	2005	2010	2020	2030	2040	2050
Developing Economies				2.9	3.2	3.7	4.1	4.8
Central and West Asia				2.0	2.3	2.5	2.6	3.0
Afghanistan	...	...	0.6	2.4	2.4	2.4	2.5	2.7
Armenia	2.0	1.1	1.5	1.8	1.9	2.0	2.1	2.6
Azerbaijan	1.4	0.9	0.9	1.2	1.2	2.1	2.2	2.4
Georgia	...	1.2	1.6	2.3	2.4	2.5	2.6	2.6
Kazakhstan	3.0	2.1	2.5	2.5	4.1	4.2	4.4	6.2
Kyrgyz Republic	4.0	2.1	2.4	3.7	3.8	3.9	4.1	4.2
Pakistan	0.9	0.7	0.7	0.8	0.8	0.8	0.9	0.9
Tajikistan	1.3	0.9	1.1	1.6	1.6	1.7	1.7	1.8
Turkmenistan	1.9	3.2	2.0	1.5	1.6	2.6	2.7	2.9
Uzbekistan	3.6	2.5	2.3	2.7	2.8	3.0	3.2	3.3
East Asia				3.4	4.4	5.5	6.9	8.5
China, People's Rep. of	1.8	1.8	1.8	2.7	4.6	5.0	7.4	9.8
Hong Kong, China	2.1	2.9	2.6	3.0	3.7	4.4	5.2	5.7
Korea, Rep. of	1.4	2.2	3.0	4.1	4.9	7.1	8.5	9.6
Mongolia	2.6	3.8	2.6	3.1	3.3	3.4	3.6	6.1
Taipei,China	3.3	3.4	3.8	4.0	5.5	7.6	9.9	11.3
South Asia				2.2	2.3	3.3	3.6	4.5
Bangladesh	1.3	1.1	1.1	1.3	1.4	1.5	1.6	1.7
Bhutan	2.7	5.3	3.2	3.5	3.6	6.1	6.6	10.0
India	1.0	1.1	0.9	1.0	1.1	1.1	1.2	2.0
Maldives	3.3	4.1	4.2	3.7	3.9	6.5	7.2	8.0
Nepal	1.4	1.3	2.0	1.9	2.0	2.1	2.2	2.3
Sri Lanka	1.6	1.8	1.9	1.6	1.6	2.8	2.9	3.0

Southeast Asia

Brunei Darussalam	2.3	2.6	2.2	1.9	2.0	2.6	2.8	3.5
Cambodia	1.0	1.3	1.5	2.5	3.0	4.0	4.8	5.8
Indonesia	0.7	0.7	0.9	1.3	1.4	1.4	1.5	1.6
Lao PDR	2.5	1.2	0.7	1.0	1.1	1.1	1.2	2.0
Malaysia	1.7	1.7	1.7	2.3	2.4	3.5	3.8	4.9
Myanmar	...	...	...	...	...	...	...	...
Philippines	1.4	1.5	1.4	1.5	1.5	1.6	1.6	1.7
Singapore	1.5	1.2	1.0	1.4	1.5	1.6	1.7	1.8
Thailand	1.7	1.9	2.3	2.9	3.2	5.6	6.1	8.9
Viet Nam	1.8	1.6	1.5	2.5	2.7	2.9	3.1	3.3
The Pacific								
Fiji	2.5	3.2	2.9	5.5	5.6	5.8	5.9	6.4
Micronesia, Fed. States of	8.7	7.3	11.3	12.6	13.0	13.3	13.6	14.3
Papua New Guinea	3.0	3.3	3.1	3.1	3.1	3.2	3.3	3.4
Samoa	3.3	4.6	4.0	5.6	5.7	5.9	6.1	6.2
Solomon Islands	3.0	4.3	7.4	6.9	7.0	7.2	7.4	7.7
Timor-Leste	...	6.3	8.8	4.3	4.3	4.3	4.3	4.4
Tonga	2.7	3.4	5.6	3.9	3.9	4.0	4.2	4.3
Vanuatu	1.9	2.7	2.4	4.6	4.7	4.8	5.0	5.2
Developed Economy								
Japan	5.6	6.1	6.7	7.4	8.5	9.4	10.0	10.5

... = data not available, Lao PDR = Lao People's Democratic Republic.
[a] Data refer to central government, except for Bangladesh, Georgia, Kiribati, the Kyrgyz Republic, Pakistan, and Tajikistan, where data refer to consolidated government or general government.

Sources: WHO and calculations by authors.

218   *Sang-Hyop Lee and Andrew Mason*

The final fiscal projection is for public spending on social security and welfare (Table 7.6). For developing Asia as a whole, the percentage of GDP devoted to social security and welfare, a simple average of values, is projected to rise from 2.8% in 2010 to 4.9% in 2050. The importance of social security and welfare spending, currently and in the future, varies considerably from government to government, however. Spending is relatively high in higher-income economies; for example, spending in the Republic of Korea and Taipei,China is projected to reach 12.0% and 10.0%, respectively, by 2050. These values represent significant growth in spending, but the values are still well short of what we find for Japan from 17.0% in 2010 to 21% in 2050. Note that spending in Singapore is quite low, but its Central Provident Fund is not included in the figures.

Mongolia is a significant outlier in the data and projections. In 2010, 12.9% of GDP was devoted to social security and welfare. This is much greater than in any other economy and less than we found in Japan for that year, but Japan has a much older population than Mongolia. By 2050, projected spending rises to 29.6% of GDP, which is much higher than the projection for Japan. Of course, this is not a realistic option, and more detailed information about the situation in Mongolia would be very helpful.

High public spending on social security and welfare is not limited to higher-income Asian economies. Armenia, Georgia, and the Kyrgyz Republic in Central Asia; Bhutan and Maldives in South Asia; and Timor-Leste in the Pacific have high levels projected for 2050.

The projected increase in social security and welfare spending is quite substantial. In many places, the percent of GDP devoted to social security and welfare is projected to double or more between 2010 and 2050. The greatest increases are concentrated in East and Southeast Asia.

These projections may be conservative. Many economies have relatively underdeveloped public pension systems. Should they choose to introduce these schemes in the future, public spending could rise much more rapidly than anticipated in the projections. Social security and welfare is also, however, a very broad category. The kinds of programs emphasized and the age structures of benefits may vary considerably from government to government in ways that are not captured by relying on the model constructed from a subset of those in Asia. This can only be assessed with more extensive data on this important component of public spending.

E. Interpretation and key implications

The projections of public sector spending are driven by changes in age structure and in the level of spending, that is, per capita spending at each age. Although the level of spending was indexed on per capita income, it would be a mistake to interpret this as a causal connection between income and the level of spending. Correlates of income may account for some or all of the changes in the level of spending.

Table 7.6 Government expenditure on social security and welfare (% of gross domestic product)[a]

Economy	1990	1995	2000	2005	2010	2020	2030	2040	2050
Developing Economies					2.8	2.9	3.7	4.2	4.9
Central and West Asia					5.0	5.7	6.8	7.4	8.1
Afghanistan	...	...	...	...	...	...	...	...	...
Armenia	...	...	2.1	2.0	7.1	8.1	9.5	10.4	11.6
Azerbaijan	3.9	1.7	3.0	2.4	2.6	3.2	4.7	5.3	5.8
Georgia	...	...	4.3	5.4	6.9	7.6	8.5	8.9	9.1
Kazakhstan	...	...	...	...	...	...	...	...	...
Kyrgyz Republic	4.9	5.7	1.7	2.8	5.0	5.6	6.6	7.3	8.1
Pakistan	...	...	...	...	...	...	...	...	...
Tajikistan[b]	...	0.1	1.8	3.2	3.5	3.9	4.6	5.1	5.7
Turkmenistan	...	...	...	...	...	...	...	...	...
Uzbekistan	...	...	...	...	...	...	...	...	...
East Asia					5.1	6.6	8.9	10.6	12.6
China, People's Rep. of	0.3	0.2	0.7	1.4	2.3	3.3	3.8	4.7	6.4
Hong Kong, China	0.9	2.5	2.1	2.4	2.3	3.4	4.1	4.5	4.6
Korea, Rep. of	1.3	1.0	3.2	3.8	4.8	5.9	10.1	11.5	12.0
Mongolia	7.7	3.6	6.2	6.1	12.9	15.3	19.2	22.7	29.6
Taipei,China	2.8	3.4	5.7	3.4	3.2	4.9	7.1	9.5	10.5
South Asia					1.4	1.5	2.2	2.5	3.1
Bangladesh	0.1	0.1	0.1	0.3	0.4	0.5	0.6	0.7	0.9
Bhutan	...	...	...	2.1	1.8	2.1	3.2	3.9	5.2
India	...	...	0.8	0.7	...	0.9	1.0	1.1	1.5
Maldives	...	1.1	1.0	3.9	2.1	2.5	3.9	4.7	5.6
Nepal	1.1	0.5	0.8	0.7	1.0	1.1	1.3	1.5	1.8
Sri Lanka	3.8	5.1	2.8	3.8	1.9	2.3	3.0	3.2	3.4

(*Continued*)

Table 7.6 (Continued)

Economy	1990	1995	2000	2005	2010	2020	2030	2040	2050
Southeast Asia									
Brunei Darussalam	1.1	1.3	1.2	...	1.0	1.2	1.5	1.7	2.1
Cambodia	...	0.4	0.2	0.4	0.9	1.2	1.8	2.1	2.6
Indonesia	...	0.9	...	...	0.5	0.6	0.7	0.8	1.0
Lao PDR	...	0.0	0.7	...	...	1.2	1.5	1.7	2.2
Malaysia	1.2	0.8	0.9	0.9	1.2	0.8	1.0	1.2	1.4
Myanmar	...	...	...	...	...	1.4	1.9	2.1	3.0
Philippines	0.2	0.4	0.7	0.8	0.8	...	...	...	...
Singapore	0.4	0.8	0.7	0.3	1.1	0.9	1.0	1.1	1.3
Thailand	0.5	0.5	0.9	1.4	1.4	1.4	1.6	1.8	1.9
Viet Nam	...	...	...	...	...	1.8	2.5	2.8	3.1
The Pacific						...	...	...	...
Fiji	0.0	0.0	0.1	0.1	1.6	1.2	1.2	1.3	1.5
Micronesia Fed States of	...	...	...	...	0.1	0.1	0.1	0.1	0.1
Papua New Guinea	0.3	0.2	0.5	...	...	...	...	...	...
Samoa	...	...	...	1.0	1.2	0.6	0.7	0.8	0.9
Solomon Islands	...	...	...	...	...	1.3	1.5	1.6	1.7
Timor-Leste	...	...	...	...	3.4	...	...	...	...
Tonga	0.4	0.5	1.6	1.5	...	3.4	3.3	3.3	3.9
Vanuatu	...	...	0.0	...	...	1.6	1.7	1.9	2.0
						0.0	0.0	0.0	0.1
Developed Economy									
Japan	7.4	9.1	10 6	13.7	17.0	18 6	19 1	20.5	21.0

... = data not available, 0.0 = Magnitude is less than half of unit employed.
[a]Data refer to central government, except for Bangladesh, Georgia, Kiribati, the Kyrgyz Republic, Pakistan, and Tajikistan, where data refer to consolidated government or general government.
[b]From 2000 onward, includes defense.

Source: Authors' estimates.

The analysis presented in Tables 7.7–7.10 is based on a simple decomposition procedure. In each table, the value in the first column of numbers, the 2010 value, is the share of GDP devoted to each sector in 2010. If the actual value was available, it was used, otherwise the projected value was used. (These values are identical when the actual is available.) The second column is the projected change in the percent of GDP devoted to each purpose between 2010 and 2050. The third column reports the effect of changing age structure calculated by holding the level of spending at the 2010 level using population age structures for 2010 and 2050. The next column reports the amount due to age-specific changes in the level of spending as the difference between the total change and the change due to age structure. The interaction between changes in the level of benefits and age structure is reported in the following column.

The final three columns in each table report the change due to age structure, the age-specific level of spending, and the interaction between the two as a percentage of the 2010 value. These values control for the large effect of the initial level of spending and allow us to focus our attention on the importance of age structure and the age-specific level of spending.

The decomposition analysis for education is presented in Table 7.7. The share of the population at school-going ages is declining in every economy; hence, the impact of changing population age structure is to reduce spending on education. The impact is quite substantial in many economies. On average, changing age structure could produce a decline in education spending by between 30% and 40% in East Asia, South Asia, and Southeast Asia between 2010 and 2050. The effects in other regions are smaller but still substantial, that is, a decline of 25% on average for Central and West Asia and by 20% in the Pacific. The smallest effect for any economy is found in Japan because the share of children in the population has already reached very low levels; the key change there is the share of adults who are elderly.

The effects of changes in the level of spending are positive (or zero) in every economy as the per capita age-specific level of spending is assumed to rise as incomes rise. The effects are largest where rapid economic growth is expected, but also they are largest in relatively high-income economies. Again this goes back to the assumptions underlying the projections which are based on the observed data.

The age-specific level effects are very small in Central and West Asia, most of South and Southeast Asia, and most Pacific island countries. Only in East Asia, Mongolia aside, do we see large effects from the level of age-specific spending. The rising level of age-specific spending is never sufficient to offset the effects of changing age structure, but in East Asia and in some other economies, the effects are large enough to greatly moderate the savings in education spending that population aging would otherwise be expected to deliver.

The interaction effect is all negative and substantial in several East Asian economies where a rise in per capita benefits is interacted with a decline in the share of children. The biggest effects are found in Taipei,China.

For health (Table 7.8) and social security and welfare (Table 7.9), the effects of changing age structure and changing levels of spending are mutually reinforcing.

Table 7.7 Government expenditure as percentage of gross domestic product, decomposition of change, education

Economy	Value in 2010	Percentage point change, 2010–2050				As a percent of 2010 value		
		Total change	Due to age structure	Due to age-specific level	Due to interaction	Due to age structure	Due to age-specific level	Due to interaction
Developing Economies								
Central and West Asia								
Afghanistan	...	...	...	0.0	0.0	...	...	0
Armenia	2.8	-0.9	-0.9	0.0	0.0	-32	0	0
Azerbaijan	2.8	-0.8	-1.0	0.3	-0.1	-36	12	-4
Georgia	2.9	-0.4	-0.4	0.0	0.0	-14	0	0
Kazakhstan	...	...	...	...	...	...	...	...
Kyrgyz Republic	5.8	-1.4	-1.4	0.0	0.0	-24	0	0
Pakistan	...	...	...	...	...	...	...	...
Tajikistan	4.0	-0.8	-0.8	0.0	0.0	-21	0	0
Turkmenistan	...	...	...	...	...	...	...	...
Uzbekistan	...	...	...	...	...	...	...	...
East Asia	**3.7**	**-0.9**	**-0.9**	**0.1**	**0.0**	**-25.2**	**2.5**	**-0.8**
China, People's Rep. of	3.1	0.2	-0.9	1.4	-0.3	-28	44	-10
Hong Kong, China	3.4	-0.2	-0.8	0.9	-0.2	-24	26	-6
Korea, Rep. of	3.2	-0.2	-1.1	1.3	-0.4	-34	41	-14
Mongolia	5.9	-0.9	-1.5	0.7	-0.2	-25	12	-3
Taipei,China	1.8	-0.3	-0.9	1.1	-0.5	-47	62	-29
South Asia	**3.5**	**-0.3**	**-1.0**	**1.1**	**-0.3**	**-31.7**	**37.2**	**-12.3**
Bangladesh	2.2	-1.0	-1.0	0.0	0.0	-43	0	0
Bhutan	6.7	-2.0	-2.9	1.7	-0.7	-44	25	-11
India	2.3	-0.5	-0.7	0.3	-0.1	-32	13	-4
Maldives	6.0	-2.5	-2.9	0.8	-0.4	-49	12	-6

Nepal	3.9	-1.7	-1.7	0.0	0.0	-44	0	0
Sri Lanka	1.9	-0.2	-0.4	0.2	0.0	-21	12	-3
Southeast Asia	**3.8**	**-1.3**	**-1.6**	**0.5**	**-0.2**	**-38.7**	**10.4**	**-3.9**
Brunei Darussalam	4.0	-0.5	-1.5	1.7	-0.7	-38	42	-17
Cambodia	1.6	-0.5	-0.5	0.0	0.0	-35	0	0
Indonesia	1.1	-0.2	-0.3	0.1	0.0	-30	13	-4
Lao PDR	1.0	-0.4	-0.4	0.0	0.0	-40	0	0
Malaysia	6.3	-1.3	-2.4	2.0	-0.8	-39	31	-12
Myanmar	...	...	...	...	...	...	...	...
Philippines	2.5	-0.7	-0.7	0.0	0.0	-27	0	0
Singapore	3.1	-1.1	-1.1	0.0	0.0	-35	0	0
Thailand	4.0	-0.9	-1.5	1.0	-0.4	-37	25	-9
Viet Nam	...	...	...	...	...	...	...	...
The Pacific	**2.9**	**-0.7**	**-1.1**	**0.6**	**-0.2**	**-35.1**	**13.9**	**-5.2**
Fiji	3.4	-0.4	-0.8	0.4	-0.1	-23	12	-3
Micronesia, Fed. States of	...	...	...	...	...	...	...	...
Papua New Guinea	5.1	-1.1	-1.1	0.0	0.0	-22	0	0
Samoa	4.8	-0.9	-0.9	0.0	0.0	-18	0	0
Solomon Islands	...	...	...	...	...	...	...	...
Timor-Leste	1.7	-0.4	-0.4	0.0	0.0	-23	0	0
Tonga	3.7	-0.7	-0.7	0.0	0.0	-18	0	0
Vanuatu	4.2	-1.0	-1.0	0.0	0.0	-24	0	0
Developed Economy	**3.8**	**-0.7**	**-0.8**	**0.1**	**0.0**	**-21.2**	**2.1**	**-0.4**
Japan	3.1	-0.3	-0.3	0.0	0.0	-8	0	0

... = data not available, Lao PDR = Lao People's Democratic Republic.

Source: Authors' estimates.

Table 7.8 Government expenditure as a percentage of gross domestic product, decomposition of change, health

Economy	Value in 2010	Percentage point change, 2010–2050				As a percent of 2010 value		
		Total change	Due to age structure	Due to age-specific level	Due to interaction	Due to age structure	Due to age-specific level	Due to interaction
Developing Economies								
Central and West Asia								
Afghanistan	...	...	...	...	...	...	...	...
Armenia	1.8	0.8	0.4	0.2	0.2	21	12	13
Azerbaijan	1.2	1.2	0.3	0.7	0.3	24	57	22
Georgia	2.3	0.3	0.3	0.0	0.0	13	0	0
Kazakhstan	...	...	...	...	...	...	...	...
Kyrgyz Republic	3.7	0.5	0.5	0.0	0.0	13	0	0
Pakistan	...	...	...	...	...	...	...	...
Tajikistan	1.6	0.2	0.2	0.0	0.0	11	0	0
Turkmenistan	...	...	...	...	...	...	...	...
Uzbekistan	...	...	...	...	...	...	...	...
East Asia	**2.1**	**0.6**	**0.3**	**0.2**	**0.1**	**16.4**	**13.8**	**6.9**
China, People's Rep. of	2.7	7.1	0.7	4.0	2.5	25	148	91
Hong Kong, China	3.0	2.7	2.3	0.1	0.3	78	4	8
Korea, Rep. of	4.1	5.5	3.4	0.8	1.4	82	19	33
Mongolia	3.1	3.0	0.6	1.7	0.7	20	54	21
Taipei,China	4.0	7.3	2.9	1.4	3.0	73	35	75
South Asia	**3.4**	**5.1**	**2.0**	**1.6**	**1.5**	**55.6**	**52.2**	**45.8**
Bangladesh	1.3	0.4	0.4	0.0	0.0	27	0	0
Bhutan	3.5	6.6	1.0	4.0	1.6	29	115	47
India	2.3	0.9	0.2	0.6	0.1	8	26	6
Maldives	3.7	4.3	1.2	2.1	1.0	32	57	27

Nepal	1.9	0.4	0.4	0.0	0.0	22	0	0
Sri Lanka	1.6	1.5	0.3	0.9	0.2	18	60	15
Southeast Asia	**2.4**	**2.3**	**0.6**	**1.3**	**0.5**	**22.7**	**42.9**	**15.9**
Brunei Darussalam	2.5	3.2	2.1	0.3	0.8	84	14	31
Cambodia	1.3	0.3	0.3	0.0	0.0	23	0	0
Indonesia	1.0	1.0	0.2	0.6	0.2	21	59	16
Lao PDR	1.2	0.2	0.2	0.0	0.0	20	0	0
Malaysia	2.3	2.6	0.7	1.1	0.9	29	49	38
Myanmar	0.0	...	...	...	...	...	...	...
Philippines	1.5	0.2	0.2	0.0	0.0	14	0	0
Singapore	1.4	0.4	0.4	0.0	0.0	27	0	0
Thailand	2.9	6.0	0.9	3.5	1.6	32	118	56
Viet Nam	2.5	...	...	...	...	...	...	...
The Pacific	**1.7**	**1.7**	**0.6**	**0.7**	**0.4**	**31.2**	**30.0**	**17.6**
Fiji	2.9	2.6	0.5	1.7	0.4	17	59	14
Micronesia, Fed. States of	...	...	...	...	...	...	...	...
Papua New Guinea	3.1	0.3	0.3	0.0	0.0	10	0	0
Samoa	5.6	0.6	0.6	0.0	0.0	11	0	0
Solomon Islands	...	...	...	...	...	...	...	...
Timor-Leste	4.3	0.1	0.1	0.0	0.0	3	0	0
Tonga	3.9	0.4	0.4	0.0	0.0	9	0	0
Vanuatu	4.6	0.6	0.6	0.0	0.0	14	0	0
Developed Economy								
Japan	7.4	3.1	3.1	0.0	0.0	42	0	0

... = data not available, Lao PDR = Lao People's Democratic Republic.

Source: Authors' estimates.

Table 7.9 Government expenditure as a percentage of gross domestic product, decomposition of change, social security and welfare

Economy	Value in 2010	Percentage point change, 2010–2050				As a percent of 2010 value		
		Total change	Due to age structure	Due to age-specific level	Due to interaction	Due to age structure	Due to age-specific level	Due to interaction
Developing Economies								
Central and West Asia								
Afghanistan	..	..	..	..	..	..	..	..
Armenia	7.1	4.6	4.6	0.0	0.0	66	0	0
Azerbaijan	2.6	3.1	2.4	0.7	0.0	92	28	-2
Georgia	6.9	2.3	2.3	0.0	0.0	33	0	0
Kazakhstan	..	..	..	..	..	..	..	..
Kyrgyz Republic	5.0	3.1	3.1	0.0	0.0	62	0	0
Pakistan	..	..	..	..	..	..	..	..
Tajikistan	3.5	2.2	2.2	0.0	0.0	63	0	0
Turkmenistan	..	..	..	..	..	..	..	..
Uzbekistan	..	..	..	..	..	..	..	..
East Asia	5.0	3.1	2.9	0.1	0.0	63.1	5.4	-0.4
China, People's Rep. of	2.3	4.1	1.7	1.7	0.8	75	73	34
Hong Kong, China	2.3	2.3	1.6	0.4	0.4	68	18	16
Korea, Rep. of	4.8	7.2	3.5	1.7	2.0	72	36	42
Mongolia	12.9	16.7	12.6	4.3	-0.2	98	34	-2
Taipei,China	3.2	7.2	2.5	1.9	2.8	76	59	87
South Asia	5.1	7.5	4.4	2.0	1.1	78.0	43.7	35.4
Bangladesh	0.4	0.5	0.5	0.0	0.0	113	0	0
Bhutan	1.8	3.4	2.2	1.2	0.0	124	65	-2
India	2.3	0.7	0.5	0.2	0.0	22	9	0
Maldives	2.1	3.5	2.9	0.7	0.0	135	32	-1

Nepal	1.0	0.8	0.8	0.0	0.0	85	0	0
Sri Lanka	1.9	1.5	1.1	0.4	0.0	56	23	-3
Southeast Asia	1.6	1.7	1.3	0.4	0.0	89.5	21.6	-0.8
Brunei Darussalam	0.9	1.7	1.0	0.3	0.5	110	34	52
Cambodia	0.5	0.5	0.5	0.0	0.0	92	0	0
Indonesia	1.0	1.2	0.9	0.3	0.0	84	29	-1
Lao PDR	0.7	0.7	0.7	0.0	0.0	95	0	0
Malaysia	1.2	1.8	0.9	0.6	0.4	72	47	29
Myanmar	..	..	..	..	..	..	..	..
Philippines	0.8	0.5	0.5	0.0	0.0	63	0	0
Singapore	1.1	0.7	0.7	0.0	0.0	65	0	0
Thailand	1.4	1.7	1.2	0.6	-0.1	87	42	-8
Viet Nam	..	..	..	..	..	..	..	..
The Pacific	1.0	1.1	0.8	0.2	0.1	83.3	18.9	9.0
Fiji	0.1	0.1	0.0	0.0	0.0	66	29	-2
Micronesia, Fed. States of	..	..	..	..	..	..	..	..
Papua New Guinea	0.6	0.3	0.3	0.0	0.0	55	0	0
Samoa	1.2	0.5	0.5	0.0	0.0	46	0	0
Solomon Islands	..	..	..	..	..	..	..	..
Timor-Leste	3.4	0.5	0.5	0.0	0.0	15	0	0
Tonga	1.5	0.6	0.6	0.0	0.0	39	0	0
Vanuatu	0.0	0.0	0.0	0.0	0.0	70	0	0
Developed Economy								
Japan	17.0	4.0	4.0	0.0	0.0	24	0	0

. . . = data not available, Lao PDR = Lao People's Democratic Republic.

Source: Authors' estimates.

Table 7.10 Government expenditure as a percentage of gross domestic product, decomposition of change, education, health, and social security and welfare

Economy	Value in 2010	Percentage point change, 2010–2050				As a percent of 2010 value		
		Total change	Due to age structure	Due to age-specific level	Due to interaction	Due to age-structure	Due to age-specific	Due to interaction
Developing Economies								
Central and West Asia								
Afghanistan	...	...	...	...	...	...	...	...
Armenia	11.7	4.5	4.1	0.2	0.2	35	2	2
Azerbaijan	6.6	3.6	1.7	1.7	0.1	26	26	1
Georgia	12.1	2.2	2.2	0.0	0.0	18	0	0
Kazakhstan	...	...	...	...	...	...	...	...
Kyrgyz Republic	14.6	2.2	2.2	0.0	0.0	15	0	0
Pakistan	...	...	...	...	...	...	...	...
Tajikistan	9.1	1.5	1.5	0.0	0.0	17	0	0
Turkmenistan	...	...	...	...	...	...	...	...
Uzbekistan	...	...	...	...	...	...	...	...
East Asia	**10.8**	**2.8**	**2.3**	**0.4**	**0.1**	**22.3**	**5.6**	**0.7**
China, People's Rep. of	8.1	11.5	1.5	7.0	2.9	19	87	36
Hong Kong, China	8.7	4.9	3.1	1.4	0.4	35	16	5
Korea, Rep. of	12.1	12.5	5.7	3.8	2.9	47	32	24
Mongolia	21.9	18.8	11.8	6.8	0.3	54	31	1
Taipei,China	9.1	14.3	4.5	4.4	5.3	50	49	59
South Asia	**12.0**	**12.4**	**5.3**	**4.7**	**2.4**	**41.0**	**42.9**	**25.0**
Bangladesh	3.9	-0.1	-0.1	0.0	0.0	-3	0	0
Bhutan	12.0	8.0	0.3	6.8	0.9	3	57	7
India	2.3	1.1	0.0	1.1	0.0	-2	48	2
Maldives	11.8	5.3	1.1	3.5	0.6	9	30	5

Nepal	6.7	−0.5	−0.5	0.0	0.0	−7	0	0
Sri Lanka	5.4	2.7	1.0	1.6	0.1	18	30	3
Southeast Asia	**7.0**	**2.8**	**0.3**	**2.2**	**0.3**	**3.1**	**27.5**	**2.8**
Brunei Darussalam	7.4	4.5	1.5	2.3	0.6	21	32	8
Cambodia	3.4	0.2	0.2	0.0	0.0	7	0	0
Indonesia	3.2	1.9	0.8	1.0	0.1	24	33	3
Lao PDR	2.9	0.6	0.6	0.0	0.0	19	0	0
Malaysia	9.8	3.2	−0.9	3.6	0.4	−9	37	5
Myanmar	0.0	...	...	...	...	...	...	...
Philippines	4.8	0.0	0.0	0.0	0.0	0	0	0
Singapore	5.6	0.0	0.0	0.0	0.0	1	0	0
Thailand	8.3	6.9	0.7	5.0	1.1	8	61	14
Viet Nam	0.0	...	...	...	...	...	...	...
The Pacific	**4.5**	**2.2**	**0.4**	**1.5**	**0.3**	**8.7**	**20.3**	**3.7**
Fiji	6.4	2.3	−0.2	2.2	0.3	−3	34	5
Micronesia, Fed. States of	...	...	...	...	...	...	...	...
Papua New Guinea	8.8	−0.5	−0.5	0.0	0.0	−6	0	0
Samoa	11.6	0.3	0.3	0.0	0.0	3	0	0
Solomon Islands	...	...	...	...	...	...	...	...
Timor-Leste	9.4	0.3	0.3	0.0	0.0	3	0	0
Tonga	9.1	0.3	0.3	0.0	0.0	3	0	0
Vanuatu	8.8	−0.4	−0.4	0.0	0.0	−4	0	0
Developed Economy								
Japan	27.5	6.8	6.8	0.0	0.0	25	0	0

... = data not available, GDP = gross domestic product, Lao PDR = Lao People's Democratic Republic.

Source: Authors' estimates.

The age structure effects are largest by far in East Asia and particularly in Hong Kong, China; the Republic of Korea; and Taipei,China. In those economies, age structure changes will lead to an increase in health-care spending of between 70% and 85% by 2050. The effects are large elsewhere as well but not nearly this large.

This may come as a surprise to those who are familiar with Asia's demography because the gains are much smaller in other economies like the PRC and Thailand that are aging rapidly. There are two reasons for this. The first is that aging in low-income economies has a smaller impact because health-care spending does not rise too rapidly with age. Their per capita health-care spending is projected to reach much higher levels between now and 2050, but the effect is captured by the interaction effect. The second factor to consider is that demographic measures of age structure count all individuals above a threshold – 60 or 65 – equally, but in advanced economies, the elderly at different ages count very differently when it comes to health spending. An increase in the 90+ population has a much bigger impact on health spending than the same increase in the number of 60 year olds. East Asia is further along in the aging process; hence a large share of the increase in the old-age population is occurring among the very elderly.

The effects of shifts in the age-specific level of health-care spending are also large but also vary widely across economies. Few effects occur in very rich economies like Hong Kong, China or Singapore or in those that are very poor or growing very slowly and hence do not reach the income threshold that leads to an upward shift in the health profile. This is the case for 20 of the economies for which projections were constructed. The upward shift in spending profiles led to a doubling of health-care spending relative to GDP in Bhutan and Thailand. The largest effects are also projected in the PRC.

As expected, the interaction effect is quite important where population aging and a rise in per capita benefits at older ages are both occurring. The effects are particularly large in Bhutan; the PRC; the Republic of Korea; Malaysia; Taipei, China; and Thailand with a decline of between 30% to 90%. In Bhutan, the PRC, Malaysia, and Thailand, the effect is even larger than the pure age-structure effect.

Many of the observations about the health-care projections apply as well to projections for social security and welfare. The age effect and the age-specific level effects are both positive and mutually reinforcing. The age effects are largest in East Asia and South Asia, but they are substantial in other regions as well. The age effects are greater for social security and welfare than for health for two reasons. The first is that spending on social security and welfare is strongly influenced by age even at low spending levels. Second, the high values are concentrated among the younger elderly rather than the oldest elderly. Consequently, the early parts of aging when the young elderly population is growing most rapidly have a large effect on spending.

The level effects for social security and welfare are similar but generally smaller than the level effects for health. In East Asia, the greatest effects are found in the PRC; the Republic of Korea; and Taipei,China. The interaction effects for social security and welfare are also big in these economies, even bigger than the interaction effects for health in the Republic of Korea and Taipei,China.

Table 7.10 presents projections for education, health, and social security and welfare combined. This is only a portion of public spending, but it is a substantial portion in most governments and the portion most likely to grow in coming years. It is certainly the portion that will be influenced by changes in population age structure.

The first observation to be made about combined spending is that as a share of GDP it is projected to decline in Bangladesh, Nepal, Papua New Guinea, and Vanuatu or to remain constant over the 40-year projection in the Philippines and Singapore. In all of these countries, education spending is high relative to health, social security, and welfare spending. Thus, the decline in education spending is sufficient to offset or more than offset the projected rise in health, social security, and welfare spending.

In most of these countries, education spending is high because they have relatively young age structures; their fertility is high or has been high until recently. In every country but Singapore, more than half of the population is under 25 years of age. Singapore is quite a different situation because of their heavy reliance on publicly mandated individual accounts to fund public pensions and health care. Thus, 55% of their spending on education, health, social security, and welfare went to education even though fertility is low and only 31% of the population was under the age of 25 in 2010.

In Fiji, India, and Malaysia, public spending is projected to rise over the next 40 years but not because of changes in age structure as measured by the age effect. In these three, education spending is also quite high ranging from 53% of the total in Fiji to 64% in Malaysia. These countries also have young populations, but not quite half of their populations are under the age of 25.

Another feature of the results that is interesting is that very low growth in public sector spending is projected for all Pacific island nations except for Fiji. Along with Cambodia, public sector spending as a share of GDP is projected to increase by less than 10% over the 40-year period. These populations are very young with 53% or more under the age of 25 in 2010.

In contrast, public sector spending by 11 governments is projected to increase by more than 50% relative to GDP by 2050. The East Asian economies lead with social spending projected to more than double as a share of GDP in the PRC; the Republic of Korea; and Taipei,China. In all three, public sector spending is driven by the confluence of rapid population aging and high and increasing incomes.

F. Policy issues and final observations

Population aging is a universal feature in Asia and the Pacific. Only the timing and speed vary from economy to economy. For those experiencing very rapid aging and for others that are "growing old before they are rich," anticipating and responding to needs of aging societies may be all the more difficult.

The data needed to document the current demographic situation and to project the course of population aging are comprehensive and widely available. Long-term projections of population age structure inevitably involve considerable uncertainty, but framing public policy is greatly aided by the availability of these data.

Data about the interface between population age structure and the economy are much more rudimentary and underdeveloped. In only a few economies and for only a few years do we have data on which age groups are being targeted by public programs. Even less is known about trends in the age patterns of public program benefits. This is a very serious gap in the information base needed to understand how population aging will influence public sector programs and spending needs over the coming decades. An urgent need is to improve the quality of data, particularly data on pension and health-care spending in Asia and the Pacific.

The results presented here for individual economies are based less on what we know about them as individuals and more on what we see as the broad patterns in the region based on selective data available for economies at different levels of development. The analyses based on these data do point to some important issues and considerations.

First, public programs are providing important sources of support for the elderly mostly in higher-income economies. The highest levels of spending on the elderly are of course found in the richest, but spending is highest relative to per capita income or to labor income in the richest economies in the region: Japan; the Republic of Korea; and Taipei,China. The exception to this generalization is Singapore which relies heavily on mandatory personal accounts to fund pensions and health care rather than publicly funded transfer systems. For these more advanced economies, Singapore aside, the key question is how to sustain or reform current systems in the face of rapid population aging. Population aging will lead to very substantial increases in public spending even if they are not enhanced.

For much of the region, the overwhelming issue is very different: how to improve existing health and social security systems in the face of population aging. Governments could choose to simply stick with the kinds of public programs they now have with modest enhancements knowing that population aging would then have only modest effects on the size of public programs. They would avoid fiscal problems that might otherwise arise, but they would have large elderly populations that will be left to their own devices when it comes to their economic security and their health-care needs. Some observers look for families to play an important role in supporting the elderly in aging societies, but this seems to be increasingly unlikely.

A very important issue everywhere is to improve our understanding of the connection between age, abilities, and needs. Current policies, for example, retirement and pension policies, often depend on definitions of old age that are arbitrary and perhaps increasingly out of touch. Policies should not rely on a "one-old-age-fits-all" approach and on age-based mandates that are increasingly out of date. Many elderly are perfectly able to work at the age of 70 or beyond, but many are not.

Some portion of population aging can be traced to people living longer lives. Hence, changes in the life cycle, for example, extending work life, are appropriate responses. The years spent in good health are increasing, but so too are the years spent in disability.

Aging is also a consequence of low fertility; it is unclear how economic flows across generations should change as the relative numbers of elderly and of the next generation of workers change. To what extent should taxes be increased to maintain net transfers to the elderly? The answer to this question is not apparent.

Demographic policies can be employed in response to population aging and concerns about the fiscal impacts. Pronatalist policies can be pursued or immigration policies can be relaxed. Immigration, however, is not likely to have a major impact on population age structure except in small economies that opt for very pro-immigration policies.

In countries with very low fertility, pronatalist policies may be advisable, but in countries with moderately low fertility, the value of pronatalist policies is unclear. The efficacy of such programs is uncertain, and the fiscal impact of population aging is only one consideration when it comes to formulating population policy.

Note

1 Organisation for Economic Co-operation and Development (OECD) projections for the PRC, Japan, the Republic of Korea, India, Indonesia, and non-OECD members up to 2060; Asian Development Bank (ADB) projections for its members up to 2030; and The International Macroeconomic Data Set from the United States Department of Agriculture (USDA) for 190 countries up to 2030. As ADB and USDA provide projections only up to 2030, OECD member and non-member projections are used as a benchmark for extended projections up to 2050.

Bibliography

Asian Development Bank. Various years. Key Indicators for Asia and the Pacific. Manila. http://www.adb.org/publications/series/key-indicators-for-asia-and-the-pacific/ (accessed 1 October 2013).

———. 2011. *Long-Term Projections of Asian GDP and Trade*. Manila. http://www. adb.org/publications/long-term-projections-asian-gdp-and-trade (accessed 1 October 2013).

Government of the United States, Department of Agriculture (USDA). International Macroeconomic Data Set. http://www.ers.usda.gov/data-products/international-macroeconomic-data-set/ (accessed 5 November 2013)

Lee, R. and A. Mason. 2011. *Population Aging and the Generational Economy: A Global Perspective*. Cheltenham, UK: Edward Elgar.

Lee, R.D. 1994a. The Formal Demography of Population Aging, Transfers, and the Economic Life Cycle. In Martin, L.G. and S.H. Preston, eds. *Demography of Aging*. Washington, DC: National Academy Press.

———. 1994b. Population, Age Structure, Intergenerational Transfers, and Wealth: A New Approach, with Applications to the US. Special Issue: The

Family and Intergenerational Relations. *Journal of Human Resources.* 29 (4). pp. 1027–1063.

Lee, R. D., S.-H. Lee, and A. Mason. 2008. Charting the Economic Life Cycle. In Prskawetz, A., D. E. Bloom, and W. Lutz, eds. *Population Aging, Human Capital Accumulation, and Productivity Growth:* A Supplement to *Population and Development Review.* Volume 33. New York: Population Council.

Mason, A., R. Lee, A.-C. Tung, M.-S. Lai, and T. Miller. 2009. Population Aging and Intergenerational Transfers: Introducing Age into National Accounts. In Wise, D., ed. *Developments in the Economics of Aging.* Chicago: National Bureau of Economic Research and University of Chicago Press.

National Transfer Accounts Project. 2013. *Country Summaries.* http://www.ntaccounts.org/web/nta/show/Country%20Summaries (accessed 1 October 2013).

Organisation for Economic Co-operation and Development (OECD). 2014. Shifting Gear: Policy Challenges for the Next 50 Years. *OECD Economics Department Policy Notes.* 24. Paris. http://www.oecd.org/eco/outlook/lookingto2060.htm (accessed 1 October 2013).

United Nations, Department of Economic and Social Affairs, Population Division. 2013a. *National Transfer Accounts Manual: Measuring and Analysing the Generational Economy.* New York.

———. 2013b. *World Population Prospects: The 2012 Revision.* New York.

World Health Organization. 2011. Health Accounts – Global Health Expenditure Database. http://www.who.int/health-accounts/en/ (accessed 1 October 2013).

8 Fiscal policy and inclusive growth in Latin America

Lessons for Asia

Sang-Hyop Lee and Donghyun Park

A. Introduction

In the past, Latin America was wracked by macroeconomic instability rooted in unsustainable government budget deficits. The Latin American debt crises of the 1980s epitomized the severe macroeconomic instability that curtailed growth in the region; however, since the early 1990s, fiscal and monetary policy has improved markedly in much of the region. The improvement sometimes took the form of a concerted and drastic policy effort. For example, in 1994 in the face of chronic inflation, Brazil implemented the *Plano Real* (Real Plan) that combined currency reform with monetary and fiscal tightening. The consequent improvement in fundamentals helped Latin America weather the global financial crisis of 2008–2009 well. Despite some major exceptions, there has been an unmistakable region-wide trend toward macroeconomic stability underpinned by fiscal responsibility. The improved fiscal performance is evident in key indicators such as fiscal balance (Figure 8.1) and government debt (Figure 8.2).

Another key fiscal trend in Latin America has been the growth of social assistance and basic social services. The region has a long history of social spending that began around 1920 and consists of three main realms: social insurance, social assistance, and basic social services. Until 1980, social policy in Latin America was dominated by contributory social insurance schemes. Social assistance programs included family allowances, non-contributory pensions and health insurance, and emergency public employment. From 1972 to 1982 in 13 Latin American countries, social assistance on average accounted for 17% of total public social spending, while social insurance consumed 83%, but severe economic crises combined with the evolution of democracy during the 1980s and 1990s fueled public spending on social assistance and basic social services which targeted poorer portions of the population while the coverage of social insurance was reduced.

The central objective of this chapter is to examine the relationship between fiscal policy and inclusive growth in Latin America with a view to drawing relevant policy lessons for developing Asia. Although the two regions are broadly comparable in terms of their income and development levels, as a result of the forces discussed in the preceding paragraph, Latin America has substantially more experience in leveraging fiscal policy to tackle inequality and poverty. This

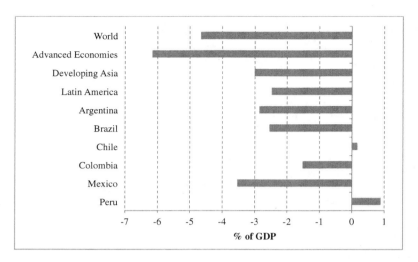

Figure 8.1 Overall fiscal balance in selected regions and Latin American countries, 2008–2013 (% of gross domestic product)

GDP = gross domestic product.

Source: International Monetary Fund. Fiscal Monitor Database.

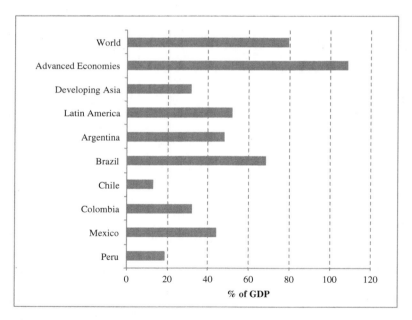

Figure 8.2 Gross government debt to gross domestic product ratio in selected regions and Latin American countries, 2013 (% of gross domestic product)

GDP = gross domestic product.

Source: International Monetary Fund. Fiscal Monitor Database.

is evident in Latin America's high level of public spending on programs that can help to promote more inclusive growth. For example, Latin American governments spend more on education which directly improves the well-being of the poor and augments their productive capacity than the governments of developing Asia spend (Figure 8.3). They also spend more on health, which also improves both the welfare and human capital of disadvantaged groups (Figure 8.4). The beneficial effects of public spending on education and health

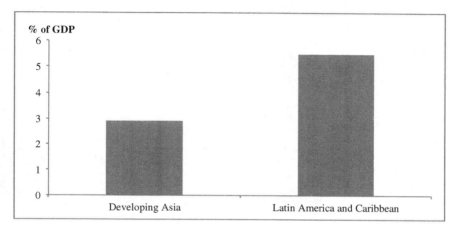

Figure 8.3 Government spending on education, 2010 (% of gross domestic product)
GDP = gross domestic product.
Source: Asian Development Bank staff estimates.

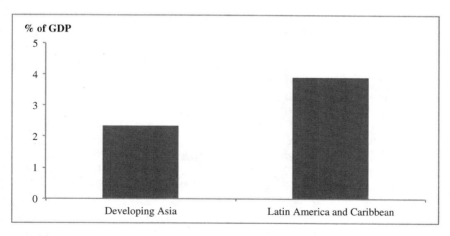

Figure 8.4 Government spending on health care, 2010 (% of gross domestic product)
GDP = gross domestic product.
Source: Asian Development Bank staff estimates.

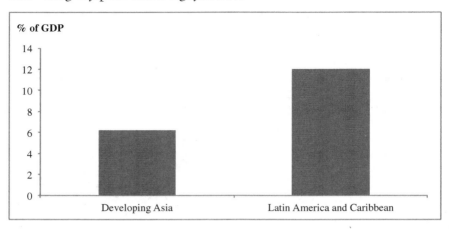

Figure 8.5 Government spending on social protection, 2010 (% of gross domestic product)

GDP = gross domestic product.

Source: Asian Development Bank staff estimates.

are likely to be disproportionately greater for the poor who tend to lack access to private education and health. Further evidence that Asia trails Latin America comes from public spending on social protection (Figure 8.5).

Latin America's greater public spending on education, health, and social protection is in line with the region's larger overall government size. From 1990 to 2000, the ratio of government expenditures to gross domestic product (GDP) was 18.6% for developing Asia and 29.9% for Latin America, and from 2000 to 2010, the corresponding figures were 21.0% and 30.6%. A bigger government requires a larger tax revenue base. Indeed, Latin America's tax revenue to GDP ratio exceeds the figure for developing Asia. The ratio was 18.1% for Latin America and 12.9% for developing Asia from 1990 to 2000. The corresponding figures from 2000 to 2010 were 21.8% and 17.8%.

While government transfers and subsidies do not directly contribute to human capital, they often provide vital protection to the most vulnerable segments of the population; however, in Asia as in other parts of the world, public transfers are often captured by the non-poor. For example, a large part of the benefits from general fuel subsidies flow to the middle and upper-middle classes. Such programs do not promote equity and are fiscally burdensome. In line with the smaller overall size of the government, the level of transfers is higher in Latin America than in Asia (Asian Development Bank [ADB] 2011). This is especially true for transfers to the elderly. Much more significantly, Latin America has become a global leader in the use of conditional cash transfers (CCTs). CCTs are usually targeted at low-income groups that can receive them only if they make human capital investments such as in education or health care. Therefore, Latin America's CCT experience offers potentially valuable lessons for inclusive fiscal policy in Asia.

The rest of this chapter is organized as follows. Part B briefly examines whether Latin America's fiscal policy has been pro-cyclical or counter-cyclical. This has significant implications for inclusive growth. Part C summarizes an in-depth study of the impact of social spending and taxes on inequality and poverty in Latin America. The study is based on six Latin American economies of varying sizes and income levels: Argentina, Bolivia, Brazil, Mexico, Peru, and Uruguay. Part D takes an in-depth look at Latin America's extensive experience with CCT programs that are widely viewed as having been effective in reducing poverty and inequality in the region. As such, Latin America's CCT experience can point the way forward for Asia as well. Part E concludes with observations.

B. Pro-cyclicality of fiscal policy in Latin America

There is a growing body of literature examining whether fiscal policy in Latin American countries has been pro-cyclical, that is, moving with the business cycle, or counter-cyclical, that is, moving against it. For example, when public spending rises when the economy is in a recession, fiscal policy is counter-cyclical. The growing interest in the subject is rooted in the fact that fiscal policy is a potentially important tool for mitigating the adverse impacts of major financial and economic shocks such as the global financial crisis of 2008–2009. In particular, crises tend to have a proportionately bigger impact on the poor and disadvantaged who often lack the resources and capacity to protect themselves from the adverse effects of shocks. Therefore, assistance from the government can be a vital means for helping the poor during crises.

Latin American fiscal policy has been dominantly pro-cyclical, focused more on preserving long-term fiscal sustainability than on responding to big macroeconomic shocks such as a financial crisis. On average, the stimulus packages implemented during the recent global financial crisis are believed to have been less than 1% of GDP, a full percentage point less than those in developed countries. Berganza (2012) surveyed seven Latin American countries' fiscal rules since the early 2000s and discussed general characteristics along with the advantages and disadvantages of different types. He used two important criteria for classifying them: long-term sustainability and diluting the pro-cyclicality of fiscal policy. While the former emphasizes reducing the deficit bias and controlling the growth of public debt, the latter emphasizes the short-term output stabilization role of fiscal policy. His findings showed that only Chile targets cyclically adjusted indicators, although the policies of Colombia and Mexico offer some stabilization properties. Many of the other countries, however, including Argentina, Brazil, and Peru, simply applied numerical rules for overall public spending without any output stabilization.

This problem may not be restricted to only Latin America but may affect developing countries as a whole. Del Granado et al. (2013) studied the cyclical behavior of public spending, particularly on education and health, in 145 countries between 1987 and 2007 and found that spending on education and health was pro-cyclical in developing countries and acyclical in developed countries. In addition, education and health expenditures follow an asymmetric pattern in developing countries. They are pro-cyclical during periods of positive output gap and acyclical during periods of negative output gap. Furthermore, the degree of cyclicality is higher the lower the level of economic development suggesting that this problem is especially pronounced for developing countries. Calderón and Fajnzylber (2009) documented that the pro-cyclicality of Latin America has improved since the early 2000s in large part due to the decline in the share of government debt as a share of GDP after 2003. The decline in public debt was in turn driven by improvements in debt management and rising fiscal revenues associated with higher global commodity prices.

Daude, Melguizo, and Neut (2011) found that this pro-cyclical bias in fiscal policy persisted in the region during the recent global financial crisis, even though many countries did implement discretionary stimuli. They note that most Latin American economies collect significantly fewer tax revenues than the Organisation for Economic Co-operation and Development (OECD) economies. Thus, a government with a debt level of 40% of GDP that collects tax revenues of only 16% of GDP can actually have a debt-to-revenue ratio of 250%. As a result, many countries in the region cannot take fiscal sustainability for granted. They also noted, however, that there are important differences throughout the region. Brazil, Chile, Colombia, and Peru seem to be effectively rebuilding their fiscal space, while Argentina and Costa Rica implemented traditional pro-cyclical fiscal policies. Zoido and Santiso (2010) also stressed this heterogeneity and the continued poor fiscal performance of some countries.

Calderón and Fajnzylber (2009) argued that pro-cyclicality has adversely affected the region's long-term growth in three ways. First, it amplifies economic fluctuations. According to estimates by Lopez-Monti (2009), the welfare cost of an amplified business cycle is not negligible. Second, governments tend to cut back on public investments during downturns. Last, pro-cyclical fiscal policy has made it difficult to expand social safety nets during economic downturns. The last adverse effect has major implications for inclusive growth as it could be especially harmful for poor and disadvantaged groups. These groups are more vulnerable during economic downturns due to their limited access to credit and limited capacity for consumption smoothing. Although, as noted earlier, the fiscal position of Latin American countries has improved greatly in the last 2 decades, the pro-cyclical bias of fiscal policy may be more difficult to alter in the short run. In this context, policy makers are beginning to pay more attention to pro-poor government expenditures, particularly to CCT programs that have become a feature of the region's fiscal policy.

C. The impact of social spending and taxes on inequality and poverty

In a recent in-depth study, Lustig et al. (2013) applied standard benefit–tax incidence analysis to estimate the effect of direct taxes, indirect taxes, and subsidies, and social spending (cash and in-kind transfers) on inequality and poverty in six countries: Argentina (transfers only), Bolivia, Brazil, Mexico, Peru, and Uruguay.

All country studies applied a common methodology to micro data obtained from household surveys (year of survey is in parenthesis). The studies for Bolivia (2009), Brazil (2009), Peru (2009), and Uruguay (2009) focused on average incidence for a particular (recent) year. The studies for Argentina (2003, 2006, 2009) and Mexico (2008, 2010) looked at how incidence has changed over a particular period of time. This study is one of the most detailed, comprehensive, and comparable benefit–tax incidence analyses available for Latin American countries to date.

We used five income concepts in our incidence analyses: market, net market, disposable, post-fiscal, and final income. Market income is total current earned income from all labor and non-labor sources before direct taxes; autoconsumption (except in the case of Argentina and Bolivia); imputed rent for owner-occupied housing; private transfers (remittances and other private transfers such as alimony); and old-age and other pensions from the contributory social security system. (We also performed a sensitivity analysis where contributory pensions were classified under government transfers.) Net market income equals market income minus direct personal income taxes on all income sources (included in market income) that are subject to taxation and all contributions to social security except for the portion going to pensions. Disposable income is equal to the sum of net market income plus direct government transfers (mainly cash transfers but can include food transfers). Post-fiscal income is defined as disposable income plus indirect subsidies minus indirect taxes (e.g., value added tax, sales tax). Final income is defined as post-fiscal income plus government in-kind transfers in the form of free or subsidized services in education, health, and housing minus co-payments or user fees. We also defined final income as disposable income plus government in-kind transfers in the form of free or subsidized services in education, health, and housing subsidies minus co-payments or user fees.

Consistent with other conventional tax incidence analyses, here we assumed that the economic burden of direct personal income taxes is borne by the recipient of income. The burden of payroll and social security taxes was assumed to fall entirely on workers. Consumption taxes were assumed to be shifted forward to consumers. Evasion of direct income and payroll taxes was taken into account in the analysis by assuming that individuals who do not participate in the contributory social security system do not pay income or payroll taxes (Brazil's survey includes a question on tax payments so tax evasion was assumed to be as reported in the survey). In the case of indirect (consumption) taxes, assumptions to take evasion into account varied. The approach to estimate the incidence of public spending on education and health followed here was the so-called benefit or expenditure incidence approach, or government cost approach. In essence, we used per beneficiary input costs obtained from administrative data as the measure of average benefits.

The following are some of the key findings that emerged from the empirical analysis.

- **Inequality and poverty reduction.** Taxes and cash transfers reduced inequality and poverty by nontrivial amounts in Argentina and Uruguay, less so in Mexico, and little in Peru. In the case of Bolivia, inequality remained essentially the same, but post-fiscal extreme and moderate poverty increased with respect to market income. In Brazil, inequality fell significantly, but poverty rose (Figures 8.6 and 8.7).

- **Direct personal income taxes.** Revenue from personal income taxes included in the incidence analysis varied from around 5% of GDP in Uruguay to 0% in Argentina and Bolivia. In all countries in which direct taxes were analyzed, they were progressive; however, their redistributive power varied. The Gini coefficient declined by 2.8%, 2.6%, and 2.4%, respectively in Uruguay, Mexico, and Brazil, while in Peru, it declined by only 1.1%. For the relatively small amount of direct taxes collected by Peru, their redistributive effect was relatively large.

- **Direct cash transfers.** Direct taxes and cash transfers reduced inequality (as measured by the Gini coefficient and with respect to market income inequality) by as much as 8.6% in Argentina (even without including direct taxes) and 7.1% in Uruguay to as little as 2% in Bolivia and Peru. Direct taxes and cash transfers reduced extreme poverty by more than 55% in Argentina and Uruguay, but by only 7% in Peru, which spent too little on

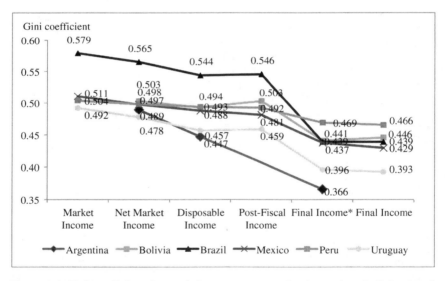

Figure 8.6 Gini coefficient for each income concept for Argentina, Bolivia, Brazil, Mexico, Peru, and Uruguay

Notes:

a. Final income* is defined as disposable income plus in-kind transfers minus co-payments and user fees. For the definition of other income concepts, see Lustig and Higgins (2013).

b. The analysis for Argentina does not include the tax side, so the disposable income Gini is gross of direct personal income taxes. The results are thus not strictly comparable.

Sources: Bucheli et al. (2014); Higgins and Pereira (2014); Jaramillo (2014); Lustig and Higgins (2013); Lustig and Pessino (2014); Lustig, Pessino, and Scott (2014); Paz Arauco et al. (2014); Scott (2014).

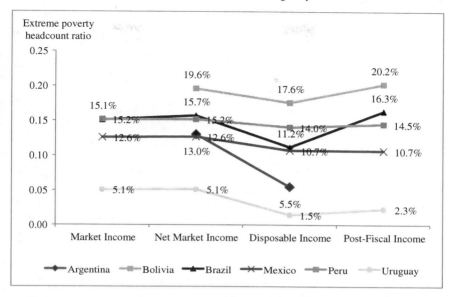

Figure 8.7 Extreme poverty headcount ratio for each income concept: Argentina, Bolivia, Brazil, Mexico, Peru, and Uruguay (%)

Notes:

a. Final income* is defined as disposable income plus in-kind transfers minus co-payments and user fees. For the definition of other income concepts, see Lustig and Higgins (2013).

b. The analysis for Argentina does not include the tax side so the disposable income headcount is gross of direct personal income taxes. The results are thus not strictly comparable.

Sources: Bucheli et al. (2014); Higgins and Pereira (2014); Jaramillo (2014); Lustig and Higgins (2013); Lustig and Pessino (2014); Lustig, Pessino, and Scott (2014); Paz Arauco et al. (2014); Scott (2014).

cash transfers to achieve much poverty reduction. Bolivia spent five times more than Peru (as a share of GDP) on cash transfers, but because funds were weakly targeted or not targeted at all to the poor, the amount of redistribution and poverty reduction has been limited. For Bolivia, the impact of these programs in terms of redistribution has been no better than Peru's and in terms of poverty reduction was only slightly higher.

- **Indirect taxes**. In Bolivia and Brazil,[1] indirect taxes wiped out the effect of direct transfers on extreme poverty which was actually slightly higher including taxes and direct transfers in income as compared to income before taxes and cash transfers. In contrast, extreme poverty rates in Mexico and Peru were virtually unchanged after indirect taxes because due to exemptions on essential goods and to informality, the poor pay little in the form of indirect taxes (Figure 8.7).

- **In-kind transfers**. Public spending on education and health was significantly more redistributive than cash transfers in all of the countries. When one adds the effect of transfers in-kind (access to free or quasi-free services in education and health), inequality declined by 14.0 percentage points in Brazil, 12.3 percentage points in Argentina,[2] 9.9 percentage points in Uruguay, 8.1 percentage points in Mexico, 5.7 percentage points in Bolivia, and only 3.8 percentage points in Peru as measured by the difference between the final income Gini coefficient and the market income Gini coefficient (Figure 8.6). Peru was the least redistributive for two main reasons: the amount of social spending was relatively small, and the total redistributive effectiveness of social spending was the second lowest (after Bolivia). In Bolivia, the limited redistributive power stems from the fact that per capita spending is practically the same for everyone. In a country with such a high incidence of poverty, we would like to observe more "pro-poor" education and health spending. The low progressivity of education spending is explained by (i) the comparatively low progressivity of primary education (due to low coverage rates among the poor) and (ii) an exceptionally high allocation of educational spending to tertiary education.

- **Unpleasant facts.** The largely positive redistributive picture in Argentina, Brazil, and Uruguay hides some unpleasant facts. In Brazil and Uruguay, spending on tertiary education is clearly "pro-rich;" in both countries, a large proportion of tertiary education spending subsidizes the rich – those with incomes above $50 per day in purchasing power parity terms – who receive a budget share significantly larger than their population share. In Argentina, government spending on progressive cash transfers is substantially less than the budget share allocated to indirect (and regressive) subsidies to agricultural producers, airlines, manufacturing, and transportation and energy. Furthermore, Argentina's social spending may not be fiscally sustainable as the sharp rise in public spending during the 2000s has been increasingly financed by distortionary taxes and unorthodox revenue-raising mechanisms.

In sum, redistribution and poverty reduction through fiscal policy is nontrivial especially in Argentina, Brazil, and Uruguay. As an important contributing factor, cash transfers were quite progressive in absolute terms except in Bolivia where programs are not targeted to the poor; however, their poverty-reducing impact, as expected, was smaller in countries that spent less (as a share of GDP) on direct cash transfers targeted to the poor (Mexico and Peru). Including the monetized value of in-kind services in income, in all six countries public spending on education and health reduced inequality considerably more than cash transfers. Direct taxes are progressive, but the redistributive impact is small because direct taxes as a share of GDP are generally low. Indirect taxes offset the poverty-reducing effects of cash transfers in Bolivia and Brazil. In Mexico and Peru the poverty-increasing effect of indirect taxes is tempered because basic goods are exempted, and there is a high level of informality (e.g., consumers are able to avoid indirect taxes).

Of the three most redistributive countries, Brazil would significantly improve its redistributive effectiveness if cash transfers were more targeted and if tertiary education for the rich were not so heavily subsidized. The latter is also true for Uruguay. Brazil would also improve its poverty reducing impact if consumption taxes were lower. In the case of Argentina, the fiscal sustainability of its redistributive model is seriously in question. Of the three least redistributive countries, Mexico and Peru reduced inequality and poverty relatively little because they spent less on cash and in-kind transfers than Argentina and Brazil. Bolivia's social spending was higher than Mexico's and Uruguay's (a high redistribution country), but because Bolivia's cash transfer programs are not specifically targeted to the poor, redistribution was small in scale.

D. Latin American experience with conditional cash transfer programs

As previously stated, Latin American countries have developed policies since 1920 for social insurance, social assistance, and basic social services. Until 1980, social policy in Latin America was dominated by contributory social insurance schemes with government efforts centered on widening coverage among urban formal-sector workers. Social assistance programs during this period included family allowances, noncontributory pensions, health insurance, and emergency public employment that had a progressive benefit incidence but were quantitatively inadequate to ease the hardship of the poor. Their ineffectiveness was exacerbated by poor design and implementation. For example, from 1972 to 1982 in 13 Latin American countries, social assistance accounted for 17% of total public social spending, while social insurance consumed 83% (McGuire 2011).

During the 1980s and 1990s, however, the combination of economic crises and new-found political democracy fueled public spending on social assistance and basic social services, both of which targeted the poorer portion of the population and reduced the coverage of social insurance. Due to a poor setup in some initial trials in the 1980s, the redesigned social spending program remained unsuccessful in reaching the poorest parts of the population. Despite this, the use of CCTs has become a unique and successful feature of Latin American expenditure policy for social inclusion since the 1990s. Countries in Latin America have adopted CCT programs at a rapid rate; nowadays virtually every country in the region has such a program. The two largest programs are in Brazil and Mexico and have covered millions of poor people.[3] (See the following box.)

Bolsa Família

In 2003, the government of Luis Inacio Lula da Silva launched a comprehensive program to stimulate growth and social progress. On the social side, the centerpiece was a sweeping reform of Brazil's social safety net, the *Bolsa Família* Program which integrated four cash transfer programs into a single program. The transfers are made preferentially to women in each family. The program supports the formation of human capital at the family

level by conditioning transfers on behaviors such as children's school attendance, use of health cards, and other social services. Since its launch, the
Bolsa Família Program has grown exponentially, and by the end of 2006,
about 50 million people were served, at least two-thirds of whom were very
poor. The *Bolsa Família* has been widely admired among developing countries because it is perceived to have reduced poverty significantly without
harming economic growth. Furthermore, the fiscal cost of the program has
been relatively small.

Sources: Lindert, Skoufias, and Shapiro (2006) and Glewwe and Kassouf (2010).

There is a huge body of literature discussing issues in CCT programs. The
most comprehensive study of them was conducted by Fiszbein et al. (2009)
and included 90 pages of detailed descriptions of CCT programs around the
world. We summarize only the most important issues in this chapter.

1. Conditional versus unconditional cash transfers

First, there is a question of whether conditionality is necessary for cash transfer
programs. Three types of programs are found in many developing countries:
unconditional cash transfers (UCTs), CCTs, and workfare programs (i.e., cash
transfers conditional on work). The workfare programs have a somewhat different purpose since they provide temporary employment opportunities. The
CCT programs are different from UCT programs, because unlike UCT programs,
CCTs impose conditions on recipients that must be fulfilled in order to gain
benefits from the program. While CCT recipients do not have autonomy to
spend the money they receive, CCTs are believed to be more effective in promoting human capital investment even though the main goal varies greatly
across countries. While most CCT programs target poor families to foster human
capital investment – especially in education and health care – CCT programs
in Bangladesh and Cambodia have been used to reduce gender disparities in
education and in Sub-Saharan African countries to alleviate HIV epidemics.

For social protection, both UCT and CCT programs are potentially more
efficient and more effective than in-kind transfers. This is clear from the broad
objective of the cash transfer programs which is to generate a sustained decrease
in poverty among some of the most disadvantaged groups. The underlying
premise is that a major cause of the intergenerational transmission of poverty
is the inability of poor households to invest in the human capital of their children. Supply-side interventions that provide in-kind transfers through the availability and quality of education and health-care services are often ineffective in
resolving this problem since the resource constraints facing poor households
preclude them from incurring the private costs associated with utilizing these

services. Unlike in-kind transfers, however, cash transfer programs that do not require large storage or transportation costs address this problem by targeting the poorest communities which, if done effectively, transforms them into human capital subsidies for poor households.

On the other hand, a well-known shortcoming of UCTs is that recipients may use the money for things like cigarettes, alcohol, or gambling as has been shown in many studies in the literature (e.g., Srisuchart 2008). The downside of the CCTs is that conditionality involves substantial administrative costs for monitoring, so the key question is whether the welfare gains from CCT programs are bigger than those of UCT programs after taking into account the administrative costs.

There are several empirical studies on this issue using various methodologies. In general, research has found that CCT programs proved to be much more successful in reaching the poor than any other form of social assistance. (See, for example, Hernanz, Malherbet, and Pellizzari 2004; Lindert, Skoufias, and Shapiro 2006; Tesliuc et al. 2006. Also see Fiszbein and Schady 2009 and Parker, Rubalcava, and Teruel 2008 for a literature review). Furthermore, most studies on Latin American countries show that benefits from conditionality can outweigh the cost of monitoring. The most successful CCT program, Brazil's *Bolsa Família* that reaches almost 50 million people, costs only 0.4% of GDP about half of which is actual transfers (Glewwe and Kassouf 2010).

We should not, however, ignore the political dimension, especially since conditionality makes cash transfers more politically acceptable to non-beneficiaries. Middle- and upper-class voters may believe that UCTs are subject to abuse unless they are tied to an improvement in specific indicators or behaviors (Febriany and Suryahadi 2012). In Indonesia, the introduction of the UCT program in 2005 generated a much higher level of public attention and scrutiny than other social protection programs had, and in some areas, it led to community conflicts, widespread protests, and even riots. Indonesia's UCT program was heavily criticized on the grounds that it would be ineffective in the long term because it would create dependency and disincentives to work.

It is also very important to understand that it is not simply a matter of UCT vs. CCT in itself. Program design, implementation, targeting, timing, and level of benefit matter as well (Bazzi, Sumarto, and Suryahadi 2012; Fiszbein and Schady 2009). For example, the programs in Bangladesh and Cambodia have several common elements. They are both poor countries with limited administrative capacity, so both programs set forth only education conditions for cash benefits and are limited in scope to secondary education for girls. Nevertheless, because of careful geographic and proxy means targeting, Cambodia was able to concentrate benefits among the poor. In Bangladesh, the program operates nationally and is targeted only by gender. In practice, the incidence of the program has been regressive largely because the base enrollment is higher among the less poor. This suggests that the program may be particularly effective in rural areas where child labor is more prevalent, that is, CCTs will be more effective in areas with high opportunity costs for children's time.

This is indeed a justification for Mexico's CCT program that is targeted in rural areas. In addition, the program allocates more to girls.

2. Impact evaluation

Conditional cash transfer (CCTs) have been praised as a way of reducing poverty and encouraging parents to invest in the education and health of their children. Many researchers and governments have investigated if empirical evidence supports this assumption. Unlike most other government programs, CCTs have been subject to rigorous evaluations of their effectiveness, using experimental or quasi-experimental methods. The assessments have addressed various aspects such as their impact on poverty reduction, employment, schooling, and health.

Several single-country studies show that CCT programs have achieved significant success in reaching the poor and bringing about short-term improvements in consumption, education, and health (Baird, McIntosh, and Özler 2011; Barrera-Osorio and Raju 2011; Behrman, Parker, and Todd 2005; de Brauw and Hoddinott 2011; Gertler 2004; Rawlings and Rubio 2005; Schady and Araujo 2008; Schultz 2004). Some reviews of the literature on CCT evaluations conclude that on the whole, these programs have had positive effects on schooling (enrollment, attendance, dropout rates); health (vaccinations, medical checkups); and child nutrition outcomes (Fiszbein et al. 2009; Saavedra and Garcia 2013). These reviews also indicate that there is substantial variation in effect between countries and among different population groups even within the same country.

One natural question is whether the results depend on the design quality of the studies. Lagarde, Haines, and Palmer (2007) reviewed the literature and selected studies that had to meet specific design criteria (randomized controlled trial, interrupted time series analysis, and controlled before and after study) and had to include a measure of at least one of the following outcomes: health-care utilization, health expenditure, or health outcomes. In all, 28 papers met the criteria and were reviewed for possible assessment. They then selected 10 of the 28 for more in-depth analysis and assessment. Overall, the evidence from these analytically rigorous, high-quality studies suggested that CCT programs were indeed effective in increasing the use of preventive services and in sometimes improving health status.

Ranganathan and Lagarde (2012) provide an updated overview of CCT programs in low- and middle-income countries and present the evidence on their contribution to improvements in health and the encouragement of health-conducive behavior. Again, several bibliographic databases and websites were used to identify relevant studies that met the criteria; especially experimental or quasi-experimental study designs were deemed suitable. They identified 13 CCT programs mostly in Latin American countries whose effects had been evaluated. Their updated results confirmed that CCT programs have indeed been effective in increasing the use of preventive services, improving immunization coverage and certain health outcomes, and in encouraging health-conducive behavior.

Despite these positive effects, many questions remain unanswered including the potential of CCT programs to function well under different conditions, to address the broader range of challenges among poor and vulnerable populations, and to prevent the intergenerational transmission of poverty. De Janvry and Sadoulet (2006) provide some insights on this issue. Using randomized experimental data from the *Progresa (Oportunidades)* program in Mexico, they showed that large efficiency gains can be achieved by taking into account how much the probability of a child's school enrollment is affected by a conditional transfer. Rules for targeting and calibration can be made to be easy to implement by selecting indicators that are simple, observable, and verifiable and that cannot be manipulated by beneficiaries. The Mexican case shows that these efficiency gains can be achieved without increasing inequality among poor households.

A recent survey study by Saavedra and Garcia (2013) using several dozens of case studies evaluated the impact of CCTs on educational outcomes along with their cost effectiveness and found a great deal of heterogeneity in both. They found that CCT programs in developing countries are more effective at increasing school enrollment and attendance with relatively low levels of baseline school enrollment and therefore are particularly effective at increasing secondary enrollment and attendance. In addition, their results indicate that program impact and cost-effectiveness are significantly larger when programs attempt to provide assistance and improve educational supply through grants, infrastructure, or other resources for schools instead of providing only family transfers. They further found that these programs have a greater impact on education when they have lower payment frequency and more stringent schooling conditions. All these results are generally consistent with previous studies and suggest that specific conditions and requirements, that is, the details, really matter in the effectiveness of CCT programs.

3. Other considerations

It is important to understand that human capital accumulation cannot be addressed solely by CCT programs. This is especially true in countries or regions where the supply of such services is insufficient or of low quality. In other words, constraints to the supply of education or health care impinge upon the effectiveness of CCTs. Cash transfers may be the right policy instrument to alleviate poverty in the short run, but their contribution to longer-term poverty reduction depends on supply-side factors as well.

In addition, although CCT programs have promoted greater consumption of education and health services among the poor, the evidence on improvements in education and health is mixed. Therefore, although there is clear evidence that CCTs increase the likelihood of access, the evidence of their impact on improving learning outcomes and nutritional standards is weaker. There are several reasons for this. One possibility is that there are important constraints at the household level that are not addressed by CCT programs. Other inputs into the production of education and health might play a substantial role as well. Another possibility is that the low quality of available services prevents increased use from leading to substantially improved final outcomes. Thus, CCT programs should be combined with other programs to improve the quality of the supply of education and health services as well as the access to these programs. This also suggests the need for more research that investigates final outcomes rather than access alone.

Some policy makers worry about the potential side effects of CCT programs such as disincentives to work, crowding out private transfers, effects on fertility and family composition, and effects on local wages and prices. The evidence reviewed in Fiszbein et al. (2009), however, suggests that these effects have generally been modest. They conclude that offsetting behavioral responses are unlikely to be large and that the marginal propensity to consume out of transfer income is high. Moreover, because transfers generally are well targeted to the poor, the effects on consumption have translated into sizable poverty reduction.

The evidence further suggests that CCT programs generally do not have large disincentive effects on the labor supply of adults. Although the results should be interpreted with caution in large part due to their short time horizon, they generally find that CCT programs do not discourage work. In addition, unlike most social assistance programs in the developed world, there is little evidence that CCT programs crowd out private transfers, and they do not appear to have had large effects on fertility either. Finally, the evidence shows that CCT programs have had no significant negative effects on wages, prices, or the receipt of other welfare payments.

In sum, the main conclusion is that CCT programs have generally worked well in Latin America. Most programs, especially those making sizable transfers, have had substantial impacts on consumption and on poverty. While effects such as work disincentives were a source of concern, they do not appear to have occurred on a scale large enough to offset the benefit of the transfers. Moreover, CCT programs generate many positive externalities. For example, monitoring and evaluating them helps to strengthen institutions and policies. This is potentially a very important issue in countries where the monitoring and evaluation systems are not very well developed.

E. Policy lessons for developing Asia from the Latin American experience

In this chapter, we looked at the Latin American experience with using fiscal policy to tackle inequality and promote inclusive growth with a view to drawing relevant policy lesson for developing Asia. The fact that Latin America, unlike the advanced economies, is more or less at similar income and development levels as Asia makes the exercise all the more opportune and timely as developing Asia is beginning to explore leveraging fiscal policy – public spending and taxation policies – to tackle the region's growing inequality, all the more so since Latin America has had a sizable head start on Asia in inclusive fiscal policy.

At a macro level, the overriding lesson for developing Asia is that fiscal policy can have a significant effect on inequality and poverty even in developing countries. In this context, the Latin American experience may be more relevant for Asia than the advanced-country experience since Asia and Latin America face a much more urgent need to preserve growth even as they use fiscal policy to promote equity. That is, both regions understandably accord a higher priority to growth relative to equity compared with advanced countries that are much richer. We should, however, remember that developing Asian economies have grown much faster than Latin America's, and as a result, poverty reduction has been much greater (ADB 2012). Therefore, of utmost importance to Asia are equity-promoting fiscal policies that do not jeopardize economic growth and in particular fiscal sustainability. Fiscal activism in the cause of equity must not impinge on growth and fiscal space.

In this context, the Latin American experience indicates that one particular instrument of inclusive fiscal policy, namely CCT programs, offers a promising way forward for Asian economies. CCT programs have proven to be an effective means of assisting the poorest and most vulnerable members of society in Latin American countries. They promote equity because they are targeted at the poor and growth because they build up human capital via investments in education and health care. A key additional attraction of CCTs is that if designed and implemented well, they need not impose large fiscal burdens that harm fiscal sustainability.

CCTs are not without potential problems. One area of concern for Asian policy makers is the impact of CCT programs in very different settings and outcomes that have not yet been studied. Although there is some encouraging evidence on the impact of CCTs in low-income countries including Bangladesh, Cambodia, and Pakistan, most evidence is still confined to the middle-income countries of Latin America. In addition, Asian evidence is limited and also more mixed compared with Latin American evidence. For example, in Bangladesh many people fail to participate in CCTs in large part due to the very low benefit level.[4] Moreover, as mentioned earlier, CCTs were more successful in Cambodia than in Bangladesh because the program was better targeted.

There is little guarantee that programs that worked well in Latin America will work well in Asia. A complex administrative structure to monitor a large-scale program does not exist in many developing Asian countries. On the other hand, the role of the community could be greater in Asia than in Latin America, so a simple pilot program that emphasizes the role of the community in implementing the programs could work in Asia.

Son (2008) warns that CCT programs are not a panacea to reduce poverty and that policy makers should be aware of their limitations. First of all, countries that provide CCTs must have the social services in place to meet the demand created by the program. This reiterates the point we made earlier about supply-side constraints to the effectiveness of CCTs. Most of all, CCT programs need to be carefully monitored and rigorously evaluated. They also need high-level political support because they are typically implemented by multiple government agencies that need to work closely with each other.

Furthermore, CCT programs are just one option among many social protection programs; they cannot be the right instrument for all poor households. Most of all, they have limited relevance for the elderly poor or households whose children are outside the age range covered by the CCT. Redistribution to those groups can be better handled with different kinds of programs. In particular for the elderly poor, since justification for further human capital development is weak, social insurance programs such as pensions are the preferred instrument to provide assistance. This is particularly important in Asia where many populations are aging rapidly.

In addition, since the focus of CCTs is long-term human capital investment, it is questionable if these are the best instruments to deal with transient and acute poverty. Programs like workfare seem to address macroeconomic shocks better than CCT programs. Finally, fiscal policy is just one part of the policy package for inclusive growth. Land reform, sound governance, and other policy instruments can give the poor greater economic security and enhance children's education and health, which in turn makes them more productive. A number of Asian governments have followed this route to greater prosperity, but many of them still have a long way to go.

Notes

1 In Brazil, however, the poverty-increasing impact of indirect taxes may be over-estimated due to the assumption of no differences in evasion rates along the income distribution.
2 It should be noted, however, that Argentina is not strictly comparable as the analysis first does not include the impact of taxes and second does not include public spending on the contributory health system.
3 CCT programs are also found in Asia in Bangladesh, Cambodia, India, Indonesia, Nepal, the Philippines, and others, but the scale is much less than in Latin America.
4 Transfers as a share of pre-transfer consumption among all beneficiaries were 0.6% in Bangladesh's Female Secondary School Assistance Project in 2000, while they were 6.1% in Brazil's *Bolsa Família* in 2006 and 21.8% in Mexico's *Progresa* (*Oportunidades*) in 2004 (Fiszbein et al. 2009).

Bibliography

Asian Development Bank (ADB). 2011. *Asian Development Outlook 2011 Update: Preparing for Demographic Transition*. Manila: ADB.
———. 2012. *Asian Development Outlook 2012: Confronting Rising Inequality in Asia*. Manila: ADB.
Baird, S., C. McIntosh, and B. Özler. 2011. Cash or Condition? Evidence from a Cash Transfer Experiment. *The Quarterly Journal of Economics*. 126 (4). pp. 1709–1753.
Barrera-Osorio, F. and D. Raju. 2011. Evaluating Public Per-Student Subsidies to Low-Cost Private Schools: Regression-Discontinuity Evidence from Pakistan. *Policy Research Working Paper Series* 5638. Washington, DC: World Bank. http://go.worldbank.org/HECT18Z2P0 (accessed 1 October 2013).

Bazzi, S., S. Sumarto, and A. Suryahadi. 2012. *Evaluating Indonesia's Unconditional Cash Transfer Programme, 2005–2006. Grantee Final Report.* New Delhi: International Initiative for Impact Evaluation. http://www.3ieimpact.org/media/filer_public/2013/10/25/evaluating_indonesias_unconditional_cash_transfer_programme_20052006.pdf (accessed 1 October 2013).

Behrman, J. R., S. W. Parker, and P. E. Todd. 2005. Long-Term Impacts of the *Oportunidades* Conditional Cash Transfer Program on Rural Youth in Mexico. *Ibero-America Institute for Economic Research Discussion Paper.* No. 122. Göttingen, Germany.

Berganza, J. C. 2012. Fiscal Rules in Latin America: A Survey. *Banco de España Occasional Paper Series.* No. 1208. Madrid: Banco de España. http://www.bde.es/f/webbde/SES/Secciones/Publicaciones/PublicacionesSeriadas/Documentos Ocasionales/12/Fich/do1208e.pdf (accessed 1 October 2013).

Bucheli, M., N. Lustig, M. Rossi, and F. Amábile. 2014. Social Spending, Taxes and Income Redistribution in Uruguay. In N. Lustig, C. Pessino, and J. Scott, eds. *Analyzing the Redistributive Impact of Taxes and Transfers in Latin America. Special Issue. Public Finance Review.* 42 (3). pp. 413–433.

Calderón, C. and P. Fajnzylber. 2009. How Much Room Does Latin America and the Caribbean Have for Implementing Counter-Cyclical Fiscal Policies? *Latin America and Caribbean Crisis Briefs Series.* Washington, DC: World Bank.

Daude, C., Á. Melguizo, and A. Neut. 2011. Fiscal Policy in Latin America: Countercyclical and Sustainable? *Economics: The Open-Access, Open-Assessment E-Journal.* 5 (14). pp. 1–29.

de Brauw, A. and J. Hoddinott. 2011. Must Conditional Cash Transfer Programs be Conditioned to be Effective? The Impact of Conditioning Transfers on School Enrollment in Mexico. *Journal of Development Economics.* 96 (2). pp. 359–370.

de Janvry, A. and E. Sadoulet. 2006. Making Conditional Cash Transfer Programs More Efficient: Designing for Maximum Effect of the Conditionality. *World Bank Economic Review.* 20 (1). pp. 1–29.

del Granado, A., S. G. Javier, and A. Hajdenberg. 2013. Is Social Spending Procyclical? Evidence for Developing Countries. *World Development.* 42. pp. 16–27.

Febriany, V. and A. Suryahadi. 2012. Lessons from Cash Transfer Programs in Indonesia. East Asia Forum. 21 February. http://www.eastasiaforum.org/2012/07/21/lessons-from-cash-transfer-programs-in-indonesia/ (accessed 1 October 2013).

Fiszbein, A., N. Schady, F.H.G. Ferreria, M. Grosh, N. Kelleher, P. Olinto, and E. Skoufias. 2009. *Conditional Cash Transfers: Reducing Present and Future Poverty.* Washington, DC: World Bank.

Gertler, P. 2004. Do Conditional Cash Transfers Improve Child Health? Evidence from PROGRESA's Control Randomized Experiment. *American Economic Review.* 94 (2). pp. 336–341.

Glewwe, P. and A. L. Kassouf. 2010. *The Impact of the Bolsa Escola/Familia Conditional Cash Transfer Program on Enrollment, Drop Out Rates and Grade Promotion in Brazil.* http://faculty.apec.umn.edu/pglewwe/documents/BrBolsa6.pdf (accessed 1 October 2013).

Hernanz, V., F. Malherbet, and M. Pellizzari. 2004. Take-up of Welfare Benefits in OECD Countries: A Review of the Evidence. *OECD Social, Employment and Migration Working Paper Series.* No. 17. Paris: Organisation for Economic Co-operation and Development.

Higgins, S. and C. Pereira. 2014. The Effects of Brazil's Taxation and Social Spending on the Distribution of Household Income. In N. Lustig, C. Pessino, and J. Scott, eds. *Analyzing the Redistributive Impact of Taxes and Transfers in Latin America. Special Issue. Public Finance Review.* 42 (3). pp. 346–367.

International Monetary Fund (IMF). 2013. Fiscal Monitor Database. http://www.imf.org/external/pubs/ft/fm/2013/01/fmindex.htm (accessed October 2013)

Jaramillo, M. 2014. The Incidence of Social Spending and Taxes in Peru. In N. Lustig, C. Pessino, and J. Scott, eds. *Analyzing the Redistributive Impact of Taxes and Transfers in Latin America. Special Issue. Public Finance Review.* 42 (3). pp. 391–412.

Lagarde, M., A. Haines, and N. Palmer. 2007. Conditional Cash Transfers for Improving Uptake of Health Interventions in Low-and Middle-Income Countries. *The Journal of the American Medical Association.* 298 (16). pp. 1900–1910.

Lindert, K., E. Skoufias, and J. Shapiro. 2006. Redistributing Income to the Poor and the Rich: Public Transfers in Latin America and the Caribbean. *Social Safety Net Primer Series.* No. 605. Washington, DC: World Bank.

Lopez-Monti, R.M. 2009. A Comparative Analysis of the Welfare Cost of Real Volatility in Latin America and Developed Countries. http://www.socialsciences.manchester.ac.uk/cgbcr/conferences/papers/documents/RLM_Conference%20Paper.pdf (accessed 1 October 2013).

Lustig, N., F. Amábile, M. Bucheli, G.G. Molina, S. Higgins, M. Jaramillo, W. Jiménez Pozo, V. Paz Arauco, C. Pereira, C. Pessino, M. Rossi, J. Scott, and E. Yáñez Aguilar. 2013. The Impact of Taxes and Social Spending on Inequality and Poverty in Argentina, Bolivia, Brazil, Mexico, Peru and Uruguay: An Overview. *CEQ Working Paper Series.* No. 13. New Orleans: Center for Inter-American Policy and Research and Department of Economics of Tulane University and Inter-American Dialogue.

Lustig, N. and S. Higgins. 2013. Commitment to Equity Assessment (CEQ): Estimating the Incidence of Social Spending, Subsidies and Taxes. Handbook (September revision). *CEQ Working Paper.* No. 1. New Orleans: Center for Inter-American Policy and Research and Department of Economics of Tulane University and Inter-American Dialogue.

Lustig, N. and C. Pessino. 2014. Social Spending and Income Redistribution in Argentina during the 2000s: The Rising Role of Noncontributory Pensions. In N. Lustig, C. Pessino, and J. Scott, eds. *Analyzing the Redistributive Impact of Taxes and Transfers in Latin America. Special Issue. Public Finance Review.* 42 (3). pp. 304–325.

Lustig, N., C. Pessino, and J. Scott. 2014. The Impact of Taxes and Social Spending on Inequality and Poverty in Argentina, Bolivia, Brazil, Mexico, Peru, and Uruguay: Introduction to the Special Issue. In N. Lustig, C. Pessino, and J. Scott, eds. *Analyzing the Redistributive Impact of Taxes and Transfers in Latin America. Special Issue. Public Finance Review.* 42 (3). pp. 287–303.

McGuire, J.W. 2011. Social Policies in Latin America: Causes, Characteristics, and Consequences. *ACSPL Working Paper Series.* Vol. 1 Article 1. Middleton, CT: Allbritton Center for the Study of Public Life, Wesleyan University.

Parker, S., L. Rubalcava, and G. Teruel. 2008. Evaluating Conditional Schooling and Health Programs. In Schultz, T.P. and J. Strauss, eds. *Handbook of Development Economics.* Volume 4. Amsterdam: Elsevier.

Paz Arauco, V., G.G. Molina, W. Jiménez Pozo, and E. Yáñez Aguilar. 2014. Explaining Low Redistributive Impact in Bolivia. In N. Lustig, C. Pessino, and

J. Scott, eds. *Analyzing the Redistributive Impact of Taxes and Transfers in Latin America. Special Issue. Public Finance Review.* 42 (3). pp. 326–345.

Ranganathan, M. and M. Lagarde. 2012. Promoting Healthy Behaviours and Improving Health Outcomes in Low and Middle Income Countries: A Review of the Impact of Conditional Cash Transfer Programmes. *Preventive Medicine.* 55 (Supplement). pp. S95–105.

Rawlings, L. M. and G. B. Rubio. 2005. Evaluating the Impact of Conditional Cash Conditional Transfer Programs. *World Bank Research Observer.* 20 (1). pp. 29–56.

Saavedra, J. and S. Garcia. 2013. Educational Impacts and Cost-Effectiveness of Conditional Cash Transfer Programs in Developing Countries: A Meta-Analysis. *CESR Working Paper.* No. 2013–007. Center for Economic and Social Research (CESR), University of Southern California.

Schady, N. and M. C. Araujo. 2008. Cash Transfers, Conditions, and School Enrollment in Ecuador. *Economia.* 8 (2). pp. 43–70.

Schultz, T. P. 2004. School Subsidies for the Poor: Evaluating the Mexican Progresa Poverty Program. *Journal of Development Economics.* 74 (1). pp. 199–250.

Scott, J. 2014. Redistributive Impact and Efficiency of Mexico's Fiscal System. In N. Lustig, C. Pessino, and J. Scott, eds. *Analyzing the Redistributive Impact of Taxes and Transfers in Latin America. Special Issue. Public Finance Review.* 42 (3). pp. 368–390.

Son, H. H. 2008. Conditional Cash Transfer Programs: An Effective Tool for Poverty Alleviation? *ERD Policy Brief.* No. 51. Manila: ADB.

Srisuchart, S. 2008. Student Loan Program, Household Credit Constraint, and Schooling in Thailand. PhD Dissertation. University of Hawai'i at Mānoa.

Tesliuc, E., D. Coady, M. Grosh, and L. Pop. 2006. Program Implementation Matters for Targeting Performance: Evidence and Lessons from Eastern and Central Europe. Unpublished manuscript. Washington, DC: World Bank.

Zoido, P. and J. Santiso. 2010. Fiscal Legitimacy, Inequality and Democratic Consolidation in Latin America. http://papers.ssrn.com/sol3/papers.cfm?abstract_id=1622686 (accessed 1 October 2013).

9 Fiscal policy and inclusive growth in advanced countries

Their experience and implications for Asia

Almas Heshmati, Jungsuk Kim, and Donghyun Park

A. Introduction

Advanced economies have a much longer history of using fiscal policy to promote inclusive growth than those in developing Asia. Addressing inequality has traditionally been one of the key strategic objectives of fiscal policy in the advanced economies which tend to use progressive taxation to redistribute resources from the rich to the poor via transfers and subsidies. Organisation for Economic Co-operation and Development (OECD) governments have actively and explicitly sought to redistribute income to achieve a more equitable income distribution. In contrast, Asian governments used fiscal policy to lay the foundation for macroeconomic stability and hence economic growth by avoiding government budget deficits. Another contribution of fiscal policy to growth in Asia has been large investments in growth-conducive infrastructure and education that have contributed to the stock of physical and human capital.

To some extent, the fundamental difference in the perception of the growth–equity trade-off between the two groups reflects a vast gap in income and development levels. As countries grow richer, they generally accord a higher priority to the quality of growth, critically including income equality as opposed to narrowly defined economic growth, that is, the citizens of high-income countries typically have a stronger preference for redistributing income to achieve a more equitable income distribution than the citizens of low-income countries. These differences in preference are consistent with the diminishing marginal utility of income. Social preferences for redistribution are evident in the relative size of the government in rich versus poor countries. The larger tax burdens and larger government size of rich countries is largely the result of the larger redistributive role of the government.

Notwithstanding the larger size of the government and the higher priority accorded to income redistribution in advanced economies, at least some of their experience with using fiscal policy for equity-promoting purposes is relevant for developing Asia. Above all, their experience can help inform and guide Asian policy makers as to whether fiscal policy can reduce inequality and thus promote inclusive growth. Furthermore, that experience will have implications about the relative effectiveness of public spending versus taxation, along with the relative effectiveness of different types of public spending – for example, education versus transfers – and different types of taxes and fiscal revenue sources – for example, personal income tax versus value-added tax. Therefore, while we must be careful to take into account the large differences between the two groups, the experience of the advanced economies can still inform and guide Asian policy makers.

Those lessons are all the more valuable at this point because the governments of developing Asia are beginning to recognize the potential of fiscal policy as a powerful tool for fostering more inclusive growth. That recognition is part of a broader, region-wide trend of visibly greater engagement of public policy for equity purposes. The Harmonious Society Initiative in the People's Republic of China (PRC) and designating inclusive growth as a national strategic objective by the Indian government are just two examples of the trend. Heightened government activism for equity, in turn, is triggered by rising inequality in the region. The Asian Development Bank (ADB, 2012) reports that the Gini coefficient rose – that is, inequality grew – from 1990 to 2010 in economies that collectively accounted for over 80% of the region's population. Therefore, now is an opportune time for Asia to take stock of the inclusive fiscal policy experience of the advanced economies and to glean the appropriate lessons.

Part B of this chapter briefly compares the fiscal policies of OECD members with those of developing Asia. Part C reviews the different types of welfare models in OECD members, while Part D takes an in-depth look at fiscal policy for inclusive growth in the OECD. The section examines various fiscal policy measures – transfers, subsidies, and taxes – and their redistributive effects. The same measures can also have regressive effects, an issue explored in Part E that also takes a look at poverty reduction effects and the growth–poverty trade-off. Part F brings the chapter to a close with some observations.

B. Brief comparison of government sizes

It is a well-known, stylized fact that the relative size of the government as measured by standard indicators such as the ratio of gross domestic product (GDP) to total tax revenue or total public expenditure tends to increase as per capita income rises. The pattern is well established both over time and across economies. That is, the government tends to expand as an economy grows richer, and richer economies have bigger governments than poorer ones do. There are a number of possible explanations for this. For one, the size of the informal sector that does not pay taxes and remains outside the purview of the government is generally larger in developing economies, while the tax administrations and hence the capacity to collect tax revenues are stronger and more effective in advanced economies. Furthermore, the demand for some public services may grow as income levels rise. For example, cash transfers to the poor could increase as a result of rising public concerns over inequality.

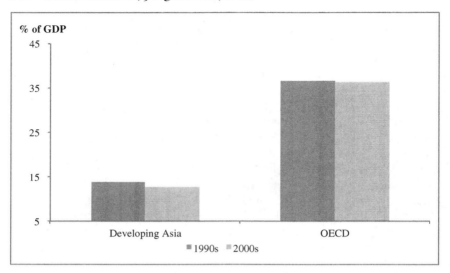

Figure 9.1 Development of tax revenues to gross domestic product ratio, developing
Asia and Organisation for Economic Co-operation and Development

OECD = Organisation for Economic Co-operation and Development.

Notes: Data are based on simple averages. Developing Asia comprises the People's Republic
of China, India, Indonesia, the Republic of Korea, Malaysia, Pakistan, the Philippines, Singapore, Sri Lanka, and Thailand.

  Following Acosta-Ormaechea and Yoo 2012, data for OECD refer to general government
owing to significant decentralization in these countries. Data for other countries mainly refer
to central government.

Sources: Acosta-Ormaechea and Yoo 2012, OECD 2013, and World Bank 2014.

This suggests that the size of government will be larger in advanced economies
than in developing Asia in light of the huge income gap between the two
groups. Their larger size gives the governments of the advanced economies
more resources to invest in public programs that promote equity like education,
health care, social protection, transfers, and subsidies. At the same time, the
larger size partly reflects a stronger public demand for equity. Figure 9.1 shows
the total tax revenue to GDP ratio in the OECD and developing Asia from
1990 to 1999 and from 2000 to 2010. As might be expected, there is a huge
gap in the relative size of the governments in the two groups. More specifically,
governments were almost three times larger in OECD than in developing Asia
during both decades, and there was little change in government size in either
group over time.

  Figure 9.2 shows the total tax revenue to GDP ratio in 2011 for selected
major economies in the OECD and developing Asia. The relative size of the
government is more or less similar for the four Asian economies. The only
noticeable feature is that the ratio is visibly higher for the Republic of Korea
than for the PRC, India, and Indonesia. This is consistent with the positive

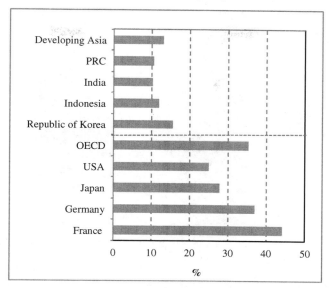

Figure 9.2 Tax revenues to gross domestic product ratio for selected countries and country groups, 2011 (and 2010)

IMF = International Monetary Fund, OECD = Organisation for Economic Co-operation and Development, USA = United States.

Developing Asia comprises the People's Republic of China (PRC), India, Indonesia, Rep. of Korea, Malaysia, Nepal, Pakistan, Philippines, Singapore, Sri Lanka, and Thailand. Data for PRC and Japan refer to 2010.

Sources: IMF 2013b, OECD 2013, World Bank 2014.

relationship between per capita GDP and government size since the Republic of Korea is much richer than the other three. On the other hand, there are marked differences in government size among OECD members. In line with the conventional wisdom of large welfare states in Western Europe, France and Germany have significantly larger governments than the United States and Japan where the role of the state in the economy is more limited.

An alternative measure of relative government size is the ratio of total public expenditure to GDP. One would expect a strong positive correlation between the tax revenue to GDP ratio and the public expenditure to GDP ratio. Figure 9.3 shows the public expenditure to GDP ratio in the OECD and developing Asia from 1990 to 2000 and from 2000 to 2010. As expected, there is a huge gap in the ratio between the two groups; more specifically, the ratio is about twice as large in the OECD. For both groups, the ratio is more or less the same during the 2 decades. The expenditure ratio is substantially larger than the tax ratio for both indicating sizable non-tax revenues as well as government borrowing. Figure 9.4 shows the total public expenditure to GDP ratio in 2012 for selected major economies in the OECD and developing Asia.

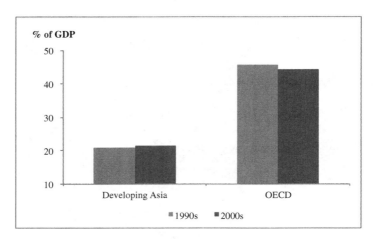

Figure 9.3 Development of government expenditures to gross domestic product, developing Asia and Organisation for Economic Co-operation and Development

OECD = Organisation for Economic Co-operation and Development.

Note: Data are based on simple averages. Developing Asia comprises the People's Republic of China, India, Indonesia, the Republic of Korea, Malaysia, Pakistan, Philippines, Singapore, Sri Lanka, and Thailand.

Source: International Monetary Fund 2013b.

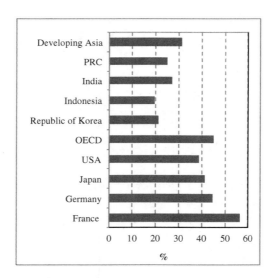

Figure 9.4 Expenditures to gross domestic product ratio for selected countries and country groups, 2012

OECD = Organisation for Economic Co-operation and Development, PRC = People's Republic of China, USA = United States.

Note: Data refers to general government.

Source: International Monetary Fund 2013b.

The pattern across countries is similar to that of the tax revenue to GDP ratio with OECD members in particular in Western Europe having larger governments than those in developing Asia. Overall, the evidence resoundingly confirms the conventional wisdom that the state is larger in OECD members than in developing Asia.

C. Social welfare models

Different groups of OECD members implement different mixes of policies to address income inequality and poverty reduction.[1] Even within the same group, there are significant differences in terms of the relative importance of various fiscal policies. To examine and compare the fiscal policy regimes of OECD members, we referred to the classification of four social welfare model systems proposed by Sapir (2006) and Joumard, Pisu, and Bloch (2012) that incorporates the latest changes in the social welfare policies. The social welfare models are the Nordic, Anglo-Saxon, Continental European, and Mediterranean and Low Income. Each model is briefly described below.

The Nordic Model (Belgium, Denmark, Finland, the Netherlands, and Sweden[2]) provides the highest levels of social protection expenditures and universal welfare cash transfers. To redistribute income, these countries adopt a high level of spending on in-kind transfers and a mix of taxes. This model features extensive fiscal interventions in labor markets, while allowing strong labor unions. Promoting employment is a key policy objective. The countries that belong to this model combine economic dynamism with comprehensive social protection and are thus widely viewed as benchmarks to emulate.

The Anglo-Saxon Model[3] includes Australia, Ireland, Japan, New Zealand, the United Kingdom, and the United States. According to Sapir (2006), the countries in this group provide relatively large levels of social assistance. Cash transfers are primarily targeted to people of working age. Measures such as employment benefit schemes that allow access to regular employment are one essential while weak unions, wide and increasing wage gaps, and a high incidence of low-paid employment are the main characteristics of this model. According to Joumard, Pisu, and Bloch (2012), Anglo-Saxon model countries make relatively less use of cash transfers and taxes to cope with income inequality. Transfers in Australia and New Zealand are targeted to low-income groups, while Japan and the United States are characterized by limited progressivity in their cash transfers which are mostly spent on old-age pensions.

The Continental European Model[4] of Austria, France, Germany, and Luxembourg depends heavily on insurance-based, nonemployment benefits and old-age pension contributions. Labor unions still remain strong, and regulations are further extended to the collective bargaining system to include non-union workers (Sapir 2006). Joumard, Pisu and Bloch (2012) report that these countries use large cash transfers targeted primarily at old-age pensions and a tax mix that does not prioritize the promotion of redistribution across individuals. A small role for personal income tax is thus one of the key elements of this model.

262 *Almas Heshmati, Jungsuk Kim, et al.*

The Mediterranean[5] and Low-Income Model[6] includes Greece, Italy, Portugal, and Spain. The model revolves around social spending on old-age pensions and permits a high segmentation of entitlements and status. Their social welfare systems feature a high level of employment protection and early retirement provisions. Their wage structure is sheltered by strong collective bargaining (Sapir 2006). Joumard, Pisu, and Bloch (2012) proposed a new model consisting of lower-income OECD members such as Chile and Turkey where the welfare system is less developed. The levels of transfers and taxes in those countries rely heavily on consumption taxes for their fiscal revenues and are far below the OECD average.

D. A review of the literature

This part takes a closer look at fiscal policy measures for inclusive growth and their effects in OECD members.

1. Overview of inclusive, equity-promoting fiscal policy measures

Rising income inequality has become one of the central issues of public debate in recent times. A large body of literature has emerged to discuss the economic and social consequences of growing inequality along with policy options to tackle the problem. While much of the discussion has centered around the determinants of rising inequality – globalization, labor market reforms, and technological progress that favor highly skilled workers – the focus of the literature is shifting to the issue of "what can be done" to mitigate inequality (Bastagli, Coady, and Gupta 2012; Kierzenkowski and Koske 2012; OECD 2008 and 2011). In this section, we review a number of relevant studies on advanced country policy experiments designed to promote inclusive growth and reduce inequality.

The single most salient finding that emerges from the existing literature is that fiscal policy – taxes and transfers – can have a large, significant impact on improving inequality and reducing poverty. This is especially true for economies with high initial levels of pre-tax and transfer inequality (Bastagli, Coady, and Gupta 2012); however, it remains unclear whether the overriding objective of fiscal policy in OECD members is income redistribution (OECD 2012a). In terms of the trade-off or complementary relationship between growth and equity, different types of fiscal policy options had different effects on economic growth. While the balance of the evidence finds a strong effect of fiscal policy on income redistribution, some studies find that redistributive taxes and transfers can produce economic inefficiencies such as tax avoidance or evasion, rent seeking behaviors, and disincentives to work.

2. Redistributive effects of fiscal policies

Bastagli, Coady, and Gupta (2012) suggest that in the 25 OECD members studied, there was on average a 15% decrease in the Gini Index of inequality from 1985 to 2005 as a result of direct income taxes and transfers. Seven economies

(Belgium, Denmark, Germany, Italy, Luxembourg, Poland, and the Slovak Republic) saw their Gini Index results reduced by over 20% while five (the Republic of Korea, Iceland, Ireland, Switzerland, and the United States) achieved approximately 10% decreases through the successful implementation of fiscal measures. A similar result was presented in the study by Joumard, Pisu, and Bloch (2012) in which they found that taxes and transfers have helped to reduce the disposable income gap in OECD members although the redistributive impact of each policy differs across members depending on the magnitude and directions of their policy instruments.

a. Public cash transfers and benefits

Regarding effective policy options, most studies took into account possible variations across countries due to differing economic and social circumstances, including political economy factors. All other things equal, the redistribution impact of public cash transfers was double the tax effect in most OECD members except for the United States[7] where taxes are more redistributive than transfers (Bastagli, Coady, and Gupta 2012; Denk et al. 2013; Krueger 2012). The major tool for public expenditures for redistribution purposes is non-means-tested transfers,[8] especially in the Nordic economies and in Austria, Belgium, Hungary, and Poland.

According to studies on the OECD[9] (Joumard, Pisu, and Bloch 2012; OECD 2012a, 2012b, and 2012c), despite smaller tax bases and welfare systems, by focusing more on income taxes and means-tested cash transfers, countries like Australia have achieved a level of redistribution that is comparable to countries with much higher taxes and transfers like Germany. Furthermore, these studies show an even greater impact of cash transfers than that of Bastagli, Coady, and Gupta (2012). They reported that the effect of cash transfers was three times greater than the effect of tax incidence[10] in reducing the level of dispersion between market income and disposable income (Joumard, Pisu, and Bloch 2012; OECD 2012a). Earlier studies by Wolff and Zacharias (2007) on the effects of US government expenditures and taxation on household incomes from 1989 to 2000 reached a similar conclusion: compared with taxes, expenditures yielded greater inequality-reducing results. Among transfers, the progressivity of housing benefits was substantial, but its redistributive impact was inadequate due to limited magnitude (OECD 2012a, 2012b, and 2012c).

Redistributive effects of transfers across countries. In comparing OECD members, the correlation between the degree of market income inequality and the redistributive impact of transfers is not obvious. In the Czech Republic, Denmark, Finland, and Sweden where the dispersion of market income is close to the OECD average, transfers have the greatest redistributive impact. The smallest redistributive impact of cash transfers was in the Republic of Korea and Chile followed by Iceland, the United States, and Portugal. Furthermore, countries with a similar dispersion in household market incomes such as Canada and Finland showed quite divergent effects of cash transfers as Finland achieved twice the impact level as Canada (Joumard, Pisu, and Bloch 2012). According to Bastagli, Coady, and Gupta (2012), the United States had the highest level of disposable income inequality among high-income economies in 2000, while central and northern European countries had the lowest income gaps.

Mixed effects of benefits. Cournède, Goujard, and Pina (2013) found that government spending on pensions helps to redistribute income. Claus, Martinez-Vazquez, and Vulovic (2012) also reported that public pension systems are on average progressive although the extent of the progressivity varied across OECD members. According to these two studies, in most of the OECD, except for Ireland, the Netherlands, and the United Kingdom and to a lesser extent Denmark, public pensions were superior in terms of income inequality reduction than other fiscal instruments were. On the other hand, reducing replacement rates – the ratio of pension benefits to pre-retirement income – can be regressive. Declines in unemployment benefits also led to more inequality, even in insurance-based systems. In the long term, however, reducing the level of unemployment benefits generally lifted employment rates.

The size of cash transfers linked with disability and sickness benefits is large, especially in the Netherlands and Nordic countries where the level of benefits was close to 3% of GDP in 2007, well above the average of 2% for other OECD members. Almost 6% of the working-age population across the OECD was covered by such benefits, and in some countries the government allocation to disability and sickness benefits exceeded unemployment benefits (Joumard, Pisu, and Bloch 2012). Reducing disability benefits would increase inequality since the replacement rate tends to be higher for low-income earners. On the other hand, poorly targeted disability benefits may increase lifetime income inequality by reducing income mobility and creating poverty traps (Cournède, Goujard, and Pina 2013; Joumard, Pisu, and Bloch 2012).

b. Redistributive and progressive effects of income taxes

The analysis of tax incidence in terms of who ultimately bears the burden of government taxes and the assessment as to whether its impact has been redistributive or progressive has been investigated in a vast body of literature. As is the case with other social benefit analyses, capturing solid evidence on the impact of different taxes remains challenging due to different economic conditions and social preferences in each country (OECD 2012a, 2012b, 2012c, and 2011). Nonetheless, in terms of overall incidence, income taxes have been found to be the most redistributive tax in many economies. In some cases, income tax has achieved an even higher impact than that of means-tested transfers (Bastagli, Coady, and Gupta 2012). Personal income tax was especially progressive although there were significant differences across countries (Joumard, Pisu, and Bloch 2012; OECD 2012a, 2012b, and 2012c).

Empirical evidence. Studies such as those by Kitao (2010) found that a reduction in income taxation stimulates an immediate incentive to work and save more which in turn raises aggregate output and consumption. Temporary tax cuts and rebates improve the overall welfare of households, and the rebates are especially beneficial for low-income households. Jara and Tumino (2013) showed that the tax and benefit systems of 27 European Union (EU) countries have a significant effect on reducing inequality especially in Belgium, Germany, and Anglo-Saxon countries (the United Kingdom and Ireland) although the size of the effect varied substantially. Immervoll and Richardson (2011) found a similar result, that is, taxes and benefits significantly reduced inequality. Other studies on income taxes found that advanced economies have a tendency to raise their tax revenues by imposing higher marginal rates on the highest income groups. Taxes on capital and wealth are also widely used in the OECD to promote equity. Changes in personal and corporate income taxes show a significant short-term output effect (Mertens and Ravn 2013). Furthermore, personal income tax is usually associated with larger multipliers than corporate income tax (IMF 2013a).

Adverse effects of taxation and tax system design. The International Monetary Fund (IMF, 2013a) argues that more progressive taxation on higher-income groups is needed to mitigate widening income gaps, but in the era of globalization, the imposition of higher tax rates on wealth and capital can provoke tax evasion and avoidance. Zucman (2013) showed that almost 8% of the global financial wealth of households was in the custody of tax havens. The OECD (2012a) reported that the size of the tax revenue to GDP ratio does not always result in the same redistributive impact. The empirical evidence found a dissimilar impact across countries with similar ratios. Some high-tax countries showed little progressivity because (i) the tax mix favored consumption taxes and social security contributions rather than progressive personal income and wealth and inheritance taxes, (ii) the progressivity of tax schedules was limited, or (iii) statutory progressivity was weakened by tax expenditures that benefitted high-income groups (OECD 2012a).

E. Fiscal policies, poverty reduction, and the equity–efficiency trade-off

We explore some evidence that fiscal policies have a regressive effect in OECD members and on poverty reduction as well as the trade-off between equity and efficiency.

1. Regressive effects of fiscal policies

In most OECD members, social security contributions, consumption taxes, and real estate taxes tend to be regressive (Joumard, Pisu, and Bloch 2012; IMF 2013a; OECD 2012a). Tax exemptions or credits pertaining to personal income tax were more likely to profit the rich except for in-work tax credits (Joumard, Pisu, and Bloch 2012; OECD 2012a). Similar evidence was found by Muinelo-Gallo and Roca-Sagalés (2013) for 21 high-income OECD members. Cutting non-redistributive expenditures was found to be the most effective fiscal policy to simultaneously stimulate GDP growth and reduce income inequality. Bargain (2012) suggested that in the absence of reforms to income support and tax credits, inequality and poverty depth would have been amplified and child poverty would not have been sharply reduced.

A study by Silva, Carvalho, and Ribeiro (2013) on the magnitude of fiscal multipliers in Europe[11] found that the tax multiplier was higher in recessions, while fiscal consolidation had a negative effect on tax multipliers. Peñalosa and Turnovsky (2011) found that tax reforms that target labor supply will affect wealth and income distribution which in turn will either reinforce or offset the redistributive impact of taxes in the US and European economies. Considering different ways of financing government expenditure, they found that policies that reduced the labor supply and output also led to a more equal distribution of after-tax income.

Kuttner and Posen (2002) investigated the effectiveness of Japanese fiscal policy from 1976 to 1999. Expansionary fiscal policies such as tax cuts or increased public expenditure did substantially stimulate the economy. The results implied that the tax cut multiplier was 25% higher over a 4-year horizon than the public spending multiplier. An analysis of historical data showed that the retrenchment of Japanese fiscal policy in the 1990s led to a significant slowdown in growth. Most of the increase in public debt was associated with declining tax revenues due to the recession. On the other hand, in an analysis of the impact of US fiscal policy on inequality, Kenworthy and Smeeding (2013) found that actual changes in tax or transfer policies did not increase the level of inequality.

2. Fiscal policy and poverty reduction[12]

Thompson and Smeeding (2013) explored trends in inequality and poverty in the United States using both market income and after-tax and transfer income between 2008 and 2010. The effects of tax and transfer policies were not uniform across the population. Poverty declined among the elderly, changed little among children, and rose sharply among the working-age population. Inequality fell across the entire population, but no change was seen among working-age households.

Gemmell and Morrissey (2005) reviewed the effect of various tax structure reforms on income distribution and poverty reduction in developing countries. The study suggested that taxes on exports and necessity goods consumed by the public – especially by the poor – proved to be significantly and consistently regressive, whereas taxes on luxury goods such as cars had a tendency to be progressive. Sales taxes were more progressive or at least less regressive than import taxes.

The OECD (2008) reported that income poverty among the elderly had declined, while the poverty level of young adults and families with children had risen. The report suggests that providing an opportunity to work is one of the most effective tools for tackling poverty. Poverty rates among jobless families were nearly six times higher than those among working families; however, work alone was not the solution for preventing poverty since more than half of the poor consisted of households with low-wage workers. In-work benefits that supplement earnings were therefore proposed as a major measure for reducing in-work poverty among this group. The mixed evidence on the impact of taxation policy and cash transfers in addressing income inequality and poverty reduction across countries has led to an investigation of the correlation between equity and efficiency in fiscal policy.

3. Equity and growth: trade-off or complementary?

Among policy makers and academics, there has been a lot of debate about the level of economic inefficiency caused by income redistribution via tax and benefit systems. The inefficiency arises because they can produce work disincentives across income distributions. Bastagli, Coady, and Gupta (2012) suggested that well-designed policies can minimize this equity–efficiency trade-off. They argue that a large part of the inefficiency is caused by means-tested social benefits due to the diminishing returns of benefits as earnings increase. More specifically, this refers to the strong disincentives for low-skilled workers to find employment opportunities (OECD 2012a, 2012b, and 2012c). Despite a vast body of theoretical literature on the link between inequality and growth, no general consensus has emerged, and the empirical evidence is rather inconclusive (OECD 2012a).

In a recent report, the IMF (2013a) suggests that among major taxes, corporate income taxes have the most negative effect on growth followed by personal income taxes, then consumption taxes, and finally property taxes. Jara and Tumino (2013) also confirmed the presence of a trade-off between income inequality and work incentives in the EU based on their analysis of the impact of fiscal policy across 27 EU member states. Empirical studies such as Berthold and Brunner (2008) found a persistent trade-off between equity and efficiency as well as a negative effect of social spending on GDP in their analysis of four different European welfare models.[13] The preferences of the citizens of each country and the electoral process determine the level of income redistribution.

4. Design of social welfare systems and equity–efficiency trade-offs

Various studies suggested that the institutional design of a welfare system to a certain extent can alleviate a degree of inefficiency (Bastagli, Coady, and Gupta 2012; IMF 2013a; OECD 2012a). Among the four social welfare models, the institutional design of the Nordic systemic has proven to be more efficient than the others and therefore faces a smaller trade-off. The OECD (2012a) reported that some tax reforms have win-win characteristics by simultaneously improving growth prospects and reducing the income gap. In contrast, many of the reforms may involve trade-offs depending on their design and targeting. The fiscal policy patterns of OECD members along with their growth and equity effects are summarized in Table 9.1 and Table 9.2.[14] Table 9.1 groups OECD members into five categories based on their levels of income inequality, while Table 9.2 outlines the growth and equity effects of different fiscal policies in the OECD.

Table 9.1 Organisation for Economic Co-operation and Development members' fiscal policy patterns

Category and Level of Inequality	Group 1[a]	Group 2	Group 3	Group 4	Group 5
	Lower[b] inequality		Intermediate inequality		Higher inequality
Member	Denmark Iceland Norway Sweden Switzerland	Belgium Czech Republic Estonia Finland France[b] Italy Slovak Republic Slovenia	Austria Germany Greece Hungary Japan Rep. of Korea Luxembourg Poland Spain	Australia Canada Ireland[b] Netherlands New Zealand United Kingdom	Chile Israel Mexico Portugal Turkey United States
Pattern	Low dispersion in labor income (high employment rate and little wage dispersion).	Average dispersion in labor income (little wage variation but low employment or high part-time rate). Highly concentrated capital and self-employment income.	Individual labor income concentrated, reflecting above average dispersion in wages and a low employment or high part-time rate.	Above average wage dispersion coupled with a high part-time rate.	High concentration of labor, capital and self-employment income.
Policy	Cash transfers tend to be universal and taxes are not highly progressive.	Cash transfers (largely insurance-based) and taxes are not highly progressive.	Taxes and transfers are not highly progressive.	Cash transfers are targeted and taxes are progressive.	The poverty rate is high.

[a] OECD (2012a) used the term cluster instead of group.

[b] "Inequality in household disposable income."

Source: Figure 5.6: Country groups with similar patterns of inequality, OECD 2012a.

Table 9.2 Summary of fiscal policy effects of Organisation for Economic Co-operation and Development members

Policy Effects	Income Inequality	GDP Growth
Increasing total tax revenues • The impact of taxes on income distribution depends on the level of taxation, the tax mix and the use of tax revenues, but if tax systems are progressive overall, equality is enhanced. • Taxes dampen incentives to work, save, and invest, and are thus detrimental to growth, but some taxes have a less adverse effect than others.	Positive (in general)	Negative
Changing the tax mix while keeping total tax revenues constant		
Moving from personal income tax to consumption taxes: • Personal income tax tends to be progressive, while consumption tax is regressive. • Personal income tax reduces work and saving incentives. A shift from direct to indirect taxes would raise GDP per capita.	Negative	Positive
Moving from labor income to property and capital taxes: 1) Wealth, inheritance taxes, and capital taxes • Wealth and inheritance taxes tend to be progressive. • The distributive impact depends on the relative progressivity of income *versus* wealth and inheritance tax.	Ambiguous	Positive
2) Real estate taxes • Real estate taxes are often less progressive than the personal income tax and can even be regressive. • Property taxes are among the least harmful for growth. Moving from income to property taxes tends to improve incentives to work and invest, and thus raise output at least in the short and medium term.	Negative	Positive
Cutting tax expenditures and marginal tax rates: • Most tax expenditures benefit high-income groups (in-work tax credits and other tax expenditures targeted at low-income groups are the exception). Cutting tax expenditure would narrow the distribution of disposable income. • Cutting marginal rates improves incentives to work, save and invest, and thus lifts the GDP per capita.	Positive in most cases but in-work tax credit is negative	Positive

(Continued)

Table 9.2 (Continued)

Policy Effects	Income Inequality	GDP Growth
Increasing the progressivity of taxes (but revenue-neutral)		
Personal income tax:	Positive	Ambiguous
In-work tax credits narrow the income distribution and raise incentives to work.		
1) Increase in top rates	Positive	Negative
• On the other hand, higher top rates may reduce working hours and productivity by undermining incentives to work, invest, and innovate.		
2) The above measure combined with expanded earned income tax credit schemes or tax free allowances	Positive	Positive
• The GDP per capita impact is thus ambiguous.		

GDP = gross domestic product, OECD = Organisation for Economic Co-operation and Development.

Source: Table 5.3 in OECD 2012a.

In order to minimize the equity–efficiency trade-offs of fiscal policies, many OECD members have implemented in-kind benefits that link the receipt of benefits to employment. Countries have also extended the use of efficient labor market programs to tighten rules for continued eligibility for unemployment benefits including tougher job search and training requirements; however, designing and implementing such policies requires a high level of administrative capacity. Furthermore, the equity effect of fiscal policies is amplified when indirect taxes and in-kind benefits are supplemented with other measures (Bastagli, Coady, and Gupta 2012).

F. Policy implications for developing Asia

Advanced countries have a much longer history and tradition of using fiscal policy to promote equity than developing Asia has. As such, their experience can provide some guidance for developing Asia in its quest for inclusive fiscal policy that contributes to inclusive growth. Given the huge gaps in income and development levels between the two groups, we must exercise a great deal of caution in making policy inferences for developing Asia from the experience of the advanced economies. Notwithstanding this important caveat, the latter's wealth of experience in inclusive fiscal policy holds some valuable lessons for the former.

The central objective of this chapter was to review that experience in order to draw relevant policy lessons for Asia. The single biggest overall lesson is that fiscal policy can be a powerful instrument for tackling inequality and creating a more equitable economy. This should give Asian governments a measure of confidence that at a very broad level, fiscal policy can be a useful tool for fostering more inclusive growth in the region. To be sure, overall government size and public expenditures that can reduce inequality are markedly higher in advanced countries than in developing Asia. Be that as it may, the significant impact of fiscal policy on inequality in the advanced economies suggests that developing Asia too can leverage fiscal policy to promote equity.

With respect to the relative effectiveness of different types of fiscal policies, the evidence from the OECD resoundingly indicates that public spending has a noticeably larger effect on inequality than taxation and other fiscal revenue policies. In particular, the OECD experience indicates that among the different components of public spending, transfers can significantly reduce inequality. Given the much larger level of transfers in advanced economies, it is unclear whether transfers can have the same equity-promoting impact in developing Asia. Furthermore, it is unlikely that the level of transfers in the region will rise to OECD levels in the foreseeable future. Nevertheless, the OECD experience suggests that well-targeted transfers that benefit poor, vulnerable, and disadvantaged groups will be effective tools for inclusive growth in Asia. For example, more public spending on pensions will protect Asia's growing elderly population which faces the risk of widespread old-age poverty.

We saw that the trade-off between efficiency and equity was an important consideration in designing and implementing equity-promoting fiscal policy measures even in the relatively rich advanced economies. The trade-off takes on a much greater significance in developing Asia where there is a much greater need for economic efficiency and growth due to low-income levels and still widespread poverty. The OECD experience indicates that generous public expenditures often create inefficiencies such as work disincentives. Its urgent need for sustained rapid growth to lift general living standards and reduce poverty means that Asia can ill afford such inefficiencies. Therefore, it is advisable for Asian policy makers to take such disincentives fully into account, for example by pursuing active labor market policies or measures to encourage work. In this sense, the Nordic model of social welfare probably contains many useful lessons for Asian economies.

Sustained rapid growth has reduced poverty on a massive scale in developing Asia in the past, and economic growth will continue to play a key role in reducing poverty. One vital element of Asia's sustained growth has been macroeconomic stability underpinned by fiscal prudence. While there are exceptions, by and large Asian governments have been fiscally responsible, which has given them fiscal space, an invaluable asset for both short-term objectives like the fiscal stimulus during the 2008–2009 global crisis, and long-term objectives like inclusive fiscal policy. The contrast with advanced economies is striking. Partly as a result of large public transfers, their government debt has reached very high levels compared to that of developing Asian economies (Figure 9.5). The salient lesson for Asian governments is that as they pursue more inclusive fiscal policies, they must tax and spend efficiently in order to maintain fiscal sustainability and economic growth.

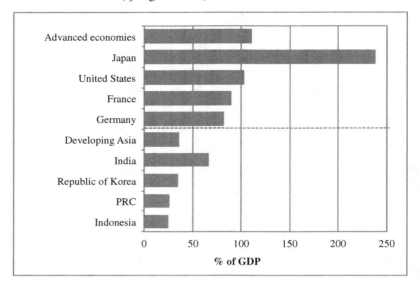

Figure 9.5 Gross government debt to gross domestic product ratio for selected
      countries and country groups, 2012

GDP = gross domestic product, PRC = People's Republic of China.

Note: Weighted by gross domestic product.

Source: IMF Fiscal Monitor Database (October 2013).

Notes

1 According to Joumard, Pisu, and Bloch (2012) welfare systems have three main
   objectives: (i) redistribution of income over the life cycle; (ii) providing income
   maintenance or insurance to cope with adverse risks; and (iii) avoiding poverty
   or a too wide dispersion in living standards. These benefits can be either universal
   or means tested.
2 Joumard, Pisu, and Bloch (2012) added Belgium into this group.
3 Sapir (2006) included Ireland and the United Kingdom, while Joumard,
   Pisu, and Bloch (2012) added Australia, Japan, New Zealand, and the United
   States.
4 Sapir (2006) included Belgium in this group, but we grouped Belgium into the
   Nordic model referring to Joumard, Pisu, and Bloch (2012).
5 Berthold and Brunner (2008) grouped the countries as Nordic = Denmark,
   Finland, Norway and Sweden; Anglo-Saxon = Great Britain and Ireland; Continental = Austria, Benelux (Belgium–Netherlands–Luxembourg) countries, France,
   Germany, and Switzerland; and South = Italy and Spain.
6 We incorporate the two models suggested by Spair (2006) and Joumard, Pisu,
   and Bloch (2012).
7 OECD (2012a) reported that the United States nearly achieved a similar redistribution effect through taxes as other countries achieved with cash transfers.
8 They include public pensions and universal child benefits.
9 OECD (2012a) and Joumard, Pisu, and Bloch (2012).

10 Tax incidence includes income tax, payroll and social security taxes, corporate income tax, taxes on goods and services, the incidence of sales taxes, value added and excise taxes, property tax, and export tax.
11 The study used tax spending and revenue variables with annual data from 1998 to 2008.
12 Poverty reduction instruments include price controls on housing rents, minimum wages and interest rate controls on deposits and loans, foreign exchange rationing, import quotas, and restrictions on exports (OECD 2012a).
13 The four models are Nordic (Denmark, Finland, Norway, and Sweden); Anglo-Saxon (Great Britain and Ireland); Continental (Austria, Belgium, France, Germany, Luxembourg, Netherlands, Switzerland); and South (Italy and Spain).
14 OECD (2012a) summarized the policy effects based on Joumard, Pisu, and Bloch (2012).

Bibliography

Acosta-Ormaechea, S. and J. Yoo. 2012. Tax Composition and Growth: A Broad Cross-Country Perspective. *IMF Working Paper.* No. 12/257. Washington, DC: International Monetary Fund.

Asian Development Bank (ADB). 2012. *Asian Development Outlook 2012 Confronting Rising Inequality in Asia.* Manila: ADB.

Bargain, O. 2012. The Distributional Effects of Tax-Benefit Policies under New Labor: A Decomposition Approach. *Oxford Bulletin of Economics and Statistics.* 74 (6). pp. 856–874.

Bastagli, F., D. Coady, and S. Gupta. 2012. Income Inequality and Fiscal Policy. *IMF Staff Discussion Note.* No. SDN/12/08. Washington, DC: International Monetary Fund.

Berthold, N. and A. Brunner. 2008. The Struggle between Equity and Efficiency: Do Nordic Countries Have a Free Lunch? *University of Würzburg Working Paper.* No. 103. Würzburg: Leibniz Information Centre for Economics.

Claus, I., J. Martinez-Vazquez, and V. Vulovic. 2012. Government Fiscal Policies and Redistribution in Asian Countries. *ADB Economics Working Paper.* No. 310. Manila: ADB.

Cournède, B., A. Goujard, and A. Pina. 2013. How to Achieve Growth- and Equity-Friendly Fiscal Consolidation? A Proposed Methodology for Instrument Choice with an Illustrative Application to OECD Countries. *OECD Economics Department Working Paper.* No. 1088. Paris: Organisation for Economic Co-operation and Development.

Denk, O., R. Hageman, P. Lenain, and V. Somna. 2013. Inequality and Poverty in the United States: Public Policies for Inclusive Growth. *OECD Economics Department Working Paper.* No. 1052. Paris: Organisation for Economic Co-operation and Development.

Gemmell, N. and O. Morrissey. 2005. Distribution and Poverty Impacts of Tax Structure Reform in Developing Countries: How Little We Know. *Development Policy Review.* 23 (2). pp. 131–144.

International Monetary Fund (IMF). 2013a. Fiscal Monitor: Taxing Times. *World Economic and Financial Surveys.* Washington, DC. http://elibrary-data.imf.org/DataExplorer.aspx (accessed 29 October 2013).

———. 2013b. Government Financial Statistics Online Database. http://elibrary-data.imf.org/DataExplorer.aspx (accessed 29 October 2013).

Immervoll, H. and L. Richardson. 2011. Redistribution Policy and Inequality Reduction in OECD Countries: What Has Changed in Two Decades? *OECD Social, Employment, and Migration Working Paper.* No. 122. Paris: Organisation for Economic Co-operation and Development.

Jara, H.X. and A. Tumino. 2013. Tax-Benefit Systems, Income Distribution and Work Incentives in the European Union. *EUROMOD Working Paper.* No. EM 7/13. Essex, UK: Institute for Social and Economic Research.

Joumard, I., M. Pisu, and D. Bloch. 2012. Tackling Income Inequality: The Role of Taxes and Transfers. *OECD Journal: Economic Studies.* 2 (1). pp. 37–70.

Kenworthy, L. and T. Smeeding. 2013. Growing Inequalities and Their Impacts in the United States. *Country Report for the United States.* January. The GINI Project.

Kierzenkowski, R. and I. Koske. 2012. Less Income Inequality and More Growth: Are They Compatible? Part 8. The Drivers of Labor Income Inequality: A Literature Review. *OECD Economics Department Working Paper.* No. 931. Paris: Organisation for Economic Co-operation and Development.

Kitao, S. 2010. Short-Run Fiscal Policy: Welfare, Redistribution and Aggregate Effects in the Short and Long-Run. *Journal of Economic Dynamics & Control.* 34 (10). pp. 2109–2125.

Krueger, A. 2012. The Rise and Consequences of Inequality in the United States. Paper presented to the Center for American Progress in Washington, DC, on 12 January.

Kuttner, K.N. and A.S. Posen. 2002. Fiscal Policy Effectiveness in Japan. *Journal of the Japanese and International Economies.* 16. pp. 536–558.

Mertens, K. and M.O. Ravn. 2013. The Dynamic Effects of Personal and Corporate Income Taxes in the United States. *American Economic Review.* 103 (4). pp. 1212–1247.

Muinelo-Gallo, L. and O. Roca-Sagalés. 2013. Joint Determinants of Fiscal Policy, Income Inequality and Economic Growth. *Economic Modelling.* 30. pp. 814–824.

Organisation for Economic Co-operation and Development (OECD). 2008. *Growing Unequal? Income Distribution and Poverty in OECD Countries.* Paris: Organisation for Economic Co-operation and Development.

———. 2011. *An Overview of Growing Income Inequalities in OECD Countries: Main Findings. Divided We Stand Why Inequality Keeps Rising.* Paris: Organisation for Economic Co-operation and Development.

———. 2012a. Chapter 5 of Part 2: Reducing Income Inequality while Boosting Economic Growth: Can It Be Done? In *Economic Policy Reforms 2012: Going for Growth.* Paris: Organisation for Economic Co-operation and Development.

———. 2012b. Inequality in Labour Income: What Are Its Drivers and How Can It Be Reduced? *OECD Economics Department Policy Note.* No. 8. Paris: Organisation for Economic Co-operation and Development.

———. 2012c. Income Inequality and Growth: The Role of Taxes and Transfers. *OECD Economics Department Policy Note.* No. 9. Paris: Organisation for Economic Co-operation and Development.

———. 2013 OECD.StatExtracts. http://stats.oecd.org (database accessed 29 October 2013).

Peñalosa, C.G. and S.J. Turnovsky. 2011. Taxation and Income Distribution Dynamics in a Neoclassical Growth Model. *Journal of Money, Credit and Banking.* 43 (8). pp. 1543–1577.

Sapir, A. 2006. Globalization and the Reform of European Social Models. *Journal of Common Market Studies.* 44 (2). pp. 369–390.

Silva, R., V. M. Carvalho, and A. P. Ribeiro. 2013. How Large are Fiscal Multipliers? A Panel-Data VAR Approach for the Euro Area. *FEP Working Paper.* No. 500. Porto: Faculty of Economics of the University of Porto.

Thompson, J. P. and T. M. Smeeding. 2013. Inequality and Poverty in the United States: The Aftermath of the Great Recession. *Finance and Economics Discussion Series.* No. 2013–51. Washington, DC: Federal Reserve Board.

Wolff, E. N. and A. Zacharias. 2007. The Distributional Consequences of Government Spending and Taxation in the U.S., 1989 and 2000. *Review of Income and Wealth.* 53 (4). pp. 692–715.

World Bank. 2014. World Development Indicators Online Database. http://databank. worldbank.org/data/views/variableSelection/selectvariables.aspx?source=world-development-indicators (accessed 31 January 2014).

Zucman, G. 2013. The Missing Wealth of Nations: Are Europe and the U.S. Net Debtors or Net Creditors? *Quarterly Journal of Economics.* 128 (3). pp. 1321–1364.

10 Summary of key findings, main policy recommendations and concluding observations

Donghyun Park

A. Summary of key facts and findings

This part lays out the key facts and findings that emerged from the analysis in this book.

- **Developing Asia is experiencing an increase in inequality.**

  Asia's sustained rapid gross domestic product (GDP) growth helped more than 700 million people escape poverty slashing the percentage of people living at or below the $1.25/day poverty line from 52% in 1990 to 21% in 2010. The Gini coefficient, a widely used measure of inequality in per capita income or expenditure, rose from the early 1990s to the late 2000s in 11 of 28 Asian countries that provide comparable data. Those 11 countries hold 82% of Asia's population. As a result of increasing inequality, there is growing popular demand for public policy, including fiscal policy, to tackle it.

- **Fiscal policy, especially public spending, can make a visible dent in inequality.**

  International experience, especially the experience of the advanced economies, indicates that fiscal policy can be a powerful tool for reducing inequality. One result that emerges consistently from the literature that is applicable to both advanced and developing economies is that public spending has a bigger impact on reducing inequality than does taxation. According to the International Monetary Fund (IMF 2014), expenditures – especially transfers without means tests – contributed more to income redistribution than did taxes. Claus, Martinez-Vasquez, and Vulovic (2014) find empirical evidence that the general pattern is also true in developing Asia.

- **Asia currently spends relatively little on equity-promoting fiscal expenditures.**

  Evidence indicates that Asian spending falls short relative to the advanced economies and to Latin America in education, health care, and social protection. Public spending on education averages 5.3% of GDP in the advanced economies and 5.5% in Latin America but only 2.9% in Asia. The difference is starker for public spending on health care, which equals 8.1% of GDP on average in the developed world and 3.9% in Latin America, but a paltry 2.4% in developing Asia. Finally, Asian governments devote 6.2% of GDP to social protection, essentially half of Latin America's 12.0% and less than a third of the 20.0% in advanced economies.

- **Public transfers remain more limited in Asia than in other parts of the world.**

  A combination of private transfers within the family and public transfers through government programs finances the gap between consumption and production in childhood and old age. For children, private transfers play a bigger role in Asia and Latin America than in Europe. The percentage of a child's total material needs covered by the family, such as education and nutrition, stands at 70% in Taipei,China; 82% in the Philippines; and 83% in India. Meanwhile, for the elderly, public transfers to cover health care and long-term care are smaller in Asia than elsewhere, especially in Indonesia, the Philippines, and Thailand.

- **Governments are beginning to explore the use of fiscal policy for inclusive purposes.**

  This is evident in countries across the region. For example, in November 2013, the Third Plenary Session of the 18th Central Committee of the Communist Party of the People's Republic of China (PRC) adopted the "Decision on Major Issues Concerning Comprehensively Deepening Reforms" that accords a high priority to improving income distribution. The Government of India has adopted a development strategy with two goals: lifting economic growth and making growth as inclusive as possible. In Southeast Asia, many governments have set promoting inclusive growth as the goal of their medium-term development plans, some with explicit and concrete targets.

- **Asian governments have been spending more on education and health in recent years.**

  The growing interest in inclusive fiscal policy is evident in the steady growth of equity-promoting public expenditures. Education and health care directly improve human welfare and are significant determinants of an individual's earning potential, especially for the poor who have limited physical capital or unearned income. Encouragingly, government spending on education and health as a percentage of GDP is on the rise in many economies in developing Asia. For example, in the PRC, public spending on education increased from 2.0% in 1995 to 3.1% in 2010. During the same period, public spending on health grew from 1.8% in 1995 to 2.7% in 2010.

- **Access to education and health remains highly unequal in the region.**

  The rich often enjoy better access to education and health than the poor in developing Asia. For example, in Pakistan, over half of the children of primary school age from the poorest families were out of school in 2006 compared with just 7% of those from the richest families. In Bangladesh, 53% of the children of secondary school age from the poorest families were out of school, nearly twice the figure for children from the richest families. While more than 60% of women in the highest income groups in the Lao People's Democratic Republic, Nepal, Pakistan, and Timor-Leste give birth attended by skilled health personnel, the corresponding share in the lowest quintile is less than 20%.

- **Public spending on education, health care, and transfers has a significant impact on inequality in developing Asia.**

  Notwithstanding unequal access, our empirical evidence indicates that both public health spending and public education spending seem to alleviate income inequality significantly in developing Asia. The poor have less access to private education and health care than the rich. Public transfers also have a significant effect on inequality. Fiscal spending on education seems to reduce inequality the most, decreasing the Gini coefficient by a cumulative 1.1 percentage points within a decade. Fiscal spending on health and transfers also has substantial impacts with Gini coefficient improvements of 0.3 percentage points and 0.6 percentage points, respectively.

- **Public spending on infrastructure has a significant effect on economic growth and can thus contribute to inclusive growth.**

  Our analysis does not find a significant link between public investments in physical infrastructure and changes in the Gini coefficient, but it does find a strong growth impact. Simulation results indicate that a one-time increase by 1 percentage point of GDP in public investment spending raises GDP growth by a cumulative 1.3 percentage points over 7 years. Growth is needed to successfully reduce poverty. For example, Kraay (2006) finds that cross-country differences in the growth of average incomes explain 60%–90% of their differing pace of poverty reduction from 1970 to 2005 making per capita income growth the single biggest determinant of success in eliminating poverty.

- **Conditional cash transfers have been effective in reducing inequality in Latin America but remain underdeveloped in Asia.**

  In recent years, conditional cash transfers (CCTs) have emerged as a promising option for magnifying the equity impact of public spending in developing countries. Currently there are CCT programs in Bangladesh, Cambodia, India, Indonesia, Nepal, and the Philippines. While evidence on the effectiveness of CCT programs in developing Asia is still limited and mixed, CCTs have become a distinctive and relatively successful form of equity-promoting public spending in Latin America where they are in use in 17 countries. Brazil's *Bolsa Família* and Mexico's *Oportunidades* accounted for about 20% of the reduction in their Gini coefficients between the mid-1990s and the mid-2000s.

- **Poor benefit incidence of government expenditures points to a need for better targeting in the region.**

   The impact of public expenditures on individual poor households depends on benefit incidence, that is, how public expenditure is distributed across different demographic groups. How much of the spending reaches the poor? The evidence from Asia underscores the need for more effective targeting. For example, in the PRC in 2009, on average, those aged 75 and in the top quartile received a pension of 11,793 yuan, while those in the second quartile received 4,000, and those in the bottom quartile got less than 250. In Indonesia in 2008, more than 90% of fuel subsidies benefitted the richest urban households, and in India in 2013, the richest 10% of households received seven times more benefits than the poorest 10%.

- **Developing Asia has been fiscally prudent in the past.**

   In line with conventional wisdom, the examination of developing Asia's past fiscal behavior confirms a generally conservative stance. There is, however, considerable diversity in government fiscal balances in the region with some like India and Pakistan running sizable deficits. Generally speaking, though, the fiscal position of many in the region and of the region as a whole is healthier than elsewhere in the world. The region's overall fiscal deficit averaged 2.2% from 2008 to 2012. The corresponding figures were 2.9% for Latin America, 6.8% for advanced economies, and 4.9% for the entire world.

- **As a result of fiscal prudence, the region currently has relatively ample fiscal space.**

   Prudent fiscal behavior in the past means that government debt is low in much of developing Asia compared with that in the rest of the world, and the region's ratio of debt to GDP compares favorably with that of other regions and the world as a whole. In 2012, the ratio was 35.9% in developing Asia, 52.0% in Latin America, 108.7% in advanced economies, and 80.8% in the world. Even taking into account that a debt ratio considered sustainable for a developing country is lower than that for an advanced economy, developing Asia's low ratio bodes well for its fiscal sustainability and fiscal space though again, India and Pakistan are among the exceptions.

- **Notwithstanding seemingly ample fiscal space at the present, developing Asia faces large fiscal demands in the future.**

  Developing Asia faces potentially significant fiscal demands from a wide range of structural challenges. For one, as income rises, public spending and government size tend to rise too, but perhaps the single biggest social and economic shift facing developing Asia is population aging. Demographic structures affect public spending because the beneficiaries are often children and the elderly. Our analysis indicates that due to rising income and to population aging, public spending on health as a share of GDP will rise from 2.4% in 2010 to 7.3% in 2050. For social security and welfare, the corresponding figures are 2.5% and 5.6%. Therefore, current fiscal space does not guarantee future fiscal space.

- **Developing Asia trails other parts of the world in tax revenue collection.**

  As with fiscal spending, Asia trails other world regions on the fiscal revenue front. Despite improvements, revenue from taxes in developing Asia remains at barely half the level of Organisation for Economic Co-operation and Development (OECD) members. The tendency of governments to expand in tandem with per capita income explains some of the gap with the OECD, but fiscal revenue mobilization in Asia also trails that in Latin America. The tax revenue to GDP ratio in the 2000s averaged 17.8% in developing Asia, 21.8% in Latin America, 31.9% in the OECD, and 28.6% in the world. This gap with Latin America suggests considerable scope for developing Asia to improve revenue mobilization.

- **Taxes are the primary source of fiscal revenues across developing Asia.**

  For developing Asia as a whole and across all of its subregions, taxes are the primary sources of fiscal revenues. Current revenues provide the vast majority of the region's fiscal revenues, and taxes dominate them. The share of taxes is higher in some subregions than others, but in no subregion of Asia and the Pacific does the share of taxes fall below 75%. The share of taxes in total fiscal revenues is higher in developing Asia, and the share of non-tax revenues is lower than in the rest of the world. Finally, the share of income taxes in total tax revenues is lower in developing Asia than in other parts of the world, and the share of taxes on goods and services is higher.

- **Indirect taxes dominate income taxes in the composition of developing Asia's tax revenues.**

  Tax composition matters because different taxes affect growth and equity differently. The GDP share of property tax in Asia is only slightly below the share in Latin America but barely half the share in the OECD. Asia's corporate income tax rate stands just below the share

in Latin America but above the OECD share. Social security contributions are lowest in Asia. Personal income tax in Asia is somewhat lower
than in Latin America and much less than in the OECD. Finally, indirect
taxes are lower in Asia than in Latin America but higher than in the
OECD. All in all, indirect taxes are more important than income taxes
in developing countries, but the opposite holds for the OECD.

- **Inherently progressive taxes, non-tax revenues, and corrective taxes are
  underutilized fiscal revenue instruments in developing Asia.**

  There are a number of inherently progressive fiscal revenue options
  that can enhance the progressive orientation of fiscal revenue systems
  across Asia. Most of them promise more equitable resource mobilization at relatively low economic cost. These include property tax, inheritance tax, and capital gains tax, yet they are underdeveloped in the
  region. For example, only four Asian countries currently have property
  taxes (Araki 2014). The GDP share of non-tax revenues such as fees
  and user charges that can have positive effects on growth and equity
  remains limited in the region relative to the rest of the world. The
  same is true for corrective taxes imposed on goods that have negative
  externalities.

B. Policy recommendations: fiscal policy for inclusive growth

The facts and findings in Part A give rise to a number of policy recommendations that can help developing Asia harness fiscal policy to promote inclusive
growth. These recommendations can be categorized into five broad groups:
(1) overall fiscal policy directions; (2) fiscal spending policy; (3) fiscal revenue
policy; (4) fiscal planning for inclusive growth; and (5) fiscal innovation for
inclusive growth.

1. Overall directions for inclusive fiscal policy

In response to growing popular demand for more inclusive growth, developing
Asian governments have begun to explore fiscal policy as a tool to tackle the
region's rising inequality. While this is a healthy and welcome trend, regional
policy makers must exercise the utmost caution to ensure that fiscal activism to
promote equity does not jeopardize fiscal sustainability or economic growth.

- **Inclusive fiscal policy should take fiscal sustainability into account.**

  Expanding the role of fiscal policy to fight inequality should not under-
  mine fiscal sustainability, but tensions are surfacing between these
  competing ends. In the Republic of Korea, a new social pension scheme
  to provide basic income support to the elderly scheduled to be introduced in July 2014 had to be scaled back in response to fiscal concerns.

A key challenge is how to leverage fiscal policy for more inclusive growth while maintaining fiscal sustainability. The fiscal space that results from fiscal sustainability is needed to tackle both short-term challenges like fiscal stimulus during the global financial crisis and long-term challenges like population aging.

- **Inclusive fiscal policy should support economic growth as much as possible.**

   For all its success, Asia still needs sustained, rapid growth to raise per capita income. The region is still home to two-thirds of the world's poor, so sustained economic growth remains critical to eliminating poverty. Inclusive growth will, however, ultimately suffer if, for example, burdensome taxes distort decisions to invest or to hire workers. Sustained rapid growth was critical to the remarkable reduction in poverty that developing Asia enjoyed between 1990 and 2010. The poverty rate fell by a staggering 32.4% in the region during this period, a far better performance than in other parts of the developing world.

2. Fiscal spending policy

In developing Asia as in other parts of the world, fiscal spending has a significantly greater impact on inequality than fiscal revenue policies. The analysis indicates that public spending on education and health can help to reduce the gap between the rich and the poor as can public transfers. Pursuing inclusive fiscal policy is not, however, just a matter of spending more: it is also better targeting spending at the poor and spending on programs that benefit the poor.

- **Governments in developing Asia should invest more in education and health.**

   Public spending on education and health is a powerful way to reduce inequalities between the rich and poor since education and health are among the most important determinants of earning potential. The rich have greater access to private education and health care than the poor do. Furthermore, education and health contribute to a country's stock of human capital and thus promote equity and economic growth, but as noted earlier, the region spends less on education and health relative to not only advanced economies but also to Latin America. Therefore, although governments in the region have been investing more in recent years, they need to invest even more.

- **Expanding public transfers, especially conditional cash transfers, can protect the most vulnerable and disadvantaged groups.**

   Public transfers – transfers from the government to households – in developing Asia trail the advanced economies and Latin America, yet empirical evidence indicates that public transfers can have a significant effect on inequality in the region. This suggests some scope for expanding them, but unlike education and health, transfers do not inherently contribute to economic growth. One promising option is to make transfers conditional on the recipient making investments that augment their human capital like sending children to school or receiving specific medical care. CCTs have proven to be relatively effective in Latin America.

- **Governments must make public investments in physical infrastructure more accessible and affordable for the poor.**

  Our analysis uncovers a sizable impact of public investments in physical infrastructure on growth. Since sustained growth is the single most significant driver of poverty reduction, this suggests that public infrastructure investments contribute to inclusive growth via poverty reduction, but it does not yield evidence of a direct effect of such investments on equality. There are ways for Asian governments to improve the equity impact of their large and growing investments in infrastructure. In particular, making infrastructure more accessible and affordable for the poor will distribute the fruits of infrastructure investments more widely.

- **Governments should better target their public spending so that the poor receive more benefits.**

  Benefit incidence analysis indicates that in many cases the poor receive a disproportionately small share of the benefits of public spending in developing Asia. Since Asian governments spend relatively little on equity-promoting expenditures compared with the rest of the world, the case for more effective pro-poor targeting is even stronger. For example, phasing out general fuel subsidies that disproportionately benefit the non-poor and using the savings to help the poor with targeted subsidies is a sensible policy option. Since such general subsidies are often fiscally costly, such reforms have the added benefit of improving fiscal sustainability.

- **Directing more fiscal resources toward programs that benefit the poor will reduce inequality.**

  Another way of ensuring that the poor get their fair share of scarce fiscal resources is to channel more public spending toward programs that primarily benefit the poor. Different types of government programs tend to benefit different income groups differently. For example, tertiary education tends to benefit the non-poor more than the poor. Therefore, according a higher priority to primary and secondary education, especially technical and vocational training which gives students the practical skills and knowledge they need for work, can maximize the equity effect of public spending on education.

3. Fiscal revenue policy

Tax and other fiscal revenue policies have a direct effect on equity. Equally important, fiscal revenues provide the resources for financing equity-promoting public spending on education, health, and social protection. The challenge for Asian policy makers is to raise sufficient revenue to support more inclusive fiscal policy without harming growth. Our analysis points to a number of promising options to raise more fiscal revenue efficiently and equitably.

- **Asian countries must improve fiscal revenue mobilization efforts across all revenue categories.**

  Despite the seemingly adequate fiscal space that developing Asia currently enjoys, it faces large fiscal demands in the future. Furthermore, the region trails not only advanced economies but also Latin America in fiscal revenue mobilization; there is thus a strong case for strengthening it across all revenue sources. There is substantial scope for improvement in all major revenue categories: income taxes, indirect taxes, property taxes, corrective taxes, and non-tax revenues. Therefore, the overriding fiscal priority for Asian policy makers must be to improve collection efforts in each and every revenue category to secure a stronger and more sustainable revenue base.

- **Personal income tax base should be broadened.**

  A large percentage of people do not pay income tax in Asia because their incomes are below the tax-free threshold. Indeed, the ratio of tax-free threshold income to gross national income per capita is generally higher in most Asian countries than in OECD members. Furthermore, the top income tax rate applies to few taxpayers, as the ratio of the top personal income tax threshold to per capita income is relatively high in Asia. Narrow bases keep personal income tax revenues low in some Asian economies that exempt certain types of income or tax them at lower rates. For example, in the PRC, only 11 types of personal income are subject to tax. The direction of reform is to broaden the personal income tax base including at the top tax rates.

- **The design of value-added tax (VAT) can be improved, especially its progressivity.**

  Of particular importance in Asia is VAT, which is a major revenue source for many governments. VAT is among the least-distortionary taxes, but it tends to be regressive. Given its importance as a revenue source, the primary policy implication is not to reduce the share of such taxes but to make them more progressive through better design. One way to improve VAT is to raise the threshold for payment. Another option for making VAT less regressive is to use the proceeds for equity-promoting expenditures such as those on education and health care. There is also scope for broadening coverage to as many goods as possible since exemptions cause distortions and inefficiencies.

- **There is a strong case for expanding corrective taxes and non-tax revenues.**

   The evidence indicates that developing Asia relies more heavily on broad-based taxes than on other taxes. There is thus plenty of scope for the region to expand its fiscal resource base by moving beyond broad-based taxes to alternative revenue sources. Individually, these alternative sources may be small, but collectively, they can make a significant contribution to a larger, more sustainable fiscal resource base. One promising option is corrective taxes because they can promote efficiency while raising revenues. In some cases, such taxes can also be progressive. Another option is non-tax revenues, an area in which the region trails other parts of the world.

- **The region should introduce naturally progressive taxes.**

   There are a number of inherently progressive fiscal revenue options that can enhance the progressive orientation of fiscal revenue systems across Asia. Most of them promise more equitable resource mobilization at relatively low economic cost. These include property taxes, inheritance taxes, and capital gains taxes. Property taxes are underused in developing Asia and thus offer scope for strengthening fiscal resources, particularly for local governments. For example, the PRC is currently exploring property tax options as a means of solving the high indebtedness of local governments. Besides inheritance taxes and capital gains taxes, removing tax expenditures, for example, tax relief, also promotes equity.

4. Fiscal planning for inclusive growth

Governments need to look beyond annual budgeting cycles to balance competing demands on public resources while guarding fiscal sustainability. Effectively using fiscal policy to reverse widening inequality requires a planning tool with explicit equity objectives: the medium-term fiscal framework for inclusive growth. The framework offers a blueprint for systematically incorporating equity objectives into fiscal policy.

- **Asian governments should consider the medium-term fiscal framework for inclusive growth as a tool for institutionalizing equity into fiscal policy.**

   The medium-term fiscal framework for inclusive growth provides a procedure to help direct more government activity to benefit low-income households over time and to review progress toward this end. The framework involves careful annual reviews of inclusive government programs and sets concrete medium-term targets and the means for financing them. Bangladesh, for example, has explicit poverty-reduction goals, so the framework could show the government's plans to boost services and assistance for low-income households over a multiyear period, while also showing how changes in spending fit within the government's fiscal targets.

- **A medium-term fiscal framework for inclusive growth requires more and better fiscal data as well as strong political commitment.**

  Effective fiscal policy for inclusive growth requires more and better fiscal data to inform evidence-based policy. Improved fiscal data will enable Asian policy makers to better track public programs and assess their effectiveness. Such data, which should ideally include at least some micro data on individual projects, will help policy makers improve the design and implementation of inclusive public spending. The framework would benefit from, for example, data on expenditures on primary, secondary, and vocational education flowing to low-income regions and neighborhoods and on the percentage of low-income students in those schools and programs.

5. Fiscal innovation for inclusive growth

Conventional fiscal policies, that is, public spending on equity-promoting programs such as education, health, and social protection financed by efficient and equitable revenues, are the cornerstone of inclusive fiscal policy, but fiscal innovation may be required to relieve the tension between inclusive fiscal policy and fiscal sustainability. A number of innovative policies can support and amplify the role of fiscal policy in inclusive growth.

- **Social public–private partnerships can contribute to inclusive growth.**

  It may be possible to expand social infrastructure such as education and health care by harnessing these partnerships, which have been a valuable tool for building physical infrastructure such as roads and power plants. While social public–private partnerships are still in their infancy in developing Asia, there are some promising developments. The Republic of Korea has successfully leveraged them to fund the construction and upgrading of school buildings. In Bangladesh, the government has partnered with nongovernment organizations to effectively deliver primary health care to poor urban children. In addition to saving fiscal space, these partnerships can lead to the more efficient delivery of services.

- **Another option is to leverage information and communication technology (ICT) to make tax administration more efficient.**

  ICT can improve and strengthen every aspect of tax administration, which tends to be weak in many developing Asian governments. Tax administration bodies in developing Asia generally have the basic infrastructure they need to apply ICT to tax administration; the potential benefits are enormous. A shift to ICT spares many taxpayers the time and trouble of traveling to the tax office to pay their taxes in person by offering electronic payments through Internet banking or electronic direct debiting from bank accounts. Furthermore, this shift reduces operating costs for tax offices and opportunities for corruption. ICT adoption must, however, be accompanied by governance reforms to be effective.

- **State-owned enterprise reform and fiscal decentralization can strengthen the role of fiscal policy in inclusive growth.**

  The reform of state-owned enterprises can expand fiscal space and foster productivity growth. Although these reforms can cause labor retrenchment and regional dislocation in the short run, they are likely to promote efficiency and growth over the longer term. In addition, if reforms pave the way for higher profits, the government can use the resulting larger dividends to fund investments in inclusive growth. Fiscal decentralization can render fiscal policy more responsive as local governments understand much better than the central government the needs of their poor communities. Decentralization also enables local governments to secure more fiscal resources, for example, through property taxes.

C. Concluding observations

Due to low initial incomes and to priorities on maximizing economic growth, developing Asia is a relative newcomer to the use of public policy to promote equity, yet the region's governments are under growing pressure from their citizens to do more to spread opportunities and the fruits of growth more widely. The same market forces that transformed the region from an economic backwater to the most dynamic part of the world economy – globalization, technological progress, and market-oriented reforms – have widened the gap between the rich and the poor. The solution is not to impede those growth-generating market forces but rather to use effective government interventions to address the market's failure to promote equality. Fiscal policy in particular is a powerful tool for promoting more inclusive growth as is evident in the experiences of other countries, especially of the advanced economies. Fiscal policy alone, however, is not enough. A constellation of public policies will be needed, but fiscal policy must lie at the front and center of government efforts to more directly tackle inequality.

To conclude, fiscal policy can and should play a bigger role in promoting inclusive growth in Asia. The specific challenges and opportunities pertaining to leveraging fiscal policy for inclusive growth will necessarily differ from economy to economy across the highly heterogeneous region; nevertheless, the broad contours of an inclusive fiscal policy with at least some relevance for the whole region emerge from the analysis:

- more and better designed and implemented fiscal spending on education, health, and transfers;
- expanding underused revenues sources such as property taxes; and
- improvements in existing sources such as VAT and personal income tax.

Developing Asia is in the midst of a transition toward a growth path that is more broadly inclusive and sustainable. Asian governments have the power to facilitate this welcome transition through the judicious use of fiscal spending and revenue mobilization. Because inclusive fiscal policy is difficult and complex, it is necessarily a long-term challenge, but one for Asia to start thinking about, discussing, and preparing for now.

Bibliography

Araki, S. 2014. Recent Discussions on Inheritance Tax in Asia-Pacific. *Asia-Pacific Tax Bulletin.* 20 (1). pp. 4–7.

Claus, I., J. Martinez-Vasquez, and V. Vulovic. 2014. Government Fiscal Policies and Redistribution in Asian Countries. In R. Kanbur, C. Rhee, and J. Zhuang, eds. *Inequality in Asia and the Pacific: Trends, Drivers, and Policy Implications.* London and New York: Routledge and Manila: ADB.

International Monetary Fund (IMF). 2014. Fiscal Policy and Income Inequality. *IMF Policy Paper Series.* Washington, DC: International Monetary Fund.

Kraay, D. 2006. When Is Growth Pro-Poor? Cross-Country Evidence. *Journal of Development Economics.* 80 (1). pp. 198–227.

Index

Note: Page numbers with f indicate figures; those with t indicate tables.

Scott, J. 170
Second Theorem of Welfare Economics 27
seigniorage: efficiency benefits of 170; as fiscal resource category 167; properties of 177*t*
selective excise taxes 175*t*
Serven, L. 13
Shapiro, M. 92*t*
Shen, K. 136–64
Silva, R. 266
Singh, Y. 12
Skinner, J. 70
Slemrod, J. 70–1, 169
small economies with special characteristics (SSC) 28; comparison of expenditures for 39–40*t*, 41*t*, 43*t*; countries with 28; income or consumption quintile, ratio of 57–8*t*; real gross domestic product growth in 54*f*; total government expenditure in 34*f*; total government revenue in 31*f*
Smeeding, T. 266
social protection spending, in Latin America 238*f*
social security taxes 173*t*
social security/welfare spending: decomposition analysis for 226–9*t*, 230–1; as percentage of gross domestic product (GDP) 218, 219–20*t*, 221
social welfare models 261–2
Solt, F. 94
Son, H. H. 251
South Africa: direct taxes in 46*f*; fiscal balance in 49*f*; government gross debt in 50*f*; government net lending/borrowing in 49*f*; gross domestic savings in 50*f*; health expenditures in 48*f*; indirect taxes in 47*f*; tax revenue in 46*f*; total government expenditure in 47*f*; total government revenue in 45*f*; total investment in 51*f*
Sparrow, R. 12
spectrum/license auctions 179
stamp duties 176*t*
Standardized World Income Inequality Database (SWIID) 93; Gini coefficients 94
state-owned enterprises, reform of 287
structural vector autoregression (SVAR): research using 91, 92*t*; shock identification strategy 92*t*

Sultana, A. 72
Swaroop, V. 72

Tang, J.-H. 72
tax and spending in Asia, sustainability of 202–33; age profiles of public spending for 208–10, 208*t*, 209*f*; aggregate controls used in study of 211–12, 212*t*; data sources for 207; education spending and 213, 214–17*t*, 218; fertility rates and 204; fiscal projections 213–21; GDP growth and 210; health-care spending and 218; inflow profiles for Philippines and 204–6, 205*f*, 206*f*; interpretation and implications of 221, 222–9*t*, 230–2; introduction to 202–7; methodology used 207–13; policy issues and conclusions 232–3; population aging and 203–4, 203*f*, 210–11, 210*t*; projection method described 212–13; public spending in low-income economies and 206–7; social security/welfare spending and 218, 219–20*t*, 221
taxes: asset 176*t*; betting and gambling 176*t*; capital gains 174*t*; corporation 174*t*; corrective 176*t*; direct, in selected economies 46*f*; domestic commodity 175*t*; economic cost of 169; on exports 176*t*; as fiscal resource category 167; on goods and services 174*t*; government spending and 77–8, 78*f*, 84–5, 84–5*f*, 85*t*, 86*t*; on imports 175*t*; on income 173*t*; indirect, in selected economies 47*f*; individual income 173*t*; on international trade 175*t*; land 176*t*; other 176*t*; properties of 173*t*; property 176*t*; selective excise 175*t*; social security 173*t*; stamp duties 176*t*; United Nations System of National Accounts definition of 168; value-added 174*t*; wealth 176*t*
tax groups to tax revenue, contribution of 20*f*
tax revenue 75*f*, 77*f*; in Brazil 46*f*; in Canada 46*f*; in Japan 46*f*; in South Africa 46*f*; in Turkey 46*f*
tax revenue indicators 74*f*
Thompson, J. P. 266
Tiongson, E. 12